FORTRESS EUROPE

FORTRESS EUROPE

European Fortifications of World War II

J.E. Kaufmann
Robert M. Jurga

Translations by
H.W. Kaufmann

COMBINED PUBLISHING
Pennsylvania

To Harvey and Tadeusz

For information, address:
Combined Publishing
P.O. Box 307
Conshohocken, PA 19428
E-mail: combined@dca.net
Web: www.combinedpublishing.com
Orders: 1-800-418-6065

Every reasonable effort has been made to insure the accuracy of the material contained in this
book. However, ongoing research continues to provide important new information to the field.
In an effort to provide readers with the most up-to-date information the authors will put
additions, clarifications and changes to the text on the following web site:
http://www.irelandnow.com/siteo/frontpage.html.

Library of Congress Cataloging-in-Publication Data available.

ISBN 1-58097-000-1

Printed in the United States of America.

CONTENTS

ACKNOWLEDGMENTS

This book would not have been possible without the help of a number of people who have done everything from giving us photographs, to sending documents and summaries, and escorting us through the fortifications. We are listing our informants in alphabetical order but we want them to rest assured that their contributions were of equal importance and greatly appreciated. Next to their names we list the area in which they contributed information. "Photos" indicates that they also provided photos of the fortifications.

John Aalbu (photos), Markku Airila* (Finland & photos), Colin Alexander (England), William Allcorn (Western Europe & photos), Captain A.D. Balgarnie, RE Press Officer, British Forces Gibraltar, Libor Boleslav (Czech), Dr. Martin Búren (Germany), Brian Burr Chin (Belgium), Jean-Louis Burtscher (France & photos), Dr. Carlo Alfredo Clerici* (Italy & photos), Olle and Colonel Gunnar Dahlquist* (Sweden & photos), Clayton Donnel (France & photos), Dr. Martin Egger (France & Russia), LTC Ove Enqvist* (Finland), Kommandørkaptein Odd Terje Fjeld (Norway), Bryan Fugate (USSR), Alessandro Gazzi (Italy), Peter Gryner (Czech), Joseph de Hasque (Belgium & photos), John Hellis (England & photos), Raul Heymes (France), Leif Högberg (Sweden & photos), Alex Horak (Czech), Herbert Jager (Germany), Anna Kedryna* (Netherlands, Poland and Russia), Dr. Machiel Kiel (Netherlands), Armin Kilian (Germany), Jurgen Kraft (Photos), Patrice Lang and his friends of the Association "Le Tiburce" (France), LTC Iikka Lansivaara* (Finland), Staff Sgt. Edmund Leizens and son (copies of AOK 1 June 1940 report), Colonel Andrezej Lisiecki (Poland), Bernard Lowry (England & photo), Michael J. Luke (Denmark), George Maistret (France), José Matrán Bea & Colonel Juan Antonio Gómez Vizcaino (Cartagena & Spain's defenses), Wes Micket (photo), Raymond Mersch (France), L.C.A. van Midden (Germany & photos), Svein Wiiger Olsen* (Norway & photos), Frank Philippart (Belgium), Margaret Pinsent (Photos), Jason Pipes (German coast defense units), Gunther Reiss* (Switzerland and Italy, photos), Charlie Robbins (German Denkshrifts), Rene Roede (Spain), LTC Nuno Rubin (Portugal), John Sloan (Russia), Dag Sundkuist* (Norway), LTC Philippe Truttmann* (France), Lucas Tsatiris*

(Greece), Lee R. Unterborn (reference material), Karol Vasata (photos), Jean-Bernard Wahl (France), Peter Waltje (Germany & Photos), Patrice Wijnands (Belgium & Germany), Charlie Woods (Belgian artillery).

The Genie of Metz, Grenoble and Nice many years ago graciously provided us with some important documentation on the Maginot Line which has always been important in our writings on the French fortifications. We also thank the various civilian associations that are preserving the forts of Hackenberg, Fermont, Rohrbach, Schoenenbourg, Simserhof, and Immerhof in France and the fort of Bouda in the Czech Republic.

We would also like to thank Brian Fugate for permission to quote from *Thunder on the Dnepr*, Medwyn Parry and Roger Thomas for permission to make illustrations of British pillboxes based on their drawings, and Herbert Jager for the use of a drawing by Robert Jurga from *Die Kustenbatterie Fort Kugelbake in Cuxhaven*.

Thanks to Maria Urbanice of the Jagiellonian Library for helping us obtain important German documents and Raymond Mersch, curator of the fortification of A10 Immerhof of Hettange-Grande, who always opened the ouvrage to us. Also, Robert Jurga's director, W. Chrostowski, made it possible for Robert to continue on the research needed for this project.

Communications were made possible with the help of Dr. Martin Egger, Jerzy Pankiewicz, and Michal Rybinski who maintained contact between us and other contributors through e-mail. Also thanks to Anna Kedryna for helping Robert process all the material needed for the drawings. Special thanks to Lee R. Unterborn not only for providing valuable reference material, but also serving as a reader of the final manuscript.

Special mention must be made for the help provided by LTC Philippe Truttmann who has continued to keep us informed on the French fortifications and clarifying details for us. Gunther Reiss, as always, was there to help us make connections and provide data. Dag Sundkuist came through with the last minute additions on Scandinavia and Spain. Dr. Carlo Clerici's books and correspondence and descriptions gave us most of the information used in the chapter on Italy. Markku Airila and Ove Enqvist handled obtaining all our material on Finland as well as translating it into English. Finally, Svein Olsen prepared special summaries of every major fortified area in Norway and the weapons employed by both Norwegians and Germans between 1940 and 1945. Like Dr. Clerici's contribution for the Italian chapter, Mr. Olsen's contribution was vital for properly completing the chapter on Scandinavia. Mr. Olsen also included additional material on Sweden and Denmark.

*Denotes those who provided a great deal of information and material to this project. Everyone's contribution was important and we hope we have not forgotten anyone's name.

INTRODUCTION

This book is a survey of most of the major and minor fortifications that were prepared and used in Europe before and during World War II. It is not meant to be a technical, in-depth study of military architecture, but rather a general overview of the subject, a reference for the professional and amateur historian. Each chapter includes a brief background section, examines the location and terrain that was defended, describes the fortifications, identifies some of the key components, and gives a brief history of those defenses in World War II.

The reader may find it necessary to refer to more detailed maps to identify some specific locations since space limitations permit us only to include a selection of illustrative material. Those who need more detailed information on individual positions and lines of fortifications will find that the bibliography contains a complete list of the resources we used as well as a complete list of suggested reading. However, many of the publications are difficult to obtain and some contain limited information.

The information on some of the fortifications in this volume may soon become outdated when additional facts come to light. In other cases, such as Rumania's, very little information was available, so we have presented all the material we were able to glean. We must caution the reader, however, that some of our sources may not have been among the most reliable.

Some countries, such as Hungary, have not been included because we were not able to find any information at all about their defenses. This does not necessarily mean that they had no permanent fortifications.

If any of our readers would like to share information with us for a future revision of this book, we encourage them to contact one of us at the following addresses:

SITE O (Fortifications and Artillery)
http://www.irelandnow.com/siteo/frontpage.html
J.E. Kaufmann, PO Box 680484, San Antonio, TX 78268, USA
Robert Jurga, Boryszyn 33, 66-218 Lubrza, POLAND

Chapter 1

FRANCE

BACKGROUND

France's World War II era fortifications date back to the close of the Franco-Prussian War in 1871. After the humiliating defeat and harsh peace terms that resulted in the loss of the province of Alsace and a large part of Lorraine, the French government and military establishment resolved to fight to restore the lost territories and national honor. Until the time for "revenge" came to pass, the French High Command decided to erect a strong defensive barrier to prevent any further intrusions that might lead to another embarrassing episode.

While the French statesmen busied themselves forging alliances, the military rebuilt the army and began establishing a series of fortifications to protect vulnerable areas and major economic centers. General Raymond-Adolphe Seré de Rivières was charged with the creation of a series of fortified rings linked together by a line of isolated forts. The most important of these rings were those of Verdun and Toul, and Epinal and Belfort. Others went up at Lille, Maubeuge, Langres, Dijon, Besançon, Grenoble, Briançon, and Nice. In addition, a number of isolated positions were established between most of these fortress rings. In most cases, Seré de Rivières positioned the guns in open positions but placed the supporting facilities, such as the magazines, in protected locales. He used narrow and/or rear facing courtyards to reduce the vulnerability of the exposed facade to high-angled fire and surrounded his forts with dry moats or fossés with coffres at the corners of counter scarps, covering them with infantry weapons.

By the mid-1880s, Seré de Rivières' forts–many far from being finished–became virtually obsolete, like most of the European fortifications of the period. This sudden disaster, called the "Crisis of the torpedo shell" by French historians, was caused by a new high explosive that triggered the development of more effective and destructive artillery shells. Beginning in 1881, the new chrome-tungsten steel shells were able to crack cast-iron armor.

As a result, between 1889 and 1914, profound changes took place in the field of military architecture. Many forts had to be redesigned and those in the final stages of construction had to be altered. After 1889 the French perfected a nickel-steel armor that could stand up to the new ammunition. They also reinforced their concrete with steel, producing a ferro-concrete that could withstand bombardment from the new shells. Other nations responded with similar developments, although methods for pouring concrete and the use of reinforcement varied from country to country. The French used metal rods near the interior and exterior edges of their concrete to prevent it from cracking badly.

In the key Seré de Rivières forts, the vulnerable open gun positions were replaced with artillery turrets. Machine-gun turrets supplanted the vulnerable infantry positions on top of the forts. The *Casemate de Bourges*, usually containing two gun rooms for 75-mm guns, was developed to protect the forts' flanks. Some of the older forts received and maintained cast-iron Mougin turrets for 155-mm guns. Only the key forts between Belfort and Verdun were equipped with the new steel 75-mm gun turrets. Fixed steel turrets or *cloches* meant primarily as observation posts were installed in many forts. Many of the features of these defenses would persist in the period between World Wars. However, technological advances were often slowed by the increasing expense of implementing them.

Before the end of 1914 the French lost confidence in the ability of their forts to resist the new heavy German artillery that had devastated Fort Manonviller and the Belgian forts[1]. Manonviller, an old fort built in the late 1870s and modernized several times, was equipped with a variety of gun turrets[2]. It served as an isolated French border fort, becoming an easy target for the new German heavy artillery in August 1914. When the Germans turned their attention towards Verdun in 1916, launching a massive offensive, they found a fortress ring that had been largely disarmed.

Three factors of this campaign would play a key role in shaping the future French fortifications. The first was the fall of Fort Douaumont to a few bold German soldiers, who quickly overpowered the skeleton garrison. It took the French army several months to recapture its own fort, after it had endured heavy bombardment and bloody close fighting before surrendering with most of its components still functional. The second factor was Fort Vaux's spirited resistance, despite the loss of its only 75-mm gun artillery turret before the battle, and eventual surrender, caused by weaknesses in its design. The third factor was the successful performance of the intermediate work of Froideterre. Its new design, consisting of dispersed positions, reduced its vulnerability to enemy artillery and assured its effectiveness. After the Great War, France was left with a large air force and tank force that foreshadowed the future in warfare.

However, aircraft and tanks, which were offensive arms, lost their popularity in the post-war peace, a period of military retrenchment for the France. Having lost a whole generation to the war, France was disenchanted with all things military. Thus France began to reduce the size of its armed forces and its High Command concluded that its best course would be to take a strong defensive stance. The crippling effects of the Versailles Treaty on their enemies notwithstanding, the French military leaders feared a resurgence of German military power. France's occupation of the Rhineland could only be expected to keep the Germans in check until the end of the 1920s. The main object was to create a barrier to protect the recovered provinces from a future German invasion. The design and layout of these new works was the subject of much discussion among the military planners in the early 1920s. The outcome was that the government approved the creation of the Maginot Line, which would later be erroneously described as a giant "concrete trench".

MAJOR FORTIFICATIONS

The Maginot Line
The Maginot Extension and Maubeuge
The Little Maginot Line (Alpine Defenses)
The Coast Defenses

LOCATION

1. The Maginot Line

When completed the Maginot Line consisted of three major sections: The Maginot Line Proper, the Maginot Extension, and the Little Maginot Line.[3] The original Maginot Line on the Northeastern Front included the Maginot Line Proper and the Rhine Defenses.

The Maginot Line Proper was divided into two Fortified Regions (Régions Fortifiées or RF) that included the RF of Metz and the RF of La Lauter. Between the two RFs the Sarre Gap, devoid of heavy defenses, relied on a system of inundations. Along the Rhine, from the vicinity of Haguenau and Seltz, a system of light fortifications known as the Rhine Defenses extended up the river to the Swiss border.

The Maginot Line Proper spanned a variety of terrain. The RF of Metz began near Longuyon in a hilly mining region of Lorraine, made a semi-circle around the previously German-fortified industrial town of Thionville, and continued on to the edge of the Sarre Gap near St. Avold. This RF covering Lorraine occupied a largely wooded plateau region. The Moselle River cut through it as it meandered from Metz to Thionville and on to the German border. These defenses covered about 75 km.

At a lower elevation than the RF of Metz, a number of small lakes and ponds occupied the Sarre Gap. This sector spanned about 25 kilometers from the vicinity of St. Avold to the east bank of the Sarre River near Sarralbe. Although this region is seldom marked on maps because of its small size, it has served as a major invasion route throughout history. The Germans had passed through it in the Franco-Prussian War in 1870. Since the terrain was not favorable for the building of subterranean fortifications, the French opted to create a defended water barrier here.

The RF of La Lauter ran from the east end of the Sarre Gap to a point near the Rhine. On a simple map of the region this RF appears to be similar to the RF of Metz. However, it contained a smaller number of fortifications and it did not constitute a continuous line because of the terrain. The Vosges creates a major natural barrier and is more heavily wooded and dissected than the plateau of Lorraine. This RF was divided into two large fortified sectors. One of the major sections of the RF extended between the Sarre Gap and a point east of Bitche, where the Vosges becomes heavily wooded. At the other end of the difficult sector of the Vosges, which was about 20 km wide, began the next set of heavy fortifications that continued to a point where the mountainous terrain met the Rhine Valley. The plain created by the Rhine was covered by lighter defenses that extended up to the river itself.

The Rhine defenses, which stretched from a point down river from Strasbourg all the way to the Swiss border, were over 120 km long. They were not part of the Maginot Line Proper and included no large fortifications except older pre-twentieth century forts. The defenses covered the low terrain of the Rhine valley, the river bank, and the line of villages behind it. To the rear, the Vosges afforded a formidable barrier. The Rhine-Rhone Canal also formed an obstacle to the rear of the river line. A gap in the Vosges, to the northwest of Strasbourg, between Saverne and Sarrebourg, afforded easy passage. There was another gap near the end of the Rhine Defenses, the Belfort gap, between the Vosges and Jura Mountains. Plans were made to build a third RF and further fortifications in this area but did not materialize.

2. Maubeuge and the Maginot Extension

A limited number of fortifications along the Northeastern Front, on the Belgian border, were also set up. However, no continuous line of major defensive positions existed between Longuyon and the North Sea. The industrial city of Lille sat astride the border, making the defense of the area around it rather difficult, especially since the low terrain of Flanders was not favorable for underground works. The old forts of Maubeuge, which defended a major invasion route that passed through Liege and Namur in Belgium, were modernized. The Maginot Extension, about 20 kilometers long, was linked to the main line by a small, 30 km-long area defended by smaller works. Part of a newer building program, it was designed to expand the line of defenses towards Sedan to block a possible German invasion through southern Belgium, via Luxembourg. It was separated from the Maginot Line Proper by a small defensive sector that relied mainly on the rough terrain for its defense.

3. The Little Maginot Line (The Alpine Defenses)

The Little Maginot Line spanned an area greater than the Maginot Line Proper, but its fortified lines actually occupied slightly less territory. In fact, almost half of the Alpine line had no fortifications, due to the forbidding nature of the terrain. This line included four major fortified positions: the first covered the city of Modane and the valley leading to the Mount Cenis Pass, the second guarded Briançon and the pass of Montgenèvre, the third protected Barcelonnette, and the fourth shielded the Larche, Pourriac, and Fer passes. Finally, an almost continuous line of fortifications defended the Maritime Alps and ended on the Mediterranean, spanning about 60 to 70 kilometers. In addition, a smaller position covered the Little St. Bernard Pass, near Bourg St. Maurice, at the northern end of the Alpine sector.

4. Coast Defenses

The most important of France's inter-war coastal defenses were built on the southern tip of Corsica to defend against an Italian invasion force crossing over from Sardinia. France also created other coastal batteries in the 1920s and 1930s at key ports and had completed some modern works by 1939. The major coastal defenses guarded French harbors such as Toulon, Marseilles, Brest, and Cherbourg. Most were designed to cover the approaches to the harbors and included forts on dominating terrain overlooking the area and on islands controlling the approaches. Many of the French coastal batteries, some dating back to the eighteenth and nineteenth centuries, were later incorporated into the German Atlantic Wall.

HISTORY

After the Great War, the French High Command took a closer look at the forts of the Verdun ring, finding a number of disquieting flaws such as a lack of gas protection and proper ventilation under heavy fire. On the other hand, the old forts also had some strong points in their favor, such as the retracting turrets and the Casemates de Bourges, which had proved their worth in combat. Forts Douaumont and Vaux had demonstrated that the forts needed better infantry positions and interior defenses. Despite emphatic disclaimers on the part of the French, it appears that the German Feste, acquired with the return of Metz and Thionville, had a decided influence on the architects of the Maginot Line.

Before the Ministry of War finally made a decision regarding the type of fortifications to build, a disagreement arose between Marshal Philippe Pétain and Marshal Joseph Joffre. In March 1920, the Minister of War, André Lefèvre, directed the *Conseil Superiéur de la Guerre* to make a study of the defensive needs of the new eastern frontier. In 1922, the War Ministry formed the *Commission de Défense du Territoire* (Commission of Territorial Defense) under the leadership of Joffre to further examine the problem. Joffre suggested building strong fortified positions like the ring of Verdun, but Pétain insisted on lighter defenses supported by a *parc mobile de fortifications* (mobile park of fortifications), which could reinforce any sector and give depth to the defenses. Other commission members such as General Louis Guillaumat, Marshal Ferdinand Foch, and General Marie Debeney, who replaced a member of Pétain's faction who had died in 1923, finally opted for two heavily fortified regions. In deference to Pétain, a compromise solution was suggested; the defenses would form a continuous line.

In 1926, the War Ministry created the *Commission de Défense des Frontiéres* (Border Defense Commission) under General Guillaumat, which prepared the plans for the new defensive system. At the end of the year the commission recommended three RFs on the Northeastern Front, but the third, the RF of Belfort, was soon eliminated. The commission recommended the creation of several Fortified Sectors (SFs) on the Southeastern Front to defend the likely invasion routes through the Alps. Most of the initial work for the new fortified line was undertaken by Minister of War Paul Painlevé and his administration. When André Maginot replaced Painlevé in 1929, the work was finally set into motion. The new defenses were given the name of the hero of Verdun, who was then in charge and had vigorously endorsed their creation. The Maginot Line was first planned and designed to act as a temporary shield that would hold the enemy at bay for several weeks, giving the army time to mobilize. However, early in the 1930s the original concept underwent a significant modification. The new fortifications would no longer serve as a temporary front, but would stop the enemy from advancing.

Maginot urged that the new line be completed before the French army was scheduled to withdraw from the Rhineland in 1935. By the time he became War Minister, the government had moved the pull-out date to 1930. The legislature appropriated a huge sum for the construction work in January 1930. However, by the time the line was completed the cost had soared to more than double the amount originally appropriated.

In 1927, the *Commission de Défense des Frontiéres* set up the *Commission d'Organisation des Régions Fortifiées* (Commission for the Organization of the Fortified Regions or CORF) to prepare the designs for various types of fortifications. General Fillonneau, the Inspector General of Engineers, was nominated president of CORF. He appointed other officers to the commission, including representatives of the artillery and the infantry. General Belhauge replaced Fillonneau in 1929, before the actual construction began, and directed CORF until its dissolution in 1935.

In 1928 work began on Rimplas in the Alps, the first fort to be built. This led to CORF making many design changes. Full scale construction work on the Maginot Line's CORF- designed installations began in early 1930. The main priority work was on the Maginot Line Proper and the Rhine Defenses, which later were designated as the "Old Fronts" after plans were drawn up for "New Fronts." As Hitler ascended to power in 1934, a new sense of urgency arose in France for the completion and expansion of the fortifications. Unfortunately, Marshal Pétain, who was the Minister of War at the time, did little to help their cause when he declared that the Ardennes were "impenetrable." In 1935, his successor began to work on the "New Fronts." By 1936, the government authorized new funds to improve the Southeastern Front when Mussolini's war with Ethiopia led to the creation of the Berlin-Rome Axis.

The military considered using new 145-mm guns with a range of about 29 km in turrets and the 340-mm naval guns from the *Normandie* Class battleships. However, these plans were indefinitely postponed, making the 75-mm gun the largest gun to be used.

The Maginot Line went on active duty in 1936, when the Germans reoccupied the Rhineland. After this crisis a number of problems, such as the organization of the garrisons and defects of design, became apparent. Since the New Fronts had not been completed by the time, and much work still needed to be done on the Maginot Line Proper and the Southeastern Front, it was possible to resolve most of these problems during the last years of the decade.

Nonetheless, a planned stop line behind the main line was never adequately completed and the linkage between the forts and the outside electrical power grid remained unfinished. Some of the weapons for the ouvrages, such as the 25-mm guns for machine gun turrets and 60-mm mortars for special bomb throwing cloches, were also not ready for installation either when the war began. Despite these shortcomings, both the Northeastern and Southeastern Fronts of the Maginot Line and their forts were practically ready for action by September 1939.

The task of protecting France's coast was turned over to the navy in 1917. However, a plan for the reorganization of the coastal gun batteries was not formulated until 1922 and was revised in 1926. The program called for the installation in concrete emplacements of artillery from warships headed for the scrap heap. These weapons included the mostly obsolete 75-mm, 138-mm (Mle 1910), 164-mm (Mle 93-96), and 194-mm guns as well as the old 220-mm cannons. Many, especially the light weapons under 138-mm caliber, were placed in open positions with light armored shields and 360 degrees of fire.

The navy also intended to use the 305-mm guns from two older classes of battleship slated for the scrap heap, but their equipment turned out to be unsuitable. Instead it ordered the newly-designed twin gun turrets from Schneider, Mle 1924, for mounting the 340-mm guns in coastal positions since the quadruple turrets of the *Normandie* Class battleships were not practical for land installations. Key ports received these new batteries during the 1930s.

DESCRIPTION

1. The Maginot Line

The Maginot Line included two Fortified Regions (RFs): the RF of Metz and the RF of La Lauter. Each RF had several Fortified Sectors (SFs).
The RF of Metz consisted of:

SF of La Crusnes (4th Brigade)	3 gros ouvrages, 4 petits ouvrages, 36 casemates, 5 observatories, and 1 abri.
SF of Thionville (3rd Brigade)	7 gros ouvrages, 4 petits ouvrages, 17 casemates, 4 observatories, and 18 abris.
SF of Boulay (2nd Brigade)	4 gros ouvrages, 8 petits ouvrages, 14 casemates (including 2 artillery),* 2 observatories and 14 abris.
SF of Faulquemont (1st Brigade)	8 petits ouvrages and 16 casemates (including 3 artillery)*.

The RF of La Lauter consisted of:

SF of Rohrbach (7th Brigade)	1 gros ouvrages, 4 petits ouvrages, 18 casemates and 3 abris.
SF of the Vosges (5th Brigade)	3 gros ouvrages, 1 petit ouvrage, 35 casemates (including 3 artillery),* 19 blockhouses, observatory, and 7 abris.
SF of Haguenau (6th Brigade)	2 gros ouvrages, 37 casemates, 2 observatories, and 15 abris.

*The artillery casemates noted above were built shortly before the 1940 campaign and were not part of CORF's original plans. They mounted either one or two 75-mm guns. Some of these were also found on the New Fronts.

The Defensive Sector (SD) of the Sarre, which occupied the gap between these two RFs, did not include any of the standard types of positions found in the RFs, except for four small artillery casemates. The sub-sectors of Kalhouse and Bining, which were part of the New Fronts built after 1935, joined the older sub- sector of Legeret to form the SF of Rohrbach, of the RF of Lauter.

Each SF was organized as a fortress brigade consisting of one active fortress infantry regiment and one artillery regiment. The SFs consisted of three or four sub-sectors. On mobilization the regiments quickly expanded into three regiments with the addition of reservists. At that time, a whole fortress infantry regiment would occupy each sub-sector. During mobilization, as the brigade expanded, an additional artillery regiment was formed, one or two battalions of which was assigned to each sub-sector. After September 1939, the SFs were dissolved. Some, mainly those outside of the Maginot Line Proper, were formed into fortress divisions.

The Maginot Line Proper consisted of a thin line of blockhouses and casemate positions with barbed wire and anti-tank obstacles. The ouvrages, which formed the backbone of its defenses, were far better built than the forts of Verdun, but their fire-power was not much different. The French classified the larger works as *ouvrages d'artillerie* (artillery ouvrages) or *gros ouvrages* (big ouvrages) and the smaller as *petits ouvrages* (small ouvrages). The former wielded the firepower of the Maginot Line while the latter, usually lacking artillery, were supplied with infantry-type support weapons.

The RFs consisted of an almost continuous line of ouvrages that covered each other with fire. The ouvrages also received support from, and in turn gave support to, the interval casemates and observatories. The abris, or infantry shelters, acted as command posts and service positions for the regiments occupying the sectors. In many cases the petits ouvrages were placed between gros ouvrages to cover gaps. In a number of places there were no artillery forts because they were not completed as originally planned and were transformed into petits ouvrages instead. This happened especially in the SFs on either side of the Sarre Gap and the SF of Haguenau on the right flank of the RF of La Lauter. The Sarre Gap was defended by positions that were mostly not designed as part of the permanent fortifications. The distinctive feature of the SD of the Sarre was its network of dams designed to create and maintain water reservoirs whose water would be released to flood the surrounding area. Most of these dams had their own defenses.

In front of the main line of defenses was an advanced line of light positions whose mission was to give early warning and delay an enemy advance. This line of *avant-postes* (advanced positions) usually consisted of small concrete structures for automatic weapons that, in many cases, also included road barriers and other obstacles. Fortified houses were located in this forward line, or probably even closer to the border. They usually stood in towns along the routes of advance from Germany. These houses varied in style, often consisting of a concrete bunker surmounted by a residential-like structure. In other instances, the residential structure was attached to a bunker on one of its ends, or was sandwiched between two bunkers.

In the Maginot Line itself, the main line ouvrages occupied key terrain. CORF selected and/or designed all the positions and components of the ouvrages, casemates, abris and special blockhouses. Interval positions were placed to cover lines of advance and relay information to the forts. The interval casemates and most of the casemates of the ouvrages were oriented for flanking fires so that they could support each other. They were also designed to engage the enemy in close combat and thus were not equipped with heavy artillery.

The artillery ouvrage had a number of standard features, even though no two forts were identical. Each ouvrage consisted of two parts; the combat section and the support section. The combat section included several concrete blocks, normally of two levels, that came in several types and usually had one main function. The block types included casemate positions, turret positions, and a combination of both. In addition, each block functioned primarily as an infantry or an artillery position. In most cases the entire block was covered with earth and rock with the exception of the casemate weapons positions. Most blocks also sported a small non-movable turret, known as a cloche, that became the trademark of the Maginot Line.

The casemate blocks could be classified under two basic types, according to their function. The first was the infantry casemate position, which usually mounted a single 47-mm anti-tank gun. However, those positions built before these weapons came into production, held a smaller 37-mm anti-tank gun. The anti-tank gun shared a firing embrasure with a water-cooled twin machine gun, known as jumelage de mitrailleuse or JM. The infantry casemate sometimes had and additional position for JM or a single automatic rifle, known as *Fusil Mitrailleur* or FM.

Along the façade, in front of the weapons crenels, a small moat known as *fossé diamant*, served as a receptacle for shell casings and the gases of expended ordnance and concrete debris off the façade caused by artillery and bomb hits. Its function was to keep the firing embrasures from being blocked. A grenade launcher, or *lance-grenade*, ejected small grenades into the fossé to prevent the enemy from crossing it and attaching explosives to the embrasures. The *fossé diamant* was a standard feature on all casemates.

On the roof of the infantry casemate could be found one or more cloches that provided small-arms and mortar fire in all directions. The firing rooms were located in the upper level of this type of block, above a rest area. The roof of the infantry casemate normally consisted of 3.5 meters of concrete with an earth covering that could resist 420-mm artillery. In addition, the rear-facing wall was usually about 1.75 meters in thickness so that it could be breached by friendly heavy artillery if the position had to be recaptured.

The second type of casemate block was the artillery casemate, which usually mounted three 75-mm guns. As in most casemates, its exposed façade faced to the rear and its firing chambers were angled so that the guns covered an angle of approximately 45 degrees to the flank. Some artillery casemate blocks featured a single 135-mm howitzer-like weapon, a special type of weapon with the characteristics of a mortar and a howitzer, known as a *lance-bombe*. Other types of artillery blocks normally mounted a pair of 81-mm mortars, but these were usually at the lower level and fired out of the fossé. Each artillery block usually had an M-3 magazine–not found in infantry blocks–equipped with a set of overhead rails that hauled ammunition cases in and out to the firing chambers.

In most infantry and artillery casemates, armored air vents attached to the wall drew air into the block's filter-room. In some of these blocks, an emergency exit allowed access to the surface and was used for patrolling the fort's superstructure. More commonly, however, the emergency exit opened into the fossé from the lower level. This exit was sealed by an armored door and was covered by an interior firing position for small arms. The length of the fossé was usually covered by an FM crenel. The turret blocks also came in two categories, according to their function: infantry turret blocks and artillery turret blocks. They included no more than one turret but could have several cloches. Most also had a small armored air vent that drew air into the filter room. Used air was normally expelled through the cloches. A *monte-charge*, or small lift, carried ammunition up to the turret. The turret–similar to the earlier models–had more armor, rotated 360 degrees, and eclipsed. Both eclipse and rotation operations could be carried out manually as well as electrically in all turrets. Different types of turrets were used for machine guns, 81-mm mortars, 135-mm howitzers and 75-mm guns. At a later date, turrets that combined different types of weapons were added to the inventory.

The infantry turret block, included one of three types of turrets: a machine gun turret and two types of mixed-arms turrets. The machine gun turret mounted a JM. Plans were made to add a 25-mm gun at a later date, however, this gun was not ready for mounting until the onset of the 1940 campaign. The mixed-arms turrets were developed for the New Fronts. One type mounted two JMs, each with a 25-mm gun. The other had two machine guns with a 25-mm gun. It also had a 50-mm mortar that fired through the roof even when the turret was retracted. The mixed-arms turret also included a periscope for observation. The turret was usually located in a commanding position above the block to give maximal fields of fire.

The largest turrets were located in artillery turret blocks for 75-mm guns. Like the machine gun turrets, they stood on a slight concrete rise that facilitated direct fire. The 135-mm howitzer and 81-mm mortar turrets sat in a small concrete depression to reduce their silhouette since these weapons used a high trajectory. The shells from the 75-mm gun and 135-mm howitzers were returned to the lower level in turrets and casemates through a funnel or hopper known as an *entonnoir*, into a toboggan, ending in a storage area inside the fort. All the artillery turrets mounted two weapons, but only the 75-mm turret had an observation position. In addition to the turrets, the ouvrage had cloches that came in several types and sizes. The GFM (*Guet* and *Fusil Mitrailleur* or observation and automatic rifle) was the most common type. It came in various sizes but normally had three or four crenels and special mounts for an episcope, an FM, and a special 50-mm breech-loaded mortar. Most cloche types also had a roof mounting for a small observation periscope. Access was by a ladder, but in most cloches the floor could also be raised and lowered. The cloches served as an exit for the fort's filtered air. The rush of air leaving the block made such a din that it was difficult to hear in cloches, besides being drafty and uncomfortable. The greatest weakness of these cloches was that they usually towered above the block, and, unless they were heavily camouflaged, they were quite vulnerable to direct enemy fire.

The JM cloches mounted a pair of machine guns that covered a limited sector across the fort's surface. These cloches had a small observation position on each side of the JM crenel. They were usually placed flush with the roof of the block and presented a smaller target than other types of cloches.

A special type of mortar cloche was designed for many of the blocks. It was flush with the surface and consisted of a special breech-loaded automatically fed 60-mm mortar. The purpose of this cloche was to shower the block's surface and surrounding area with bombs. These cloches, called *cloches lance-grenade*, were never ready for use because their weapon was not perfected. In addition to the GFM cloches for observation, CORF designed special observation cloches that mounted no weapons. One type had narrow observation slits and a small roof periscope. The other type was flush with the surface and mounted a huge periscope that rose above the ground. When not in use, the periscope was lowered and the cloche opening was sealed with an armored covering. Some ouvrages had special observation blocks exclusively endowed with these special cloches. In this case, the command post was usually situated below the observation block.

In each combat block the crew, whose number varied from twenty to forty men, slept in a special rest area situated at the lower level. These men were rotated back to the service area in shifts, but during the war many simply preferred to stay in their block rather than haul their gear back and forth. Each block had a filter room, rest area, storage for small arms ammunition, latrine facilities, and a stairway connecting it to the subterranean level of the fort. Some of the smaller blocks–those for observation only that had just a single cloche or weapons position–did not always have these features. However there were few of this type in the Maginot Line Proper. Most artillery blocks had a chamber for an M-3 magazine and elevators for hauling ammunition from the subterranean gallery to the combat level.

The underground gallery system was situated below most of the blocks, especially the artillery blocks, at a depth of twenty to thirty meters, depending on the terrain. The gallery system consisted of secondary access tunnels that connected the combat area to the main gallery, which was normally at a depth of about thirty meters. Additional facilities for the artillery blocks were located in the tunnels below, and included a machine room for operating the elevators, an M-2 magazine for maintaining a larger supply of ammunition for the guns above, and a room for expended shells. The access tunnels were usually sealed off from the main gallery by a set of armored air-pressure doors. In the majority of the ouvrages the main command post was located near the main gallery together with offices for the artillery, infantry, and engineer commands and a communications room. Telephone lines linked the command post to all parts of the ouvrage and order transmitters were found in the firing chambers of the gun rooms. In only a couple of ouvrages was the command post situated at a level between the subterranean works and the combat blocks.

A power sub-station, located near a point where the combat area of the fort began, received electrical power from the service area. Its transformers and converters stepped down the power for redistribution to the combat blocks and other facilities. The power lines and the communications wires ran back to the service area along the main gallery. With few exceptions, the ouvrages had a rail system that connected the service area to the access tunnels through the main gallery. This was necessary since the length of the main gallery between the combat and service areas was up to 500 meters long, and the distance between the entrance block and the most distant combat blocks could easily exceed 1,000 meters. The train engine normally operated only in the main gallery, where it received its power from overhead cables and carried almost exclusively supplies and ammunition. The troops had to walk, or in the case of larger forts like Hackenberg, they were supplied with folding bicycles. At one or more points the main gallery was sealed off by armored doors designed to halt any enemy soldiers that might penetrate that far. In addition, at several points along the gallery there were special explosive-filled niches that would block the gallery when detonated. There were even internal blockhouses in a few of the forts.

All galleries had a slight incline so water could flow out of the fort through a drain located beneath the floor, which emptied at the side of a hill. Most drains were large enough for a man to crawl through and could serve as an emergency exit. A weapons position covered the length of the drain. The main gallery was usually wide enough or two sets of tracks near the EM, but the secondary tunnels only accommodated one set of tracks.

Most ouvrages were also provided with a secret emergency exit that was invisible from the surface because its upper chamber was filled with sand. When this sand was released into an empty room below, it allowed the men to enter the upper chamber and climb a ladder to the surface.

The main gallery began in the service area, near the entrance block. The gros ouvrages normally had two entrance blocks: one for the munitions called *entrée des munitions* or EM, and one for the men, called *entrée des hommes*, or EH. The EM was a large block that faced the rear and contained one or two firing chambers for anti-tank guns, JM and FM like the infantry blocks. The roof of this block usually had two GFM and a lance-grenade cloche. A diamond fossé protected the exposed face of the block in front of the weapons crenels and the entrance. A permanent concrete bridge spanned the narrow fossé and a heavy iron grating barred access to the entrance tunnel. The grating was covered by a firing position for an FM at the end of the tunnel, adjacent to a heavy armored door. In front of the armored door and weapons position was a sliding bridge over a deep pit, known as a tank trap. This arrangement was standard for EMs designed for train cars of a narrow-gauge military railroad and for trucks. Those entrances that were not designed for railroad use had a slightly different design. Trucks and rail cars could be off loaded behind the armored doors, where the small train cars of the ouvrage awaited. This unloading area was defended by one or two interior blockhouses located in front of a second armored door leading to the main gallery. Depending on the elevation, access to the main gallery was either direct, by an incline using a special engine to move the cars at an angle, or by elevator. The incline was considered to be the most desirable for the EM, while the elevator was preferred for the EH.

The EH was smaller than the EM and had an "L" shaped entrance, a narrower entrance corridor, and no tank trap. A removable metal bridge spanned the fossé and the armored door sealed the end of the "L" shaped entrance, out of the direct fire of the enemy. In a few ouvrages a single entrance was used both for supplies and men and was called *entrée mixte* or mixed entrance. It resembled the EM rather than the EH, which was too small for the protected unloading and movement of supplies.

The service area housed the *caserne*, or barracks area, and associated facilities. The caserne was designed to accommodate about one third of the garrison. It included showers, latrines, a large filter room, a well, water storage, kitchen, storage rooms for food stocks and wine off the kitchen, an infirmary, and, more often than not, a small detention area. The larger ouvrages also had an operating room and a dentist's office. Since there was no mess hall, the troops had to eat in the corridors, on shelves attached to the walls. The officers, however, were allowed the luxury of their own mess area. Electric heaters kept the temperatures in the caserne at comfortable levels.

In addition, the service area normally contained the *usine*, or engine room. In the gros ouvrages it held four diesel engines, two of which were used to maintain operations and the remaining two were kept in reserve. These engines supplied the fort's electrical needs. The fumes from the usine were expelled into the fossé of an entrance block, through special escape vents. In rare cases, when the usine was too far from the entrances, a special chimney block had to be built. Associated with the usine were the fuel and water storage areas, the converters, the transformers, and a work room. In peacetime or prior to combat, power arrived from the National Grid by underground cables after leaving a special fortified military sub-station by aerial cables.

Another important feature of the service area were the magazines. The M-1, or main magazine, was usually located near the EM. It had smaller annexes for fuses and other types of explosives. Most ouvrages had an M-1, except Schoenenbourg, one of the most prominent exceptions, which had a special M-1/M-2 magazine near its combat blocks. To protect the rest of the ouvrage from the effects of accidental explosions, special protective measures were taken. They included a sprinkler system and curved access galleries to deflect the force of the explosion. In addition, the main gallery could be quickly sealed by a special seven ton armored door that was designed to slam shut automatically in the event of an explosion.

Finally, the service area housed workshops and garages for the maintenance, repair, and storage of the underground train located in the main gallery.

The surface of the ouvrage was protected by wire and anti-tank obstacles. Normally, the service and combat areas were surrounded by separate sets of obstacles. However, in some cases the individual blocks were similarly protected. The anti-tank obstacles consisted of several rows of rails embedded at various heights which connected most of the ouvrages. In the few ouvrages with two separate sets of combat areas, each set was covered by these obstacles. In some cases an anti-tank ditch and/or wall ran between the two areas and covered their individual blocks as well.

Originally, plans for the ouvrages called for encircling moats, but these turned out to be too expensive, especially during a period of economic depression. As a result only a few small sections were actually built, as mentioned. There were no mine fields because the French had not developed anti-personnel mines, but some anti-tank mines and booby-traps (anti-personnel) were implanted. The petits ouvrages were similar to the gros ouvrages but they had fewer combat blocks, and the few that had artillery mounted no more than 81-mm mortars. A number of petits ouvrages had originally been planned as gros ouvrages but were not completed as such. In most cases, their mission was either altered or became more circumscribed.

The few petits ouvrages that had a separate entrance block either had a very small entrance for men, like Lembach, or a mixed entrance, like Immerhof. This entrance was smaller than the EM of a gros ouvrage, and looked more like the EH. In most petits ouvrages, there was no special entrance block, but two or more of their infantry casemates included a regular entrance. Most petits ouvrages consisted of one to six blocks. The monolithic ouvrages were rather large because they had no subterranean galleries. Consequently, all their service facilities and mortars, which fired through the fossé, were at the lower level. In some petits ouvrages, the underground facilities could not be placed thirty meters below the surface because of the terrain. The usines of the petits ouvrages held fewer engines, and all their facilities but the combat blocks were built on a smaller scale.

The following is a list of gros and petits ouvrages with their main armament:

OUVRAGES	ENTRANCES	ARMAMENT
RF of Metz		
PO Chappy	—	1 Inf Cas, 1 MG-Tur
GO Fermont	2	1 Inf Cas, 1 75-Tur, 1-75 Cas, 1 81-Tur, 2 MG-Tur, 1 Obs
GO Latiremont	2	2 75-Cas, 1 81-Tur, 2 MG-Tur, 1 Obs
PO Mauvais Bois	—	2 Inf Cas, 1 MG-Tur
PO Bois du Four	—	1 Inf Cas/MG-Tur
GO Bréhain	2	2 75-Tur, 1 135-Tur, 1 81-Tur, 2 MG-Tur, 2 Obs
PO Aumetz	—	2 Inf Cas, 1 MG-Tur
GO Rochonvillers	2	2 75-Tur, 1 75/135 Cas, 2 135-Tur, 2 MG-Tur, 1 MG Tur/Inf Cas, 1 Obs
GO Molvange	2	3 75-Tur, 1 135-Tur, 1 81-Tur, 2 MG-Tur, 2 Obs
PO Immerhof	1	1 81-Tur/Inf Cas, 2 MG-Tur
GO Soetrich	2	2 75-Tur, 1 135-Tur, 2 MG-Tur, 1 81-Cas
PO Karre	—	1 Inf Cas/MG-Tur
GO Kobenbusch	2	1 75-Tur, 1 75-Cas, 1 81-Tur, 2 MG-Tur, 1 Inf Cas, 1 Obs
PO Oberheid	—	1 Inf Cas/MG-Tur
GO Galgenberg	2	1 135-Tur, 1 81-Tur, 1 MG-Tur, 2 Inf. Cas, 1 Obs
PO Sentzich	—	1 Inf Cas/MG-Tur
GO Métrich	2	1 75-Tur, 1 75-Tur/Inf Cas, 1 75-Cas, 1 135-Tur, 1 81-Tur, 1 MG-Tur, 1 Inf Cas/MG-Tur, 1 Inf Cas, 2 Obs
GO Billig	1	1 75-Tur/75-Cas, 1 75-Cas, 1 81-Tur, 1 MG-Tur, 2 Inf Cas, 1 Obs
GO Hackenberg	2	1 75-Tur, 2 75-Cas, 1 135-Tur, 1 135-Tur/135 Cas, 2 81-Tur, 1 MG Tur, 2 MG Tur/Inf Cas, 2 Obs, 5 Inf Blocks in AT obstacle
PO Coucou	—	1 Inf Cas/MG-Tur, 1 Inf Cas

GO Mont des Welches	2	2 75-Tur/Inf Cas, 1 81-Tur, 1 MG-Tur, 1 Obs
GO Michelsberg	1	1 75-Tur, 1 135-Tur, 1 81-Tur, 1 MG-Tur, 1 Inf Cas
PO Hobling	—	1 MG-Tur, 1 Inf Cas, 2 Obs
PO Bousse	1	1 Inf Cas/MG-Tur, 1 Inf Cas, 1 Obs
GO Anzeling	2	2 75-Tur, 1 135-Tur/135-Cas, 1 81-Tur, 1 MG-Tur/Inf Cas, 1 MG-Tur 1 MA Tur/Inf Cas
PO Behrenbach	—	1 MG-Tur/Inf Cas, 1 Inf Cas, 1 Obs
PO Bovemberg	—	1 MG-Tur, 1 Inf Cas, 3 Obs
PO Denting	—	1 MG-Tur, 2 Inf Cas
PO Village de Coume	—	1 MG-Tur, 1 Inf Cas, 1 Obs
PO Coume-Annexe Nord	—	1 MG-Tur/Inf Cas
PO Coume	—	1 MG-Tur/Inf Cas, 1 Inf Cas
PO Coume-Annexe Sud	—	1 81-Cas, 3 Obs
PO Mottemberg	—	1 MG-Tur, 1 Inf Cas, 1 Obs
PO Kerfent	—	1 MG-Tur, 2 Inf Cas, 1 Obs
PO Bambesch	—	1 MG-Tur, 2 Inf Cas
PO Einseling	—	1 MG-Tur/Inf Cas
PO Laudrefang	—	1 81-Cas, 1 MG-Tur, 2 Obs
PO Téting	—	1 MG-Tur, 1 Inf Cas
RF of Lauter		
PO Haut Poirier	1	1 AM-Tur, 2 Inf Cas
PO Welschoff	—	1 AM-Tur, 2 Inf Cas
PO Rohrbach	1	1 AM-Tur/Inf Cas, 1 MG-Tur/Inf Cas
GO Simserhof	2	1 75-Tur, 2 75-Cas, 1 135-Tur, 2 MG-Tur/135 Cas, 2 81-Tur/Inf Cas
GO Schiesseck	2	1 75-Tur, 1 135-Tur, 1 81-Tur, 1 81-Cas, 1 MG-Tur, 1 Inf Cas, 3 Obs
PO Otterbiel	1	1 81-Tur/Inf Cas, 1 MG-Tur, 1 Inf Cas, 1 Obs
GO Grand Hohékirkel	2	1 75-Tur, 1 MG-Tur, 2 Inf Cas, 1 Obs
PO Lembach	1	2 Inf Cas, 1 Obs
GO Four à Chaux	2	1 75-Tur, 1 135-Tur, 1-81 Tur, 1 MG-Tur, 1 Inf Cas, 1 Obs
GO Hochwald	3	2 75-Tur, 2 75-Cas, 1 135-Tur, 1 135-Tur/135-Cas, 1 81-Tur, 2 MG-Tur, 2 75-Cas in fossé, 9 blocks on AT ditch
GO Schoenenbourg	2	2 75-Tur, 1 81-Tur, 1 MG-Tur, 2 Inf Cas

NOTES: GO=Gros Ouvrage, PO=Petit Ouvrage, Obs=Observation and/or GFM cloches, Cas=Casemate, Tur=Turret, / = combination, Inf=Infantry, MG=Machine Gun, 81=81-mm Mortar, 135=135-mm Howitzer, 75=75-mm Gun, AM=Mixed Arms. Only entrance blocks not serving as combat blocks are listed under Entrances. Some PO entrance blocks were very small.

Another type of structure in the Maginot line was the interval casemate found in the main line between ouvrages and designed by CORF. These casemates followed standard blueprints and were similar to some of the infantry casemates of ouvrages mounting anti-tank guns, JM and FM. The main difference was that the CORF casemate had its own small usine since it was an independent position. Some were double casemates, meaning they had firing positions on both flanks. Only the cloches were devised for observation and defensive firing to the front. Like the casemates of most petits ouvrages, the CORF casemates had an armored door entrance that faced to the rear and often a diamond fossé. Each casemate sheltered a garrison of about two dozen men and one officer. Communication was by telephone, via underground cable linked to adjacent positions and ouvrages.

The CORF observatories were smaller than the casemates and were manned by a few men with communications equipment. They were located at key points with a good view of the surrounding terrain. Their job was to keep the artillery ouvrages informed of the enemy's movements.

Abris, or troop shelters, were found to the rear of the other positions of the main line. They were like small casernes with facilities for a command post and came in two types: the cavern abri and the monolithic surface abri. The cavern abri generally had two small entrances, each defended by a small arms position that led to the subterranean facilities below.[4] The monolithic abri generally consisted of two levels and had two GFM cloches above. This type of abri was similar to the casemates of an ouvrage in that it was covered by a layer of earth, (except on its rear-facing façade), and was usually built into a reverse slope or a hill.

When the war began, new types of non-CORF positions appeared and still newer types were added when work began on the New Fronts. These included a mixed variety of non-CORF casemates and blockhouses. Many old FT-17 tank turrets and chassis set in concrete became observatories and small bunker-like positions. During the war, the army built many non-standard blockhouses throughout the line.

The Sarre Gap was defended not only by dams for flooding, but also by a number of small blockhouses. The *Service Techniques du Génie* (STG), or Technical Service of the Engineers, designed fortifications to cover areas not protected by CORF works and, after 1938, built some STG type casemates mainly in the Sarre Gap. These STG positions were smaller and usually held fewer weapons. A few were designed to mount a cloche that was not installed in time for the campaign.

The support positions, which included permanent casernes, were generally located behind the main line of resistance. However, there were small temporary casernes near each ouvrage. Only the RF of Metz had fortified sub-stations for relaying power from the National Grid to the ouvrages. Supply, ordnance, engineer depots, and even some positions for heavy artillery were also located in the rear area. At Thionville the French rearmed the gun turrets of the three old German Feste of Illange, Koenigsmacker and Guentrange with 105-mm guns to support the main line.[5]

Although they were not a part of the Maginot Line Proper, the Rhine Defenses were built at the same time. They included no forts along the Rhine, except for old ones, and consisted mostly of casemates located along the river and behind the river line. These casemates consisted of a single level because the water table did not allow for underground construction. Each was a typical CORF casemate with its own facilities to operate independently with a platoon-sized force. Most had a GFM cloche. Over a hundred casemates occupied the river and village lines, but even those on the river provided only flanking fires. These river positions covered the key crossing points and had to be heavily camouflaged, yet they were not difficult to detect. The village line had the largest casemates. A large number of smaller block-houses mostly occupied a position between the casemates of both lines. The block-houses in the Rhine sectors were similar to the many non-standard types built by the army and only held a few men. Between the river and village lines a number of abris and blockhouses guarded key points, and roughly, formed a second line in the heavily wooded terrain. In a few sectors defensive positions near the Ill River created a fourth line.

The SF of Haute Alsace, with only seven casemates and over forty blockhouses running from Sierentz to Folgensbourg and then parallel with the Swiss border, was the only sector not dependent on the Rhine as a natural barrier. Here the French established a defensive line southeast of Blotzheim and south along the Swiss border.

2. The Maginot Extension and Maubeuge

The Maginot Extension was part of the New Fronts built to extend the western terminus of the Maginot Line. The new ouvrages lacked some of the features of the Old Fronts and were slightly different. Some of the changes included a new type of entrance block that no longer used a rolling bridge, but a heavy metal portcullis that came up from the floor near the entrance. In addition, whereas the forts of the Maginot Line were designed to support each other and create interlocking fires, those of the extension were spaced so far apart that they could not adequately do so, not being able to assist more than one neighboring ouvrage at a time. The sub-sector of Marville (part of the SF of Montmédy and attached to the SF of La Crusnes when the war began) was a heavily wooded and hilly region with a number of STG casemates and other smaller positions to defend it. The 75-mm gun turret of the ouvrage of Veslones in the extension covered the entire sector. The 75-mm gun turret of the ouvrage of Fermont, the last artillery fort on the Maginot Line Proper, also covered much of this sector.

The sub-sector of Montmédy held four of the new ouvrages: two petits ouvrages, and two gros ouvrages. One of the two petits ouvrages was protected by both gros ouvrages, while the last ouvrage on the line, La Ferté, was covered only by one of the two gros ouvrages. Furthermore, the gros ouvrage were not within range of each other and could not provide mutual support. The two gros ouvrages had a single 75-mm gun turret block each. One was outfitted with an older turret of World War I vintage, and a mixed arms turret block that was basically an infantry position. Both ouvrages had several mixed arms cloches, but these forts were not as powerful as those of the main line. The petit ouvrage of Thonnelle, located between the two larger forts, had a mixed arms turret block, two other infantry blocks and an entrance block. The smallest ouvrage, at the end of the extension, was La Ferté with only two combat blocks, one of which mounted a mixed arms turret.

The main differences between the ouvrages of the main line and those of the Maginot Extension, were the extensive use of mixed arms turrets and cloches and the new and more economical type of entrance block. In addition, the artillery ouvrages were smaller in size, had fewer artillery blocks, and were not designed to support each other effectively. Finally, the petits ouvrages of the Maginot Extension were generally better armed than many of those in the Maginot Line Proper.

The New Fronts also included, among other areas, the SF of Montmédy, the SF of Maubeuge, and the lightly defended SD of the Ardennes. The SF of Maubeuge received new fortified works in 1936, after work had already begun on the New Fronts elsewhere. Four petits ouvrages were added to four old forts that partially surrounded the town of Maubeuge. Of these, three consisted of two blocks, and one of three blocks and all four included one mixed arms turret. A similar ouvrage was built in the SF of Escaut. Even though these forts are identified as Maginot ouvrages, they were of inferior quality and were even less suited to function within the Maginot scheme of defense than those of the Maginot Extension.

The ouvrages in these New Fronts included:

OUVRAGES	ENTRANCES	BLOCKS
SF of Escaut		
PO Eth	—	1 AM-Tur/Inf Cas, 1 Inf Cas
SF of Maubeuge		
PO Les Sarts	—	1 AM-Tur/Inf Cas, 1 Inf Cas
PO Bersillies	—	1 AM-Tur/Inf Cas, 1 Inf Cas
PO Salmagne	—	1 AM-Tur/Inf Cas, 1 Inf Cas
PO Le Boussois	—	1 AM-Tur/Inf Cas, 2 Inf Cas
Maginot Extension		
PO La Ferté	—	1 AM-Tur/Inf Cas, 1 Inf Cas
GO Le Chesnois	1	1 75-Tur, 1 AM-Tur/Inf Cas, 2 Inf Cas, 1 Obs
PO Thonelle	1*	1 AM-Tur/Inf Cas, 1 Inf Cas, 1 Obs
GO Veslones	1	1 75-Tur, 1 AM-Tur/Inf Cas, 2 Inf Cas

NOTES: Obs=Observation and/or GFM cloches, Cas=Casemate,Tur=Turret, / = combination, Inf=Infantry, MG=Machine Gun, 75=75-mm Gun, AM=Mixed Arms. *These entrance block served as a combat block. Cas=Casemate, Tur=Turret, / = combination,Inf=Infantry, AM=Mixed Arms

3. The Little Maginot Line (Alpine Defenses)

The Alpine or Southeastern Front included some of the most impressive Maginot fortifications. Three SFs ran from the Swiss border to the Mediterranean Sea. Mountainous terrain formed almost impenetrable gaps between the fortifications. The SFs included the following from north to south:

SF of Savoie	5 gros and 5 petits ouvrages, 1 casemate, 4 abri and 7 avant-postes
SF of Dauphiné	4 gros and 12 petits ouvrages, 1 observatory, 5 abri and 4 avant-postes
SF of Alpes Maritimes	14 gros and 17 petits ouvrages, 27 casemates, 2 observatories 1 abri, and 14 avant-postes*

*The sub-sectors of Tinée-Vesubie and Mounier are included here, but when the war began they were part of the 65th Division and detached from the SF of the Alpes Maritimes. A Demi-Brigade of Alpine fortress troops occupied most sub-sectors of the Alpine Front.

The ouvrages of the SF of Savoie sealed the Arc Valley and the approaches to Modane. Other works defended the Valley of the Isère leading to Chambéry. The ouvrages of the SF of Dauphiné blocked the approaches to Briançon. The largest sector, the SF Alpes Maritimes, closed the southern approaches through the Maritime Alps and shielded Nice. The entrance block of its last ouvrage rested near the beach adjacent to Menton, while the rest of the ouvrage perched at a higher elevation directly above. Several more ouvrages of the SF of Alpes Maritimes actually overlooked the sea.

The Alpine ouvrages did not conform to the CORF designs of the Maginot Line Proper. In fact, they were usually smaller and held smaller garrisons. In addition, their service areas lay virtually within the combat areas. The firepower of the gros ouvrages usually equaled that of the forts of the Northeastern Front, but some petits ouvrages were more like shelters than actual combat positions.

Some ouvrages were located in hilltop positions in valleys, while others were either built into mountain sides or on mountains tops. Some had two subterranean gallery levels instead of a single level, but none had train engines since the wagons needed to be pushed only short distances. Their usines normally held three diesel engines, but did not rely on the outside electrical power grid. Because all the facilities were so close together, their entrance blocks were always of the mixed type, and were normally located close to the combat blocks. However, they were quite secure because the mountain terrain permitted much greater overhead cover than in the Maginot Line Proper. The combat blocks usually consisted of two floors and housed artillery combinations unlike similar blocks in the Northeast Front. Indeed, in the Alps it was not unusual to find an artillery block with 81-mm mortars and 75-mm guns or mortars. Many blocks had firing chambers on both levels often covering two different directions. Monte Grosso, the largest ouvrage of the Little Maginot Line, housed the only 135-mm casemate and turret in the Alps. In the SF Alpes Maritimes, Monte Grosso, L'Agaisen, and Mont Agel mounted the only 75-mm gun turrets in the Alps. The latter ouvrage had two of these turrets.

Many of the Alpine gun casemates faced forward, requiring additional concrete protection and added armor. The artillery was concentrated in two or three blocks in most cases. Turret blocks were seldom used in the Alps because the surrounding terrain did not allow a 360 degree unobstructed field of fire. Like the Maginot Line Proper, the Little Maginot Line relied on interlocking fields of fire for its defense. In most cases the terrain was so rugged that anti-tank obstacles were unnecessary, although wire obstacles remained in use.

The garrisons of the gros ouvrages averaged 160 men in the SF of Savoie, 200 men in the SF of Dauphiné, and 290 men in the SF of Alpes Maritimes.

The petits ouvrages of the Southeastern Front were small and unlike similar positions in the Northeast Fronts. Normally, they mounted nothing larger than JMs and held no diesel engines. They were also classified as active abris since they seldom had more than a few cloches or embrasures and usually mounted only light weapons.

Most of the Alpine ouvrages were not finished because priority was given to the Northeast Front. In addition, the construction of such positions in the Alpine sectors involved a great deal of money because of their location and the ruggedness of the terrain. Some of the ouvrages were almost inaccessible in the winter because of the snow and in the spring because of landslides that often blocked their access roads. A few, located high in the mountains, were reached by a type of ski lift with small cable cars known as a *téléphérique*.

The Alpine defenses also included a line of avant-postes that were, however, very different from those of the Northeast. They were designed by the STG and usually built by military labor (Main d'oeuvre or MOM)[6]. Seventeen of the twenty-five avant-postes built after 1935 were sited near the frontier of the SF Alpes Maritimes. Many were multi-block and connected by trenches or tunnels, but none could be considered as strong as an ouvrage. Their main defensive advantage was in their location, since many lacked roofs over their thin walls.

In some places the advance line included upgraded older fortifications. For instance, in the early 1930s the late nineteenth-century fort of La Turra, located on a ridge dominating the pass of Mont Cenis in the SF of Savoie, received a new caserne and two gun casemates for 75-mm field pieces that opened onto the rock cliff overlooking the plateau below.

Some older fortifications to the rear of the main line were also modernized to support the newer positions. Thus the two-block gros ouvrage of Barbonnet was built into the old fort of Suchet whose old 155-mm Mougin turrets served as long range support.

The Alpine ouvrages consisted of the following:

OUVRAGES	ENTRANCES	BLOCKS
SF of Savoie		
PO Chatelard	—	1 Inf Cas
PO Cave à Canon	—	1 Inf Cas
GO Sapey	1	2 75-Cas (1 gun each), 1 75-Cas, 1 Obs
GO Saint Gobain	1	2 81-Cas, 2 Inf Cas, 1 Obs
GO Saint Antoine	1	1 75+-Cas/81-Cas, 1 Obs
GO Le Lavoir	2	2 75+-Cas, 1 75+-Cas/81-Cas, 2 Obs
GO Pas du Roc	1	1 75+-Cas, 1 81-Cas, 1 Inf Cas, 1 Obs
PO Arrondaz	1	2 Obs
PO Les Rochilles	2	2 Inf Cas, 1 Obs
SF of Dauphiné		
GO Janus	1	1 95-Cas, 1 75+Cas 1 81-Cas, 2 Inf Cas, 2 Obs
PO Col du Buffere	1	1 Inf Cas
PO Col du Granon	1	1 Inf Cas, 1 Obs
PO Les Aittes	1	3 Inf Cas
PO Le Gondran	1	1 Inf Cas, 1 Obs
GO Roche Lacroix	1	1 75-Tur/75+/81 Cas, 2 Inf Cas, 2 Obs
GO Saint Ours Haut	1	2 81-Cas, 1 Inf Cas, 2 Obs
PO Plate Lombarde	1	3 Obs
PO NW de Fontvive	—	2 Inf Cas
PO NE de Saint Ours	—	2 Inf Cas
PO Bas de Saint Ours	—	1 Inf Cas
PO Restefond	—	1 75-Cas/75+-Cas, 2 Obs
PO Col de Restefond	—	3 Inf Cas
PO Granges Communes	—	1 Inf Cas
PO La Moutière	—	2 Inf Cas, 1 Obs
SF of Alpes Maritimes		
PO Col de Crous	—	1 Obs
GO Rimplas	1	2 75-Cas/75+-Cas, 1 81-Cas, 1 Inf Cas, 1 Obs
PO Fressinea	1	1 Inf Cas, 1 Obs
PO Valdeblore	1	1 Inf Cas, 1 Obs
PO Col du Fort	—	1 Inf Cas, 1 Obs
GO Gordolon	1	1 75+-Cas/81-Cas, 1 81-Cas
GO Flaut	1	1 75-Cas, 2 81-Cas, 1 Inf Cas
PO Plan Caval	—	2 Inf Cas, 1 Obs
PO La Beole	2	1 Obs
PO Col d'Agnon	2	1 Obs
PO La Dea	2	1 Obs
GO Col de Brouis	1	2 81-Cas
GO Monte Grosso	1	1 75-Tur, 1 75-Cas, 1 135-Tur, 1 81-Cas, 2 Inf Cas
PO Champ de tir de L'Agaisen	2	1 Inf Cas
GO L'Agaisen	1	1 75-Tur/81-Cas, 1 75+-Cas/81-Cas, 1 Inf Cas
GO Saint Roch	1	1 75-Cas/81-Cas, 2 Obs

GO Le Barbonnet	1	1 75-Cas/81-Cas
GO Castillon	1	1 75-Cas/81-Cas, 1 81-Cas, 2 Inf Cas
PO Col des Banquettes	2	1 Inf Cas
GO Sainte Agnés	1	1 135-Cas/75+/81-Cas, 75+-Cas, 1 Inf Cas
PO Col des Gardes	2	1 Inf Cas, 1 Obs
GO Mont Agel	3	2 75-Tur, 1 Inf Cas, 1 Obs
GO Roquebrune	1	2 75+-Cas/81-Cas, 1 Inf Cas
PO Croupe du Reservoir	—	1 Inf Cas, 1 Obs
GO Cap Martin	—	2 75-Cas, 1 81-Cas

NOTES: Obs=Observation and/or GFM cloches, Cas=Casemate, Tur=Turret, / = combination, Inf=Infantry, MG=Machine Gun, 81=81-mm Mortar, 135=135-mm Howitzer, 75=75-mm Gun, 75+=75-mm Mortar. Many of the ouvrages were not completed and those POs with only an entrance block completed are not listed.

4. The Coast Defenses

The French coastal defenses did not receive the same priority as the Maginot Line because it was unlikely the Germans would present a serious threat from the sea. From 1932 the 3,000 kilometers of coast line were divided into four naval districts, each commanded by an admiral. During the First World War many of the large guns were removed to be used at the front and they remained with the army after the war. Nonetheless, the French continued to maintain coastal fortifications, which were mostly concentrated in their major ports. However, with few exceptions, these installations had become obsolete before 1939.

The 1st Naval District extended from Dunkirk on the Belgian border to St. Malo, covering most of the 1,100 kilometers of the North Sea and Channel coast line. Dunkirk, Calais, and Boulogne were relatively small ports. The navy set up light defenses at Dunkirk where sand dunes and embankments dominated a large part of the coast. To the east of Dunkirk, a coastal battery and searchlight unit occupied a position north of the old Fort des Dunes (west of Zuydcoote), and further east was the Battery of Bray-Dunes. West of Dunkirk lay gun batteries at Ouvrage Ouest and at Fort Mardyck, also equipped with a searchlight. All these defenses were oriented seaward.

Further along the coast, the port of Calais included the Battery de la Digue, located opposite its West Mole and guarding the approach to the port. The ship basin on the northeast end of the town was covered by a battery and searchlight position at Bastion II. A battery at Bastion XII, defended the channel entrance toward the city in the proximity of old Fort Risban. A battery position with turret guns lay west of Calais at old Fort Lapin. In 1928 there were eight old 240-mm and 190-mm guns and four railway pieces at Calais. By the beginning of the war, the defenses included no gun heavier than 120-mm. However, many weapons were in open emplacements with a 360 degree field of fire like the battery of 138-mm guns at Cap Gris Nez. The French made little effort to protect either Calais or Dunkirk from land assault. However, they did plan some water barriers for the protection of Calais.

The port of Boulogne was more extensively protected than Dunkirk or Calais. At the east end of its ship basin, north of the town, stood the gun battery of La Crèche with its searchlight. Batterie de la Digue was located on the mole and Batterie du Bassin lay inside the port. Batterie du Mont de Couple, with a searchlight, and Batterie d'Alprech were on the southwest side of the town, on either side of Le Portel. Batterie d'Equilen stood about three kilometers to the south. Landward defenses were absent and the town had to rely on its old medieval walls for protection.

Further down the coast lay the two most important seaports of the 1st Naval District: Le Havre and Cherbourg. Le Havre in particular was not only an important commercial sea port, but also the key to the Seine and, therefore, to the important inland port of Rouen. The harbor of Le Havre was defended by three batteries, and the mouth of the Seine by two. Two old forts from the Vauban era overlooked the northern part of the city. In 1928 its weapons included four old 240-mm guns, two 140-mm naval guns, and two 95-mm coast guns. However, these guns may have been retired and not part of the batteries mentioned, before the war began. On the south side of the mouth of the Seine, the small harbors of Trouville and Deauville were given a battery of guns. All of these defenses overlooked the net and mine barriers installed at the mouth of the river. All these important measures were taken because the Le Havre area was considered to be one of the most important access points on the northern coast.

However, Cherbourg, which served as a naval base and headquarters for the admiral commanding the district, was the most heavily defended port in the district. Here, the moles created an inner and outer anchorage area. The outer moles linked several islands defended by forts. On the coast, up to ten kilometers east and west of the city, stood the artillery batteries. To the east lay Batterie Brulay, with its 135-mm guns and large, but still unfinished concrete observation post. There were two more batteries between Batterie Brulay and the city. Additional batteries were still under construction when the war began, including Batterie Tourville with its 340-mm Mle 1912 guns originally intended for the *Normandie* class battleships. Work on this position stopped in June 1940. Three others were situated west of the city. Old Fort du Roule, on the south side of the city, overlooking Cherbourg and its harbor, was one of the old Vauban positions protecting the city.

The 2nd Naval District began at St. Malo and ended south of Brest on the southwest corner of Brittany. It encompassed the easily defended major naval base of Brest, headquarters of the commander of the 2nd Naval District. Its old Vauban forts formed part of the outdated defenses of the landward and seaward fronts. However, sixteen newer battery positions protected the approaches to the anchorage outside of Brest. Not all the positions were completed in time of the war. For instance, the battery of Minou had only four of its guns. To the west of Minou lay Batterie Toulbroch with its 240-mm guns in open and unshielded concrete positions. South of the anchorage of Brest, on the southern end of the Crozon Peninsula, was the Batterie of Cap de la Chèvre with its modern concrete command post completed in 1939. The guns of this battery, like the others, were mounted in armored shields, on pedestal positions. A mobile anti-aircraft and searchlight battery was also used. To the west of the Brittany Peninsula, the island of Ouessant served as an advance post with a gun battery on its eastern and western ends. The old fort of St. Michel, located on an island near Brest, had received two 75-mm gun turrets in 1910, one of which was still operational when the Germans incorporated the fort into their Atlantic Wall.

The 5th Naval District covered about 1,300 kilometers of Atlantic coast. It began where the 2nd Naval District ended, and continued to the Spanish frontier. The naval port of Lorient, almost defenseless in 1928, was fortified with batteries at the mouth of the river leading to the harbor. Additional defenses were being erected along this stretch of the coast when the war began.

The mouth of the Loire, leading to St. Nazaire, was covered by a battery of 194-mm guns. Further down the coast La Rochelle and La Pallice were also protected by battery positions that included the batteries on the Island of Ré. Batteries for 164-mm and 240-mm guns were projected for Royan, at the mouth of the Gironde. Their mission would be to cover the approaches to Bordeaux. Most of these positions, including those of the 1st and 2nd Naval Districts, were improved, completed and incorporated into the German Atlantic Wall between 1942-1944.

The 3rd Naval District, which included the major seaport of Marseilles and the main naval base of Toulon, encompassed the entire Mediterranean coastline and Corsica. Marseilles, like Toulon, was heavily defended by fortifications going back to the Vauban era. In addition, it was protected by a number of coastal batteries mostly concentrated on the fortified islands of Ratonneau and Pomeque that guarded the harbor entrance. The most notable of these defenses were a 305-mm gun battery, consisting of weapons from a *Danton* Class battleship, located outside the port and a few 240-mm coastal guns.

Toulon was protected by a number of gun batteries, including eight 240-mm coastal defense guns. Its defenses were increased during the latter part of the 1920s. Two new twin gun turrets with 340-mm guns were taken from the *Normandie* Class battleships and installed in the Cepet Battery at Toulon. The other minor ports along the coast up to Menton were given smaller batteries that included no gun larger than 120-mm. As in the other districts, all the batteries of the 3rd Naval District were also designed for landward defense. Unfortunately most of these batteries were also obsolescent. In 1943 they were modified and put to use by the Germans.

WEAPONS AND EQUIPMENT

MAGINOT LINE ARMAMENT:	MAXIMUM RANGE (METERS)
95-mm naval guns model 1893	8,000
75-mm gun*	
Model 1929, 1932, & 1933 (casemate)	12,000
Model 1933 (turret)	12,000
75-mm howitzer* R Model 1932 (casemate)	9,100
R Model 1932 (turret)	9,200
R Model 1905 (turret)*	8,200
135-mm lance-bombes (howitzer- casemate & turret)*	
Model 1932	6,000
75-mm mortar*	
Model 1931 (casemate)	5,900
81-mm mortar (casemate & turret)*	
Model 1932	3,600
50-mm mortar	
Model 1935	1,075
47-mm anti-tank gun	
Model 1934	1,000
37-mm anti-tank gun	
Model 1934	?
25-mm cannon	1,000
13.2-mm Hotchkiss machine gun	7,000
MAC 31 JM (twin machine gun)***	1,200
FM (automatic rifle) Model 24/29	600

*All of these weapons were water cooled and drew the water from a reservoir that served all the weapons of the block. Most weapons were simply sprayed with water by a crewman with a hose and water can.
***The MAC 31 JM was a combination of the air-cooled FM Model 24/29, but its high rate of fire required a water cooling system.
Artillery of older forts

155-mm Model 1887 (turret)	9,000
105-mm Model (German Metz forts)	9,700
105-mm Model (Re-armed forts of Thionville)	10,800-13,000

Supporting Field Artillery 105-mm Model 1935	10,300
120-mm L Model 1878	9,000
155-mm L Model 1932	27,500
280-mm Mortar	10,000

Railroad Guns (reinforced Maginot and coastal defenses)	
274-mm Models 1987-93	26,400
320-mm Model 1874	24,800

370-mm Model 15 Howitzer	16,000
400-mm Model 15 and 16 Howitzer	16,000
520-mm Model 16	14,600
(also all the coast defense guns listed below)	

Coastal Defenses

95-mm Model 1893	8,000
194-mm Model 1875 gun	18,300
240-mm Model 1884 gun	17,400
240-mm Model 1893-96 gun	22,700
340-mm Model 1912 gun	30,000

Turrets

	Diameter (meters)	Roof thickness (mm)
Gun 75-mm/33	4.0	350
Gun 75-mm/32	3.04	300
Howitzer 135-mm	2.90	300
Mortar 81-mm	2.35	300
Mixed Arms (old 1904 75-mm gun turret)	2.90	285
Mixed Arms w/50-mm mortar	2.55	350
Machine Gun	1.98	300
Cloches		
GFM Model 1929		
Petit (2 types)	1.20	200
Grand (2 types)	1.20	300
GFM Model 1934		
Petit	1.30	250
Grand	1.30	300
JM Model 1932		
Petit	1.39	200
Grand (2 types)	1.39	250 & 300
Mixed Arms Modele 1934		
Petit	1.5 to 1.9	300
Grand	1.5 to 1.9	300

Other types of cloches had a minimum armor thickness of 250 mm. (Source: *La Muraille de France* by Truttmann). The French engineers set up several categories for thickness of concrete and armor.

Protection	Concrete Thickness	Resists weapons of
1	1.75 meters	160-mm
2	2.25 meters	240-mm
3	2.75 meters	300-mm
4	3.50 meters	420-mm

THE MAGINOT LINE IN WORLD WAR II
1. The Maginot Line and the Extension

In September 1939, as the army mobilized, the troops of the Maginot Line quickly occupied their defenses. However, as no German attack materialized in 1939, the defenders of the Maginot Line soon became bored with garrison duty. The only major action at that time consisted of a barrage of German propaganda. While waiting for something to happen, the Maginot troops were put to work creating a number of intermediate positions of non-standard type and improving the existing defenses.

When the German offensive finally took place in May 1940, the French fortress troops were ready, only to find that they would not be in the main theater of operations: the Maginot Line had forced the Germans to avoid a direct assault on the French frontier and seek a different invasion route.

In the meantime, the garrisons of the ouvrages of Schoenenbourg and Hochwald, bored with routine operations, sought and received permission to install old 120-mm guns in open positions on their forts and fire upon German positions. Some forts of the RF of Lauter, which were within reach of the German border, also fired occasional volleys from their 75-mm turrets.

As the German offensive broke through the Ardennes, a German infantry division went after the last ouvrage on the Maginot Extension, the petit ouvrage of La Ferté, with heavy artillery and air support. On May 17, 1940, two huge 210-mm mortars joined in the bombardment, inflicting little damage to the ouvrage, except to the surrounding obstacles. On May 18 the two nearby casemates with 75-mm guns were abandoned by their garrisons. German assault engineers worked their way up to Block 2 of La Ferté. The neighboring ouvrage of Le Chesnois strove to drive them off with its 75-mm gun turret but it was too far away to be effective. The mixed arms turret of La Ferté was partially blown out of its well and its weapons destroyed with hollow charges. By May 19, after a whole day of fighting, the Germans penetrated Block 1 and found the crew dead, apparently asphyxiated in the subterranean gallery. Between June 12-14 the garrisons of the other three ouvrages received orders to sabotage them, and the extension was abandoned completely. Thus came about the Germans' first victory against the Maginot Line, a victory that had more value in the war of propaganda than in actual fact.

On May 14 the Germans bombarded the ouvrage of Schoenenbourg with 280-mm guns, and later with a 420-mm, in an effort to divert attention from their offensive through the Ardennes[7]. It wasn't until a few days later that it became clear that the Germans were crossing the Meuse between Sedan and Dinant and had no intention of assaulting the Maginot Line.

Between May 20 and May 23 the four petits ouvrages at Maubeuge fought valiantly until they were eliminated one by one. In some cases the Germans deployed Stuka bombers, assault engineers, flame throwers and/or heavy artillery against them. Further north, the isolated petit ouvrage of Eth lasted until May 26, fighting off the German attacks for four days. Ironically, while the men of the Maginot Line resisted undaunted, the Germans continued their race to the sea and the bulk of the Allied forces floundered and retreated.

The interval troops had been on the defensive since the campaign began, and were in the process of being removed from the Maginot Line Proper and the Rhine Defenses when the German Army Group C finally struck in June. At the time, German Army Groups A and B had already started a new campaign, breaking through the final defensive positions between the Maginot Line and the sea. The German infantry divisions that had begun to move around the Maginot Line in the vicinity of Longuyon were engaged by the gros ouvrage of Fermont.

In a retaliatory move, Fermont was placed under heavy bombardment. High-velocity German 88-mm flak guns, which proved successful in penetrating the cloches of La Ferté, were trained on the rear face of Fermont's artillery casemate. They almost succeeded in penetrating the concrete wall after firing repeatedly at the same spot, but they withdrew one round too soon. The crew of the damaged block effected repairs under cover of darkness. A few days later, on June 21, Fermont withstood another heavy bombardment and beat back a German ground assault.

The Germans showed little interest in engaging the great forts in the RF of Metz. On June 14, Operation Tiger was launched in the Sarre Gap. Several German divisions forced back the remaining French covering forces and fanned out behind the Maginot Line. On June 21, the Germans laid siege to several petits ouvrages on the end of the RF of Metz, which were well beyond the artillery range of the gros ouvrages. A couple of these small forts were saved by the 81-mm casemate mortars of the petit ouvrage of Laudrefang. Nonetheless, the Germans, attacking from the rear, were able to reduce and capture a few of these petits ouvrages with the help of their high-velocity 88-mm guns. Two of the petits ouvrages on the Sarre end of the RF of the Lauter also fell between June 21-24.

In the RF of the Lauter, German troops were able to penetrate through the lightly defended gap in the Vosges, between Bitche and Lembach. Heavy artillery, including the 420-mm howitzer, was trained on the ouvrages of Hochwald and Schoenenbourg. The latter, heavily bombarded between June 20 and 23, sustained only one damaging hit when a shell penetrated near an artillery block leaving a fracture in the combination M-1/M-2 magazine below. The aerial Stuka bombardment only succeeded in damaging the fossé of an infantry block.

June 15 marked the beginning of Operation Bear, an assault across the Rhine. The undermanned garrisons of the Rhine Defenses strove to repel the invaders, but were no match against the 88-mm guns that quickly knocked out the vulnerable casemates on the river. The Germans succeeded in taking the first line and penetrating the next line of casemates because most of the supporting troops had been ordered to withdraw with the French Second Army Group.

When France surrendered, many ouvrages still held on, not giving up until directed to do so by a representative of the French government. The Germans soon occupied the forts and began to exploit them for propaganda purposes. They removed many of the weapons and some of the equipment for use elsewhere. The Germans also found other uses for a few of the forts. For instance, Hackenberg became an underground factory and Four-à-Chaux was used as a target for weapons tests.

In 1944, the Germans failed to use the Maginot Line systematically even though the ouvrages could have been useful against the advancing Americans since many of their weapons fired toward the flanks and rear. One of the few ouvrages to be turned against the Allies was Hackenberg, whose artillery casemate (Block 8) with its three 75-mm guns stopped the American advance in November. The day was saved by a French officer who directed the Americans to a blind spot from which 155-mm self propelled artillery blasted away the weak rear wall of the block.

The Germans made a belated attempt to defend their old forts of the Metz ring, previously renovated by the French for use as headquarters and support bases. They also defended the forts of Thionville, which had been rearmed by the French to support the Maginot Line. The Americans had a difficult time eliminating these forts, but they succeeded in capturing both Koenigsmacker and Guentrange.

In the RF of Lauter, the ouvrage of Simserhof and Schiesseck changed hands in combat in 1944. The American 100th Division found these ouvrages impervious to their artillery despite the fact that they were not fully armed. Finally, a major battle raged over Simserhof. The American troops had to fight on its surface, destroying the positions occupied by the Germans one by one with explosives.

2. The Little Maginot Line

Since the Southeast Front had been stripped of most of its divisions even before the Germans embarked on the last phase of their campaign in the West, the Italians, who entered the war in early June, believed they could easily penetrate the French defenses. However, they soon found out how wrong they were. On June 20, when the Italians launched their assault, many parts of the Alpine front were still covered with snow, severely hampering their maneuvers. Their effort to penetrate the Arc Valley and take Modane failed dismally. They never even penetrated the line of avant-postes at Mont Cenis. The old masonry fort of La Turra, firing its two 75-mm guns through galleries in the cliff brought them to a standstill. One gun was pulled out and positioned to fire down on an advancing column of Italian light L-3 tanks. Further down the front, on June 24, Italian troops tried to overrun the two ouvrages of Pas du Roc and Arrondaz near the border south of Modane. However, the two forts, mutually supporting each other, successfully repelled the attack.

At Briançon the French ouvrages engaged in a duel with the huge Italian fort of Chaberton, despite the fact that they had not been designed for this purpose. With the help of the ouvrages' observation positions, a battery of French 280-mm mortars destroyed most of the 149-mm gun positions on top of Mount Chaberton between June 21-24.

In the Southeast the Italians concentrated their effort against the SF of Alpes Maritimes. Here again, the main attack, which began on June 22, failed to even break the line of avant-postes. Near Menton the tiny avant-poste of Pont St. Louis held out until the end of the campaign, denying the Italians the use of the coastal road. However, despite Pont St. Louis's valiant stand, the Italians took the railroad tunnel beneath it and attempted to advance behind it to take Menton. Alas, victory would elude them once more. As they emerged from the tunnel, they ran into a barrage of fire from several of the ouvrages in the area. To counter the cannonade, the Italians brought forth a naval artillery train, which was promptly damaged. Italian forces actually managed to storm the last ouvrage of the line, Cap Martin, but had to withdraw after a desperate fight. It must be recognized, however, that during the attack the Italians achieved something the Germans never did: to reach the superstructure of a gros ouvrage.

Thus the Alpine forts remained undefeated. Unfortunately, their victorious campaign was negated by the surrender of the French armies and government to the Germans.

3. The Coast Defenses

Some of the coastal defenses took part in the defense of Dunkirk, Calais, and Boulogne. At and near Dunkirk the Battery of Bray Dunes fired its three 164-mm guns at German troops from May 28 until its ammunition was expended on June 4, 1940. The Battery of Zuydcoote, with three 149-mm and two 75-mm cannons, did likewise. The 155-mm guns of the 3rd Naval Mobile Battery also took part in the action until June 3, when they were destroyed. If the events of the Pas de Calais area took on epic overtones, those off the coast of Menton owed more to the comic opera. In late June 1940 the Italians assembled an armada of fishing boats, motor boats, and other private vessels as well a squadron of MAS (motor torpedo) boats, and two submarines. The armada departed on June 22, but it soon became clear that the mismatched fleet would not be able to travel in unison. The smaller vessels were soon left behind, some, not equipped for such a long voyage, were actually stranded in high seas. By the time Menton was sighted, what remained of the small armada was too widely scattered to be effective. In addition, it became apparent that the engines on many of the vessels were too loud to approach the French coast undetected. Finally, the troops on board were too exhausted by the long trip and seasickness to consider swimming ashore. Thus the operation was aborted with no bloodshed.

After the fall of France, the Germans worked on the unfinished defenses and restored the completed ones for use in their Atlantic Wall by 1942.

GO of Hackenberg. Main Gallery. Access gallery to the left enters the M-1. (Kaufmann)

PO Immerhof. Mixed Entrance. Interior showing JM removed and the 47-mm AT gun, attached to overhead rail, in the firing position. Raymond Mersch, curator of the ouvrage for many years, holds a round for the weapon. (Kaufmann)

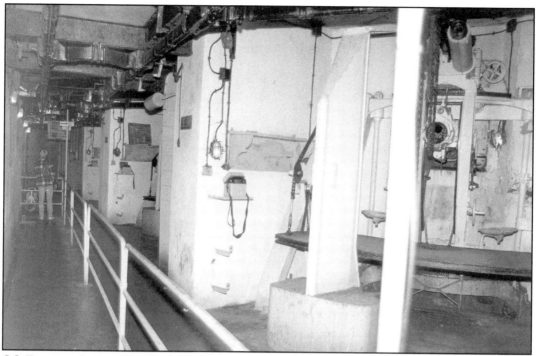

GO Fermont. Block 4, Artillery Casemate. Interior view back at all three gun positions. The gun can be seen in the first position with gunners seats and platform for loaders. (Kaufmann)

GO Metrich. Block 1, Artillery Casemate. 3 x 75-mm guns. (Kaufmann)

Above: GO Soetrich. Block 5, Artillery Turret. Turret for 2 x 75-mm guns. This was the largest type of turret in the GOs. Note armored air vent to left rear flush with the surface of the block. (Kaufmann)

Below: PO Bois du Four. Monolithic ouvrage with MG turret and weapons positions on both flanks. The upper embrasures are for a 47-mm gun with a JM and FM. The two below were in the fossé and each mounted an 81-mm mortar. This was the standard position for the mortar in the casemates of both French and Czech positions. (Kaufmann)

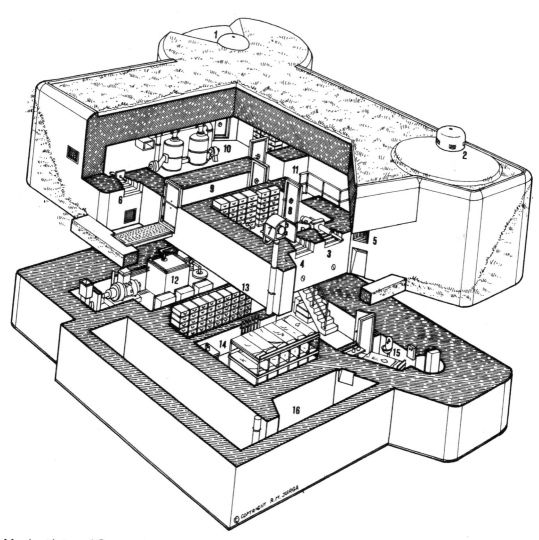

Maginot Interval Casemate:

1. JM (MG) cloche
2. GFM cloche
3. 47-mm AT gun (JM removed to side)
4. JM
5. FM (automatic rifle)
6. FM covering entrance & portable footbridge
7. Armored Searchlight of 350-mm
8. Firing chamber with ammo boxes against wall
9. Entranceway
10. Filters and ventilator
11. Stairway (WC behind stairs on lower level)
12. Usine
13. Food stores
14. Crew quarters
15. CO's room
16. Fosse

1. EM (2 x GFM cloche, 1 x 47-mm AT)
2. EH (1 GFM cloche, 1 x 47 mm AT)
3. Blocks 5 (75-mm Gun Turret, 1 GFM cloche)
4. Block 4 (135-mm Howtz. Turret, 1 GFM cloche)
5. Block 1 (MG turret, 1 MG cloche, 1 GFM cloche)
6. Block 2 (MG turret, 1 GFM cloche, 1 Obsv cloche)
7. Block 3 (2 GFM cloche, 2 x 81-mm mortars, 1 x 47 mm AT)
8. Block 6 (75-mm gun turret, 1 GFM cloche, mortar cloche*)
9. Small gallery serving as a drain and cable entrance

10. Magazine M-1
11. Position for armored door which closes by pressure from explosion of magazine to protect caserne - also includes a bypass around armored door.
12. Caserne
13. Kitchen
14. Position for explosives to block gallery
15. Command Post
16. Usine
*Weapon never perfected

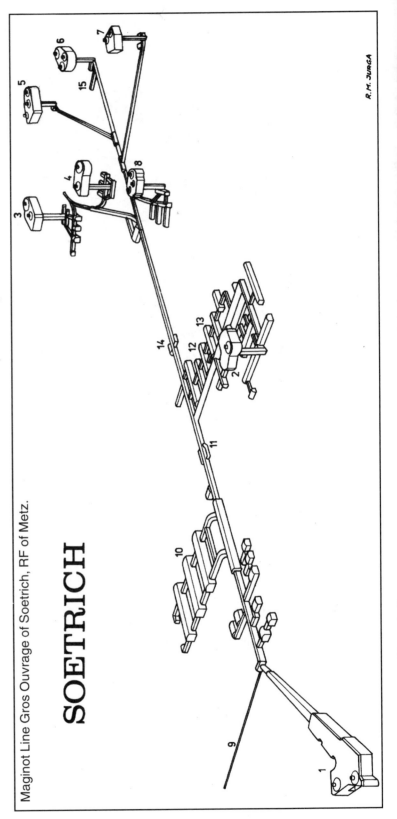

SOETRICH

Maginot Line Gros Ouvrage of Soetrich, RF of Metz.

R. M. JURGA

48

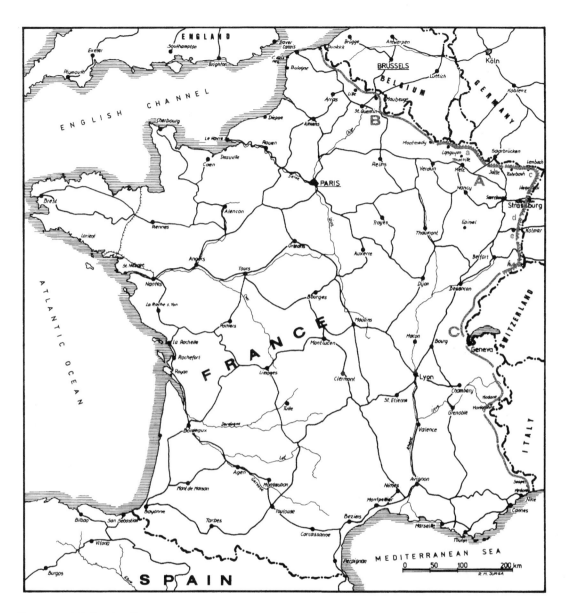

France and defensive lines

Hackenberg, Block 5 Artillery casemate for 3 x 75-mm guns.

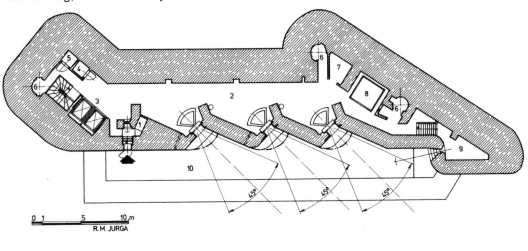

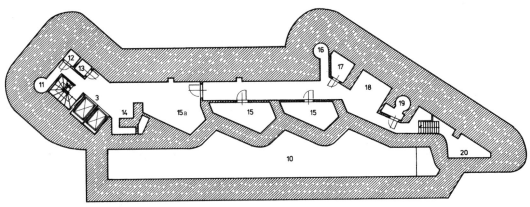

1. Defended exit with decontamination area
2. Firing chambers for 75-mm guns
3. Munitions elevators
4. Munitions
5. Munitions
6. Cloche (the two on the ends are GFM, the center one is for an automatic mortar that was never perfected)
7. Munitions
8. Water reservoir
9. Flanking coffre for light MG
10. Fosse

11. Storage
12. Magazine
13. Storage
14. WC
15. Rest area
15a. Ventilator and Filters
16. Storage
17. Officers room
18. Rest area
19. Storage
20. T.S.F. (Radio Room)

Propaganda illustration of Maginot Line from 1930s.

Plans of Maginot Line Ouvrages

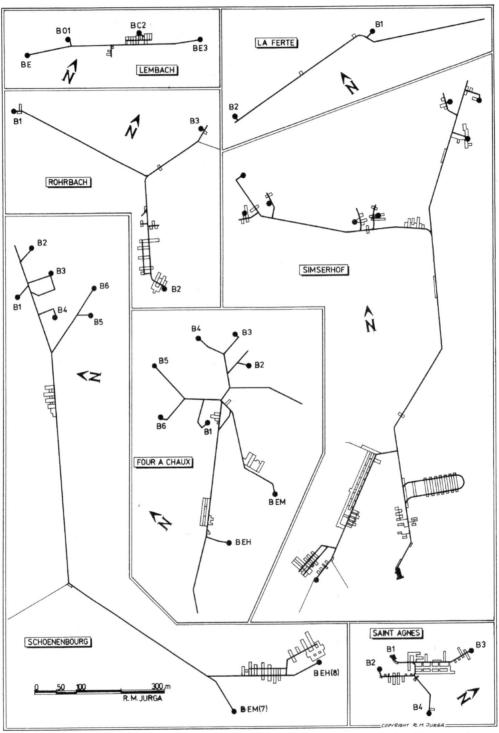

E = Entrance
EH = Men's Entrance
EM = Munitions Entrance

Inf = Block covering AT Wall
Obsv = Observation Block
T = Turret (type of guns)

Cas = Casemate (number 8 type guns)
Cl = Cloche (only AM included)
AM = Mixed Arms (25-mm gun w/MG)

Plans of Maginot Line Ouvrages

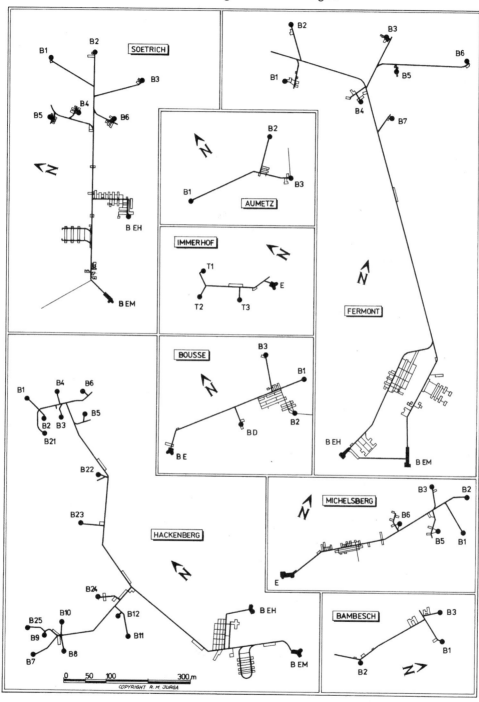

E = Entrance
EH = Men's Entrance
EM = Munitions Entrance
Inf = Block covering AT Wall
Obsv = Observation Block

T = Turret (type of guns)
Cas = Casemate (number 8 type guns)
Cl = Cloche (only AM included)
AM = Mixed Arms (25-mm gun w/MG)

Command Center in Maginot Line Gros Ouvrage.

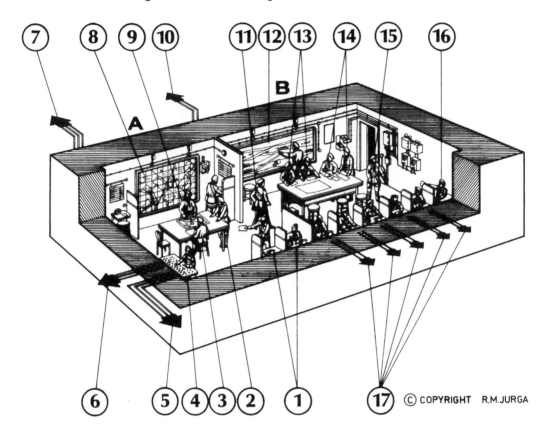

© COPYRIGHT R.M.JURGA

A. Fire control room:
1. Fire control section
2. Fire control officer
3. Secretary
4. Telephone exchange
5. Lines to artillery blocks
6. Lines to observers
7. Direct line to artillery blocks
8. Maps
9. Artillery commander
10. Lines to Group Artillery Command Post

B. Intelligence section:
11. Runner
12. Panoramic photos
13. Secretaries
14. NCOs
15. Intelligence officer
16. Telephone center of ouvrage
17. Lines to observers

Turret crews for Maginot Ouvrages based on estimates of LTC Ph. Truttmann.

TURRET FOR MG BLOCK

Chief Gunner

2 controlmen   Ammo handler

2 controlmen

TURRET FOR 75 MM GUN BLOCK

Chief Gunner   2 loaders

Chief Controlman   2 monte charge   2 ammo handlers

2 controlmen

TURRET FOR 81 MM MORTAR BLOCK

2 loaders

2 controlmen   2 monte charge and ammo   Chief

3 controlmen

TURRET FOR 135 MM HOWITZER BLOCK

2 loaders

Chief   2 controlmen   2 monte charge
2 powder men   2 fuses & charges

4 controlmen

TURRET FOR MIXED ARMS BLOCK

Chief   4 loaders

Chief   2 controlmen
2 monte charge   Ammo handler

6 controlmen

R.M.JURGA

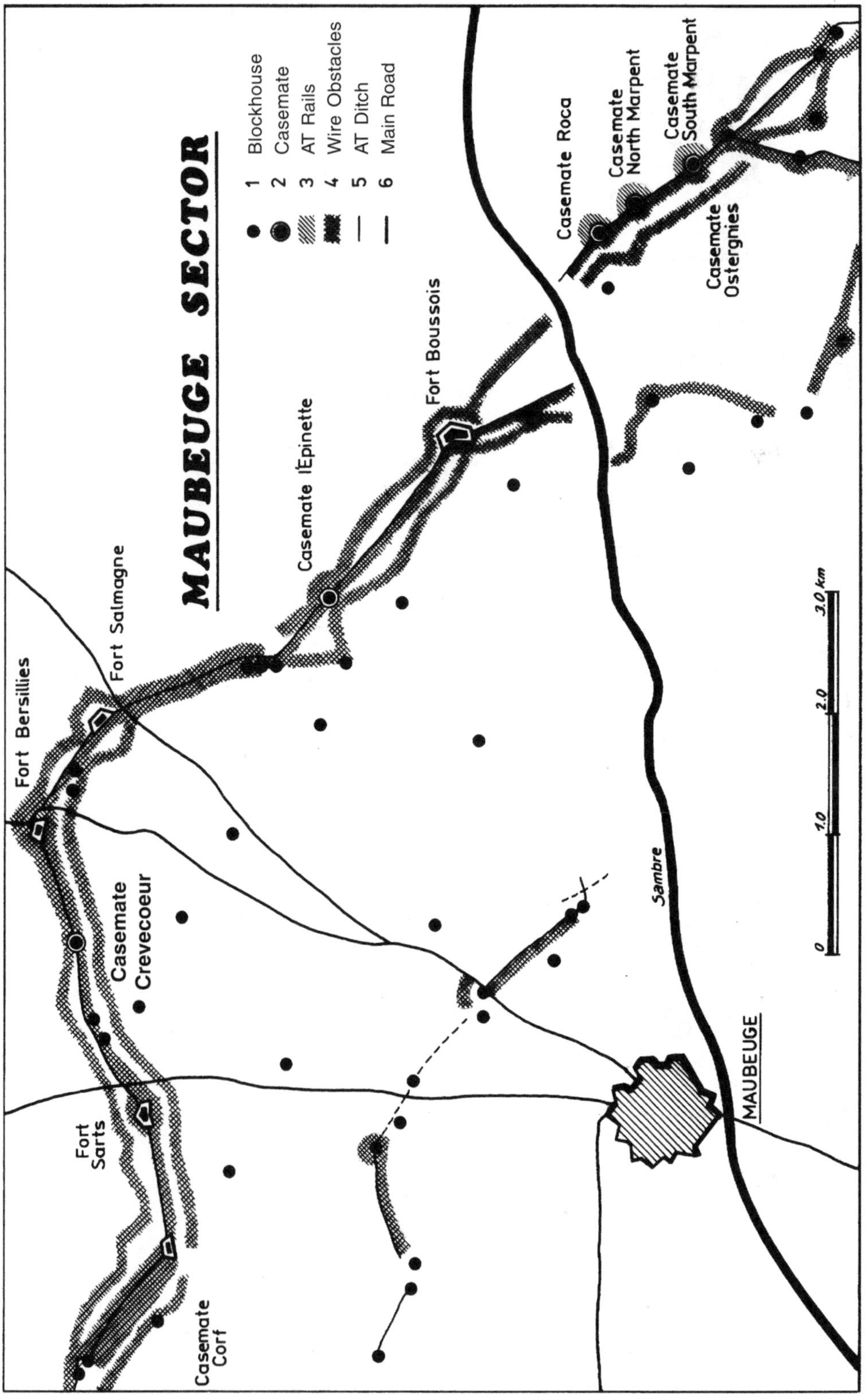

Maubeuge Sector with four Petit Ouvrages built onto old forts.

MAUBEUGE SECTOR

1	Blockhouse
2	Casemate
3	AT Rails
4	Wire Obstacles
5	AT Ditch
6	Main Road

Casemate Roca

Casemate North Marpent

Casemate South Marpent

Casemate Ostergnies

Fort Boussois

Casemate l'Epinette

Fort Salmagne

Fort Bersillies

Casemate Crevecoeur

Fort Sarts

Casemate Corf

Sambre

MAUBEUGE

3.0 km

2.0

1.0

0

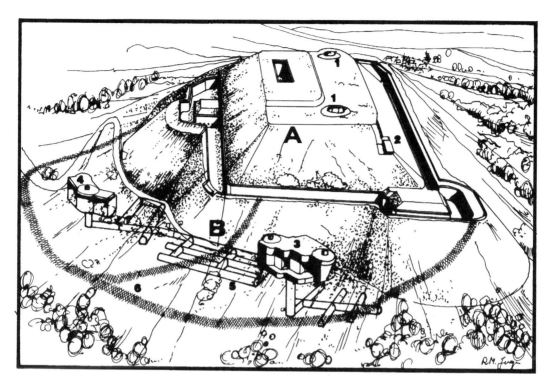

Fort Suchet and Gros Ouvrage of Barbonnet in Alps.
A. Ft. Suchet
  1. Turret with 2 x 155-mm guns
  2. Observation position
B. GO of Barbonnet
  3. Block 2 artillery casemate with 2 x 75-mm guns,
     2 x 81-mm mortars, and 1 GFM cloche and 1
     Lance Grenade cloche
  4. Entrance - Block 1 with 1 cloche
  5. Caserne
  6. Anti-Infantry Obstacles

Section A - filled with gravel.
Section B - gravel from Section A was
     released into this empty
     chamber so exit could be used.

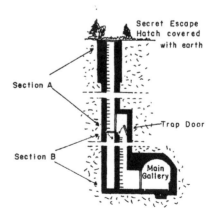

SECRET EMERGENCY
EXIT of the Ouvrage
of ANZELING
Each Gros Ouvrage had one.

Kaufmann

Abri of Coucou in RF of Metz.

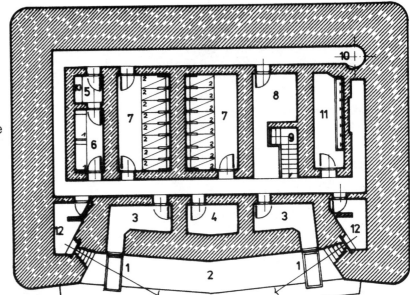

1. Footbridge of entrance
2. Fosse
3. Entrance corridor
4. Office
5. Telephone exchange
6. Room for 2 Officers
7. Chamber for 16 men
8. Infirmary
9. Stairway
10. GFM cloche
11. WC
12. Embrasures for light MG covering entrance,
13. Gallery to Petit Ouvrage of Coucou
14. Munitions
15. Food stores
16. Usine
17. Kitchen
18. Magazine
19. Reservoir
20. Urnial
21. Latrine
22. Coal for stove

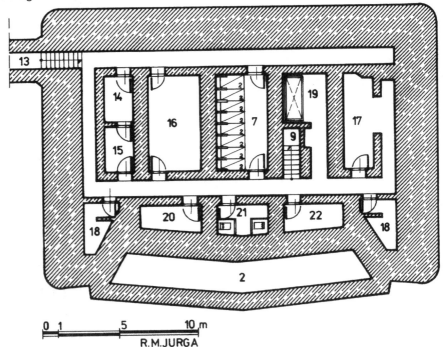

R.M.JURGA

Chapter 2

GERMANY

BACKGROUND

After the Franco-Prussian War, the leaders of the Second Reich (1871-1918) expected France to seek retribution for its losses. In addition, fearing that a potential Franco-Russian alliance could lead to a disastrous two-front war, they decided to create a number of forts and associated defenses on both the eastern and western borders of Germany. In the west, the Germans established fortress rings around Strasbourg and Metz, often building on old French forts, as in the case of Metz.

By the turn of the century, the Germans, responding like the French to advances in warfare, developed new and stronger forts. They extended the defenses of Strasbourg to Mutzig and those of Metz to Thionville. They also developed a new type of fortification known as *Feste*. The preliminary work at Mutzig consisted of triangular type forts and detached batteries employing turret positions. The Feste was further refined at Thionville and Metz. Located at prominent points and usually covering much of a hill top, it consisted of one or more large batteries of four guns, each in an armored turret. All its other facilities were built into the ground, including the large earth-covered casernes. Only the rear façades, a number of coffres, infantry positions, and observation points were exposed. Most of the *Feste* was surrounded by a ditch or moat, and infantry obstacles. A tunnel system linked most of the concrete positions, and an engine room, or usine, provided the needed power. When World War I began, these forts were still unfinished. None of them had a chance to participate in combat until World War II. At the end of the Great War, virtually all of the German *Feste* in the west ended up in France. The only one remaining in German territory, Istein, was destroyed, since Article 42 of the Treaty of Versailles specified that:

"Germany is forbidden to maintain or construct any fortifications either on the left bank of the Rhine or on the right bank to the west of a line drawn 50 kilometers to the East of the Rhine."

Thus the Treaty of Versailles left the Rhineland virtually defenseless. In the west only the obsolete fortresses of Ulm and Ingolstadt were allowed to stand, in East Prussia, the obsolete defenses at Königsberg and Lötzen, and in the east, the outdated fortifications of Küstrin, Breslau, and Glogau.

In addition, the treaty directed that "The fortifications, military establishments, on the Islands of Helgoland and Dune shall be destroyed," thus unmasking the approaches to the mouth of the Elbe and Wesser Rivers and associated ports as well as the Kiel Canal. However, Article 195 allowed Germany to maintain certain coastal defenses in their "existing condition." Those defenses included positions at Cuxhaven and Wilhelmshaven on the North Sea, and Pillau and Swinemünde on the Baltic Sea. Thus, during the 1920s Germany had been virtually stripped of its defenses. With a navy of six obsolete battleships and an army of ten divisions, the armed forces could do little to defend its naval bases or frontiers.

Nonetheless, the Germans did not give up easily. After World War I, the outlawed General Staff surreptitiously continued to operate, but defense was not its primary concern. Despite this attitude the German fortress engineers not only continued to maintain the few remaining fortifications, but also illegally improved their condition. However, the Inter Allied Commission, set up after the war, foiled several German attempts to build defenses on the eastern frontier. Until 1935, the German army was unable to build anything more than some bunkers along the Oder River and create water defenses on the Nischlitz-Obra Line, which later became part of the future Oder-Warthe-Bend Line. On the western frontier they completed only a small number of positions along the eastern side of the Rhineland, as allowed by the restrictions of the Versailles Treaty. After 1933 the situation changed, but fortifications remained of secondary importance as the General Staff concentrated on resurrecting the German army and transforming it into an offensive machine to be reckoned with.

MAJOR FORTIFICATIONS

The East Wall
The West Wall
The Coast Defenses

LOCATION

1. The East Wall

In East Prussia, Pomerania, and parts of Poland, glaciation from the last Ice Age left a region of moraines dotted with lakes with no unusually rough features. Nonetheless, on the edges of the North European Plain, there was no lack of natural defenses, despite the fact that most of the moraine did not exceed more than a couple of hundred meters in elevation. In fact, the terrain turns to mud after heavy rains, seriously impeding progress off the roads. To overcome this problem the German government built an autobahn running from Berlin past Breslau and Stettin to Königsberg and Elbing. The segment between Königsberg and Elbing remains in its original state to this very day, only one double lane completed for most of its length. Another autobahn ran from Berlin to Frankfurt-on-the-Oder, making possible rapid reinforcement of all the defensive positions in the east.

The East Wall occupied large sections of the frontier, including the isolated defensive positions of East Prussia primarily protecting Königsberg. Although it continued to be developed throughout the war, it was never actually completed. The East Wall consisted of three distinct lines: the Fortified Front of the Oder-Warthe-Bend, the Pomeranian Line, and the Oder Line. In addition, the Ortelsburger, Lötzen and Christburg Positions formed the border defenses of East Prussia. Finally, the position known as Fortress Samland constituted the final interior line running from the Frisches Lagoon (Vistula Lagoon) to the Kurisches Lagoon (Courland Lagoon) well in front of Königsberg. The small positions of the Heilsberg Triangle south of the fortress area, which were of little value by the end of the 1930s, are usually overlooked. At Königsberg, the old fortress ring acted as the last line of defense.

The main defensive line of the East Wall was the Oder-Warthe-Bend (OWB) Line, which was intended to cover the direct route to Frankfurt-on-the-Oder and Berlin. Intended to be the main defensive front, this position received the most attention. It was planned as a quadrangle extending from Küstrin on the Oder, along the Netze River to the Warthe. Directly to the south the main lines of fortifications covered the gap between the Warthe and the Oder rivers. The intended path of the defenses followed the Oder downstream past Frankfurt to Küstrin. Most of the area consisted of hilly and swampy terrain dotted with a number of lakes.

Before 1939 the OWB Line was the only German fortified front, representing the main defenses on the Eastern Front. It extended for approximately 80 km. The sides of the quadrangle remained uncompleted. The heavily defended sections began near Schwerin (Skwierzyna), at the confluence of the Warthe and Obra Rivers and ran south along the west bank of the Obra to the vicinity of Meseritz (Miedzyrzecz). The line then continued southward to the Oder passing west of

Schwiebus (Swiebodzin), a road junction on the main highway toward Frankfurt on the Oder, and then reached the Oder east of Krossen (Krosno Odrz).

The OWB Line included three sectors: Northern, Central, and Southern. The Central Sector, about 15 km long, was the shortest, occupied the terrain with the most relief, and had the heaviest concentration of modern fortifications. Dominated by hills more than any other, this sector was covered by fields, and had hardly any woods at all before the war. The other sectors, also running in the midst of fields, relied heavily on the many lakes and watercourses for defense.

The Oder Line hugged the river between the cities of Glogau and Breslau and was located over 20 km behind the border in most places. South of Breslau the terrain became hilly and more easily defended, especially in the industrial region of Upper Silesia. Between Breslau and Frankfurt there were some low and marshy patches along the river, particularly on the east side of the Oder, down river from Glogau.

The Pomeranian Line began where the Netze River merges with the Warthe River and followed the line of lakes to a point north of Scholochau where the terrain became hilly and began to resemble the morainic regions of East Prussia. For the most part, the main positions were not near the river but ran close to the border. The small wooded moraines that dominated the region were amenable to defense. The plan to extend the line to the sea was never carried out.

The main border defenses of East Prussia began east of Elbing, near the coast at Braunsberg (Braniewo), followed the Passarge River to Wormditt, turned eastward along the Alle River to Bartenstein (Bartoszyce), then hooked around and covered the town of Allenstein. They were known as the Christburg Position.

The Lötzen Position ran north to south using the heavily wooded Masurian Lake Region for defense. An intricate network of marshes and lakes and a tangle of moraines turned much of the area into a wilderness. This formidable terrain, which extended from Lyck to Osterode and included the Ortelsburger Forest Position, covered the border southeast of Allenstein, joining the Lötzen Position. Access through this region was via easily defended narrow defiles. Both of these positions ran from 20 to 40 km behind the border. The main line, Fortress Samland, began near the sea at Brandenburg, hugged the Frisching River to its source, turned north to Tapiau, and followed the Deime River to the sea.

2. The West Wall

According to German propaganda, the West Wall ran from the Swiss border to the point where the Rhine enters the Netherlands and consisted of the Army Position, which closely followed the border, and the Air Position which was further back and formed an air defense zone. In reality, the strength of the first position was grossly exaggerated and the second position was never developed beyond an elementary stage. Nonetheless, in World War II the West Wall was the fortified line with the greatest depth in relation to its length.

The West Wall ran along the Rhine and the elevated terrain of the Black Forest in the Upper Rhine Valley and through the wooded and low rolling terrain of the Saar region. Further north it passed through the wooded and rough terrain of Hunsrück and Eifel, along the remainder of the Belgian border to the Dutch border, and on to the sea[1]. The West Wall almost ceased to exist along most of the relatively flat terrain near the Dutch border, before it reached the point where the Rhine enters the Netherlands.

The West Wall, which spanned over 400 km, consisted of four major sections: Aachen, Trier, Pfalz (the Palatinate), and Oberrhein (Upper Rhine). The main defensive positions were the Aachen Advanced Position, the Orscholz Position in the Trier sector, the Hilgenbach Position, the Sprichern Position in the Pfalz, the Fischbach Position, the Ettlinger Position, and the Korken Wald (Forest) Position on the Upper Rhine. Most of these positions formed switch lines or oblique lines running off the main line of the West Wall.

The West Wall was located in excellent defensive terrain consisting of hills, many woods, and forests with the Rhine barrier forming a front line on the Upper Rhine or a final defensive position in other sectors. Only in some sectors, such as the Pfalz, did the Germans sacrifice the advantage of good defensive terrain to move their fortifications closer to the border at the insistence of Hitler[2].

3. Coast Defenses

In the North Sea, the German island base of Helgoland was restored to its role as the main position for the protection of the approaches to the ports of Wilhelmshaven, Cuxhaven, and Hamburg. It was located about 50 km from both the mainland to the south, southeast and east. The East Frisian Islands, beginning with Borkum Island in the west and Wangerooge in the east, covered the North Sea coast up to the approaches to Wilhelmshaven. Borkum, Norderney, and Wangerooge mounted the main defenses. The North Frisian Islands, with Sylt Island serving as the main defensive position, shielded much of the coastal region along Schleswig-Holstein. This coastal defense region was known as the *Coast Defense–Naval Command North Sea*. The fortress commander for the East Frisian Area was headquartered at Wilhelmshaven and the commander of the North Frisian Area, in Cuxhaven. In September 1939 the fortress commands became coastal commands and in February 1941 the two regions were unified as the *Coast Defense, German Bight*.

On the Baltic Sea, the pre-war *Coast Defense–Naval Command Baltic* included three autonomous zones: the *West Baltic Coastal Command*, which covered the coast of Schleswig-Holstein, Mecklenburg, and the main defenses near Kiel, the *Pomeranian Coastal Command*, concentrated at Swinenmünde (Swinoujscie), and the *East*

Baltic Coastal Command, centered at Gotenhafen with additional sections at Pillau (Baltikysk) and Memel (after the annexation of the latter in 1939).

HISTORY

Until 1934, German improvements of their defenses were rather trivial or insignificant, not only because of the treaty restrictions, but also because the military leadership was not very interested in investing in fortifications. The eastern frontier, considered by the Germans to be vulnerable to an attack from Poland, received a limited amount of work until 1934.

This work began on the Oder Line after 1927 because the Inter Allied Commission had not specifically mentioned the building of fortifications on the west bank of the Oder. Until 1930, the German engineers contented themselves with reconnaissance work for the planning of future fortifications. The most important work carried out between 1926 and 1930 was the so-called "land reclamation and flood control project" that involved the construction of sluices, canals, and a water barrier for the future OWB Line. After that, work was initiated on the Nischlitz-Obra Line, which followed the river and defended crossing points. By 1936 this line became part of the new OWB Fortified Front, one part of it being incorporated in the main line and the remainder becoming part of the rear line.

Work on Fortress Samland had began in 1932, and shortly afterwards the border defenses of East Prussia became a priority operation, because only a single corps could be spared to defend the isolated province.

Serious work on fortifications began after Hitler took power in 1933. Concerned about the size of the Polish armed forces, he ordered the army to proceed with the construction of the East Wall despite the restrictions of the Versailles Treaty. Already in 1932 the General Staff had suggested that fortifications were necessary to protect the eastern border and East Prussia from Polish aggression. The General Staff also claimed that the German army would not be ready for offensive operations until 1942. General Otto Förster was appointed Inspector of Engineers and Fortifications in October 1934, and he directed the construction of the East Wall until 1939.

Priority was placed on the Oder, Pomeranian, and OWB Lines. The Fortress Engineers Corps, only seven battalions strong, was given the task of directing the work of civilian construction firms. In the beginning Hitler and his chief military engineer apparently set out to outdo the Maginot Line, but in 1938 Hitler had second thoughts, and decided to apply his own personal touch to the final design.

Before 1936, only a limited amount of work was done along the border with Czechoslovakia and the eastern part of the Rhine valley, in accordance with treaty limitations. After the reoccupation of the Rhineland in 1936, Hitler ordered the creation of a Limes Position that would eventually become the West Wall. It would run from Aachen to the Rhine. Even before German troops marched into the demilitarized zone, the Fortress Engineer Corps sent its men in to survey the region for the future line of fortifications. Hitler ordered the main defenses to be established between the Mosel and Rhine Rivers with light fortifications elsewhere. The work, which was undertaken between 1936 and 1937, did not include a continuous anti-tank barrier, but relied mostly on natural features.

In 1937 the West Wall consisted mostly of simple light defenses, including forward-firing bunkers. General Förster, Major Erich von Manstein of the General Staff, Minister of Defense Field Marshal Werner von Blomberg, and Commander of the Army F.W. von Fritsch debated the best method of defense for the Reich. The disagreement between them centered mainly on whether to build a line of fortification, sectors defended in depth, or other types of fortifications altogether. Hitler, the arbitrator, settled the matter by deciding on defense in depth, but allowed the engineers to plan for heavy fortifications.

A number of the largest German fortifications, known as *Werkgruppen*, were already under construction on the OWB Line in the East.[3] In 1937 plans were made for a number of Werkgruppen on the West Wall, some of which neared completion early in the war. In addition, work began in 1937 on the huge subterranean fort of Istein, beneath the site of Feste Istein, which was destroyed after the Great War.

Work progressed apace on the East Wall and the Pomeranian Line where the first bunkers went up in 1934 on the OWB Line. These early bunkers included two-level models, called "Hindenburg Stands," whose lower floor was built of "fortress brick" instead of concrete to cut costs. The situation improved in 1935 after work began on the first B-Werke, large bunkers of Type B strength also known as *Panzerwerke* when they included one or more armored cupolas.[4]

Hitler visited one of these positions in October 1935, examined the plans for the fortifications and for a gigantic tunnel system, and then gave Förster a free hand. The engineer general was given approximately fifteen years to complete the fortifications. Despite this fortuitous order, work slowed on the East Wall, due mostly to competition for resources with the West Wall. The OWB Line was transformed into a fortified front in 1936 and was nearly completed by 1939. Between 1939 and 1940 the heavy A-Werke planned for the East Wall were begun, but they were never completed. Most of these fortifications were planned as batteries of three single-gun turrets for 105-mm guns and 150-mm howitzers.

Interestingly, the work on the massive tunnel system was so well camouflaged that it went undetected by the Polish agents who observed the construction of the German fortifications. The subterranean galleries linked a number of the

Werkgruppen and large artillery battery blocks, which were barely laid down and never completed when the war began.

In 1938 Hitler returned to visit the site and was infuriated by the amount of money and effort that had gone into the building of a tunnel system that he deemed useless and Werkgruppen that held no artillery weapons. The Führer further criticized the type of weapons used in the Werkgruppen and stated that the OWB Line would be a hiding place for war shirkers. After this visit, construction was drastically curtailed and Hitler dashed off a memorandum on the construction of fortifications.

German industry could not produce the needed cupolas for the gun battery positions planned for the East Wall in the mid-1930s, so plans for their installation were postponed until after 1938. German industry was able to produce no more than two turrets a year. Work on the first positions began just before the onset of the war, but the short Polish campaign obviated the need to complete them in a hurry.

In 1938 General Förster felt that the Limes Position, or West Wall, was little more than an "improvised line of border defense." Hitler, dissatisfied with the army's work in the West, ordered Dr. Fritz Todt of the Reich's Labor Service to take over the construction, albeit under the supervision of Förster's engineers. At this point, Hitler demanded that the defenses run right along the border and not behind it, where better defensive sites existed because he did not want the enemy to be able to set foot on German soil.

Hitler's memorandum of July 1938 set up the guidelines for all defensive structures before the war. He condemned the type of tunnel system built on the East Wall and stated that there was no need for concrete protection able to resist guns heavier than 220-mm since the enemy would not be likely to concentrate heavier weapons against small fortifications. He also called for the installation of flame throwers, which would demoralize the enemy, and gas protection devices that were already in use in the French defenses.

The summer of 1938 was hectic, as work continued on the fortifications on both fronts, many reserve units took up positions in the unfinished West Wall, and the army prepared for an invasion of Czechoslovakia. By the time the Czech crisis was over, 5,000 bunkers stood on the West Wall because the Reich's Labor Service had increased the work force on the fortifications to 342,000 men in October 1938, a number ten times larger than in June. In November plans were drawn up for ten small Werkgruppen and 14,600 more bunkers. In 1939 the numbers were increased to twelve Type A-strength Werkgruppen, fifty small Type B-strength Werkgruppen, twelve battery positions, and over 60 km of galleries. This growth was due to the "Aachen to Saar Program "that called for upgrading the quality of positions, and building the new S-100 type bunker. When the war broke out, over 22,000 positions were completed on the West Wall, forming a long, almost continuous concrete anti-tank barrier and massive mine fields. The famous concrete "dragon's teeth," and a wooden pole version, appeared both on the East and West Walls. The mine fields of the West Wall consisted mostly of anti-personnel mines and were the first major such fields to be laid by any nation before 1940. During 1940 the War Expansion Program called for the construction on the West Wall of new A- and B-strength S-400 bunkers with Czech weapons and armor and the B-strength S-500 bunkers. Few of the B strength Werke were ready, and the Werkgruppe of Istein–called the "Gibraltar of the West" by Hermann Göring in the spring of 1938–was far from complete.

In the late 1930s the East Wall was all but ignored while German propaganda concentrated its attention on the West Wall. The German government released photographs and films of construction on the West Wall in order to impress the enemy. Included in the propaganda material was a film showing troops entering Panzerwerke Scharnhorst and a view of its interior. This was not the Werkgruppe on the OWB Line, but a simulated position created to misinform the world about the German defenses in the west.

DESCRIPTION

1. The East Wall

The East Wall was the heaviest pre-war fortification system built by the Germans, who concentrated the largest positions on the OWB Line. The weapons, equipment, and construction materials were tested at a secret engineer site northeast of Magdeburg, which included the Wandern and Hillersleben testing grounds in the Krupp Polygon. The East Wall positions served as prototypes for the positions on the West Wall and other places.

The OWB Fortified Front, which consisted of three sectors and blocked the direct route to Frankfurt and Berlin, was the heart of the East Wall. Its 16-km long Central Sector contained a number of strong points or werkgruppen that formed the core of the OWB Line. After 1936, many of these Werkgruppen were linked to the vast tunnel system, which was excavated by civilian labor. The 27-km long Northern Sector consisted of a few Werkgruppen and a number of water defenses. The 34-km long Southern Sector relied heavily on defensive terrain and water obstacles, including fourteen dams and sluices. The OWB numbered a total of eleven Werkgruppen that consisted of B-Werke linked to each other by underground tunnels.[5] Smaller bunker positions and individual bunkers and associated anti-tank obstacles also occupied the entire front. The entire OWB Line consisted of just over 100 positions, including heavy works. There was an advance line at about 10 to 12 km in front of the main line and a third line at about the same distance to the rear, but the latter only comprised a few small structures.

A German fortress battalion trained troops for garrisoning the East Wall, but the only positions that needed a permanent garrison were the Werkgruppen. The individual bunker positions were designed for field troops who only needed to provide maintenance and technical support when the positions were unoccupied. This was also true for the fortifications of the West Wall and accounts for all the simple instructions found painted on the walls of even the oldest bunkers. These inscriptions enjoined the soldiers to "close the armored shutter while using the latrine" to prevent the enemy from seeing the light, not to block vents, and to take other such practical precautions.

The Pomeranian Line covered a larger front that extended for about 275 km and included several thousand positions and eight Werkgruppen.[6] Like the OWB, it comprised three lines: the main line sandwiched between a forward and a rear line of light bunkers. The positions consisted of small bunkers with anti-tank gun shelters, like in the OWB Line. The underground links of the Werkgruppen were not as long or as deep as those of the OWB Line, and often consisted of a single Panzerwerke with detached cupolas.

A total of twelve Panzerwerke were built in the Pomeranian Line. These two-level structures had 1.5 meter thick concrete walls, housing a garrison area and usine on the lower floor and usually two weapons positions behind steel walls, and a half cloche on the upper floor[7]. They accommodated a garrison of about thirty-five men. Only a few Panzerwerke were not an integral part of the eight Werkgruppen of the Pomeranian Line. In many cases, the Werkgruppen had bunkers that were not classified as Panzerwerke. In general, no specific name was assigned to the Werkgruppen, which are referred to in current literature by the name of their location:

TOWN NEAR WERKGRUPPE (POLISH NAME)	NUMBER OF BLOCKS
Deustch Krone (Walcz) - "Kamel"	6 including an entrance
Deustch Krone (Walcz) - near quarry	2 and 2 detached cloche
Strahlenberg (Strzaling)	7 including an entrance
Tütz (Tuczno)	3 including an entrance
Eulenburg (Silnowo)	2 entrances and 2 detached cloche
Eulenburg (Silnowo)	6 including an entrance
Rederitz (Nadarzyce)	No data - position covered by earth
Neu Stettin (Szczecinek)	Unknown

The Oder Line spanned about 150 km, excluding the lightly defended area of Upper Silesia[8], and numbered no heavy works among its 778 positions. Its first line of bunkers went up on top of the dike of the Oder River between 1930 and 1932. Even though it was vulnerable, this line continued to be integrated into the defenses of the area. A second line of smaller bunkers was erected about 10 km behind the main line. Later, more bunkers were added to the main line. However, this time they were built into the dike, in less conspicuous and vulnerable positions. In most cases their weapons were able to cover each other's flank and fire along the river. All the bunkers had a single level, and every third bunker mounted an observation cloche that barely rose above the surface. All in all the Oder Line consisted of small, light bunkers for heavy and light machine guns, troop shelters, and observation posts. The river served as the main obstacle but at certain points, such as bridges, the defenses were heavily reinforced.

Before 1935, the Germans devised a classification system for defensive works for both East and West Walls based on concrete thickness. Four main types of construction were established: Type A (the heaviest), Type B, Type C, and Type D (the lightest). Type A structures had roofs 3.5 meters thick (although a variant, A1, was not as thick) while those of Type D had a concrete thickness no greater than .30 meters. Types C and D were discontinued after the summer of 1940 because they were considered to be too weak.

This classification system was also extended to the armor plate. Thus Type A armor was from 400-mm to 600-mm thick while Type D positions used nothing greater than 20-mm. It must be noted that the thickness of Type A concrete, 3.5 meters, was identical to the thickness of the heaviest French positions. Nonetheless, the French and the Germans used different methods of concrete mixing and reinforcement, coming up with far different results. Thus Type A armor could resist weapons of 520-mm and direct hits from 1,000 kg bombs while the French walls could only withstand guns of 420-mm. Except for a bridge position on the autobahn between Berlin and Königsberg, no Type A positions were completed on the East Wall.

Since most German Type A positions, with the exception of a few on the West Wall, never passed the planning stage, Type B became by default the more common type of position. Called B-Werke, Type B positions were capable of resisting a single 300-mm artillery round and continuous fire from 210-mm guns and withstand a hit from a 500 kg bomb, as Hitler had desired. The older variants of Type B, only 1.0 meter thick, could only withstand bombardment from 150-mm artillery pieces. The old Type C could resist weapons under 105-mm caliber while the Type D could only stand up to the lightest weapons. However, Types C and D could not withstand any direct bomb hit.

The *Panzerwerke* made up most of a fortified group, known as *Werkgruppen*. Panzerwerke were single- or multiple-level structures usually designed to fire in all directions, mounting their armament in the roof. This armament normally consisted of one or more heavy machine guns and, on Hitler's insistence, also a flame-thrower and a mortar after July 1938. However, only a few dozen flame-throwers and mortars were actually installed.

A 50-mm breech loaded automatic mortar (designation M-19 automatic granade launcher) with a frequency of fire of 30 to 60 rounds per minute, was developed for mounting in a cloche flush with the ground[9]. It was operated by an officer and seven men, including a gunner and two assistants on the controls in the cloche.

The rotating nozzle of the flame-thrower projecting through the steel collar and mounted in the roof, was able to spray its flames in a full 360 degree arc on the surface. Its fuel supply was stored in a large room beneath the control room. In a few rare instances the fuel room was on the same level as the control room. The whole mechanism was operated by a three-men crew.

Each Panzerwerk needed its own power source to operate some of its specialized weapons and other supporting equipment. The Panzerwerke that formed part of a Werkgruppe received their power from an usine located in the subterranean facilities. The automatic weapons could also be operated manually, but with less efficiency.

The entrances to the Panzerwerke usually consisted of an "L" shaped hall with a decontamination shower at the end nearest the outside entrance. Another armored door with a crenel for small arms at the other end of the corridor, covered the entrance. In addition, part of the entrance floor leading to the interior door consisted of a trap several meters deep that was exposed when the floor was pulled up like a drawbridge to cover the interior doorway. These positions had garrisons of 50 to 70 men.

None of the Werkgruppen had rotating turrets, but had full (six embrasure) on the roof and/or half (three embrasure) cloches projecting from a wall instead.[10] The ubiquitous cloches, found in most major fortification of Europe of the time, varied in size and function. The smallest were an observation cloches and the largest, in France, were capable of holding a small cannon. The cloches of the Panzerwerke were among the largest in Europe. They had six crenels for two heavy machine guns that could be rotated to each crenel individually and small observation points for periscopes in between. Many had a small roof periscope and a searchlight (used in the weapons embrasures) with a range of about 300 meters. Several men occupied the rotating floor with two serving each machine gun. The cloche was made of chrome molybdenum steel with about .5% to .7% molybdenum content imported from the U.S. The first cloche was tested in late 1934 at Meppen, and installation began in 1938.

The half cloche was not set above the roof of the bunker, but projected from the wall, its roof jutting just below that of the bunker and its rear opening into the bunker. Its three embrasures together could cover almost 180 degrees.

The weapons rooms for heavy machine guns and anti-tank guns were actually armored casemates with a steel plate wall and sometimes a similar armored plate roof. The main weapon in both cloche and casemate was a machine gun, but casemates with 37-mm and 50-mm anti-tank guns, and 105-mm guns were projected.

Most Werkgruppen had underground facilities that included a caserne area with all necessary facilities such as the living quarters, usine, and storage areas. The subterranean facilities were located between 15 to 20 meters below the level of the Panzerwerke and were connected to them by a staircase and an elevator. The whole position was gas-proofed with filters and airtight doors. A transformer room located at the lower level of the Panzerwerke converted power from the civilian grid. Each Panzerwerke included one to three emergency exits that led to the surface and were filled with sand that had to be shovelled out before use. These positions, and most bunkers, were connected by underground telephone lines. Few Werkgruppen had special entrance blocks like the Maginot ouvrages. Werkgruppe Ludendorff in the Northern Sector is a rare exception to this rule. Plans were made to connect most Werkgruppen in the Central Sector that had two to four Panzerwerke, to the underground tunnel system. Seven of the nine Werkgruppen in the area were actually linked to it.

On the East Wall, 83 Panzerwerke were completed, 41 of which were located in the Central Sector of the OWB Line. Of these, 23 were grouped into 9 Werkgruppen. The Northern Sector included 24 Panzerwerke, 8 of which formed 3 Werkgruppen. The Southern Sector comprised 18 Panzerwerke that could also be classified as B-Werke, 4 of which formed a single fortified group:

WERKGRUPPEN	NUMBER OF BLOCKS
Northern Sector	
Ludendorff	6
Roon	1
Moltke	1
Central Sector	
Schill	3
Nettelbeck	3
Lützow	4
York	5
Gneisenau	2
Scharnhorst	3
Friesan	1
Jahn	4
Körner (no tunnels)	3
Southern Sector	
Lietzmann	4

The fortified group of Ludendorff was the first to be built and was used to test new types of Panzerwerke. By 1944 it included five Panzerwerke and a special entrance block. Werkgruppen Roon and Moltke were unusual in that both consisted of a single Panzerwerke, but had underground works and two detached cupolas. A tunnel of about 30 meters connected Moltke's two detached positions, consisting of half cloches, with the Panzerwerke. The usine and caserne occupied the lower level of this large bunker. Additional positions were added to the defenses as the Russians advanced westward in 1944.

One of the most striking features of the East Wall was the vast tunnel system built in great secrecy in the Central Sector that would have become a veritable underground city if it had been completed. The German engineers took advantage of the numerous old mine shafts that honeycombed the area, connecting some of them to form the tunnel and using others as dumps for the spoil from new excavations. Workers completed 32.5 km of underground works and more were planned.

The main galleries were wide enough to accommodate an underground railroad that was to extend for several kilometers. A small underground train would haul supplies from the entrances to the access galleries leading to the various Werkgruppen. Only a small section of track was laid and the train engine and cars were never delivered. The main tunnel of the underground system, 4.0 meters wide and 4.2 meters high, included twenty-two stations spread over a distance of about 10 km. The entrances to the tunnel were located over 2 km behind the main line. The secondary galleries were smaller and led to chambers for two-level magazines and casernes and usines for four to six diesel engines. The subterranean works were located 20 to 40 meters below the surface. In 1938, as most of the tunneling was being completed and the equipment was being installed, Hitler demanded all work to cease. Thus none of the entrances with level access, allowing trucks to drive straight in, were completed. All heavy loads had to use the elevators that were part of the positions already completed with the Werkgruppen. At key points in this complex blockhouses and iron gratings controlled access. Efficiently designed water drains beneath the floor kept the galleries dry and are still mostly functional today. Ventilation was assured through eleven tall chimneys towering above the complex. In accordance with German military planning, the entire elaborate system was primed for destruction thanks to special niches for explosives located throughout the network of galleries.

When he visited the project, Hitler concluded that it was a massive waste of resources, particularly because the dozen Werkgruppen connected with the tunnels mounted only light armament. Actually several large Panzer batteries were planned and would have been installed in A-Werke of three individual blocks mounting a single 105-mm turret gun each. Seven of these batteries were projected for the Central Sector, which was also supposed to include four similar batteries of 150-mm howitzers. The turrets, similar to those used on the Feste, were non-retracting and were designed for long barrel weapons. Each cupola was to be mounted on the end of a rectangular-shaped block. Each battery would have required about 470 men. Work actually began on Panzer Battery 5 and the foundations for a couple more blocks were poured by 1940. The lower level of a massive entrance block for this battery that led to the tunnel system below was completed, and was changed into the principal entrance, after work stopped on the tunnel system. A complex of munition rooms and supporting facilities encircled by a gallery was built in the tunnel system below the battery. Plans for positions with 50-mm guns in rotating turrets and special cloches for 105-mm howitzers were also projected, but none of these positions were built.

The first bunkers built in the Nischlitz-Obra Line were Type C-strength. The earliest, the two-level Hindenburg Stands, served as troop shelters and had a garage for a 37-mm anti-tank gun that was rolled out into an open position when needed. Some of these bunkers included a forward-facing machine gun position. The German firing positions on both the East and West Walls usually comprised a large armored 60-mm shield that formed most of the exposed façade and a rear entrance covered by a crenel for a light weapon. The small doors on these positions were similar to those of a ship and those of the B-Werke.

Late in the war, log machine gun bunkers with a concrete façade and open to the rear were created on the Pomeranian Line. Also in 1944 thousands of prefabricated one-man bunkers were deployed on the East Wall.

Other defenses employed on the OWB Line included rows of concrete dragon's teeth to stop tanks. Set at different heights they were usually poured in four rows and covered approximately 20 km of the Central Sector of the OWB Line in front of the werkgruppen.

According to a 1944 document, the hundred positions of the OWB Line required a garrison of about 4,300 fortress troops, including a regiment-size formation that would operate the vast tunnel system and service the fortifications. The subterranean complex would need up to 6,000 men, the Pomeranian Line, 7,500 fortress troops for its 4,000 positions, and the Oder Line another 7,500.

In East Prussia the strongest concrete positions were the older fortifications of Königsberg. The terrain was the best defensive asset so that most positions set up in the area were of Types C and D. The Hohenstein Position relied on obstacles, water defenses and flooding devices for its defense, but also included a small number of concrete positions. It covered the border with Danzig, along the Vistula River. Christburg, a similar position, ran east of Elbing to Allenstein where it merged with the Ortelsburg Wald Position. Here, concrete bunkers covered the forest paths. Finally, the Lötzen and Hohenstein positions, much stronger than Christburg, relied mainly on the terrain for protection.

2. The West Wall

The older positions of the West Wall included light machine gun bunkers along the Upper Rhine and the Ettlinger Barrier, which became a switch-back position after the West Wall was built. The Ettlinger Barrier was built before the occupation of the Rhineland and included an anti-tank ditch and over fifty bunkers–mostly Type C–and the standard wire obstacles. Additional switch positions encircled the cities of Aachen and Saarbrücken.

The West Wall consisted in actuality, of three positions: the forward position, the main line, and the rear position. The forward position was 2 to 20 km deep, depending on the terrain. The main line, on the other hand, had a depth of 3 to 8 km. The rear position was a few kilometers behind the main line.

The West Wall is usually divided into three sectors: Northern, Central, and Southern. The Northern or Aachen Sector, which ran from the point where the Rhine entered the Netherlands to the cities of Aachen and Trier, was lightly defended. The Central Sector, sometimes identified as the two sectors of Trier and Pfalz, covered the area between Trier and Karlsruhe on the Rhine and concentrated its heaviest defenses in the Pfalz.[11] The Southern or Oberrhein Sector covered the Upper Rhine and included Werkgruppe Istein and mostly light defenses covering the river crossings. By the time the war began the entire West Wall included 22,000 positions and an almost continuous anti-tank barrier.

Behind the three positions of the West Wall collectively known as the Army Position, lay the Luftwaffe Position, whose existence owed more to propaganda than actuality and was purported to bristle with anti-aircraft weapons capable of shielding Germany from aerial attacks.

Most of the bunkers built on the West Wall were standardized models that could mount a machine gun or a 37-mm anti-tank gun. A large number of troop shelters built for the Army came in sizes that could accommodate ten to twenty-six men as well as a machine gun position. Artillery observation positions for six men occupied key sites.

Of the few large Werkgruppe actually completed, the largest was Besseringen, near Edingen, a B-Werk with eleven blocks mounting no weapon larger than mortars and machine guns. A great deal of work was lavished on the huge fortress of Istein, which, nonetheless, never reached completion. Many of its subterranean works were excavated 60 meters below a ridge and the tunnel leading off to the rear support area, if completed, would have extended for over 2 km. The access gallery was beneath the ridge and opened into the railway tunnel that passed through it. The usine and service centers were also in this forward area. Six machine gun casemates were completed, some overlooking the Rhine and others, Istein. The types of cloches and weapons used on the East Wall were employed here and in other positions of the West Wall as well.

A number of blockhouses built along the river, were not linked by galleries to Werkgruppe Istein.

If completed according to specifications, Istein would have required a garrison of 2,600 men and been able to accommodate another thousand. The Werkgruppe would have incorporated a total of fifty combat positions, including emplacements for the new 50-mm automatic mortars, a 75-mm gun turret, two 170-mm gun batteries, and two 88-gun batteries. Plans also called for support facilities that included workshops, magazines, a huge tank garage, and so on.

In addition to Istein, eleven more A-Werke and a large number of B Werke were planned for the area west of the Rhine. One Type A Werkgruppe would have consisted of six or more combat bunkers, a pair of entrance blocks, and a subterranean gallery system that would have rivaled the ouvrages of the Maginot Line. In fact, the plans for Werkgruppe Gerstfeldhöhne, a few kilometers south of Zwibrücken, were very reminiscent of a Maginot ouvrage, except for its blocks, which appear to have been smaller. Werkgruppe Gerstfeldhöne was to have had two underground levels: the lower serving the entrances and the upper with a 4 km long tunnel linking fourteen combat positions for machine guns and howitzers. Work began on this Werkgruppe sometime in 1937.

Plans were also drawn up for fourteen heavy Type A turret batteries similar to the ones designed for the East Wall, over 170 small B-Werke called Kleinstwerke, and twelve battery positions.[12] Subterranean positions were to be used where needed, but no massive tunnel complex was projected. Blueprints were also drafted for a 50-mm AT gun turret. Instead of being located at the end of each block as on the East Wall, the 105-mm gun turrets on the West Wall were to be located centrally on the block.

About thirty-two B-Werke were completed, twenty-two of which were in the Pfalz Sector along with forty-eight B-Kleinstwerks (small B-Werke). The A-Werke and turret batteries were not begun and most such positions under construction in 1940 were never completed.

Since the West Wall was designed for defense in depth, its key elements included massive mine fields and anti-tank obstacles defended by bunkers. The small number of large concrete bunker complexes was not a drawback because the small positions could effectively slow, stop, and entangle the enemy thanks to the massive obstacle barriers before them and artillery support.

By the time the war began, the Todt Organization laborers were working on over 600 positions for light and heavy batteries, troop shelters, and munitions bunkers. The guns were usually placed in open positions. Five 170-mm gun batteries, a 240-mm gun battery, a 280-mm coast battery and a 305-mm gun battery, heavy rail guns, and several batteries of Czech 150-mm weapons supported the West Wall."

According to Dieter Bettinger, the number of structures actually completed as of May 1940 was smaller than the official 22,000 claimed in 1939. Bettinger estimates that there was a total of 11,820 positions for infantry, 1,192 for anti-tank guns, 2,673 for artillery, and 1,544 for air defense. His figures also include 44 casemates for 47-mm anti-tank guns, 24 casemates for 75-mm Flak guns, 24 positions for 83.5-mm guns, 50 casemates for 88-mm Flak, 1 casemate for 105-mm Flak, 15 casemates for 170-mm naval guns, 2 casemates for 240-mm naval guns, 15 positions for 280-mm coastal defense howitzers, a pair of positions for 305-mm coastal defense guns, and 99 gun positions with crew quarters and munitions rooms. These numbers include 32 B-Werke that were also Panzerwerke.

The famous concrete dragon's teeth of the West Wall were similar to those in the east but covered a greater distance. From the Rhine to the Aachen sector they covered 280 km. The 1938 type was usually poured in two bands of four rows and was able to stop a 20-ton armored vehicle. The new 1939 type usually formed five to six rows and could halt a 36-ton vehicle. The newer 1942 model was designed to check a 52-ton tank. Near crossing points they were five deep and flanked a concrete gate holding a huge steel beam.

To conclude, the West Wall was essentially a position of relatively light defenses with great depth and formidable obstacles. The individual bunker positions, like those of the East Wall, normally housed about five days of supplies, whereas Werkgruppen had larger stores. The fortifications were manned by the field army and were not intended to remain isolated in battle for long periods of time.

3. The Coast Defenses

The North Sea approaches to the Elbe and the ports of Pillau and Swinemünde in the Baltic Sea, were the most vulnerable to attack in the event of war. These coast defenses could not be considered formidable by 1940 standards. They lacked sufficient artillery, had no anti-aircraft defenses, and had to rely on the new Kriegsmarine for defense rather than their own weapons. Thus the navy was the first line of defense and, although many of its vessels were new, it remained a small surface force. Its main advantage was in the Baltic, where its potential naval opponents were not much stronger.

In the North Sea, Section Borkum Island, Section Norderney Island, and Section Wangerooge were assigned a naval artillery detachment, a naval anti-aircraft detachment, and a small flotilla each. Section Wangerooge activated a second naval artillery detachment after the war began. Section Emden had two naval anti-aircraft detachments, and Section Wilhelmshaven a flotilla and the 2nd Naval Anti-Aircraft Regiment. Section Wesermünde included two naval anti-aircraft detachments and Section Cuxhaven one anti-aircraft detachment and a flotilla. The small key island of Helgoland comprised a naval artillery detachment and a naval anti-aircraft detachment. Section Brunsbüttel covered the west end of the Kiel Canal with the 14th Naval Anti-Aircraft Regiment. Section Sylt on the island off the Danish coast, had the 8th Naval Anti-Aircraft Regiment and three additional naval anti-aircraft detachments.

In the Baltic, the West Baltic Command was assigned a naval artillery detachment and the 1st Naval Anti-Aircraft Regiment, at Laboe, on the east end of the Kiel Canal. In addition, eight more naval anti-aircraft detachments operated in the same area. The Pomeranian Command at Swinemünde included the 3rd Naval Anti-Aircraft Regiment and a naval artillery detachment, the East Baltic Command, two naval anti-aircraft detachments, Section Gotenhafen and Section Pillau, two naval anti-aircraft detachments and a naval artillery detachment, and Section Memel both a naval artillery and anti-aircraft detachment.

The weapons used for coast defense included a number of older pieces from World War I, some of which were mounted on pedestal-type mounts with or without gun shields, and a few were in turrets or casemates. The old 240-mm SK (naval) guns were mounted in open barbettes and turrets. At Borkum a pair of old Russian 280-mm guns occupied open emplacements. The elderly 170-mm SK guns on pivot mounts formed batteries at Helgoland and Kiel. Forty 50-mm tank guns mounted on pivots in concrete pits supported the small 37-mm dual purpose Flak gun batteries.

The heavy gun batteries defending the German coast when the war began included:

North Sea			
	Frisian Island		
	Borkum	Battery Oldenburg	2 x 240-mm SK guns
		Battery Coronel	4 x 280-mm SK guns
	Norderney	Battery Hamburg	4 x 240-mm SK guns
	Wangerooge	Battery Graf Spee	4 x 280-mm SK guns
		Battery Friedr. August	3 x 305-mm SK guns
Sylt		Battery Skagerrak	4 x 240-mm SK guns
Heligoland		Battery Jakobsen	3 x 170-mm SK guns
Baltic Sea			
	Kiel	Battery Ehrhardt Schmidt	3 x 170-mm SK guns
		Battery Tirpitz	3 x 280-mm SK guns
	Fehmarn	Battery Prinz Heinrich	2 x 280-mm SK guns
	Swinemünde	Plantagenbatterie	4 x 210-mm SK guns
		Battery Goeben	4 x 280-mm SK guns
	Pillau	Battery Grosser Kurfürst	4 x 280-mm SK guns

In the 1930s the navy modernized some of the old forts retained after World War I, such as Fort Kugelbake at Cuxhaven. Kugelbake and neighboring Fort Grauerort, served as munitions depots in the 1930s since most of their weapons, such as the 280-mm guns, had been removed for use on the Western Front during the Great War.

Additions were made to the fort to accommodate its new role. By 1939 positions for a Naval Flak Battery were set up at Kugelbake, which may have included 88-mm guns with gun shields. Four 105-mm guns in turrets replaced these weapons by 1942. This battery was part of sixty others that formed the Luftverteidigungszone (Air Defense Zone) West in 1939.

WEAPONS AND EQUIPMENT

FORTIFICATIONS	MAXIMUM RANGE (METERS)
150-mm Heavy H* (turret)	24,000
150-mm Heavy FH* (casemate)	15,300
105-mm gun K* (casemate & turret)	7,000
105-mm Light Turret H	6,000
105-mm Light FH (casemate)	10,600
105-mm Flak 38	17,500
105-mm K (casemate)	5,000
88-mm Flak	14,800
75-mm Flak gun75-mm FK 16*	11,900
50-mm Anti-Tank gun (casemate & turret)	8,000
47-mm Anti-Tank gun Fortress Model 36 (Czech)	6,000
37-mm Anti-Tank gun	
Model 35/36 (casemate)	7,500
Model K (casemate & turret)	6,400
50-mm Mortar M-19	750
Fortress Flame-thrower	40
MG 37 (Czech)*	2,000
MG 34	3,500
MG 08	3,500

*FH= field howitzer, FK= field cannon, H= howitzer, K= cannon, MG= 7.92-mm machine gun
Note: the above artillery weapons from 75-mm to 150-mm were not installed in the East Wall or West Wall because the positions for them were never built or completed. The exception were the weapons used in open firing stands.

SUPPORTING ARTILLERY	MAXIMUM RANGE (METERS)
305-mm SK**	48,000
240-mm SK	26,700

170-mm SK   27,000

COASTAL ARTILLERY

305-mm SK	48,000
280-mm SK L/45	36,100
240-mm SK	26,700
170-mm SK	27,200
150-mm SK C/28	23,500
150-mm SK L/40	20,000
105-mm SK C/32 (Dual)***	15,300
105-mm SK L/60 (Dual)	13,500
88-mm SK C/35	12,300
75-mm Anti-Tank gun	9,800
50-mm Tank gun	6,500 (horizontal)
37-mm Flak gun	6,000

**SK= naval gun
***Dual= for both surface and Flak use.

ARMORED POSITIONS FOR EAST AND WEST WALL

	Diameter (meters)	Roof Thickness (mm)
Turrets		
Artillery*+		
50-mm AT (A and B strength)	3.1 to 3.35	250-600
105-mm Gun (A and B strength)	3.8 to 4.15	250-600
105-mm (long) Gun and		
150-mm Howitzer (A strength)	4.15	600
Cloches - selected examples.		
Observation		
Infantry types	1 or less	60-250
Artillery types	1 to 6.5	100-250
MG Half Cloches (A and B strength)		
(3 embrasures)	1.8 to 2.6	125-440
MG Cloches (A, B and D strength)		
(6 embrasures)	1.8 to 2.7	50-650
Mortar Cloche (A and B strength)	1.7	250-705*

+No artillery turrets were ever installed.

Type	Concrete Thickness*++	Steel Thickness	Resists weapons
A	3.5 meters	600 mm	520-mm
A1	2.5 meters	350 mm	
B	2.0 to 1.5 meters	250 mm	210-mm

B1	1.0 meters	120 mm
C	6 meters	60 mm
D	.3 meters	20 mm

*++Inner walls were thinner and the roof could be the same or less.

Mine fields formed the key element in the West. They included the following types:

Anti-Tank	Teller mine 35
Anti-Personnel	Schrapnel mine 35

German armor was coded according to an ingenious system: the first number referred to the Type, the letter P for Panzer or armor, and the following number to the year of production. For example, 10P7 meant Type 10 Armor for 1934, 424P01 means Type 424 Armor for 1937.

The Germans also established a Standard Design or Regelbau for each type of bunker, which came into use for the building of the West Wall since most of the East Wall positions were built to meet the demands of the specific situation. The Inspectorate of Fortifications created numerous standard types that helped speed up construction on the West Wall. These standards allowed the use of prefabricated parts and equipment that included everything from armored pieces to doors. The Luftwaffe and Navy used the same Regelbau, but designed their own bunkers if the existing designs did not suit their needs. In 1939 the Series S-100 type was introduced followed in 1940 by S-400 and S-500 types. Selected types used on West Wall:

REGELBAU	DESCRIPTION	GARRISON
Bunkers 1937/38 B Strength		
1	MG Bunker	5 men
2	MG Bunker & Squad Shelter	18 men
3	MG Bunker with Small Cloche	7 men
8	Double MG Bunker with Small Cloche and Squad Shelter	25 men
9	MG Bunker*	5 men
15	Double MG Bunker with Small Cloche*	12 men
20	AT Gun Shelter with MG	10 men
25	Bunker with MG Cloche	10 men
27	Battalion Combat Bunker with MG	18 men
Bunker 1935/36 C Strength		
1	MG Bunker	5 men
2	MG Bunker with Squad	18 men
6a	AT and MG Bunker	10 men

Older Bunkers D Strength

1 to 5	MG Bunker (each type different size)	

Luftwaffe Bunkers for West Wall

B	MG Bunker	6 men
F	Command Bunker	18 men
M	Munitions Bunker	
Pz	AT Gun Shelter with Small Cloche	15 men
U	Double Squad Shelter	12 men

Bunkers 1938 for Limes Program (future West Wall)

1	MG Bunker	5 men
3	Double MG Bunker	10 men
19b	Artillery Observation with Cloche	8 men
20	37-mm AT Gun Bunker	8 men
2a	75-mm Flak Bunker	6 men
30	170-mm Naval Gun Bunker	9 men

Bunkers 1939   100 Series

104a	MG Bunker and Squad Shelter with Small Cloche	18 men
105a/b	MG Casemate	6 men
107a/b	Double MG Casemate	12 men
115a	Bunker with MG Cloche and Squad Shelter	24 men
139a	47-mm AT Gun Casemate and Twin MG	18 men

Bunkers 1939/40   500 Series

501	Squad Shelter	14 men
503	MG Casemate and Squad Shelter	18 men
505	AT Gun Casemate	6 men
514	MG Casemate	6 men

Bunkers 1944   600 Series

687	Shelter with Panther Tank 75-mm Gun Turret[13]	

*Roof armor over firing chamber as well as firing wall.

(NOTE: See *Der Westwall* by Bettinger and Büren for complete listing).

WORLD WAR II

1. The East Wall

When the war began in 1939, the East Wall consisted of a number of lightly armed Werkgruppen. The Frontier Guard Corps that garrisoned much of the line watched the war pass it by. In East Prussia the defenses were equally inactive. After 1942 much of the equipment in the east was shipped westward in response to the demand for armament on the new Atlantic Wall. In addition, some of the underground facilities were converted into factories.

When Army Group Center on the Eastern Front was destroyed in the summer of 1944 by the Soviets, the Germans, realizing that their situation was becoming precarious, decided to quickly revitalize the East Wall. Trenches were dug and new Tobruck positions–small concrete shelters for small arms with a circular opening in the roof serving as the firing position–were built.

Despite these last-ditch efforts on the part of the Germans, the Soviets moved relentlessly forward. In late January 1945, a Soviet armored formation penetrated the OWB Line. By April the Soviets crossed the Oder, many of the positions of the OWB were destroyed, and much of East Prussia was overrun, the final showdown taking place around Fortress Samland. German resistance in the East was fierce in most cases, but hopeless because their poorly armed positions were no match for the Russians.

2. The West Wall

The West Wall was first manned during the Czech Crisis of 1938, growing much stronger in the following year with additional construction. When the invasion of Poland began, the West Wall was entrusted to German frontier and reserve units backed by a few regular formations. As the Polish Campaign wound to a close, army divisions were rushed back to the West Wall.

However, before the switch could happen, the French launched their Saar Offensive in support of Poland. Even though it was a half-hearted operation, the French should have been able to overcome the small German force in the West. Instead, the French invasion ground to a halt when the French units made their acquaintance with one of the most devastating weapons ever invented: the anti-personnel mine used in massive mine fields. Following this disastrous incursion, the French were accused of lack of aggressiveness, which is partially true, but what has been forgotten is the catastrophic psychological effect of a weapon that was only then making its debut in modern warfare.

Many pre-war analysts expected the Second World War to revolve around the Maginot and Siegfried (i.e. West Wall) Lines. As history has shown, this did not happen. The Germans manned the West Wall with a weak army group and concentrated their efforts on a revised version of the Schlieffen Plan.

Once victory was assured in the West, the Germans promptly lost interest in the completion of the West Wall. The grandiose plans for large A-Werke and B-Werke were soon abandoned. Much of the equipment used in the West Wall was removed and sent to the Atlantic Wall; only the mine fields and obstacles remained in place.

However, the Germans did not completely abandon the idea of building fortifications. Late in the war they still designed the Regelbau 687 Bunker, mounting a Panther tank turret with its 75-mm gun, some of which were actually built on the Eastern Front (not the East Wall), and on the Gustav Line in Italy.

In 1944 the Allies advancing upon the West Wall found its depth to be the greatest problem. It was the last barrier that remained between Germany and the Allies in late 1944 and was only breached after the massive offensives of 1945.

3. The Coastal Defenses

The anti-aircraft batteries on the North Sea ports saw little activity until 1941, except for their limited action against British bombers in 1939. Some of these positions were later improved and incorporated into the Atlantic Wall. The Germans moved most of the heavy coastal defense batteries of the North Sea and Baltic to other locations, after the fall of Norway and France. By 1944 these coastal areas of Germany were considered less vulnerable to invasion than the conquered territories, so they were not significantly updated, receiving only new Flak.

Left: West Wall "Dragon's Teeth," Type 1938.
(Archives of Jürgen Kraft)
Below: West Wall Luftwaffe Regelbau 11
Doppelgruppenunterstand of the Air Defense Zone
(LVZ) with flanking defensive embrasure. Located
near village of Eisen near Berkenfeld. The LVZ
included over 1500 bunkers by 1940.
(Peter Waltje)

Above: OWB tunnel system. An example of the difference in size of the main tunnel and access tunnels. The installation of the rails for the subway was never completed. (Kaufmann)
Below: East Wall. Wooden Dragon's Teeth. These were usually placed where concrete ones could not be placed, especially in shadow areas near river banks. A metal bank was placed around the top of each of these. (Kaufmann)

Above: One of many portable concrete bunkers for one man created late in the war. Robert Jurga standing next to the entrance. (Kaufmann)
Below: Tobruk position used on OWB. These were used on most fronts. The entrance can be seen in the depression. Dragon's Teeth in the rear. (Kaufmann)

Map of Germany

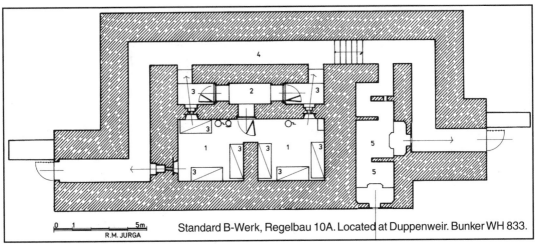

Standard B-Werk, Regelbau 10A. Located at Duppenweir. Bunker WH 833.

1. Crew's quarters
2. Gas lock
3. Defended entrance
4. Corridor,
5. Firing room for heavy MG-08 behind armored plate.

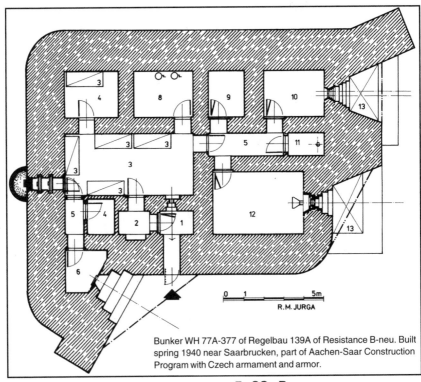

Bunker WH 77A-377 of Regelbau 139A of Resistance B-neu. Built spring 1940 near Saarbrucken, part of Aachen-Saar Construction Program with Czech armament and armor.

1. Defended entrance
2. Gas Lock
3. Crew's quarters (12 men) and emergency exit
4. Storage
5. corridor
6. Firing room for MG-08 behind armored plate 422PO1, for flanking fire
7. COs Room
8. Filter and Ventilation Room
9. Magazine
10. Firing room for heavy MG zw. MG 37(t)
11. Observation room with periscope
12. Firing room for 47-mm PAK(t)
13. Diamond fosse.

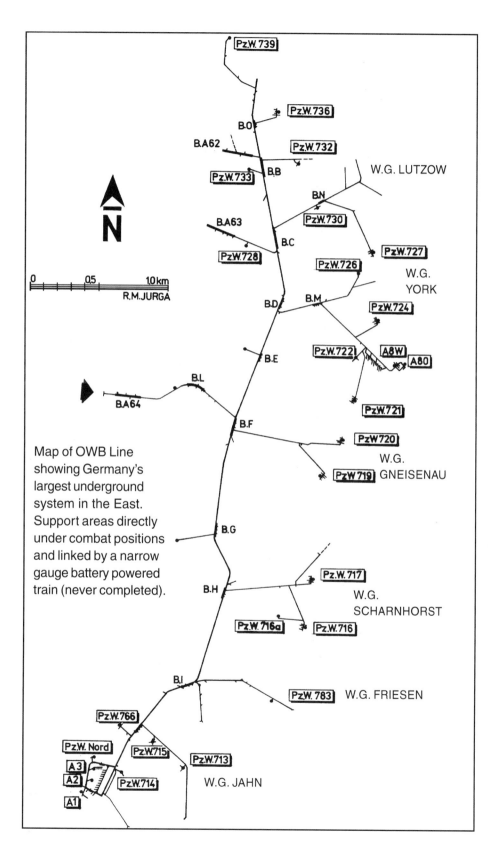

PzW.739

PzW.736

B.O

B.A62

PzW.732

B.B

W.G. LUTZOW

PzW.733

B.N

B.A63

PzW.730

B.C

PzW.727

PzW.728

W.G.
YORK

PzW.726

B.D B.M

PzW.724

B.E

PzW.722 A8W A80

B.L

B.A64

PzW.721

B.F

PzW720

W.G.
GNEISENAU

PzW719

Map of OWB Line
showing Germany's
largest underground
system in the East.
Support areas directly
under combat positions
and linked by a narrow
gauge battery powered
train (never completed).

B.G

Pz.W. 717

W.G.
SCHARNHORST

B.H

PzW.716a Pz.W.716

B.I

PzW. 783 W.G. FRIESEN

PzW.766

Pz.W. Nord

PzW.715

A3

PzW.713

A2

PzW.714

A1

W.G. JAHN

0 0.5 1.0 km
R.M.JURGA

N

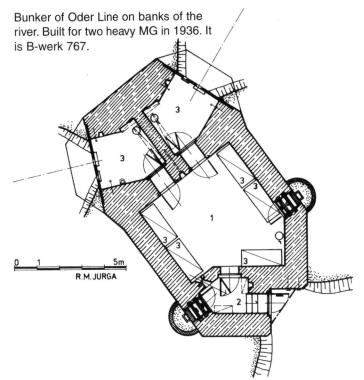

Bunker of Oder Line on banks of the river. Built for two heavy MG in 1936. It is B-werk 767.

R.M. JURGA

Left:
1. Crew's quarters (15 men) with emergency exit
2. Defended entrance with emergency exit
3. Firing room for heavy MG-08 behind armored plate 7P7 (10-cm thick)

Below:
1. Defended entrance with emergency exit
2. Crew's quarters (12 men)
3. Firing room for heavy MG-08 and armor plate 7P7 with additional quarters for 9 men
4. Infantry observer position with 9P7 Kleinstglocke (small observation cloche)

Bunker of Pomeranian Line near Bugno. Standard position built in 1935 with resistance B-1 for heavy MG and observation position.

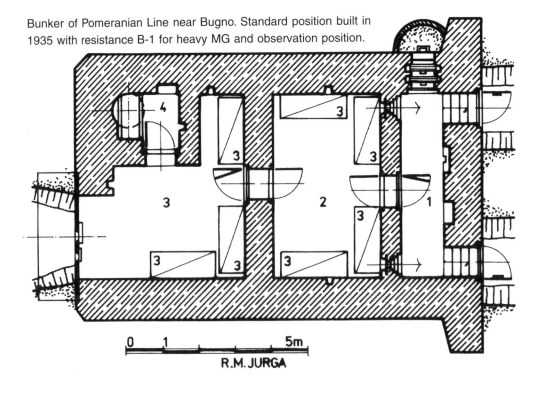

R.M. JURGA

Plans of Pomeranian Line Werk Gruppes.

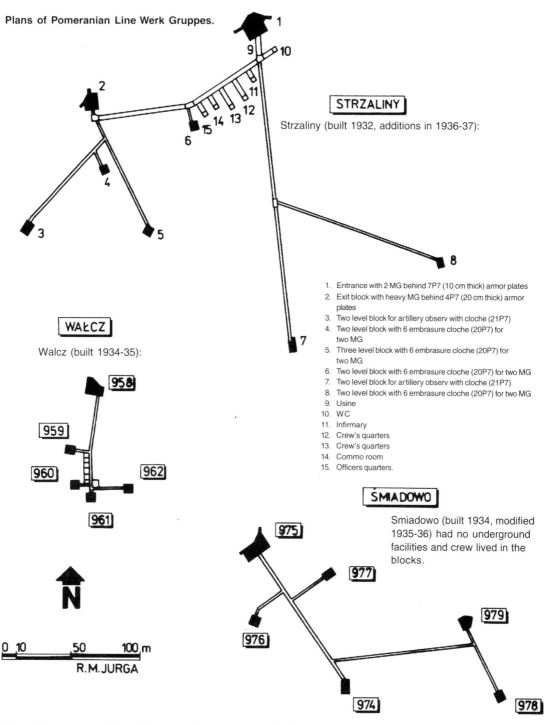

STRZALINY

Strzaliny (built 1932, additions in 1936-37):

1. Entrance with 2 MG behind 7P7 (10 cm thick) armor plates
2. Exit block with heavy MG behind 4P7 (20 cm thick) armor plates
3. Two level block for artillery observ with cloche (21P7)
4. Two level block with 6 embrasure cloche (20P7) for two MG
5. Three level block with 6 embrasure cloche (20P7) for two MG
6. Two level block with 6 embrasure cloche (20P7) for two MG
7. Two level block for artillery observ with cloche (21P7)
8. Two level block with 6 embrasure cloche (20P7) for two MG
9. Usine
10. WC
11. Infirmary
12. Crew's quarters
13. Crew's quarters
14. Commo room
15. Officers quarters.

WAŁCZ

Walcz (built 1934-35):

SMIADOWO

Smiadowo (built 1934, modified 1935-36) had no underground facilities and crew lived in the blocks.

N

0 10   50   100 m

R.M.JURGA

PzWerk 958- Entrance block with heavy MG behind 7P7 armor plate
PzWerk 959 - 6 embrasure cloche (20P7) for two MG
PzWerk 960 - Infantry Obsv cloche (52P8)
PzWerk 961- 3 embrasure, half cloche (2P7)
PzWerk 962- 6 embrasure cloche (20P7) for two MG.

PzWerk 975 - Entrance block with usine & magazine. 6 embrasure cloche (20P7) for two MG and 1 MG behind armor plate (7P7)
PzWerk 976 - MG behind armored plate (7P7)
PzWerk 977 -same as 976
PzWerk 978 - 2 MG behind armor plate (7P7)
PzWerk 979 - 1 MG behind armor plate (7P7) and infantry observ position.

Plans of West Wall Werks.
The last two fortifications were not completed except for small sections.

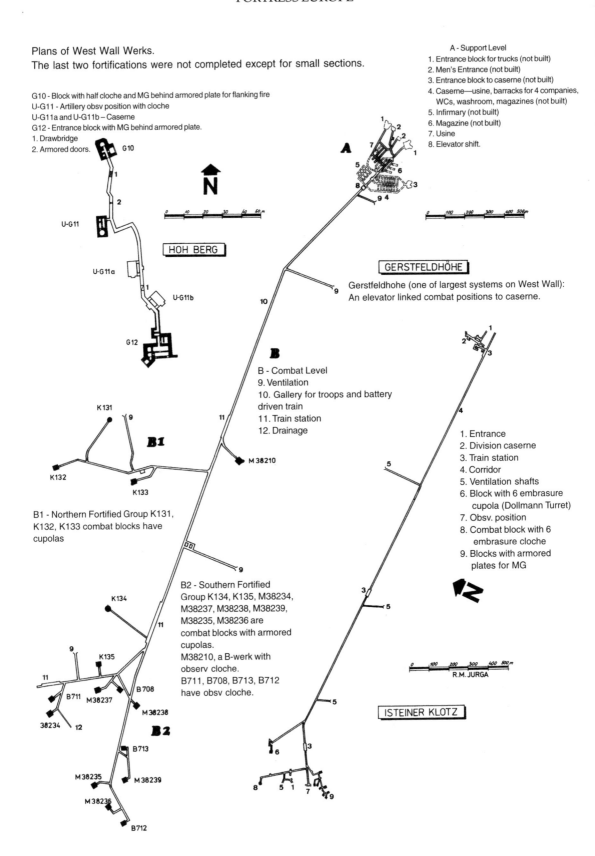

G10 - Block with half cloche and MG behind armored plate for flanking fire
U-G11 - Artillery obsv position with cloche
U-G11a and U-G11b – Caserne
G12 - Entrance block with MG behind armored plate.
1. Drawbridge
2. Armored doors.

G10

U-G11

U-G11a

U-G11b

G12

HOH BERG

N

A - Support Level
1. Entrance block for trucks (not built)
2. Men's Entrance (not built)
3. Entrance block to caserne (not built)
4. Caserne—usine, barracks for 4 companies,
   WCs, washroom, magazines (not built)
5. Infirmary (not built)
6. Magazine (not built)
7. Usine
8. Elevator shift.

A

GERSTFELDHÖHE

Gerstfeldhohe (one of largest systems on West Wall):
An elevator linked combat positions to caserne.

B

B - Combat Level
9. Ventilation
10. Gallery for troops and battery
driven train
11. Train station
12. Drainage

K131

B1

K132

K133

B1 - Northern Fortified Group K131,
K132, K133 combat blocks have
cupolas

M 38210

1. Entrance
2. Division caserne
3. Train station
4. Corridor
5. Ventilation shafts
6. Block with 6 embrasure
   cupola (Dollmann Turret)
7. Obsv. position
8. Combat block with 6
   embrasure cloche
9. Blocks with armored
   plates for MG

K134

B2 - Southern Fortified
Group K134, K135, M38234,
M38237, M38238, M38239,
M38235, M38236 are
combat blocks with armored
cupolas.
M38210, a B-werk with
observ cloche.
B711, B708, B713, B712
have obsv cloche.

K135

B 708

B 711

M38237

M 38238

38234

B 713

B2

M 38235

M 38239

M 38236

B712

R.M. JURGA

ISTEINER KLOTZ

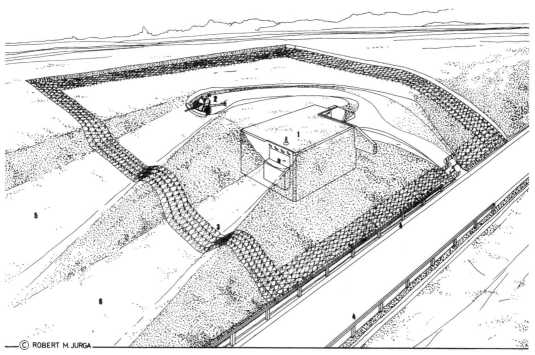

© ROBERT M. JURGA

FFOWB Line Nieslyz-Obra.

1. Hindenburgstand with Garage for 37-mm AT guns
2. AT gun firing position
3. Anti-infantry obstacle
4. AT obstacles on road
5. Field of fire for AT gun
6. Field of fire for MG in casemate

© COPYRIGHT R.JURGA

German Panzer Nest.
Position for a MG in the defensive
lines of the West and in Italy.

1. Panzer position
2. Periscope
3. Air vent
4. Moving embrasure cover
5. MG mounting
6. Shelves
7. Air filter
8. Pedal operated fan (Moved into
position by placing axle through
ventilator opening and rolling it.)

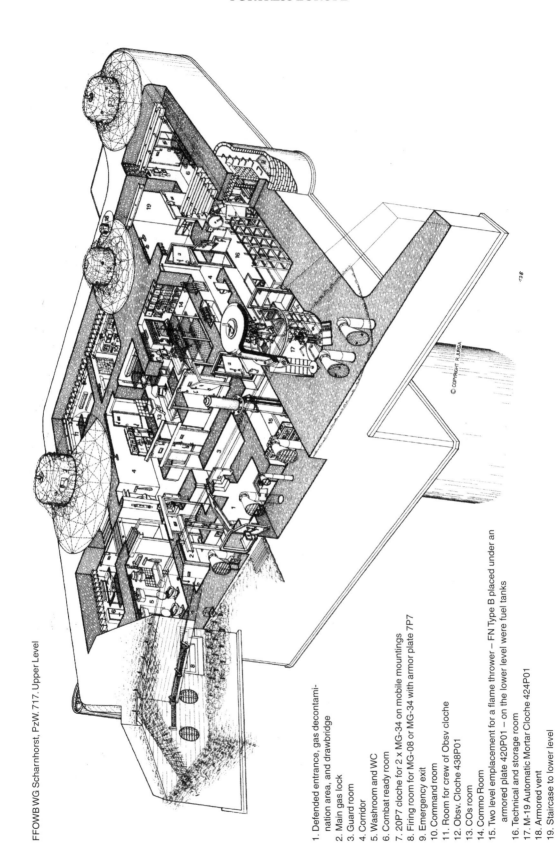

FFOWB WG Scharnhorst, PzW. 717. Upper Level

1. Defended entrance, gas decontamination area, and drawbridge
2. Main gas lock
3. Guard room
4. Corridor
5. Washroom and WC
6. Combat ready room
7. 20P7 cloche for 2 x MG-34 on mobile mountings
8. Firing room for MG-08 or MG-34 with armor plate 7P7
9. Emergency exit
10. Command room
11. Room for crew of Obsv cloche
12. Obsv. Cloche 438P01
13. COs room
14. Commo Room
15. Two level emplacement for a flame thrower – FN Type B placed under an
    armored plate 420P01 – on the lower level were fuel tanks
16. Technical and storage room
17. M-19 Automatic Mortar Cloche 424P01
18. Armored vent
19. Staircase to lower level

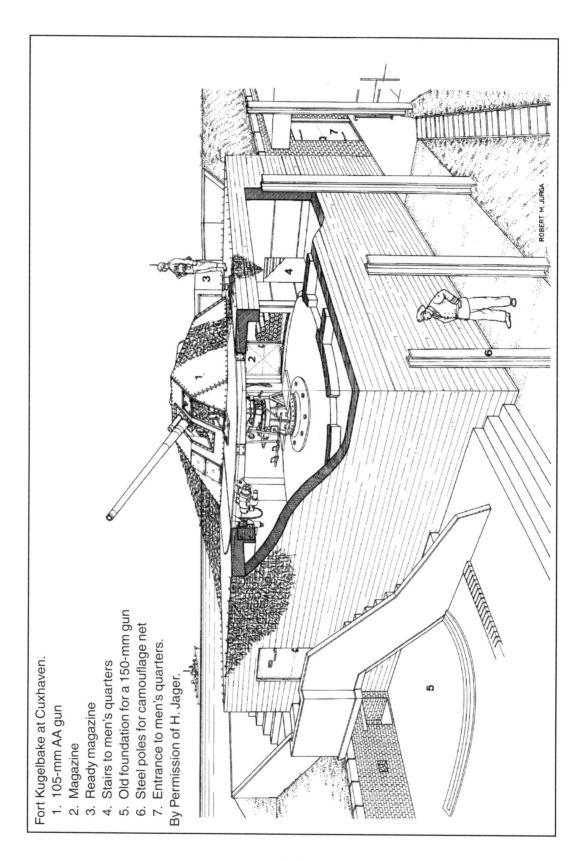

Fort Kugelbake at Cuxhaven.
1. 105-mm AA gun
2. Magazine
3. Ready magazine
4. Stairs to men's quarters
5. Old foundation for a 150-mm gun
6. Steel poles for camouflage net
7. Entrance to men's quarters.
By Permission of H. Jager.

ROBERT M. JURGA

West Wall, MG Bunker. Simple open position for a MG with light armored crenel.

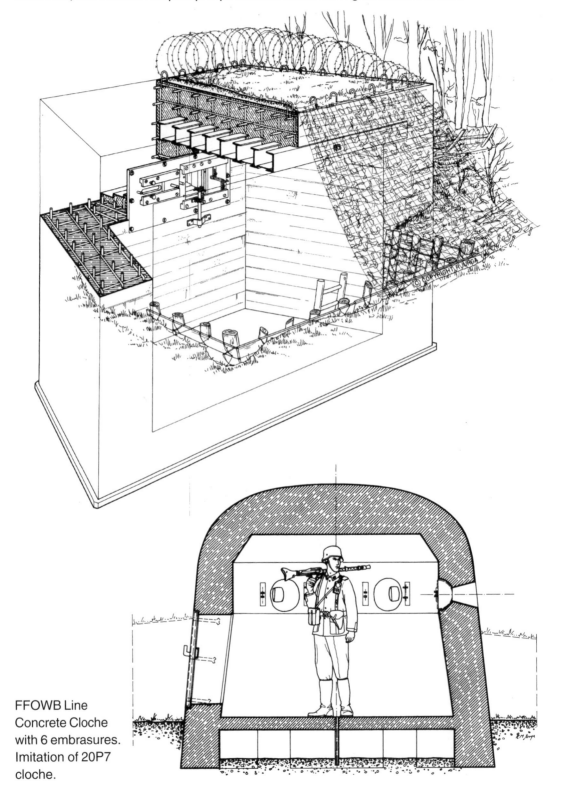

FFOWB Line
Concrete Cloche
with 6 embrasures.
Imitation of 20P7
cloche.

Cross section of 6 crenel cloche 20P7 for two MG and observation.

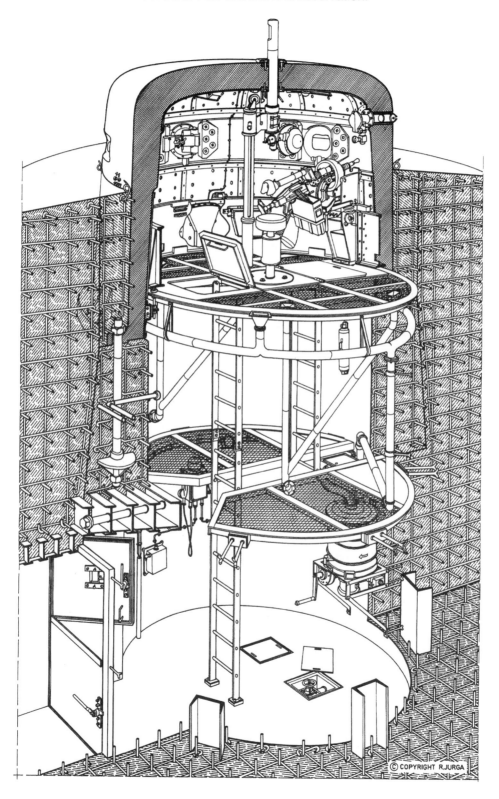

FFOWB WG Schill designed for flanking fire. Built 1937. 1. PzW 757

1. PzW 757 with 20P7 cloche (2 MG each) and observation cloche, M-19 automatic mortar, fortress flame thrower, MG behind armor plate 6P7
2. PzW 754 with 20P7 cloche and obsv cloche, and M19 automatic mortar
3. Underground caserne
4. Corridor
5. Magazine for mortar
6. Railroad
7. Overpass

© ROBERT M. JURGA

Chapter 3

BELGIUM

BACKGROUND

Born out of revolution in 1830 when it successfully broke away from the Netherlands, Belgium quickly gained recognition from other European nations, which guaranteed its neutrality. The last battle it fought in Europe in the nineteenth century was when it drove a Dutch invasion force from Antwerp. After that, Belgium saw no necessity to modernize its armed forces. However, twice in the twentieth century, its neutrality failed to keep it safe. Unlike Switzerland, Belgium could not rely on its geography for its security even though a 1839 treaty had removed the Dutch threat. The fact remained that its other borders continued to be vulnerable to its more aggressive neighbors. To complicate the situation, Belgium occupied a major invasion route between the German states and France.

The southern part of Belgium, occupied by French-speaking Walloons, was dominated by the hilly wooded terrain of the Ardennes. The rest of the country, occupied by the Flemish-speaking Germanic population, lay in the open North European Plain where some wooded regions and a few watercourses offered some limited defense and where most of the industry was located.

After the 1870 Franco-Prussian War, Belgium, concerned about future relations with the newly formed German Second Reich, decided to take steps to ensure its security. The task was assigned to the military engineer Henri Brialmont, who soon became one of the most prominent designers of fortifications of the century.

After 1871 rings of forts were created to protect Liege, which blocked the invasion route from Germany, Namur, which guarded the road from France, and Antwerp, which was not only the largest city in Belgium but also a vital seaport. The capital, Brussels, located near the center of the triangle formed by these three fortresses, had no major defenses.

Each of the fortress cities received a ring of new forts by the end of the nine-teenth century. Although Antwerp already had an older ring of forts, it got a newer ring by 1914 to keep the city outside the range of newer models of enemy artillery. The Brialmont forts of Liege and Namur, mistakenly believed the best of the time, did not, in fact, compare favorably with the French and German forts of the period. In the first place, the Belgian method for pouring concrete and the lack of reinforce-ment made their forts vulnerable to heavy artillery. Secondly, Brialmont made the fatal error of concentrating all the heavy gun cupolas in a central citadel, making them easy targets for enemy fire. Infantry positions, added to the surface of the forts, had a limited value. The army neglected to set up defensive positions in the gaps between forts, which allowed an enemy to pass between the forts unhindered.

By 1914 Belgium's defenses were virtually complete, but its army's equipment was obsolete. Despite all these precautions, the new forts failed to deter the Ger-mans. In fact, the Germans, having every intention of violating Belgium's neutrality in order to outflank the French, designed heavy artillery such as the 420-mm Big Berthas to smash the Belgian fortifications. In August 1914 the Schlieffen Plan was implemented and the German armies raced through Belgium, investing Liege by penetrating the undefended gaps between the forts. On August 8, the first of the Belgian forts fell to German artillery, even before the Big Berthas arrived from Ger-many. The arrival of the 420-mm guns on August 12 only speeded up the process. On August 18 the central citadel of Fort Loncin suffered a hit by a shell that pen-etrated an ammunition magazine and detonated it, creating a huge crater across the right center of the fort. Several gun turrets were shattered, popping out of their shafts, and/or toppling into the crater. The commander of the Liege defenses was pulled from the rubble and forced to surrender. The remaining forts of Liege fell soon after this debacle. Namur's forts resisted only four days. Antwerp lasted a little longer, but also succumbed to the heavy German guns.[1]

After the Great War, Belgium remained an active ally of France to secure its future. In the late 1920s, as France completed plans for the Maginot Line, Belgium committed itself to its own security. If both countries had worked in concert on the new defenses, and Belgium had not returned to neutrality in 1936, the course of World War II might have been different.

MAJOR FORTIFICATIONS

The Liege Defenses
The Namur Defenses
Albert Canal Line

Antwerp's Defenses and the National Redoubt
The KW Line
Coast Defenses

LOCATION

1. The Liege Defenses

After World War I Belgium's situation changed little, since Liege remained on the most convenient invasion route from Germany into France. Thus the Belgians resolved to establish their main defenses in the area, taking advantage of the surrounding terrain. The region to the north and east was mostly open with some woods and rolling terrain, but the Meuse River, which flowed east from Namur through Huy and Liege, created a steep sided and narrow valley cutting through the heart of the city before turning on a northerly route toward Maastricht. It served as a major anti-tank obstacle and was incorporated into the defensive scheme. To the south of the city the terrain became rougher as it neared the Ardennes, also facilitating defense. Fortified Position of Liege II (*Position Fortifiée de Liège* or PFL II), the second line of defense, consisted of revitalized forts of the World War I era and new bunkers to fill the intervals.[2] These forts occupied the rolling terrain that surrounded the city. The main line, the PFL I, was anchored on the Meuse river behind the Dutch frontier, opposite the roads to Maastricht, swung southward toward Verviers in the gentle terrain astride the Aachen to Liege highway, then curved westward towards a point south of Liege where the terrain had more relief, was more heavily wooded, and easily defendable. The entire line covered about 50 km and was situated mainly on the Herves Plateau. It acted as an outer defense line for Liege and a major barrier blocking not only the approaches from Aachen, but also Maastricht in the event of Dutch neutrality being violated."

2. The Namur Defenses

Namur, like Liege, sat on a major road junction that included the main route from Aachen to France via Belgium. The main defenses consisted of old forts that occupied the high ground around the city. Here the Meuse River created a well defined valley as it passed through the steep-walled city. Although it might appear that the Belgians refortified this city to deter French aggression, the decision was made while the two countries were still allies. It appears, therefore, that Namur was intended to be a final block against a German penetration along the main highway from Aachen.

The Meuse River continued on to Huy and Liege, forming steep sided banks rising an average of about 100 meters above the valley floor. Although, less pronounced than in many places in the Ardennes, it still presented a formidable obstacle. This well-defined valley continued on towards the Dutch border past Liege.

3. The Albert Canal Line

This line picked up where the Meuse defenses of Liege ended as the river entered the Netherlands. The main part of the Albert Line ran from Liege to a point north of Maastricht, and from there relied upon a series of canals and the Campine between Maastricht and Antwerp. The new canal formed a formidable anti-tank obstacle opposite the Maastricht Appendage (the narrow strip of Dutch territory separating Belgium from Germany). The Albert Canal turned back and ran west to Antwerp where the Meuse returned to form the Dutch-Belgian border near Lanaken.

At the point where the Albert Canal turned away, another canal, the Schelde-Maas (Meuse) continued to parallel the Meuse River and then turned northwestward almost again paralleling the border where it was replaced by a barrier formed by the marshes and woods of the Campine region, after the Meuse turned into the Netherlands. The canal and this rough terrain formed a good defensible barrier along the Dutch border all the way to Dessel. It covered a large part of the Dutch border up to the point where the canal turned toward Antwerp. Although the ground was level here, much of it was heavily wooded, especially in the vicinity of the Dutch border. This was the region where Allied troops got bogged down as they attempted to relieve the airborne troops dropped at Arnhem in 1944.

4. Antwerp's Defenses and the National Redoubt

Antwerp, a major urban center, served as Belgium's main port. In the 1920s, Belgium undertook a dredging operation up to Flushing in order to turn Antwerp into the largest seaport in Europe. The old forts of the inner ring, already obsolete, could no longer adequately defend the growing city. New positions had to be created in the outer ring. The main component of the outer ring was the new anti-tank ditch that defended the eastern half of the city. These defenses formed the Fortified Position of Antwerp (PFA). The terrain around Antwerp was relatively level but dipped to the northwest of the city, near the Schelde River. The Schelde flowed through Antwerp, gave access to the sea, and formed marshes that served as a major obstacle and last line of defense.

The army created the *Tête de Pont de Gent* (TPG), or Bridgehead of Ghent, on the Schelde River and linked it to the defenses of Antwerp to form the *Réduit National* or National Redoubt. This line, which ran through low terrain, had few natural obstacles to back it up beyond the low sandy terrain and polders along the coast.

5. The KW Line or Dyle Line

The KW Line extending from Koningshooikt to Wavre, included the Dyle River to the east of Brussels and was linked to the PFA and to the PFN. Its northern section ran through a lightly wooded area and its southern part passed through mostly open level to rolling terrain.

6. Coast Defenses

The coastal region of Belgium was limited since the wide mouth of the Schelde River was entirely in Dutch territory. As long as the Netherlands remained neutral, the approaches to Antwerp along the Schelde would remain open for sea going ships. Ostend was the only sizable port on the Belgian coast. A second, smaller, port on the entrance to the Leopold Canal was Zeebrugge of World War I fame. The coastal region consisted mainly of dunes followed by polders (land reclaimed from the sea). Canals crisscrossed the area.

HISTORY

In the 1920s the Belgian military decided to set up new defenses and restore a few old ones, assigning the task to the Belgian Superior Council of National Defense. As is often the case in such circumstances, its members disagreed over the steps that should be taken to defend the southern province of Luxembourg. They finally decided to concentrate the defenses on the Flemish lands of the north, where most of the country's eight million people lived. The less numerous Walloons of the south immediately complained about being abandoned. However, the government, which maintained an army of only 72,000 men at the end of the 1920s, was unable to defend both the north and the south and decided to shield the most vulnerable area, the approaches to Liege.

Between 1928 and 1931 a special commission, led by the Minister of War, planned the new defenses of Belgium. The commission finally settled on creating fortified bridgeheads on the Meuse at Liege and Namur, restoring some of the old forts (eight at Liege and seven at Namur), and preparing only token defenses in the south. However, it evinced no interest in linking up the Belgian defenses with the French Maginot Line. The commission also called for the creation of the Ghent Bridgehead and the formation of a National Redoubt, but gave this project low priority.

The Meuse between the Namur and Liege bridgeheads would not be heavily defended. The PFL II was built between 1928 and 1932, followed in 1934 with the construction of a second line, PFL I, which was 5 to 8 km in advance of the of the old forts. PFL I received four new and modern forts by the mid-1930s to secure the vulnerable flank facing the Maastricht Appendage and stop a German advance on Liege along the main road from Aachen.

Among the new generation of forts was Fort Eben Emael, which was built on the recommendation of General A.G. Galet of the special commission. Its mission was to secure the flank opposite Maastricht, which was open to a surprise attack by the Germans who could quickly cross the narrow strip of Dutch territory and force a crossing of the new Albert Canal. Fort Eben Emael was completed in 1935 while work continued until 1939 on other forts whose construction had not begun until later. Unfortunately, Eben Emael may not have not been a great secret to the Germans because the Belgian contractor sub-contracted work to two German companies.

New and deeper galleries made for the old forts were added at Namur and Liege, new turrets mounting different weapons replaced the older ones. At Antwerp many turret positions were transformed into simple machine gun casemates. The newest work at Antwerp consisted of an anti-tank ditch defended by special bunkers. Some canals, such as the Albert Canal, were fortified. The KW Line, which later became the main defense line, received less attention until the end of the 1930s.

In 1936, when the new king decided to restore his country to a state of neutrality, all hopes for joining with the French defenses vanished. The defense of the Ardennes was virtually neglected even though some small bunkers were built along the main routes. On the other hand, positions like Antwerp and the National Redoubt received more attention. Brialmont had warned against building three fortress rings because Belgium could not raise enough troops to adequately defend them, and maintain a field army at the same time. However, his warning was ignored and by the late 1930s the military ended up with a greater number of defensive positions than in Brialmont's time and with an army too small to defend it all.

By 1939 the defenses of Liege were complete except for a fifth fort that had been planned for the PFL I. Actually, in addition to this proposed fort of Remouchamps, plans for two other small forts at Comblain-du-Pont and Les Waides were dropped even earlier. Most of the other positions were also ready, but work continued through the early part of the war on the KW Line.

The Belgian attempt to fortify much of their country turned out to be of little value in view of later political developments. Indeed, the defenses of Liege and the Albert Canal Line had been conceived with the idea that France would support Belgium. However, when he declared the neutrality of his country, the king adamantly refused to consider French intervention, even in secret. Denied their original plans, the Belgian generals had no recourse but to turn these defenses into delaying positions. If French help could not be gotten without advance preparation and French troops could not enter the country before an invasion, the only line that could be used as the main line of defense would be the incomplete Dyle or KW Line.[3]

DESCRIPTION

1. The Liege Defenses

The PFL II around Liege consisted of eight restored forts of the original twelve. Two of these, Pontisse and Flémalle on the left flank of the Meuse, stood on the heights overlooking the river valley.[4] The remaining forts formed the bridgehead position on the right bank.

Each fort was given new deeper galleries and an improved ventilation system. One interesting feature found in a few of these forts was a new air intake block located beyond the fort's fossé. This block, disguised as a concrete water tower, had its own defenses. The infantry positions on the forts were eliminated based on a mistaken evaluation of their future role. Thus, each fort was manned only by artillery men and had no infantry component as in the past. The garrisons of the forts numbered up to 500 men in the larger forts and 300 men in the smaller ones. In addition to replacing the old wrecked turrets, the army installed more effective long-range weapons. The old 210-mm howitzer turrets were replaced by 150-mm gun turrets. Machine gun and 120-mm mortar turrets took the place of the old twin 150-mm gun turrets. The 120-mm gun turrets positions received twin 105-mm gun turrets. The old 57-mm Quick Fire gun turrets were replaced by a more powerful 75-mm howitzer turret. Cloches were not included in the refurbishment of these forts.

The old forts of the Liege bridgehead consisted of:

FORT	TURRETS	MACHINE GUN EMBRASURES
Pontisse	1 x 105-mm gun	22
	8 x 75-mm gun	—
Barchon	2 x 150-mm gun	26
	2 x twin 105-mm gun	—
	2 x twin 120-mm mortar	—
	5 x 75-mm gun	—
Evegnée*	1 x 150-mm gun	25
	1 x twin 105-mm gun	—
	1 x twin 120-mm mortar	—
	3 x 75-mm gun	—
Fléorn	2 x 150-mm gun	26
	2 x twin 105-mm gun	—
	4 x 75-mm gun	—
	2 x 81-mm mortars (turret ?)	
Chandfondtaine	1 x 150-mm gun	22
	1 x twin 105-mm gun	—
	2 x twin 120-mm mortar	—
	4 x 75-mm gun	—
Embourg**	4 x 75-mm gun	20

Boncelles**	4 x 75-mm gun	20
Flémalle*	1 x 150-mm gun	25
	1 x twin 105-mm gun	—
	2 x twin 120-mm mortar	—
	4 x 75-mm gun	—

*One 120-mm gun turret not restored or replaced.
**One 210-mm howitzer, one 150-mm twin gun and two 120-mm gun turrets not restored or replaced. Two 210-mm howitzer turrets at Boncelles not restored either.

The main defense against direct assault was the fossé. Intermediate positions consisting of bunkers and obstacles protected the gaps between the forts. Fifty-five bunkers, most mounting only machine guns and only nine including an anti-tank gun, covered these gaps. There were three different sizes of bunkers. The heaviest, which were very few, had walls of up to 1.5 meters of concrete, the intermediate had 1.0 meter thick walls, and the lightest were as little as 0.5 meters thick. Both lines of Liege had anti-tank rails, up to five rows deep.

The PFL I included two large and two small forts built in the 1930s. A third small fort, which was to secure the right flank of the line, was never built. The two large forts occupied the key positions. Eben Emael secured the left flank on the Albert Canal, opposite the Maastricht Appendage, Battice dominated the main route from Aachen.

Fort Eben Emael, the pride and showpiece of the Belgian defenses, was built into a plateau overlooking the newly constructed Albert Canal, which cut through the plateau as it reached the Meuse River. From the air, Eben Emael looked like a slice of pie with the canal and its steep walls forming its eastern and northern sides, a man-made water filled anti-tank ditch delineating part of its western side, and an arching anti-tank wall outlining its southern side. A single entrance block gave access on the west side. Like the French entrance blocks, it included a rolling bridge obstacle and protective weapons crenels. The galleries were at two levels, the upper gallery virtually circling around the center of the fort. This was a design favored by the Belgians as opposed to the French design of a single main gallery taking a straight path. The lowest gallery was approximately 60 meters below the surface.

A large subterranean caserne accommodated the garrison. A wooden barracks located adjacent the fort in peacetime was to be removed in time of war. The interior facilities were complete with a large barracks, a kitchen, an infirmary, a mess hall, storage areas, and a well. The usine contained six diesel engines to meet the heavy demands of this large fort. During peacetime an outside power connection was used. The intermediate level had 4 km of galleries that led to the combat blocks. Here also, the two air intakes on the face of the Albert Canal fed in the fresh air, which passed through purification filters. The ammunition magazines were on this level, and unlike the French and many others, the Belgians decided not to keep a large supply of ammunition inside their combat blocks.

The fort had multi-level blocks for machine guns and anti-tank guns at different points along the anti-tank wall and fossé. Two blocks occupied positions at the level of the canal's footpath. The fort's surface, which was well above the entrance, and anti-tank ditch and wall were covered by two machine gun blocks and an open position for anti-aircraft guns. These blocks formed what was known as the fort's defensive battery.

The offensive battery, located on the fort's surface, consisted of four artillery casemates and three gun turrets. The main weapons were two 120-mm gun in a non-eclipsing turret. Even though they had the range to reach Maastricht, they were partially masked by St. Peters Hills on the opposite side of the Albert Canal. The range of these cannons reached the outskirts of Liege, but fell short of the large fort of Battice.

Two eclipsing twin 75-mm gun turrets occupied positions on the southern end of the fort. The four artillery casemates were identified as either Maastricht 1 and 2 and or Vise 1 and 2, according to the direction they fired. These 75-mm gun casemates faced the direction in which their guns fired unlike the French casemates, whose facade faced to the rear while their guns fired to the flank. The embrasures for these long barrel weapons allowed a traverse of 70 degrees as opposed to the French 45 degrees. Each three-gun casemate not only had the mission of protecting the fort's flanks, but also of covering vital river and canal crossings. These weapons were semi-automatic, firing at a rate of 10 rounds per minute, half the rate of the turret's automatic guns.

All the blocks of the fort contained air filters and latrines, but all ammunition came from below and was sent up to the weapons by means of monte-charges. Expended shells were quickly evacuated by a slide to a lower level to prevent fumes from fouling the air. Most of this equipment was similar to the French. Many of the blocks, especially those of the defensive battery, included a small observation cloche. Some cloches included an opening in the roof for a small periscope. Not all the cloches were the small observation type, some mounted machine guns. The garrisons of most of these blocks consisted of 25 to 35 men.

Eben Emael was the only Belgian fort with artillery casemates. It was also the only new fort whose subterranean facilities were completely enclosed within its perimeter, surrounded by the canal and an anti-tank wall. With a 1,200 man garrison it was by far the largest Belgian fort. This was also a larger garrison than any ouvrage of the Maginot Line. Another unusual feature of Eben Emael was that two of its combat blocks, Block Canal Sud and Fortin O1, were located outside the defended area. Canal Sud covered the other end of the Albert Canal while Fortin 01, lightly armed, provided observation beyond Lanaye, along the Meuse, and into the Netherlands.

Eben Emael's blocks included:

Cupola 120	–	twin 120-mm gun turret
Cupola Nord	–	twin 75-mm gun turret
Cupola Sud	–	twin 75-mm gun turret (attached to Block 5)
Vise 1	–	3 x 75-mm casemate guns
Vise 2	–	3 x 75-mm casemate guns
Maastricht 1	–	3 x 75-mm casemate guns
Maastricht 2	–	3 x 75-mm casemate guns
MI Nord	–	machine gun block
MI Sud	–	machine gun block
Block 1	–	Entrance with machine guns and 2 x 60-mm anti-tank guns
Block 2	–	machine guns and 2 x 60-mm anti-tank guns
Block 4	–	machine guns and 2 x 60-mm anti-tank guns
Block 5	–	machine guns and 1 x 60-mm anti-tank gun
Block 6	–	machine guns and 2 x 60-mm anti-tank guns
Canal Nord	–	machine guns and 1 x 60-mm anti-tank gun
Canal Sud	–	machine guns and 1 x 60-mm anti-tank gun
Fortin 01	–	machine guns and 1 x 60-mm anti-tank gun

All of the defensive positions above included searchlights and a cloche.

The northern part of the fort was partially covered by woods. Nonetheless, the fort was clearly visible from the air because of the canal and anti-tank ditch. South of the fort, farmers' fields helped highlight the location of the fort from the air. The three dummy cupolas apparently showed up well because the Germans marked them as real on their maps. The other large fort of the PFL I was Battice, only slightly smaller in acreage than Eben Emael, but no less powerful. Although Battice had no artillery casemates, it mounted more turret guns: 2 x twin 120-mm gun turrets and 3 x twin 75-mm gun turrets. It was enclosed by a dry fossé with only one small open side of about 60 meters in length. This section was located inside a railroad cut defended by two coffres on its two ends, and was used as the peacetime entrance. Supply trucks left the main highway and drove about 30 meters into the railroad cut, turned into the fossé, and drove a short distance to the entrance block. In wartime anti-tank obstacles closed the entrance to the fossé.

The tunnel complex went around the fort and also cut across its center. A usine with a group of diesel engines was located near a special chimney that discharged the fumes into the fossé. The command post was near the entrance, and ammunition storage areas were near the blocks. The main subterranean works, located about 50 meters outside the fort's anti-tank ditch, comprised the caserne, similar in many ways to the Eben Emael's. A secondary tunnel about 100 meters long led from the main gallery to the wartime entrance and an air intake block well outside the fort's perimeter. Another air intake also located outside, but on the opposite side of the fort was used as an auxiliary position. The garrison used surface barracks during peacetime like at Eben Emael.

The other two smaller forts had a similar layout. At Battice there were no defensive blocks on the surface, only along the fossé. The armament of Battice was similar to Eben Emael, except that not all of the defensive blocks had 60-mm anti-tank guns. Some of its cloches mounted a machine gun.

The two small forts of Aubin-Neufchâteau and Tancrémont (Pepinster) were not as large as Eben Emael and Battice. They were more regularly shaped than the two big forts and were surrounded by a fossé. Tancrémont was polygonal in shape with four straight sides, while Neufchâteau was triangular. Tancrémont had originally been designed to take a 120-mm gun turret, but as a result of cost cutting, it ended up having a block with three cloches for machine guns. Both forts followed the general subterranean plan of Battice with regard to the caserne, usine, entrances, air intakes, and other facilities.

Aubin-Neufchâteau had a single and a double coffre that covered the three sides of triangular fossé. A detached coffre outside the fossé covered the entrance to the fort. A central block mounting three 81-mm mortars covered three different directions, and the other two artillery blocks mounted a twin 75-mm gun turret each.

The armament of the small Belgian forts was standardized. At Aubin-Neufchâteau, the 81-mm breech loaded mortars that fired through a well-like position similar to the French Maginot positions were actually of French origin. The Belgian positions were designed to give a 90 degree field of fire instead of the 65 degree attained in the French positions. The defensive blocks, including the entrance block, mounted one to two 47-mm anti-tank guns each and a number of machine guns. Tancrémont was similarly equipped. The proposed fort of Sougne-Remouchamps would have had two 75-mm turret gun blocks and a mortar block like these two forts. These smaller forts had garrisons of over 600 men, which was more than many Maginot artillery forts.

If not well designed, the Belgian forts were certainly well protected. Like the French and Germans, the Belgians used up to 3.5 meters of concrete on the walls and roofs of their forts. At some points—near cupolas,for instance—they used up to 4.5 meters of concrete. Their rear walls, no less than 2.75 meters thick, were not made intentionally weaker as in the Maginot Line. In the case of armor, it appears the Belgians attempted to make up for failings of earlier forts with mantles in some places up to 500-mm thick and roofs of 120-mm gun turrets up to 460-mm (two layers of armor). The 75-mm gun turrets had roofs of up to 450-mm of armor, which was greater than the 330-mm used by the French. The cloches had roofs of up to 350-mm of armor, also thicker than most of the French ones. Some cloches were the simple observation type that rose above the roof of a block. The machine gun and 47-mm anti-tank gun cloches were usually designed to be flush with the concrete block roof. Their field of fire cut through the roof in a fan shape. Block C-3, outside the entrance to Aubin-Neufchâteau, was very unusual because it was located beyond the perimeter of the fort and had a searchlight cloche and two cloches for 47-mm guns. The interior positions of the forts were equipped with girder beams and sand bags that could be used to block the interior armored doors if an enemy penetrated from above. The entrances of the smaller forts were similar to Eben Emael's with its rolling bridge trap. Only Tancrémont lacked such a device because it was finished too late to receive this addition.

In addition, the forts' surface was secured by anti-infantry obstacles. Both old and new forts were surrounded by wire obstacles encircling the forts. In the old forts they ran in some depth from the counterscarp along the glacis. The air intake blocks of the new forts also had their own individual wire protection that was not found on combat blocks within the fort's fossé.

Steps were also taken to assure communication with the forts. In addition to underground telephone cables, radios were used, but there is no data available on their effectiveness. Although the guns were mostly Belgian models, much of the optical equipment was French. Each fort could operate independently for several weeks.

Between the forts of the PFL I were the interval positions. Along with the anti-infantry and anti-tank obstacles, 162 bunkers, only 8 with anti-tank guns, closed the intervals. Three of these bunkers were for observation and the remainder mounted machine guns. As in PFL II, light, medium and heavy types were included, although here too only a few were of the heavy type with walls 1.5 meters thick. The bunkers used in both PFLs included the combination anti-tank and machine gun bunkers placed at key points such as bridges and roads. These heavy bunkers were often multi-storied and equipped with a cloche and a searchlight. Their main armament was a 47-mm anti-tank gun and a machine gun, and their garrisons consisted of about fourteen men. The observation bunkers, fewer in number, were equipped with an observation cloche but housed no weapons. An anti-tank barrier consisting of ditches and obstacles ran from the Meuse to Fort Barchon and on to most of the other forts on the bridgehead line.

2. The Namur Defenses

At Namur the Belgian army restored and modernized seven out of nine of the old forts. A bridgehead created at Namur on the right bank of the Meuse was similar to the one at Liege. The army restored fortifications on the left bank, which, in effect, created a ring defense. Namur was primarily a second position against a German penetration through southern Belgium or past Liege. It was also prepared for an attack from the left bank of the Meuse in the event of a French violation of Belgian neutrality. The armament of the old forts was modernized. Although the old 210-mm howitzer gun turrets were not rearmed, initially, 105-mm guns replaced the weapons in the old twin 150-mm gun turrets, but later most were replaced with 75-mm GP guns. A pair of heavy machine guns or two 120-mm mortars replaced the old 120-mm cannons. Other changes, mostly internal, were similar to those made at Liege. The armament of the Namur forts included:

FORT	TURRETS	MACHINE GUN EMBRASURES
Marchovelette*	1 x 75-mm GP twin gun	16
	3 x 75-mm GP gun	—
	2 x 120-mm twin mortar	—
Maizerat*	1 x 105-mm twin gun	21
	4 x 75-mm gun	—
	2 x 120-mm twin mortar	—
Andoy*	1 x 75-mm GP twin gun	17
	4 x 75-mm GP gun	—
	3 x 120-mm twin mortar**	—
Dave*	1 x 75-mm GP twin gun	19
	3 x 75-mm GP gun	—
	1 x 120-mm twin mortar	—
St. Héribert+	1 x 75-mm GP twin gun	19
	4 x 75-mm GP gun	—
Maloone*++	1 x 75-mm GP twin gun	20
	4 x 75-mm GP gun	—
	1 x 120-mm twin mortar	—
Saurlée+	1 x 75-mm GP twin gun	19
	4 x 75-mm GP gun	—

*One 210-mm howitzer turret position not restored or replaced.
**One of these turrets had only one mortar.
+Two 210-mm howitzer and two 120-mm gun turrets not restored or replaced.
++One 120-mm gun turret not restored or replaced.

The abandoned forts of Eminer and Cognelée, that formed part of the all around defense of Namur, were turned into munitions dumps and given a pair of machine gun positions each.

Over two hundred bunkers completed the defense of the Fortified Position of Namur or PFN, almost the same number as at Liege; however, they covered a smaller area. This meant that the PFN had slightly more depth that the PFL. Its northeastern and southeastern segments actually included a second line. Anti-tank ditches and barriers almost completely encircled the position.

3. The Albert Canal Line

Besides PFL-I, from 1936 until 1939 the Albert Canal Line was the most advanced defensive line and considered the main position for the army field divisions, until it was realized that the French could not help defend it if neutrality were maintained until after Germany attacked. This line linked the PFL to the PFA or Fortified Position of Antwerp and joined the Schelde and Turnhout Canal defense lines near Antwerp to complete a continuous barrier facing the Dutch border.

This line ran along the newly constructed Albert Canal and included bunkers with machine guns and anti-tank guns placed into its embankments. Each bunker covered a large stretch of the canal and, usually, a crossing point as well. A total of more than 200 bunkers were built, over 60 of which were on the Schelde and Turnhout Canals.

The bunker types ranged from light to medium constructions (0.5 to 1.0 meters of concrete thickness), many of which were designed for flanking fires and were placed on the bank where the enemy was expected to appear. Fire from the friendly side was expected to cover these positions because the anti-infantry obstacles did not provide sufficient defense. The bunkers were about 1,200 meters apart, but the army, deciding that they were too far away from each other, began adding additional bunkers just before the war.

Nearby, anti-tank bunkers covered bridges already prepared for demolition. One of the main obstacles used to block these crossings was "Element C" (Elements Cointet invented by French Colonel Cointet) better known as Belgian Gates. These large anti-tank obstacles were rolled into position on wheels that were removed when the gates were locked together.

4. Antwerp's Defenses and the National Redoubt

Less priority was attached to this area because of the experiences of World War I. With the fall of Liege and Namur, this position became almost untenable although it held on for many weeks.

Between the world wars only twenty-two of the original thirty-two forts and redoubts of the outer ring returned to active service. The forts of the inner ring were removed from Antwerp's defenses. Since the Germans had removed most of the 57-mm and 75-mm gun turrets and scavenged the remaining turrets in 1917, and the forts of the PFL and PFN had received the bulk of the funds allotted for new turrets, the army replaced the PFA fort's turrets with concrete machine gun positions. The old defenses were not abandoned because they occupied man-made platforms that dominated the level terrain.

From the Schelde River to the Albert Canal, a water filled anti- tank ditch formed the major obstacle in the PFA. As on the Albert Canal, bunkers using flanking fire covered most of the ditch and were embedded on the enemy side of the canal. The bunkers were of several types.

The army engineers had prepared the canal locks and dikes for demolition to create a zone of inundation in front of the PFA. The south front of the PFA included the Nerthe and Rupel Rivers that flowed into the Schelde. The southern banks of these rivers were marshy and served as a final line of defense since the line of forts ran about 5 km south of these rivers. Other tributaries leading to these rivers added to the forward defense and numerous bunkers were concentrated along them (some as part of the KW Line). Between 1935 and 1937 the army added many double embrasure machine gun bunkers to the PFA.

The PFA consisted of the following:

	Forts	Redoubts	Bunker
Schelde River to Turnhout Canal (linked by AT ditch)	4	3	40
Turnhout Canal to Lierre (linked by AT ditch to the Albert Canal; marshes cover remainder of area to Fort Lierre)	5	2	40+
Lierre to Mechelen	3	3	100+ (most in KW Line)

The defenses ended near Mechelen with only water barriers covering the remainder of the PFA. Between the town of Lierre and Fort Koninghyndt an anti-tank barrier of Element C formed the most significant obstacle. The Ghent Bridgehead occupied the south side of the Schelde River and was linked up to the PFA by the Schelde and Lys Rivers to form the National Redoubt, but no bunkers were built along those rivers. Over a hundred casemates defended the bridgehead with three special casemates for 75-mm field guns.

5. The KW Line

This line ran from Koningshooikt to Wavre and was later extended to Namur. It was the last of the major fortifications to be erected in Belgium, since it did not begin to go up until 1938. Its main defense was formed by the River Dyle, which, unfortunately, did not run along the entire line. To compensate for the lack of natural obstacles, the army had to set up man-made anti-tank defenses at the point where the river turned away from the line. Over 190 bunkers were built along three lines and more field fortifications added. A line of Belgian Gates between Wavre and Namur, almost completed by May 1940, formed an anti-tank barrier that was, unfortunately, virtually undefended since no bunkers had been built to cover that section.

6. The Coastal Defenses

The coastal defenses consisted of a few defended points and dikes located in the polders behind the coastal sand dunes that were prepared for demolition to inundate the low lying areas. A single battery of four old German 280-mm guns constituted the main defensive artillery. The few installations created by the Germans in the Great War were reactivated.

WEAPONS AND EQUIPMENT

WEAPONS OF THE PFL II AND PFN:	MAXIMUM RANGE
150-mm L/50 Cannon	17.0 km
105-mm L/33 Cannon	11.0 km
75-mm GP Cannon	11.0 km
120-mm Mortar	?
81-mm Mortar Model 32	3.6 km

WEAPONS OF PFL I:	
120-mm Cannon FRC Model 1931	18.0 km
75-mm Cannon in turret FRC Model 1934	10.0 km
75-mm Cannon in casemate	11.0 km
60-mm Anti-Tank Gun FRC Model 1936	3.0 km
47-mm Anti-Tank Gun Model 32	2.0 km
Maxim 7.65 Machine Guns	———
Field Artillery:	
280-mm Cannon	32.0 km
170-mm Cannon	24.0 km
150-mm Cannon	20.0 km
105-mm Cannon	12.3 km

	DIAMETER (METERS)	ROOF THICKNESS (MM)
Turrets		
Gun 120-mm	5.7	460
Gun 75-mm	4.0	450
Cloche		
Observation	1.39	350-370
Anti-Tank 47-mm	2.30	350
Machine Gun	2.30	350

Obstacles employed:
Anti-tank
Element C: 3 meters high, 2 meters wide, 1 1/4 tons Over 100 km.
Iron Pyramid: 2.5 meters wide and 1.5 meters high. Sometimes set in concrete. Used in most forts and other positions.

Concrete Triangle	3 meters wide and 1.3 meters high (hollow inside) Used near Arlon in south.
Concrete Walls	1.5-2.0 meters high and 1.2-1.5 meters thick. Used as road blocks.
Round Concrete Barrier	
Concrete pillars	50 meters in diameter and 2.0 meters high (half beneath the ground). Used in two rows in southern Belgium.
AT Rails	Same as the French. 2.0 meters high (half sunk into the ground), but height not as varied as the French. Used at Liege and Namur in five rows.
AT Ditch	1.5 meters wide and 1.5 meters deep.

WORLD WAR II

When the war began, Belgium frantically worked to complete the Dyle Line (KW Line) while struggling to remain neutral. A special regiment was assigned to each of the three fortress cities. The army, on the other hand, took up positions near the German border after it mobilized. The 1st Chasseurs Ardennais Division was stationed to the Ardennes, near Arlon, while the 2nd Chasseurs Ardennais Division was located near Huy, on the other side of the Meuse. Between these two divisions stood the 1st Cavalry Division and several cyclist companies armed with 47-mm anti-tank guns. These troops could probably have used the few obstacles and bunkers built in southern Belgium to seriously impede the German advance, but their orders did not call for a protracted resistance. The majority of the Belgian army took up positions along the Albert Canal and near the Dutch border. The King refused to allow the coordination of Belgian defenses with the Allies, so the Belgian army was only able to prepare for delaying action on the advanced positions and then withdraw to the still incomplete KW Line. Furthermore, coordination between the Netherlands and Belgium was also non-existent, which forced Belgium to deploy its army along the border with the Netherlands instead of concentrating it near Liege.

The German assault began on May 10, 1940, when German paratroopers, carried in over 40 gliders from airfields near Cologne, silently approached three key crossings of the Albert Canal and Fort Eben Emael even before the ground invasion began. Meanwhile, another German relief force, consisting of a special company wearing uniforms of the Dutch military police, crossed the Dutch border in an attempt to take the bridges at Maastricht. This contingent was followed by an advance force consisting of an infantry regiment and the 4th Panzer Division.

The assault on Eben Emael was meant to draw the world's attention away from the other, more significant operations. The ploy succeeded beyond expectations since the other operations were barely noticed by the world. There was not even much attention paid to the risky landing of troops in several light Storch aircraft to capture key points in the Ardennes for the main thrust of the campaign.

The glider-landed paratroopers took the bridges over the Albert Canal at Veldwezelt and Vroenhoven, but the Belgians blew up the bridge at Kanne. The attempt to take the Dutch bridges in Maastricht failed, but the spearhead continued to advance. The special engineer assault group landed on top of Fort Eben Emael taking the garrison by surprise. The Belgians were still preparing the fort for action at the time of the attack, but their biggest problem was a lack of defenses on the fort's surface. The Germans used the new, and still secret, hollow charges designed to penetrate most armor of Eben Emael. Thus the Germans successfully neutralized the key positions on the fort that included most of the artillery turrets and casemates. They encountered little resistance from the two ineffectual infantry blocks on the fort's surface and the Belgian artillery men, who were not trained to engage in infantry combat on the surface. Forts Pontisse, Barchon, and Evegnée pounded the surface of Eben Emael with their 105-mm guns to no avail. By the end of the day the Germans neutralized the fort. They even penetrated one block and descended into the gallery below, causing the garrison to seal the access to the tunnel. Canal Nord temporarily checked the crossing of the Albert Canal by German troops until the evening. By the next day the situation became hopeless as the German troops poured across the Albert Canal. A Belgian relief force had been repelled on the first day and there was little left for the commander of Eben Emael to do but surrender the pride of the Belgian forts.

The Allies rushed to the Dyle Line, believing the main German thrust was coming across the Albert Canal. Other forts of the PFL I were soon engaged. The Belgian forces in the Ardennes were ordered to withdraw quickly, abandoning the region to the main German spearhead.

On May 10 the Germans engaged other positions of the PFL I, Fort Aubin-Neufchâteau opened fire against them, but by the evening of that day the fort was surrounded. German heavy artillery pounded the fort on May 11 and their numerous infantry assaults were driven back. The Luftwaffe joined the heavy artillery in the bombardment and finally breached the fort's defenses by May 15. On May 20 another German infantry attack was beaten back with the help of Battice, but the fort was badly damaged. After another major assault on May 21, the fort surrendered having expended most of its ammunition.

During the first days of the invasion the Germans brought up 355-mm and 305-mm weapons to bombard the PFL I. On May 13, 305-mm mortars fired almost 200 shells on Fort Battice, causing no significant damage. General Fedor von Bock, commander of Army Group B, unhappy with the waste of lives on both sides after the fierce battle for Aubin-Neufchâteau, on May 20-21, demanded both Battice and Tancrémont to surrender. Both forts had held out for about a week and a half without hope of support or relief as the Belgian army withdrew from the Albert Canal Line. Battice surrendered on May 22, the day after Aubin-Neufchâteau but Tancrémont continued to hold out. Little more could have been expected from them, and although some of the tactical decisions might appear to be a repeat of 1914, these forts were better built and performed much better than their predecessors.

The Germans simply bypassed Tancrémont. It did not surrender until May 29, one day after the Belgian army was ordered to lay down its arms. For the other forts, those of the PFL II the story was different because the lines of communication through Liege had to be opened.

The forts of the PFL II had been in action since the first day. Some tried to support Eben Emael. Belgian army units had withdrawn from Liege by May 12 leaving the forts isolated. General von Bock stated that two of the forts of Liege had fallen by May 14, but all the Meuse bridges were down. His main concern was to open the road and he preferred to avoid tangling with the forts if possible. To von Bock the whole PFL position represented a threat to his line of communications far behind the front lines. On May 15, dive bombers attacked Fort Flémalle, and damaged its 120-mm mortar turret and breached the counterscarp. The garrison surrendered the next day. On May 18 the same engineer battalion that spearheaded the relief force for the paratroopers on Eben Emael assaulted Fort Barchon. A Czech 420-mm howitzer bombarded the fort. The engineers breached Barchon and, with demolitions and flame throwers supported by 88-mm anti-aircraft guns, they eliminated most of the fort's turrets and machine gun positions. Barchon surrendered the same day as did the nearby forts of Pontisse and Fléron. Bock claimed the latter gave up without a fight, and on May 19 he visited Fort Pontisse where he found its heavy armored turrets overturned as a result of Stuka attacks. Only the air vent, disguised as a water tower, outside of Barchon continued to resist. Fort Evegnée succumbed the next day. The forts south of Liege remained, with Tancrémont, isolated.

The Belgians withdrew from the Albert Canal Line and frontier defenses as the Allies took up positions on the Dyle Line. The position was not strong and in the south the Germans found it easy to breach undefended sections of the Element C anti-tank obstacles. In other places the gates themselves offered the assault engineers protection from the defenders small arms fire.

As the main German thrust through the Ardennes gained momentum and crossed the Meuse by May 14, German troops engaged the defenses of Namur. By May 16 Allied troops were disengaging from the Dyle Line and by May 18 the Belgian army was taking up positions on the Dender River as the PFN was left to its own devices. By May 22 most of the PFNs forts had fallen, and on that morning 88-mm anti-aircraft guns supported the attack on Fort Maizeret. These weapons helped eliminate most of the fort's turrets and cloches. Assault troops crossed the moat and forced the garrison to surrender.

The Belgian army fell back upon the Ghent Bridgehead on May 19. On May 17 the key fort of Lierre on the PFA was taken by a *coup de main*. Antwerp was abandoned by May 18. By May 26 the Ghent Bridgehead had fallen and the army was clinging to defenses along the Lys River. Surrender soon followed. Except for the PFL I and the Albert Canal, most of Belgiums defensive positions proved of no significant value. Building so many other defensive positions, failing to commit a reasonable force to defend southern Belgium, and insisting on a policy of strict neutrality until the last moment, assured the collapse of Belgium.

Top Right: One of the largest canal casemates on the outer bank of Antwerp's AT ditch (which ran north from the Albert Canal to the Schelde). Many of the 22 restored forts and redoubts were on the ditch. These two-level casemates fired to the flanks and their sluices controlled the water level. (Kaufmann)
Bottom Right: Ft. Eben Emael. Fortin 01. 60-mm AT gun, 3 MGs, and 3 searchlights. Observation cloche can be seen above. (Wes Micket)

Above: Rolling Gate. Designed to be used locked together in line or singly as AT obstacles. They were also used in the Atlantic Wall. (Kaufmann Collection)

Left: Ft. Barchon. Air intake. Ft. Barchon was one of the old restored forts of PFL-2 which received a new concrete air intake located beyond the fort's perimeter. The defensive weapons embrasures can be seen on the block which is designed to appear as a water tower. (Kaufmann)

Map of Belgium

Cloche for Hvy MG.
Note: Periscope position
can be seen behind MG
position.

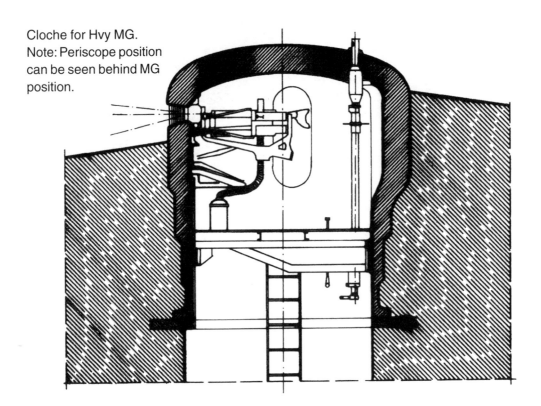

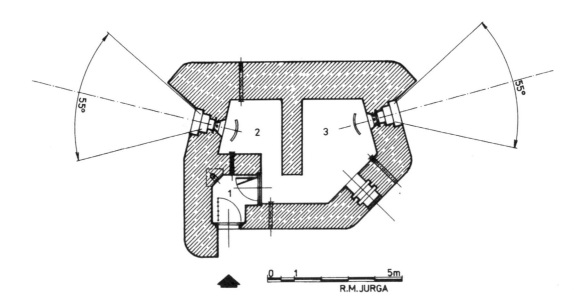

R.M. JURGA

Standard Belgian Flanking Bunker
1. Entrance
2. MG Room
3. MG Room and Emergency Exit
In the walls 4 tubes for grenade throwers for close defense are marked

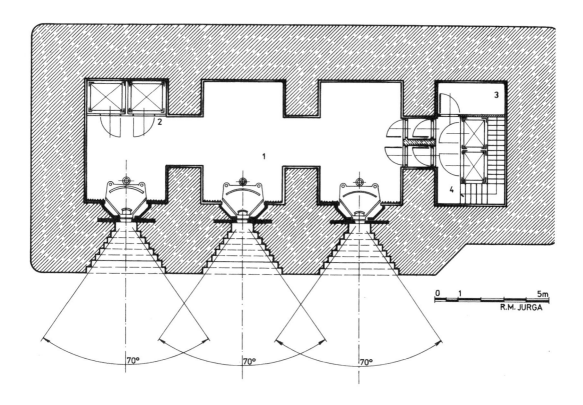

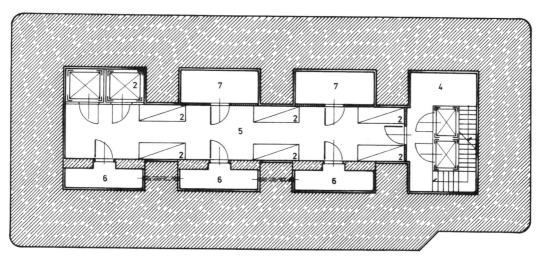

Eben Emael Artillery Casemate VISE 2. Upper floor:
1. Firing rooms for 3 x 75-mm guns
2. Monte Charges
3. CP
4. Elevators and staircase down

Lower floor:
5. Crews quarters
6. Magazines
7. Technical rooms

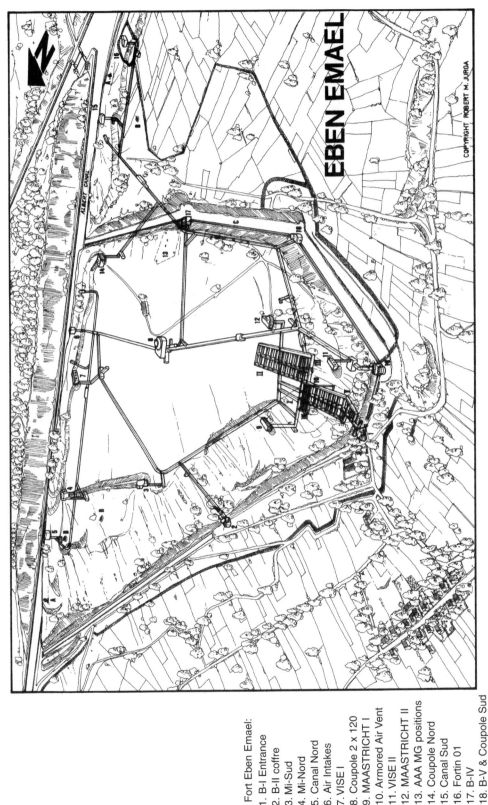

EBEN EMAEL

COPYRIGHT ROBERT M. JURGA

ALBERT CANAL

Fort Eben Emael:
1. B-I Entrance
2. B-II coffre
3. Mi-Sud
4. Mi-Nord
5. Canal Nord
6. Air Intakes
7. VISE I
8. Coupole 2 x 120
9. MAASTRICHT I
10. Armored Air Vent
11. VISE II
12. MAASTRICHT II
13. AAA MG positions
14. Coupole Nord
15. Canal Sud
16. Fortin 01
17. B-IV
18. B-V & Coupole Sud
19. B-VI, A. Searchlight Position, B. Dumrny Turret, C. AT Ditch and Concrete Scarp, Underground System I. Infirmary, II. Caserne, III. Officers quarters, IV. Commanders quarters, V. Magazines.

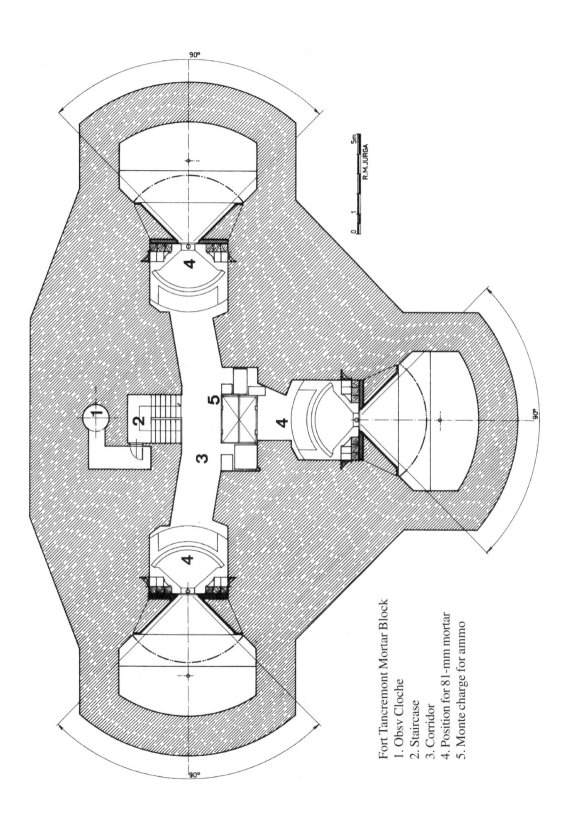

Fort Tancremont Mortar Block
1. Obsv Cloche
2. Staircase
3. Corridor
4. Position for 81-mm mortar
5. Monte charge for ammo

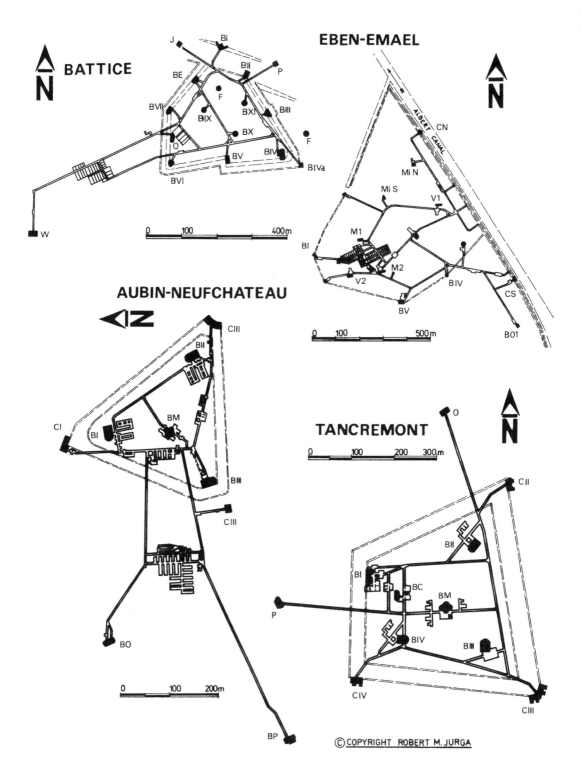

Plans of Battice, Eben Emael, Aubin-Neufchateau,
Trancremont: B=Block, C=Coffre, BM=Mortar Block,
BE=Entrance Block, J,O,P,W=Air Intakes (P&W also entrances)

Chapter 4

NETHERLANDS

BACKGROUND

On September 18, 1939, LTC Robert Brown, American Military Attache to Brussels, reported that in the event of war between the Germany and Britain, "Holland will be invaded." In addition, he stated, "It must not be excluded that the Great National Redoubt of the Netherlands will be attacked from the rear." The war was not a month old when even a foreign observer could see that the situation in the Netherlands was precarious.

Born out of a religious revolution during the Reformation, the Netherlands had had an unusual history compared to most European nations. Their fortified cities, which relied upon their remarkable water defenses, had foiled the invading Spanish Army during the Eighty Years War that ended in 1648. The new nation became one of northern Europe's first republics and one of the leading sea powers of the seventeenth century. Thanks to windmill-powered pumps used in the construction and maintenance of polders, the country grew in size by reclaiming land from the sea. However, the low-lying land could quickly be returned to the sea to deter invaders. The last major European conflicts in which the Netherlands participated were the wars of the Napoleonic Era. The defeat of Napoleon and the restoration of the Netherlands' independence transformed this former republic into a monarchy, and left the former Austrian Netherlands, or Belgium, under its aegis. However, this territorial expansion lasted only until the Belgian Revolution of 1830, the last European campaign in which the Dutch Army would be involved until 1940.

As Europe prepared for a new war in the aftermath of the Franco-Prussian War of 1870-71, the Netherlands made some effort to modernize their antiquated fortifications. Previously they had relied on individual positions that could be used for creating water barriers. However, with the exception of the Old Waterline, no actual continuous fortified line existed in the Netherlands before the mid-nineteenth century. The Old Waterline was a hastily improvised position set up in the 1670s to stop the invading French army with inundations. It ran west of Utrecht and was designed only to defend the province of Holland.

In the nineteenth century the New Water Line, to the east of Utrecht, was created as the main line of defense. It ran from the Zuider Zee to the banks of the Maas and Rhine Rivers where a bridgehead was created. This line relied heavily on massive inundations. Its heaviest fortifications had to be placed on the high ground near Utrecht that took more time to flood. The modernization of this position began between 1866 and 1871.

Meanwhile, Prussia created the Second Reich, establishing a major power on a large part of the Dutch border. The Netherlands responded by erecting several new forts, one of the largest of which was Fort Rijnauwen, built between 1868 and 1879.

In the 1880s, the Netherlands adopted the fortress rings already prevalent in France, Belgium, Germany, and Austria-Hungary. While the New Water Line became the main line of Fortress Holland, the key city of Amsterdam received a protective ring beginning in 1883 with the construction of Fort Abcoude. This ring eventually became the National Redoubt. Once more, inundations played a key role in the new defense by creating a barrier several kilometers wide. Numerous other forts, most of which sat on artificial high ground, filled out the line, occupying key points near roads and along canals among the numerous polders.

While the new forts were built, many older forts were modernized. East of the fortified town of Gorkum, on the end of the New Water Line on the Waal (Rhine) River, the new fort of Vuren built in the 1840s was refurbished in the 1880s. South of the Waal, the old bridgehead with its medieval works continued in service, and its defenses were supplemented with sluices at Woudrichem and Bakkerskil. Fort Bakkerskil, built earlier in the century at the Papsluis (a key sluice in the area) was renovated in the 1880s. The bridgehead position from the old defenses was advanced to higher ground southeast of Woudrichem and was strengthened with the addition of Fort Giessen in 1880. This fort had large, earth covered, brick barracks and twelve guns that stood high on its walls. In addition to these and other forts, the Dutch also built small supporting gun battery positions.

Near the north end of the New Water Line, the old fortress of Naarden was modernized in the 1880s and became part of the World War I era defenses. Not far from Naarden the second line of defense began at the fortress of Muiden, near the mouth of the Vecht River. During the middle of the nineteenth century, a coastal battery was set up at Muiden and later it received a bombproof tower, one of nine built in the forts of the New Water Line by 1860. By the 1870s these towers became virtually obsolete and had to be given earth cover to meet the demands of the ever-changing war technology[1]. Muiden protected several of the most important sluices for flooding the northern part of the water line.

The Dutch completed a total of 42 forts in the Amsterdam Position at the end of the nineteenth century. They adopted the Belgian method of using non-reinforced concrete in their construction. Each fort included two retracting 60-mm gun turrets and a casemate mounting two 110-mm guns that covered each flank. Large caliber guns occupied separate battery positions behind the defensive line. At the end of the century sluices for flooding the land in front of the line were completed. It took half a day to fully inundate this area.

Coast defenses included a number of forts, complete with moats. The French built Fort Prins Frederik and Fort Sabina Henrica near Willemstad during the Napoleonic Wars. The Dutch modernized them in 1860 and the 1880s, by adding eight 240-mm Krupp guns to Fort Sabina Henrica and five to Fort Frederik. Not far from these forts in 1883, Willemstad, on the Holland Deep, received two four-gun batteries of 240-mm coast defense guns and new shelters. The Willemstad Position, created in 1860, encompassed Fort Sabina Henrica and the small position of Fort Hell. In 1874 the Willemstad Position was modernized and enlarged to form the Holland Deep Position.

New weapons rendered many of these fortifications obsolete after World War I. However, the Netherlands remained firmly convinced that they could maintain their neutrality, secure behind their water defenses.

MAJOR FORTIFICATIONS

The Grebbe Line and Fortress Holland
The Frontier Lines

LOCATION

1. The Grebbe Line and Fortress Holland

The Grebbe Line and Fortress Holland constituted the core of the Dutch defensive system. The Grebbe Line, which kept Amsterdam beyond the range of modern artillery, passed through the highest part of the country where the elevation rose up to 30 meters, and the Grebbe Berg constituted the highest point of the Netherlands. The Grebbe Line relied on water barriers that passed through the area for its defense, and was in part protected by some woodland areas. As in the rest of the country, the land was mostly level and devoted to agriculture.

Fortress Holland's New Water Line paralleled one of the country's major canals and stretched from the Zuider Zee to the Lek and Waal Rivers, both channels of the Rhine. The country behind the New Water Line was low and included much of the country's polder lands from the Holland Deep to Walden Sea. Over 20% of the region's level land was below sea level with only the road embankments and scattered trees rising above it.

The New Water Line joined the South Front that stretched along the Waal River to the North Sea. Along the South Front much of the land had been reclaimed from the sea, and guns placed on top of the old forts had a commanding field of fire over the level terrain.

The West Front, which covered the coastline up to the Den Helder Position, included large areas of sand dunes similar to parts of the Belgian coast. All the major Dutch ports were inside Fortress Holland: Amsterdam on the Zuider Zee and Rotterdam on the Lek River. Den Helder, Ijmuiden, and Hoek van Holland on the coast included some facilities for naval vessels. They occupied part of the same coast line from which the Spanish Armada had been unable to pick up troops in 1588, because lighters were needed in the shallows.

The Den Helder Position, which defended the northern sectors, was sometimes considered part of Fortress Holland. On the other hand, the fortress ring of Amsterdam, occupying many positions in the polder lands, formed part of the Northern Front.

Finally, the country's only new heavy fortifications stood at two points on the Great Dike, barring the entrance to Fortress Holland from that quarter.

2. The Frontier Lines

Border defenses were established in places where natural obstacles existed already, otherwise they turned inward to find such features. The F and Q Lines covered the open northern quarter of the country and used the few watercourses present. The Ijssel Line followed the river of the same name which flowed up to 40 km behind the border at most points. It connected to the Maas Line which ran along the Maas River, south to the Belgian border. Sometimes these two lines are referred to as the Maas-Ijssel Line or Ijssel-Maas Line. Fort Pannerden was located near the point where the lines joined. Further south of the Maas Line, the city of Maastricht, with its defenses, incorporated the Juliana Canal to form a major obstacle.

The Peel-Raam Line, a few kilometers behind the Maas Line, paralleled a major canal and passed through the Peel Marshes. The land in this region was also relatively level and unobstructed, the marshland constituting one of its few natural barriers.

Finally, the isolated positions of Bath and Zendijk on the neck of South Beveland were separated by polders that could turn the peninsula back into an island if necessary.[2] South Beveland was more important in helping the Belgians than the Dutch because it covered the mouth of the Schelde River, which led to Antwerp.

HISTORY

The Dutch, feeling secure in their neutrality for a few years after the Great War, did not plan new fortifications or work on them until the 1930s. The only exception was the northern part of Fortress Holland where the Great Dike (Afsluitdijk) was being built. The States-General approved the damming and draining of large sections of the Zuider Zee in 1918, planning to drain the Northeastern Section by 1941. The dike, which sealed the Zuider Zee in 1932, was wide enough to carry a roadway and offer a new approach into Fortress Holland. Thus the country's two newest forts went up on either end of the dike early in the 1930s.

The New Water Line, which formed the old East Front of Fortress Holland, was too close to the major population centers of the country to adequately defend the area from long range artillery. Thus it was time to create a new defensive position, the Grebbe Line, 25 km in front of the New Water Line. The original Grebbe Line, which had been used since the eighteenth century, consisted of a series of canals and dams that could inundate the area, and of earthen redoubts that defended the key positions. It was abandoned as a major defensive line after the Napoleonic Era. In 1935 the army commander became interested in extending the East Front defenses forward to the old Grebbe Line. When war became imminent in 1939, General Willem Roell, commander-in-chief, called for its activation, turning it into the main position by early 1940. Construction on most of the line's defensive works, including an anti-tank ditch, began in 1939. By the spring of 1940, the inundation mechanisms were completed.

Between 1929 and 1938, Fortress Holland received thirty new heavy bunkers, and the Maas and Ijssel river lines forty after 1936. The largest of these bunkers, known as river casemates, had two to four levels and mounted an anti-tank gun and machine guns. However, no more than two stories rose above ground level facing the enemy. At first thirty large bunkers were built, but after 1938, smaller, more economical three-man bunkers, over 2,000 of which were built throughout the Netherlands, became more common.

The New Water Line of the East Front got the most attention prior to 1936 where some of the heaviest fortifications were built at Fort Kijkuit in 1935. The South Front, based on the great river barriers, required few improvements. It received anti-tank and machine gun bunkers between 1936 and 1937 to protect the bridgehead at Moerdijk.

The main part of the North Front, which consisted of the Amsterdam Ring or

Amsterdam Position, did not receive significant improvements since most work was done near the Great Dike.

The Ijssel Line and Maas Line were renovated between 1936 and 1938, when key points received heavy bunkers. However, most construction took place later when many smaller fortifications and obstacles were added to form a continuous line.

The Peel-Raam Line was built at the end of the decade to serve as a possible main line of defense in conjunction with the Grebbe Line, in the event the Belgians decided to secure its right flank.

The first 2.5 km section of the Afsluitdijk (Great Dike) was completed on the island of Wieringen in 1926 and the remaining 25 km were finished in 1932. Man-made islands were created to house the sluices, locks, and two new forts of this line.

Four phases of Dutch construction can be identified in the 1930s. During the first phase, the two new forts were built on the Great Dike in the early 1930s, and new casemates were placed on old forts in 1935. During the second, which lasted from 1936 to 1938, the large anti-tank and machine gun bunkers were built to protect the bridges over the Maas and Ijssel Rivers and other key crossing points. During the third, which lasted from 1939 to 1940, the majority of the bunkers for the Grebbe, Maas, Ijssel, and Peel-Raam Lines were begun and the new armored turrets were put in place. During the fourth and final phase, which took place in 1940, the East and South Fronts of Fortress Holland were improved.

Like the Belgians, the Dutch created a multitude of defensive lines that they could not complete in time for war, nor adequately man with their small army.

DESCRIPTION

1. The Grebbe Line and Fortress Holland

The Dutch army leaders had replaced the New Water Line as the main line of defense for Fortress Holland, with the Grebbe Line in 1940.[3] The line included 144 of the new armored turret positions, which consisted of a fixed turret similar to a cloche but with a distinctive shape and weapons embrasure. The armor made of chromium nickel steel was 100-mm thick for the simplest turrets and up to 170-mm thick for the heaviest type. These turrets were meant to be placed on a small concrete structure and were designed in such a way that they could be placed at different firing angles, depending on the needs of the position. The turret included a gas proof mount for the embrasure and a gas proof door. The intended weapon was a heavy machine gun. A Belgian firm at Liege produced those turrets designed for 47-mm and 50-mm fortress anti-tank guns, but most were not delivered in time for installation. The Grebbe Line also included 130 positions, mostly small three-embrasure machine gun bunkers, and only four anti-tank bunkers.

The Grebbe Line consisted of two defensive belts. The area in front of the first belt which could be inundated, varied from several hundred meters to a few kilometers in width. The Grebbe Berg, although only about 37 meters high, dominated the area, and the dense woodlands offered some protection for the troops. The hills averaged about 30 meters in height across most of the position. At one critical point in front of the Grebbe Berg, eighteenth century fortifications reinforced with new works protected the flood gate.

In the spring of 1940, Major William Colbern, American Military Attache to the Hague, who was taken on a tour of the Grebbe Line, described it as a main position protected by an inundation and an outpost line. According to him, the main position followed the west bank of the Een River from the Zuider Zee to Amersfoort, encircling that town on the east, following the west bank of the Luntersche Beek to the confluence of the Grebbe, and then running along the west bank of that river to the Rhine River. An inundation zone, only partially prepared for flooding, occupied the 5 km that separated the outpost line from the main position. Colbern also reported that the area north of Amersfoort could be flooded within six hours, but that the area to the southeast, which was slower to inundate, was already awash in about 45-cm to 60-cm of water. According to Colbern complete inundation was to be achieved in twelve hours at a depth of about 100-cm, covering anti-tank ditches and barbed wire obstacles. The outpost line was not a solid line, but a number of positions placed at intervals of up to 400 meters apart for early warning and mutual support. The defensive positions in the outpost line were not permanent, but instead used wood and sand platforms.

Some of Colbern's descriptions are not confirmed by post-war sources. In addition, a few of his comments obviously indicate that the Dutch had misled him. For instance, he claimed that the main position consisted of three lines about 500 to 800 meters apart, each made up of a continuous trench and of bunkers incorporated in a sand dike. The trenches, reported Colbern, were revetted with wooden planks and without overhead cover and the bunkers were placed about every 300 to 400 meters. Some of the few large bunkers sheltered seven men with a couple of heavy machine guns and an anti-tank gun. Some contained a hand operated air pump for the air filter to prevent infiltration of poison gas. Colbern claimed that the armored turrets were sunk into the dikes without concrete and questioned their stability under bombardment. He also noted that they were not only gas proof, but had bullet-proof glass covers. Most of the work appeared to have been completed at the time he visited the defenses, the positions were camouflaged with earth, bushes, and small trees, and the trenches were covered with green netting interwoven with burlap.

Colbern's evaluation of the entire position reveal some serious weaknesses not always mentioned in more recent sources. Most positions, he correctly concluded, appeared incapable of resisting direct hits from medium artillery. The Dutch reportedly had only four regiments of 105-mm guns that could fire beyond the outpost line from behind the main position since the distance was between 7 to 12 kilometers to that line.

The Grebbe Line was extended to cover the gaps between the Lek and the Waal Rivers and the Waal and Maas Rivers, to form a position called the Ocheten Spa and Putuijk Positions respectively by the Germans in 1940.[4] These positions included some of the bunkers, which were included in the count for the Grebbe Line, and inundation mechanisms. An additional position, known as the Waal-Linge Line, extended back from the Grebbe Line to the New Water Line, using inundated areas and the river to close the gap on the exposed southern flank of the Grebbe Line. The small Linge River flowed through the sluices at Fort Asperen where its waters could be backed up to flood the area between the Waal and Lek. The remainder of Fortress Holland was heavily dependent upon its system of inundations and, to a smaller extent, on the numerous small bunkers and other fortifications that had been added to defend key positions. The special armored turret positions that had been installed on the Grebbe Line were placed here too, sometimes on old forts such as Vechten and Rijnauwen near Utrecht. In early 1940 field fortifications were still being prepared and some of the old fortresses such as Muiden, Naarden, Utrecht, Vianen and Gorinchem had been refurbished with the addition of new positions. Only the eastern part of Muiden was modernized between 1934 and 1940: three heavy machine gun casemates were added in 1934, a number of lighter machine gun casemates in 1934, and a number of lighter machine gun casemates with Belgian made cloches between 1939 and 1940.

Fort Kijkuit guarded the route created by the new state highway that ran through the swampy region of the New Water Line from Hilversum to Harlem via Vreeland. Fort Kijkuit and Fort Spion, which occupied positions on artificial islands among the marshes, were over a hundred years old and modernized in the 1880s. Fort Kijkuit received a large reinforced concrete casemate whose roof and some walls were up to 2.5 meters thick, and an armored shield mounting two light guns that covered the causeway. Similar concrete casemates were placed near the road, but only this one was built of reinforced concrete.

In the New Water Line some of the restored forts included Fort Rijnauwen and Fort Vechten. Rijnauwen built in 1876, had old armament that included ten 150-mm cannons, six 120-mm cannons, and even older weapons. Special armored turrets for a machine gun were added before the war. Between the world wars reinforced concrete positions were added to cover the road and terrain in front of the fort.[5]

The newest fort in the Amsterdam Ring of 42 forts, was completed in 1912 with two 105-mm Krupp cannons in a turret. Old Fort Walmer included a casemate for 100-mm guns. Panzer Fort Pampus, built in 1879 and situated on an artificial island outside of Amsterdam, mounted two turrets with 240-mm cannons, two positions with a pair of embrasures for old 57-mm QF guns, and an observation cloche. Other forts of the ring included Fort Hoofdorp, Fort Velsen, and Fort Spijkerboor completed in 1904, 1900 and 1911 respectively. Each mounted two disappearing 60-mm gun turrets and two flanking casemates for a pair of 110-mm guns. Some forts like Spijkerboor had more weapons, in this case a 105-mm gun turret, and Fort Velsen had a 150-mm gun turret. Batteries of two 150-mm howitzers and four 150-mm howitzers occupied positions behind the forts. Many of the Amsterdam forts had a long, thin design and their bomb-proof barracks and associated buildings had concrete walls only 1.9 meters thick. They lacked electricity and running water so the garrisons obtained their drinking water from cisterns that collected runoff from the roof when it rained.

The inundation system at Amsterdam, and other positions was required to produce a sheet of water 50-cm deep, which would make the area impassable to troops using boats. Unfortunately the elevation of the polders varied from .5 meters to 7 meters and in Amsterdam alone required eighty different inundation levels. To protect the flood gates, armored ships were maintained in the vicinity.

The two new forts of Kornwerderzand and Den Over consisted of two lines of fortifications that included a number of bunker positions. Because of the low water table, these bunkers could not be linked by subterranean works, but they represented nonetheless the most modern fortified groups in the Netherlands.

Fort Kornwerderzand comprised seventeen and Fort Den Over, thirteen structures that included machine gun casemates, anti-tank gun casemates, flak storage bunkers, a searchlight bunker, a command post bunker, and a combination infirmary and usine bunker. Fort Kornwerderzand lay on the eastern end of the dike and Fort Den Over on the western end. The forts occupied two islands apiece. The first line of each fort was located on the easternmost island of its group and the second line on the island behind it.

The forts' bunkers were mostly on one level and occupied small sand hills on the man-made islands. The standard roof and wall protection was 2.0 meters of reinforced concrete. More vulnerable positions were 2.5 to 3.0 meters thick, while only the walls of the Flak bunkers had less than 2.0 meters. The ceilings were lined with teak wood from the Dutch East Indies. The bunkers varied in size and held ten to twenty men. Each fort held a total garrison of about 200 men, which included artillery men, engineers, infantrymen, and signal men. Many of the individual positions were partially surrounded by their own concrete trench which comprised firing steps for one or more machine guns in open positions, especially those found on the end of a jetty. Dutch-made periscopes were used in the roofs of the bunkers for observation. Some bunkers even included large cloches, also manufactured in the Netherlands, that used episcopes through their narrow vision slits.

The anti-tank bunkers mounted one or two guns. The one at Kornwerderzand had two floors and a special observation embrasure between the gun rooms. The Flak bunkers housed a small anti- aircraft weapon and served as a storage and rest area for the crew. The diesel engines in the usine bunker served as a secondary power source for the locks. All the bunkers had an underground telephone link, and in some cases, trenches were dug to connect them.

The army maintained the Wons Position in front of Fort Kornwerderzand on the Friesland coast, a bridgehead consisting mainly of earth and wooden defenses in the form of field fortifications. The Wons Position consisted of about ninety-five bunkers, a third of which had only rifle embrasures, and only six anti-tank gun bunkers. The Wons Position and the forts on the Great Dike formed the Den Helder Position, a defensive area which included five old forts near Den Oever that protected the naval base and supported the new forts. One of these old forts mounted two 150-mm Krupp guns and ten obsolete 240-mm guns. Another was a panzer fort endowed with two outdated turrets, each mounting a pair of 305-mm guns.

The West Front of Fortress Holland consisted mainly of coastal defenses guarding the access to the river mouths, the ports, and the open coastline. Some of its old forts, the newest of which was Panzer Fort Hoek van Holland built in 1888, still maintained a defensive role. Fort Hoek van Holland had two turrets mounting a pair of 240-mm cannons each and a turret with a pair of 150-mm cannons. Its 10-meter wide moat was of limited value since the fort's main protection consisted of an armored gallery with rifle embrasures. Fort Ijmiden, located on a small island near the town of the same name, included a turret with two obsolete 150-mm guns, five emplacements for ancient 240-mm guns, and two positions for 75-mm guns."

The main type of bunker throughout the Dutch defensive lines was the small three man machine gun casemate with walls 0.7 to 1.2 meters thick and roofs 1.0 meter thick. The three-embrasure bunker called the "Spider" or "Porcupine" included firing crenels for light machine guns and had enough space for three men. Unlike the casemate, which gave flanking fires, the "Spider" faced the enemy and was found mostly in the major lines, including those on the frontier. A few larger types of bunkers were also built for machine guns.

The troop shelter or "Pyramid," which served as a shelter and command post, included a defended entrance and a periscope in the roof for observation. Its roof was up to 2.15 meters thick and angled to deflect bombs. It was found in several locations in Fortress Holland and, in some cases, it was placed in lines adjacent to roads where obstacles were prepared to bar an enemy's advance.

On the South Front of Fortress Holland, the bridgehead at Moerdijk included river casemates built early in the 1930s. Later in the decade pyramids were erected behind the dike near its base on the north bank across from the bridgehead. Armored turrets mounting machine guns had their concrete emplacements built into the dike of the north bank. The bridgehead included many special turrets and pyramids and a inundation zone on the south bank.

The inlet sluices on the Lek River at Fort Honswijk controlled the water level in front of the fortifications of Utrecht. However, the new Amsterdam-Rhine Canal, which passed through the New Water Line, could interfere with the flooding. To prevent this problem the Plofsluis sluice was built at the same time as the new canal in 1934. It had five huge containers that could quickly block the canal when their contents of 40,000,000 kilograms of rubble were released, allowing the main sluice to flood the area as planned. The position was bombproof and gas proof so that its garrison could continue to carry out its duties. The Plofsluis also had flood gates to control the flow of water in either direction if the enemy was able to take control of the Lek Dike.

Other key facilities for inundation included the Diefdijk, which regulated the Waal and Lek Rivers with sluices at each end. Fort Everdingen was located at one end of the dike on the Lek, adjacent to the main sluice. Fort Asperen was at the other end of the dike, on the small Linge River. In the 1930s the Diefdijk was broken by a new road that connected Utrecht to 's-Hertogenbosch. A bridge that included a special gate known as a "guillotine," which could be dropped across the road to close the dike, was built at the point where the dike was broken. Thus the area in front of the dike could still be flooded when needed. Across from Fort Everdingen lay Fort Honswijk. Both forts, built in 1860 and modernized in the 1870s, controlled a main sluice on either side of the Lek. Fort Everdingen was given additional concrete shelters during the Great War. Several lines of shelters were added east of Fort Honswijk in 1916, and "pyramids" and two road blocks in 1940.

2. The Frontier Defenses

The Ijssel and Maas Lines included 480 machine gun bunkers (including 337 of the smallest type), 352 armored turrets, and 22 anti-tank gun bunkers. Many of these bunkers had special armored turrets, a few had a ready room and cloche or an anti-tank gun. The large river casemates generally had two levels: one below and one above ground level. There were also four-story bunkers with two floors for embrasures above ground. These large structures usually defended bridges and crossings at places like Zwolle, Deventer, Doesburg, Arnhem, Nijmegen, Venlo, and Roermond. The defensive positions built in front of main lines, virtually on the frontier, were rather insignificant, meant mainly to preserve a neutral stance.

Between the frontier and the Maas-Ijssel Lines, roadblocks were readied for quick installation. They included concrete and steel obstacles, and, in some cases, freshly felled trees that were booby trapped. In addition, all the bridges were mined before the war began.

One key position, almost linking the Maas and Ijssel Line, was the old fort of Pannerden, built in 1872 and refurbished between world wars. Its importance lay in the fact that it occupied the point where the Rhine River forked to become the Waal and Neder (Lower) Rhine.[6] Fort Pannerden included three armored batteries: one of five 150-mm guns, two with two 105-mm guns. The garrison of 300 men occupied a large brick fort with a massive moat that was not bombproof by modern standards. Only the earthen cover and new armored plate for the gun batteries and some new concrete casemates kept the fort from being totally obsolete.

Fort Westervoort, which stood further down the Rhine near Arnhem where the Rhine forked again into the Ijssel, was renovated in the 1930s when several casemates were added to it. Between Arnhem and Nijmegen, the fortifications were extended to link the Ijssel and Maas Lines, taking advantage of the fork of the Rhine. The position was very close to the German border.

The Dutch also resorted to passive resistance, removing all road signs and markers within about 75 kilometers of the frontier months before the invasion in order to confuse the enemy and force him to pass through the rather featureless and unmarked terrain.

The Peel Line, not actually a frontier position, was designed to join with the Grebbe Line. However, since the 1940 strategy was to withdraw into Fortress Holland, it should be included with the border positions. It backed up the Maas Line and ran from the small Raam River which entered the Maas River in the north near Grave and then took a southerly course to Griensaveen and Weert, and then on to the Belgian border. It consisted of three lines. The first included field works and bunkers located at intervals of 300 meters, the second field fortifications, and the third, which followed the Zuid Willems Canal from 's-Hertogenbosch to Nederweert (northeast of Weert), bunkers and field works. The Zuid Willems Canal, which was navigable, had a width ranging from 30 to 35 meters. The first two lines occupied positions among the Peel Marshes. The first line included the newly completed canal from Grave to St. Anthonis to Griendsveen, which was designed for the defense. This defensive canal passed through the marshes to link the Raam River in the north with the Maas in the south. Since the canal had to rise over some of the high ground in the Peel Marshes, it had sluices. The spoil from the 10 meter wide canal were used to build earth works on one of its banks. This canal zig zagged through the swamp land and its sluices could be used to flood large parts of the Peel Marshes. Small porcupine (three embrasure) bunkers were placed along the canal. Machine gun casemates for flanking fire, and armored turret positions were placed on every bend of the canal and covered key points.

Large anti-tank bunkers protected key crossing points in the Peel Line, as on the frontier lines. The Dutch used great ingenuity in camouflaging their bunkers as houses, hay stacks, and a variety of other things. The Peel Line covered almost three times the distance of the Grebbe Line, but comprised only about 290 machine gun bunkers, 245 of which were of the light three embrasure type. There were also 79 special armored turrets but only 13 anti-tank gun bunkers. The water barriers and the swampy terrain of the Peel Marshes formed the main barriers, but on either end of the line the terrain could not be flooded. The gaps on the northern and southern end of the line left it vulnerable, especially since there were no additional army units to defend them. Between Weert and the Belgian defenses on the Albert Canal a 45 km gap was left open.

The F and Q Lines, built along the main water courses in the north, were only intended for delaying actions. The Q Line, which followed several canals, ran from southeast of Delfzij on the mouth of the Ems to Veendam and Emmen. The F Line began a little further south of Emmen and followed the Hoogeveensche Canal to Meppel and the Zuider Zee. Fortifications were few in this region.

WEAPONS AND EQUIPMENT

	Range in meters
Coastal Defense Ships Guns:	
240-mm	unknown
150-mm	unknown
Coast Defense Guns:*	
280-mm (Krupp)	12,800
150-mm QF (Krupp)	14,300
120-mm	unknown
75-mm	7,500
105-mm Flak (Bofors)	unknown
75-mm Flak (Vickers)	10,000 (vertical)
Army Weapons:	
75-mm (3 types)	8,200, 8,450 & 10,600
80-mm Model 1880	3,500
105-mm	16,500
120-mm Model 1880	7,600
120-mm L/14	7,250
150-mm	8,650
Infantry Weapons:	
50-mm AT Gun (Bofors)	800
47-mm AT Gun (Rheinmetall)	600
37-mm AT Gun (Rheinmetall)	600
81-mm Stokes Mortar	2,100
Heavy MG, 7.9-mm	1,700
Light MG, 6.5-mm (Madsen)	1,000

Water barriers: width   depth
    Maas River   150 meters   3 meters
    Ijssel River   150 meters   3 meters
    Juliana Canal   46 meters   5 meters
    Maas-Waal Canal   60 meters   5 meters

Bunker classifications:

  First Generation -works built before 1936.

  Second Generation

    River casemates -Large bunkers of two to four levels. No standard type, but usually held 50-mm gun and machine guns. On Ijssel and Maas Rivers at crossings. Over 80 built.

  Third Generation

    Type S (Stekelvarken or Porcupine) - shelter with walls only .80 meters thick and roof 1.0 meter thick. Several types with positions for 1, 3 and 7 machine guns. Three gun type most common. About 780 built.

    Type B -single machine gun for flanking fire. Walls 1.2 meters thick. About 215 built.

    Type G -armored turret of cast steel placed in concrete position. One heavy machine gun for two men. Over 570 emplaced.

    Pyramid shelter -Over 2.0 meters of concrete in roof. Heavy wooden door protected by crenel. Held a dozen men. About 700 built.

*At the beginning of 1923 all of the coast defense guns mounts for the guns produced by Krupp in Germany in the mid-1880s, were installed. The gun elevation was not greater than 20 degrees and all were low velocity short range guns. These weapons included many Krupp 280-mm guns which had not been mounted, although the army intended to use them as railway guns.

WORLD WAR II

American attaché LTC Brown's prediction came true, probably even faster than he believed possible. The Dutch only resisted for four days in May 1940. Although the German invasion of the Netherlands was a secondary operation compared to the invasion of Belgium, it was carried out with astounding efficiency. Early in the morning of May 10 the German 7th Air Division and 22nd Air Landing Division began their descent over Holland by parachute and in aircraft. The leading assault force had successfully surprised the defenders of the key bridges over the rivers of the Southern Front leading into Fortress Holland. Meanwhile, on the frontier, special German troops, the Brandenbergers, disguised in Dutch uniforms and followed by armored trains, attempted to capture some of the key bridges near the border so an armored force could race through to relieve the paratroopers. They succeeded in taking only one bridge, but it proved to be enough.

At the time of the attack as many as twenty-five Dutch frontier battalions manned the frontier defenses, nine of which were stationed on the Maas Line, three on the Ijssel Line, five on the open eastern border area, between the Ijssel and F Lines, six in the Maastricht Appendage of the province of Limburg, five in Friesland, four in Zeeland, three on the South Front of Fortress Holland, two at Fort Den Helder, one at fort Den Oever, and one at fort Kornwerderzand. Of the ten army divisions most were located in the vicinity of Fortress Holland and four manned the Peel Line.

General Henri G. Winkelman, commander-in-chief of Dutch forces, and his superiors had made the decision that if a German invasion came they would withdraw the army into Fortress Holland and abandon the defenses of the Brabant. The heavy concentration of Dutch forces in Fortress Holland after a fighting withdrawal should have made it possible to successfully resist German assaults. Unfortunately, the events of the war did not unfold as predicted. In the first place, the weather did not cooperate that winter and spring and it did not rain enough to make the water obstacles efficient. In the second place, the Germans did not behave as predicted. They attacked swiftly and suddenly, leaving their opponents with too little time to activate their water defenses.

Elements of the German 7th Airborne and 22nd Air Landing divisions launched the initial paratrooper assault on the bridges of Moerdijk, Dordrecht, and Rotterdam to breach the Holland Deep, the Waal, and the Lek River, in an attempt to open a back door into Fortress Holland for air-landed elements who were to land near The Hague and capture the government and military high command. However, the Germans failed to take the bridge at Dordrecht so that only the south side of the Rotterdam crossings fell on the first day. The landings inside Fortress Holland were not as successful, but with the bridge at Moerdijk solidly in German hands, the river barriers were effectively breached.

The German endeavor to force crossings of the Maas and Ijssel, and to penetrate the Grebbe Line failed when several armored trains were destroyed by the Dutch. At Gennep, on the other hand, the Brandenbergers' trick succeeded so that an armored train passed over the Maas and was shortly followed by the 9th Panzer Division which began its race across the North Brabant to relieve the paratroopers.

In the North, the German 1st Cavalry Division quickly crossed the Q Line, reaching the Wons Position by May 11. Here it came face to face with the 650 men of the Dutch 33rd Infantry Regiment, who were later joined by additional troops. The fighting raged around Rotterdam and Dordrecht from May 11 to May 12. The first elements of the 9th Panzer Division passed over the Moerdijk on May 12, crossing the river in the afternoon. The Maas and Peel Lines had been penetrated and generally abandoned after the first day. On May 12, the Wons Position collapsed and the Germans were at the approaches to the Great Dike. By that time, other German forces had already penetrated the Ijssel Line and were attacking the Grebbe Line, which was breached by a German SS regiment. On May 13, two German divisions continued the advance, breaking through the line and forcing the Dutch to fall back on the New Water Line. Their swift success was due to the fact that most of the Dutch reserves had been tied up in fighting the German air landed troops.

When Fort Kornwerderzand was attacked, Fortress Holland stood on the verge of collapse. Despite the odds, the fort's garrison of 225 men soundly repelled the German assault with the help of the 150-mm guns of a gunboat from Den Helder. The fort did not surrender until it was ordered to do so by the Dutch commander-in-chief on May 14, when the rest of the army also laid down its arms.

Only the Dutch battalions in Zeeland held out until May 18 when the last French divisions withdrew, having arrived too late to help the Dutch. The German SS Verfügungs Division, a regiment-size unit, attacked the Bath Position on May 14 and the Zandijk Position the next day. When the Dutch forces surrendered, their last defense line had already fallen.

Most of the invading German troops involved in this operation were not first rate, and the Dutch might have held out longer had it not been for the air assault.

The Germans put some of the Dutch defensive positions, including coastal positions like Hoek van Holland, back into operation after the surrender of the Netherlands. In 1940 they also restored the fortress and added casemates at Willemstad, built a couple of casemates on to the forts of the Great Dike and converted other positions for their own use throughout the country.

Den Oever, Block IX. One of the fort's larger blocks which mounted MG. Near the cloche a seam can be seen where this position was built in two parts. In the rear (left side of photo) an open position for a MG and behind it two doors which were the latrines (Dutch kept them outside the blocks). (Kaufmann)

Ft. Pannerdern. Above the old walls in the fort's moat can be seen an armored artillery casemate for two guns. (Kaufmann)

Dutch MG turret mounted in concrete position. There was usually enough space for 2 to 3 men. (Kaufmann)

Dutch "Pyramid." These shelters were usually found in lines and used as shelters and CPs. The entance was covered by a firing position, but there were no external weapons embrasures. (Kaufmann)

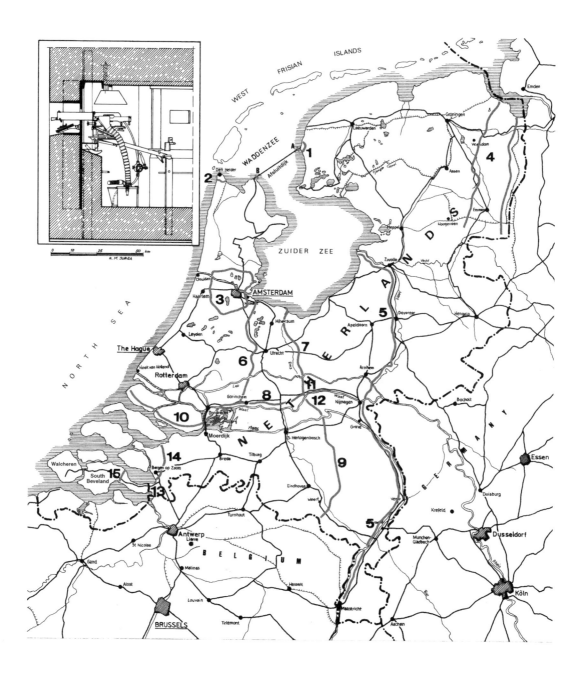

The Netherlands Fortifications:
1. Wons Position
A. Fort Kornwerderzand
B. Fort Den Oever
2. Den Helder Position
3. Amsterdam Position
4. Q Line
5. Maas-Ijssel Line
6. New Water Line
7. Grebbe Line
8. Waal-Linge Line
9. Peel-Raam Line
10. Southern Front of Fortress Holland
11. Ochten Spees Position
12. Putuijk Position
13. Bath Position
14. Eendracht Position
15. Zendijk Position

Heavy MG behind armored plate in light bunker.

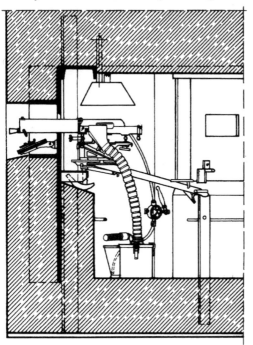

Dutch Three Embrasure Bunker Type SZW 100.

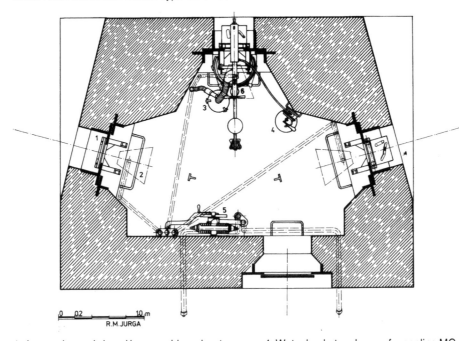

R.M.JURGA

1. Armored crenel closed by cover hinged on top
2. Drain for removal of shells
3. Water filter for MG

4. Water bucket and pump for cooling MG
5. Hand ventilator & filter
6. M-8 Heavy MG on fortress mount

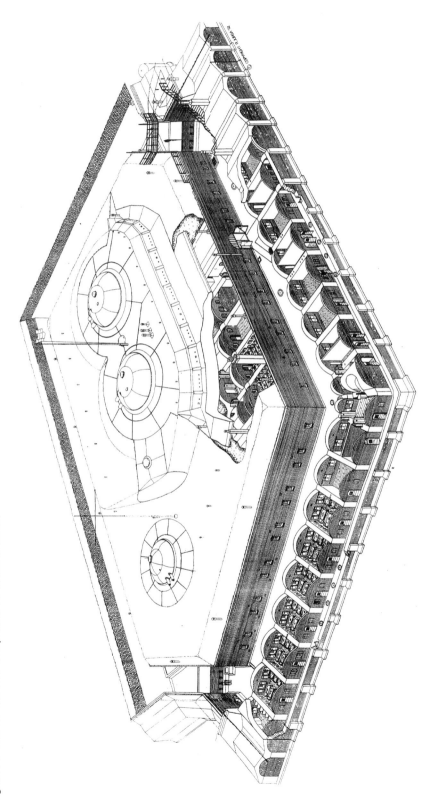

Fort Hoek van Holland. Built in 1888 the Dutch mounted two twin gun turrets with 240-mm guns and one with 150-mm guns. The surrounding ditch was 11 meters deep and 10 meters wide.

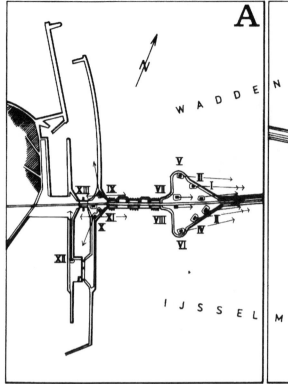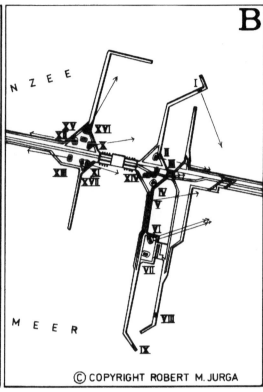

Forts Den Oever (A) and Kornwerderzand (B):

Den Oever 1st Line:
Block I - MG
II - MG & Cloche
III - 50-mm AT & MG
IV - 2 x 50-mm AT
V - 50-mm AT, MG & Cloche
VI - MG & Cloche
VII - AAA Gun Shelter
VIII - MG & Cloche
2nd Line:
Block IX - 3 x MG & Cloche
X - 3 MG
XI - AAA Gun Shelter
XII - MG
XIII Usine

Kornwerderzand 1st Line:
Block I - MG
II - 50-mm AT
III - Usine & Infirmary
IV - CP, MG & Cloche
V - MG
VI - 2 x 50-mm AT
VII - Searchlight & Cloche
VIII - MG, IX - MG
2nd Line:
Block X - MG
XI - MG
XII - MG
XIII- MG
XIV - AAA Gun Shelter
XV - AAA Gun Shelter
XVI - MG
XVI- Searchlight

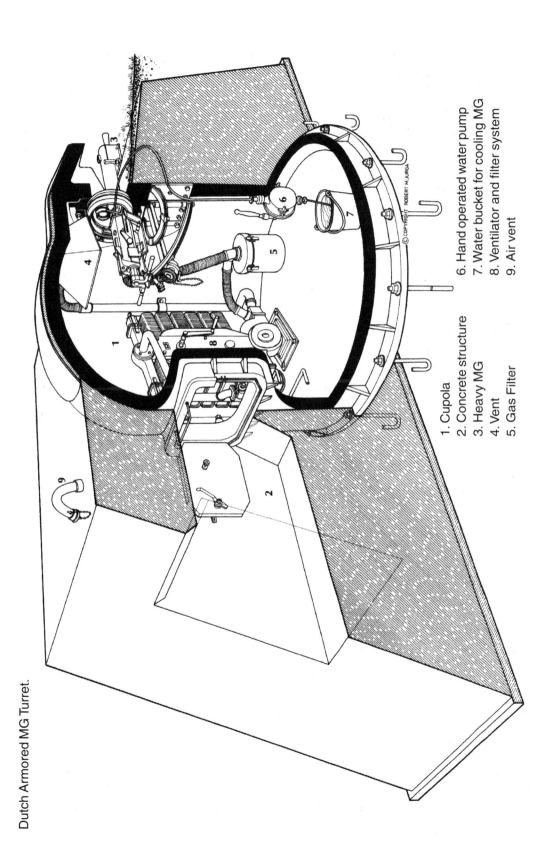

Dutch Armored MG Turret.

1. Cupola
2. Concrete structure
3. Heavy MG
4. Vent
5. Gas Filter

6. Hand operated water pump
7. Water bucket for cooling MG
8. Ventilator and filter system
9. Air vent

© COPYRIGHT ROBERT M.JURGA

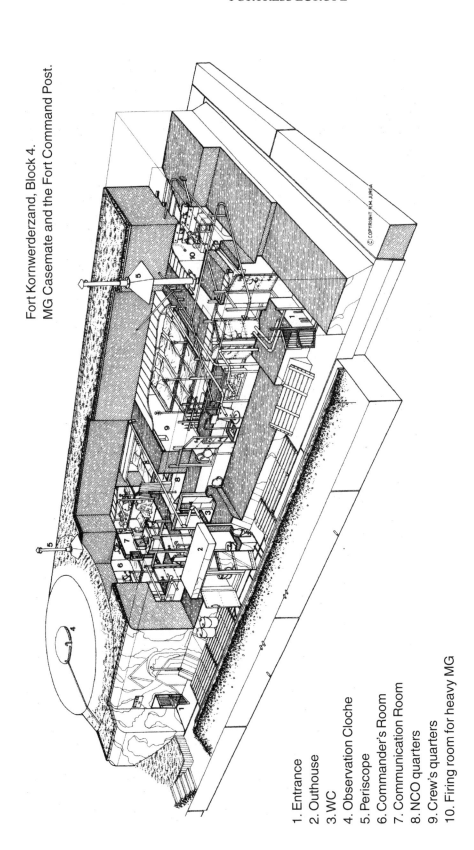

Fort Kornwerderzand, Block 4.
MG Casemate and the Fort Command Post.

© COPYRIGHT R.M. JURGA

1. Entrance
2. Outhouse
3. WC
4. Observation Cloche
5. Periscope
6. Commander's Room
7. Communication Room
8. NCO quarters
9. Crew's quarters
10. Firing room for heavy MG

Chapter 5

SWITZERLAND

BACKGROUND

The Swiss military forces engaged in their last major conflict during the Napoleonic Era and saw their last combat action in 1846, during a minor civil war that inflicted few casualties. Beginning in the thirteenth century, the country's rugged terrain had made it possible for Switzerland to defy the authority of the Holy Roman Empire until its cantons formally achieved their independence in 1648. The Congress of Vienna in 1815 formally recognized Switzerland's neutrality, which it has preserved ever since. Nevertheless, in 1856, 1870, 1914, and 1939 the Swiss army, mostly a militia force, mobilized to prevent external conflicts from spilling over their borders.

In the past, fortifications had not been the key to Switzerland's success, as much as the character of its tough mountain people. However, after 1870 the situation changed because the traditional methods of defense were no longer enough against the new massive conscript armies equipped with long-range weapons.

The socio-economic and political heart of Switzerland occupied the western third of its territory, on the Mittelland Plateau, shielded on one side by the Jura Mountains and on the other by the Alps. It was through this very area that the main invasion route passed, leading from the Bodensee to Geneva. The northern sector of this heartland, extending along the Rhine, starting at Basel, was not as easily defended and did not present a formidable barrier against modern weapons. This does not mean that this terrain was indefensible, but rather no longer impassable.

Since Switzerland had become industrialized, the likelihood of its armed forces abandoning its new and growing cities to pull back into the mountain fastness and resist in the old manner diminished. Thus fortifications grew in importance since they made it possible to close off key valleys and form solid lines of defense.

The Swiss fortifications in the western region ranged in age from the Middle

Ages to the Renaissance. More defensive works were added in the nineteenth century, but, with the advent of the torpedo shell in the 1880s, they soon became totally obsolete. Thus special commissions were appointed in 1880 and 1882 to study the problem. The work of these commissions resulted in the creation of two defensive zones: one for the populated areas of the west and the other for the Alpine region. This remained the basis of the Swiss defensive scheme through the first part of the twentieth century. To design the new fortifications, Swiss officers were sent to investigate German, Austrian, and Belgian techniques. What emerged from these investigations was an eclectic style that combined elements of the various schools of fortification. Even the equipment reflected this eclectic style. For instance, the Swiss combined German guns with French carriages, and adopted the German Gruson gun turret.

First priority went to defending the St. Gotthard area where a new railroad tunnel had been completed in 1882. Work on a series of forts and defenses for the St. Gotthard Pass began in 1887. The year of 1890 saw the completion of Forts Airolo and Galenhütten that included characteristics of the Belgian Brialmont forts. Forts Brühl and Bäuzberg were built shortly after that on the other side of the valley. They included armored gun turrets cut into the rock.

The defense of the region southeast of Lake Leman or Geneva had second priority. Here "mobile" 53-mm gun turrets were used to economize on some of the positions. Fort Savatan on the lower plateau and Fort Dailly on the higher plateau formed Fortress St.Maurice in 1894. Curiously, Fortress St. Gotthard and Fortress St. Maurice appear to have defended areas that should not have been considered too vulnerable at a time when a conflict was looming between Germany and France. These fortresses were two of the cornerstones of the National Redoubt created by the commission of 1882. Work and improvements continued on all the fortifications during the Great War.

MAJOR FORTIFICATIONS

The Army Position and Border Line
The National Redoubt

LOCATION

1. The Army Position and Border Line

This position stretched from Vallorbe on the French border, to the west of Neuchâtel to Basel, then eastward, to Konstanz and the Bodensee. At a short distance behind the Border Defenses,which ran close to the frontier, was the Army Position. At Koblenz the Army Position followed Lake Zurich, joining with the Border Defenses at Fortress Sargans. This last segment formed part of the National Redoubt. An additional section, considered part of the Army Position, covered the region of Bellinzona in the southeast.

The Swiss built only two forts between Vallorbe and Basel because the rugged Jura Mountains presented a serious obstacle. The forts at Vallorbe and Porrentruy commanded major road junctions where access through the mountain barrier was less difficult. The Rhine formed another natural barrier between Basel and the Bodensee. Here the roads passed through many easily defended defiles, even though the hills south of the Rhine did not reach great elevations. The other end of the Bodensee was covered by Fort St. Margrethen. The northern frontier with Germany was the most vulnerable to invasion.

2. National Redoubt

The National Redoubt had three key anchor points: Fortress St.Maurice, Fortress St. Gotthard, and Fortress Sargans that formed the southern and eastern bulwarks of the region. Between St. Maurice and St. Gotthard was the Rhone Valley that included the highest sections of the Swiss Alps, with elevations of over 3,000 meters above sea level. This fortress region followed most of the border with Italy up to the St. Gotthard area and the Rhine Valley northward to Sargans. At this point it abandoned the mountainous eastern quarter of the country.

The remainder of the redoubt area extended northward from St. Maurice, around the Alps to Thun, and along the line of lakes to Lake Zurich, where it turned eastward, to Sargans. Only two major roads cut through the massive Alpine barrier between St. Maurice and Sargans. Fortress St. Gotthard stood at one end, dominating both of these passages.

HISTORY

As in other countries, national defense in Switzerland became part of the economic recovery program from the depression. In 1934, the Swiss Parliament authorized the construction of defenses to employ the jobless. Since the government had recently drained the Linth Plain, opening a new route for the enemy, Fortress Sargans had to be set up to protect it. The new fortress underwent four construction phases between 1938 and 1942, resulting in the most heavily defended area in Switzerland. The other two fortress zones of the National Redoubt were also improved, receiving additional forts.

Site surveys for the new forts in the National Redoubt and the Border Line were carried out in the latter half of 1935 and construction began in 1937. The new forts neared completion by the summer of 1939. New heavy bunkers were also created to defend both positions. The new Border Line Position, where five forts were erected, was completed between 1939-1940.

Furthermore, in 1937 the Swiss government committed funds and men to positions on the French and Italian borders to avoid giving the impression that only Germany was being singled out as a potential threat. Most road bridges near the borders were prepared for demolition, obstacles were readied, and key bridges were outfitted with capped holes. In time of war troops would be able to quickly replace the caps with steel anti-tank rails.

Soon after the war began, the Swiss army leaders concluded that the Border Line was too weak, so work resumed on the Army position. Between October 1939 and the summer of 1940, construction continued on this position, and the Border Line increasingly took on the role of an advance position.

Late in the 1930s, the government reorganized the army into nine divisions and three independent brigades that formed three corps initially. During the war these three corps were reorganized into four, each retaining a mountain brigade. The III Corps defended Fortress St. Gotthard and most of the National Redoubt.

The frontier guard consisted of only 1,800 men and the army required two days to mobilize. According to military writer B. H. Liddel Hart, it would have been a simple matter for the enemy to launch a surprise attack on Switzerland and overwhelm its border defenses, especially between November and February when fewer men were on active duty.

DESCRIPTION

1. The Army Position and Border Line

The most common type of structure in the Army Position and the Border Line was the heavy, two-level bunker. Its lower level included crew quarters, munitions storage, and a filter system for protection against gas. The firing rooms, which were on the upper level, mounted machine guns or machine guns and an anti-tank gun. Their concrete thickness was of approximately 2.0 meters with rock work used for reinforcement.

The Border Line consisted of a line of machine gun bunkers stretching from Basel to Schaffhausen. The bunkers were laid out to create interlocking fields of fire and were spaced 500 to 760 meters apart. The intervals between the bunkers were filled out by blockhouses-also found in the Army Position-that were not self-sufficient. In addition to these fortified positions, the Border Line included a variety of obstacles. Bridges were prepared for demolitions and outfitted with obstructions, and barbed wire obstacles were deployed along the length of the Rhine.

In addition to the bunkers and the blockhouses, the Border Line included forts built after the Great War. Each of these forts consisted of machine gun blocks and normally included two gun casemates mounting a single 75-mm gun. Fort Pré-Giroud had an additional 75-mm gun casemate that housed a 47-mm anti-tank gun. Fort Heldsberg, larger than the others, had four 75-mm gun casemates instead of the regulation two. The Swiss border forts were much smaller than the French Maginot ouvrages and had smaller blocks and subterranean facilities. Their entrance block was normally combined with a machine gun block. Where possible, one block was outfitted with an escape exit. The Swiss forts were not as strong as the French forts and they probably would not have withstood heavy bombardment as well as the Maginot forts.

Fort Pré-Giroud, built on a mountain slope, dominated the railroad tunnel through Mont d'Or and the Joux Valley at Vallorbe, across from the French border. Some of its blocks, like those for the 75-mm guns, were camouflaged as rock outcroppings and had no close defense weapons. The machine gun blocks were disguised as chalets.[1] Wire obstacles and concrete anti-tank barriers covered the approaches. The garrison consisted of about 100 to 150 men.

The new Swiss forts had some standard features in common. For instance, they had two-level gun casemates with the firing chamber on the upper level, and machine gun blocks with firing chambers on one or two levels. However, there appears to have been no standard for the location of blocks and facilities. Thus at Pré-Giroud the caserne, usine, and all other facilities were located 30 meters below the entrance where feasible. In addition, the caserne was a two-level complex behind and below the entrance. At Fort Reuenthal, on the other hand, the caserne consisted of several single-level chambers because the fort was located on the hills overlooking the Rhine and it had not been practical to dig out deep and extended galleries. Furthermore there were two magazines at Pré-Giroud, but only one at Fort Reunethal.

The equipment of the forts, ranging from diesel engines, to ventilation systems, and weapons, was relatively standard. A decontamination shower was placed in the entrances. An underground telephone system linked the fort to other units. The weapons included old models of water-cooled machine guns and the 75-mm guns of the latest design. A pantograph with an attached magnifier was mounted on the machine gun and cannon to help aim the weapons at targets in the surrounding area.

In the blocks of the forts there were special hookups for the crews' gas masks that supplied the men with oxygen. There were also hand-operated ventilators. Power was supplied by an usine in the fort and by the civilian grid to which the fort was hooked up by cables. Each fort maintained two months worth of supplies.

The forts included:

Pré-Giroud	3 blocks for 75-mm guns	2 MG blocks
Plainbois	2 blocks for 75-mm guns	? MG blocks
Reuenthal	2 blocks for 75-mm guns	3 MG blocks
Ebersberg	2 blocks for 75-mm guns	? MG blocks
Heldsberg	4 blocks for 75-mm guns	5 MG blocks

At least one infantry fort, Fort Flueholz near Baden, somewhat similar to the Border Line fort's but without artillery was built on the Limmat River section of the Army Position. Actually three artillery forts with gun turrets were planned in the Limmat sector since 1938, but none were built as a result of the German attack on the Eben Emael. The military felt that line gave them more flexibility in holding back an invasion.

Ethnic and linguistic diversity, a problem unique to Switzerland, was solved by assigning French-speaking crews to the two forts along the Jura, where the local language was French, and German-speaking garrisons to the forts located in German cantons.[2]

2. The National Redoubt

The National Redoubt contained the greatest variety of Switzerland's defenses: from the largest forts to the blocking positions prepared for demolition. After the war began, more forts were built in the redoubt. Even as the twentieth century comes to a close, and most of the forts in other countries have slid into obsolescence, a number of the Alpine forts in Switzerland have been refitted with modern weapons and their number, size, and locations remain officially secret.

When World War II began, Switzerland was near completing or had completed twelve new artillery forts, five of which covered the important northern and western fronts. There was one fort at Tessin, one at Grisons, and four in Valais and Fortress Sargan. Nineteen large artillery forts were under construction and cavern positions for older 75-mm field guns were being prepared. The weapons mounted in the new forts included 75-mm, 105-mm, and 150-mm guns. The 150-mm gun was not installed until late in the war and still remains in service. Some of these forts even mounted cloches.

Today Fort Fürigen, one of the small forts guarding the approaches to the redoubt, is open to the public but it probably is not typical because it was built into the rock, over the lake shore near Lucerne. It includes three machine gun blocks, one of which is located at a higher elevation than the others and is equipped with a searchlight. The fort also has two 75-mm gun blocks that include an observation position.

It has the same facilities and equipment as the border forts, but its layout is very different.

The Fortresses of St. Gotthard and St. Maurice contained the oldest forts, built at the end of the last century. Their artillery included:

1. Fortress of St. Gotthard*
   St. Gotthard Pass
      Fort Airolo

	1 turret - 2 x 120-mm guns
	4 turrets - 1 x 53-mm gun
	5 x 84-mm guns in casemates
Additions	
	1 turret - 1 x 120-mm howitzer
	53-mm gun casemate

       Redoubt Hospiz   2 turrets - 1 x 120-mm gun
       Battery Motto Bartola   4 x 120-mm guns
     North side of Urserne Valley
       Fort Bühl

	2 turrets - 1 x 120-mm gun
	2 turrets - 1 x 120-mm howitzer
	3 turrets - 1 x 53-mm gun
	observation turret

       Fort Bäzberg

	3 turrets - 1 x 120-mm gun
	4 turrets - 1 x 53-mm gun
	2 observation turrets

     Oberalp Pass
       Fort Stöckli   2 turrets - 1 x 120-mm gun
     Furka Pass
       Fort Galenhütten

	1 turret - 1 x 120-mm howitzer
	2 x 120-mm guns in casemates

2. Fortress of St. Maurice**
       Fort Savatan

	5 turrets -1 x 120-mm howitzer
	turrets for 53-mm guns
	4 x 84-mm guns in caponiers

       Fort Dailly

	6 turrets - 1 x 120-mm gun
	open positions for 120-mm guns
	2 x 75-mm casemate guns
	turrets for 53-mm guns

3. Fortress of Sargans
     Rhine barrier forts (built 1938)***
       Fort Shollberg   3 x 75-mm casemate guns
       Fort Anstein   2 x 75-mm casemate guns
     Major forts (built 1939)
       Magletsch

	3 turrets - 1 x 105-mm gun
	4 x 75-mm casemate guns

       Kastels

	3 turrets - 1 x 105-mm gun
	2 x 75-mm casemate guns

Furkels	4 x turrets - 1 x 105-mm gun
Passatiwand	2 x 75-mm casemate guns
Southern Front (built 1941)	
Molinära	2 x 75-mm casemate guns
Haselboden	4 x 75-mm casemate guns
Rhine barrier forts (built 1941-1942)	
Tschingel	1 x 75-mm casemate gun
Nussloch	1 x 75-mm casemate gun
Tamina Ragaz	1 x 75-mm casemate gun

*The forts on the pass included central citadels like Brialmont's in Belgium. Those on the north side of the valley had scattered positions, most of which were built into the rock. The 53-mm gun turrets were considered mobile because they were mounted on a 60-cm railway track, and were rolled out of their shelter.

** Fort Savatan was on a plateau lower below the Plateau of Dailly.

*** Planned as border forts.

In the redoubt special caverns were carved out in the mountains to accommodate small magazines and store anti-tank guns, machine-guns, and munitions. Two to four rows of holes were drilled and capped in narrow defiles to create anti-tank obstacles similar to those used on the bridges. In certain narrow passages small chambers secured by a door were prepared and loaded with explosives, ready to be detonated by the local militia. The rail tunnels were also readied for destruction. Thus passage through this Alpine fortress was easily controlled and blocked with a judicious use of forts and explosives.

WEAPONS AND EQUIPMENT

Much of the equipment for the new forts was locally produced, especially the weapons and optical instruments. However, armor plate for the border forts initially came from the German Krupp Works, but slow or delayed deliveries before and during the war forced Switzerland to produce its own. Many of the cloches for machine-guns and observation for the National Redoubt were purchased from Czechoslovakia, about a year before the Munich Crisis. However, the turrets for 105-mm guns, the guns themselves, and the 75-mm anti-aircraft guns were manufactured in Switzerland. The 75-mm ant-aircraft guns were built under license from the French Schneider Creusot Company. The 105-mm and 150-mm guns were produced under a license from the Swedish Bofors Company. The 75-mm guns, used in casemates (BK or BunkerKanone), were designed in Switzerland but derived from the Bofors 75-mm mountain gun.

WEAPONS	TURRET MANUFACTURER	RANGE
150-mm Bofors Kanone		20+ km
150-mm Howitzer 1916		8.8 km
120-mm Krupp Cannon 1882	Gruson (German)	10.5 km
120-mm Howitzer 1912		6.4 km
105-mm Kanone	Swiss	9.5 km
84-mm Krupp Cannon		5.0 km
75-mm Kanone 1938 L 30	Swiss	11.0 km
53-mm Cannon	Gruson (German)	3.0 km
47-mm Anti-Tank Gun IK 35/41		3.0 km
24-mm Anti-Tank Rifle TB 41		————
Machine Gun Model 1911		1.5 km

WORLD WAR II

The Swiss army mobilized as soon as the war began. In 1938, secret talks concerning a French advance into Switzerland to head-off a possible German attack took place between the military leaders of both countries. Some Swiss officers inspected the Maginot Line and information was exchanged.

During the summer of 1939, the army took over the newly completed border forts and the frontier brigades took up defensive positions on the border. However, many soldiers returned home during the Phony War but the defenses remained fully manned. In March 1940 about 60,000 border troops returned to active duty. It is at this time that the Swiss fortifications caught media attention. The press coined the name of *Winkelried Line* for the Army Position or, perhaps, for the Army Position and the Border Line combined.

After the collapse of France in the summer of 1940, the Swiss commander-in-chief, General Guisan, decided to concentrate on the defense of the National Redoubt since the country was now surrounded. Since he did not think that the border could be held for more than a couple of days, he decided to redeploy the army. At the same time new infantry and artillery forts and other defenses were added to the redoubt. In addition to casemated artillery, a number of turret positions in the rock with underground facilities were set up. Swiss manufacturers produced new 75-mm, 105-mm and 155-mm guns for these positions, replacing the older 120-mm and 150-mm howitzers.

Nonetheless, the frontier positions were not abandoned and additional work was done there. By 1941 Fort Pré-Giroud received three new bunkers that were not connected with underground galleries. At Fort Reuenthal a non-linked bunker with a 47-mm anti-tank gun was added. Some forts, such as those in the Redoubt, received Bofors anti-aircraft guns. Finally, in 1942, the Corps de Garde de Fortifications replaced the border brigades in the fortifications.

Switzerland's war preparations were not unwarranted. Indeed, the German General Staff had drawn up "Operation Tannenbaum" for the invasion of Switzerland in 1934. The 1940 version of the plan involved a surprise assault that would bring Switzerland to its knees within one week with the participation of only eleven divisions and an Italian army attacking from the south. Documents show that the German strategists were concerned about their ability to take the Swiss border forts, which indicates that there might have been intelligence gaps on the subject. If the German invasion had materialized, the Swiss would most likely have destroyed many vital points on the lines of communications, such as tunnels, crippling the main rail routes between the Reich and Italy. This contributed to the Germans abandoning their invasion plans.

Ft. Reuenthal on German border near Koblenz (Switz.). The guard post and entrance, located beneath the large MG block (see plan). (Kaufmann)

Swiss 75-mm fortress gun on mount inside an artillery block. Note the metallic map above the gun with a pointer and magnifying glass which shows where the weapon is pointed. The Czechs used a similar device on their weapons, but the French did not. (Kaufmann)

Ft. Pré-Giroud. One of the fort's MG blocks covered with artificial metal trees for camouflage. (Kaufmann)

Ft. Pré-Giroud. Main gallery leading down to one of the fort's 75-mm blocks and a MG block. (Kaufmann)

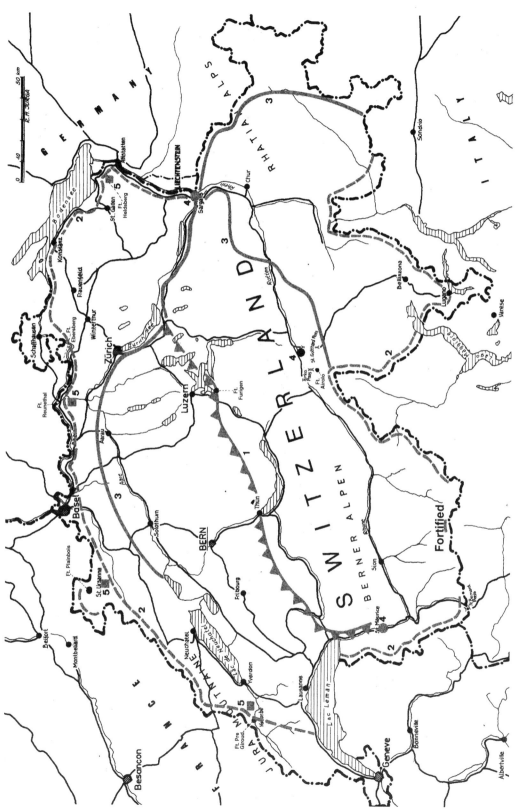

Swiss Fortified Lines 1. National Redoubt, 2. Border Line, 3. Army Position, 4 Alpine Fortress, 5. Artillery Fort, 6. Intermediate Position

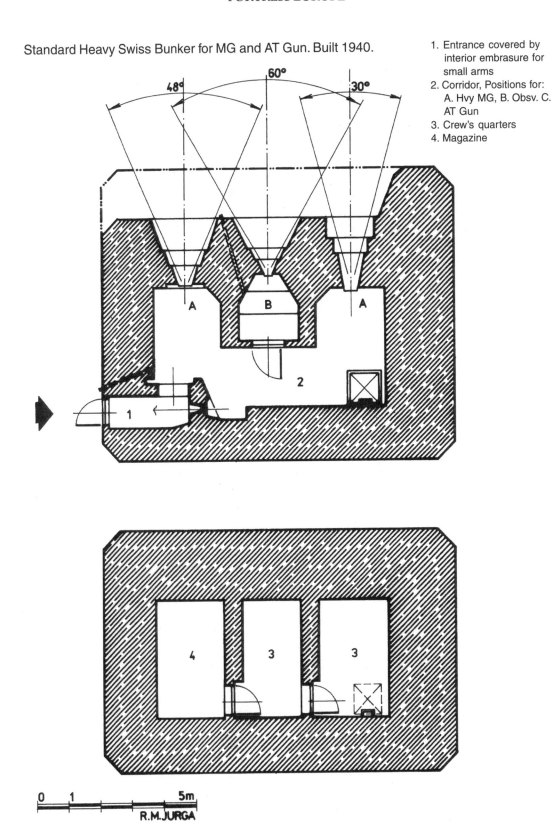

Standard Heavy Swiss Bunker for MG and AT Gun. Built 1940.

1. Entrance covered by interior embrasure for small arms
2. Corridor, Positions for: A. Hvy MG, B. Obsv. C. AT Gun
3. Crew's quarters
4. Magazine

0   1   5m

R.M. JURGA

Three Swiss Border Forts:

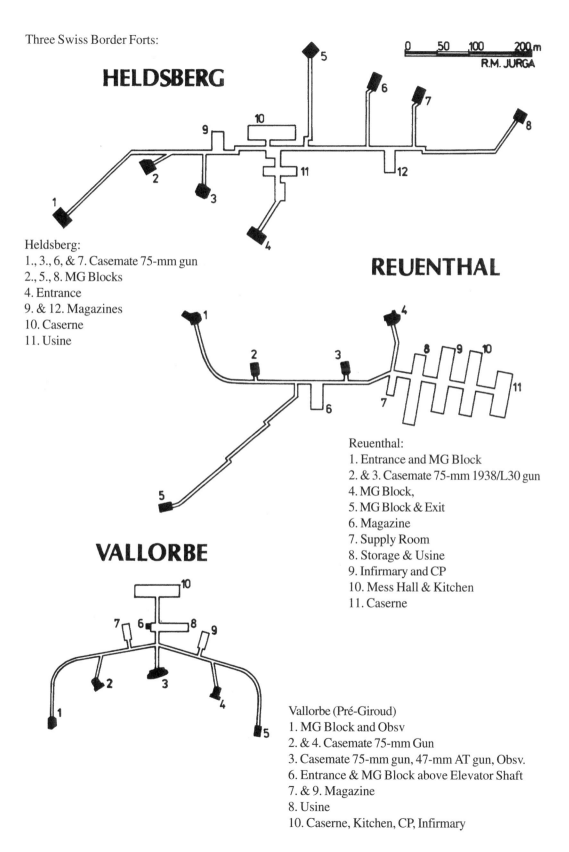

HELDSBERG

REUENTHAL

Heldsberg:
1., 3., 6, & 7. Casemate 75-mm gun
2., 5., 8. MG Blocks
4. Entrance
9. & 12. Magazines
10. Caserne
11. Usine

Reuenthal:
1. Entrance and MG Block
2. & 3. Casemate 75-mm 1938/L30 gun
4. MG Block,
5. MG Block & Exit
6. Magazine
7. Supply Room
8. Storage & Usine
9. Infirmary and CP
10. Mess Hall & Kitchen
11. Caserne

VALLORBE

Vallorbe (Pré-Giroud)
1. MG Block and Obsv
2. & 4. Casemate 75-mm Gun
3. Casemate 75-mm gun, 47-mm AT gun, Obsv.
6. Entrance & MG Block above Elevator Shaft
7. & 9. Magazine
8. Usine
10. Caserne, Kitchen, CP, Infirmary

Swiss Fort Fürigen:

1. Entrance
2. Gallery
3. Interior blockhouse
4. Hvy MG
5. Obsv. Position
6. Pump
7. Radio Room
8. 75-mm Gun
10. Magazine
11. Filter Room
12. Air Intake
13. Access Shaft
14. Usine
15. Storage
16. Pantry
17. WC
18. Caserne, CP, Mess Hall
19. Water Reservoir
20. Searchlight.
NOTE: Small road adjacent fort is on edge of lake.

Chapter 6

GREAT BRITAIN

BACKGROUND

For centuries Great Britain depended on the sea for its first line of defense. Ever since William the Conqueror's successful invasion in 1066, no force larger than a raiding party had struck the British coastline. Napoleon Bonaparte's planned invasion in the early 1800s, which never materialized, forced the British to prepare for war on their own shores. When Napoleon III took power, just as the steam powered ship increased the capabilities of the navy, the British became alarmed again. So the army undertook the construction of coastal defenses. However, by the 1880s Parliament reaffirmed its confidence in the navy, allowing it to remain the first line of defense.

By the turn of the century, however, the winds of war were sweeping through Europe again and Britain deemed it prudent to prepare for the protection of its empire. Thus the Committee of Imperial Defence was founded in 1904 and given the task of advising the prime minister on the best means and methods of defense. Nonetheless, little changed in Britain's defensive policy, since on the eve of the Great War the Committee was still declaring that:

> The maintenance of sea supremacy has been assumed as the basis for the system of Imperial Defence against attack from over the sea. This is the determining factor in shaping the whole policy of the defence of the Empire and is fully recognized by the Admiralty, who have accepted the responsibility of protecting all British territory abroad against organized invasion from the sea.

The first significant shift in British defensive philosophy occurred during World War I, when fortified positions went up on the coast. These new positions included battery positions with modern weapons as large as the 9.2-inch guns, emplacements for land-launched torpedoes, pillboxes or bunkers, and barb wire obstacles near likely landing sites.[1] Trenches created Stop Lines beyond the likely invasion sites such as the vicinity of the Medway. A mine barrage across the Channel blocked the passage of German vessels during the war.

The advent of the airplane brought a new element to the defenses of the Britons, who concluded that aircraft must become the first buffer against invasion.

The other key British positions in Europe requiring special attention included Gibraltar, acquired during the War of the Spanish Succession early in the eighteenth century, and the island of Malta taken from the French in 1814. These two outposts guarded the route to the Suez Canal and allowed the Royal Navy to maintain a presence in the Mediterranean.

MAJOR FORTIFICATION

Coastal Defenses
The Stop Lines
Gibraltar
Malta

LOCATION

1. Coastal Defenses and Stop Lines

Great Britain was divided into six commands in addition to the London District. The Scottish Command covered Scotland, the Northern the east-central half of the island, the Western Command the west-central half, the Eastern Command the area between the Wash and the Thames, the Southeastern Command the coastline of Kent to Portsmouth, the Southern Command the area from the Isle of Wight to Land's End, including many of the sectors of the GHQ Line.[2] The main beach defenses and Stop Lines occupied the southern part of the island south of a line running from the Wash to the Bristol Channel.

The majority of the coastal positions protected the south and east shores of England, from Cornwall to Northumberland. A large part of the coastline between Devon and Kent was dominated by the cliffs that are part of the white chalk hills behind the coastline. A number of excellent ports on the south coast were the probable targets of any invader who would need to secure them to establish a supply line. A German invasion force attempting a landing on the south coast of England would have faced many of the problems faced by the Allies after 1941. However, the English coastline had a greater concentration of ports suitable for the establishment of a secure beachhead.

The east coast was less favorable to invasion even though its concentration of major ports was similar to the south coast's. Indeed, its ports were not as evenly distributed so that the defenders would be able to concentrate their defensive efforts around clusters of harbors. Further north, the Scottish coast, with its jagged coastline broken by numerous sunken valleys known as lochs and firths, was less vulnerable. The west coast of Great Britain, which consisted of Welsh, English, and Scottish territory, was also rugged in many places. Its major ports were concentrated in a few areas.

The advent of air-power turned these sections of Great Britain into secondary targets. Before the war, the British had been uncertain of Germany's capabilities as they planned their own defenses. However, it became apparent in 1940 that no German invasion force would be able to penetrate very far north as long as any part of the Royal Air Force (RAF) remained operational because it would be far beyond the range of its own air support. Fortunately for Great Britain, the pre-war planning became irrelevant because no major work was begun until 1940.

The western part of England, most of Wales, and Scotland was mountainous. Much of the heavy industry was concentrated in the west and central part of England, in the Midlands. This allowed some room for maneuver in the event of an invasion of the south coast. The GHQ Line, which ran between Bristol and London and was to be extended northward to Edinburgh, was located 25 to 80 km behind the coastline. It was considered the final defensive position that could be held or Stop Line. In addition to the GHQ Line, a number of smaller Stop Lines were prepared by lower formations of the army, such as corps, who made the most of the terrain located between the coast and GHQ Line.

2. Gibraltar and Malta

Gibraltar and Malta guarded the line of communications through the Mediterranean to the Suez Canal. Gibraltar allowed the British to control Axis shipping into or out of the Mediterranean. Although submarine transit could not be effectively blocked from Gibraltar, it could be made difficult. The anchorage on the "Rock" sheltered a sufficient naval force to stop the passage of surface units with the help of the artillery.

The limestone mountain of Gibraltar, honeycombed with caves and manmade tunnels, occupied much of a peninsula little more than a kilometer wide and no more than about 5 km long. The mountain rose sharply from the sea on its east side to a maximum elevation of 426 meters. The town and anchorage were found along the western, more gently sloping side of the mountain. The only low ground was on the north end of the peninsula, where more than half of the airfield extended into Gibraltar Bay.

Located south of Sicily, the islands of Malta and Gozo served as a British base. Thanks to the advent of aviation, they were at the mercy of whoever controlled Sicily. The main city, Valletta, occupied the site of the Grand Harbor, strategically the most important part of the island. A number of large bays were found around the hilly island offering potential invasion sites. The beaches between Valletta and St. Thomas Bay on the southeast coast, and those between Valletta and St. Paul's Bay on the east coast were the most vulnerable invasion sites. The southwestern coast included a large area of beaches suitable for invasion, while the hills in the west precluded any type of major operation in that area. The north had only a few suitable landing beaches. Southern Italy could easily serve as an assembly area for an invasion force, which had only a short distance to travel to reach Malta.

HISTORY

1. Coastal Defenses and Stop Lines

Some of the defensive works built in Great Britain during World War I included a number of pillboxes that remained in place. The old coastal defense positions, dating from the latter part of the nineteenth century and modernized somewhat at the beginning of the twentieth, had received few improvements since then. When rearmament began in 1934, the navy gave some consideration to the coast defenses. Since the main concern was air defense, the Reorientation Committee decided in 1935 to orient the air defense zone toward the east and Germany rather than France. The Aircraft Fighting Zone ran from the River Tees (south of Newcastle), to a point west of Harwich, Dover, east of London, and Portsmouth. Air defense served as Great Britain's first line of defense. In 1935 radar became the main asset of the warning system. By 1936, the first line of twenty stations was set up between the River Tyne and Southampton. A second group of radar stations for detecting low flying aircraft was set up later.

Until the creation of the RAF, the Royal Navy had been the main deterrent against invasion. After the advent of the airplane, the navy took on a secondary role, at least in the areas within the range of enemy air cover. The Royal Navy's mission was to prevent any successful landings. After the war broke out, most of the capital ships of the Home Fleet moved to northern ports such as Rosyth and Scapa Flow to avoid constant Axis air attacks.

Late in 1939, after examining the situation, General Kirke, the commander of the Home Forces, designated the area between the Wash and Sussex as the most vulnerable to invasion. He ordered, therefore, the improvement of the defenses of key ports and airfields as part of the Julius Caesar plan, which remained in effect until about the time of the German campaign in the west in 1940.

The German airborne operations in Norway and then the Low Countries in the spring of 1940 greatly concerned the British. From Scotland to British Somaliland, British troops were soon alerted against parachute and glider troop assaults. As a result, a considerable amount of effort was wasted on the creation of obstacles throughout the British countryside, along roads, and around bridges to prevent any type of airborne operation. Many roads were so effectively blocked, that they hindered the movement of British troops.

The Emergency Battery Program, which went into effect to protect the coast line, involved the installation of about 600 pieces of artillery, mostly in open concrete emplacements. The most important of these positions consisted of four gun batteries of 6-inch guns.

Since the coastal gun positions, built during the pre-war era and early in the war lacked overhead cover, the army had to create casemate-like positions with walls about 1 meter thick to protect them. As the Germans began to install heavy artillery in the Calais area, the British responded with a pair of old 14-inch naval guns and two 15-inch coast-defense guns. However, the largest coast defense weapons consisted of 9.2-inch guns. During the summer of 1940, Falmouth, Plymouth, Portland, Portsmouth, Newhaven, and Dover were strengthened, becoming the strong points of the south coast. Over forty battery positions were set up between these ports.

In May 1940, General Edmund Ironside, who had just become the commander of the Home Army, decided to commit his forces to a static defense since his army lacked the ability to undertake a mobile defense. He created many positions along the coast and inland to the Stop Lines that included pillboxes, anti-tank barriers, and wire obstacles.

The work continued as General Alan Brooke replaced Ironside in late June 1940. However, Brooke did not believe that the army had sufficient strength to defend such an extensive position, especially after its material losses at Dunkirk. He went back, therefore, to an emphasis on a mobile defense, concentrating his troops near the GHQ Line but moved his limited number of anti-tank guns up to the coast.

The British defensive situation was precarious, at best, in the summer of 1940. Many of the bunkers were built and located somewhat haphazardly. Many of the coastal bunkers fired only forwards rather than to the flank, others, which stood in towns or roadblocks, had no embrasures covering routes of approach. Some of the coastal bunkers built on unstable terrain collapsed into the sea. Sea walls were reinforced with sand bags, becoming defensive positions, and wire was strung all along the beaches. As the situation improved, more concrete barriers known as pimples—

the British version of dragon's teeth—began to cover large stretches of the coast. Meanwhile, Brooke ordered the removal of many of the obstacles blocking the inland villages so the army could move around unhindered.

New and more inventive devices such as scaffolding placed below the high water mark to hinder landing craft came into use. They also set up makeshift flame weapons. As the British situation improved and the German offensive opened in the East in 1941, the likelihood of an invasion evaporated.

By the end of 1940, the last of over 150 emergency coastal batteries were completed. By June 1942, the last large artillery batteries near Dover were also finished.

One of the most prominent features of the British coastal and air defenses was the creation of the Sea Forts. They had been planned in 1941, but not built until the following year. They occupied positions in the Thames Estuary and when completed they were used in an air defense role to replace flak ships and to give early radar warning.

2. Gibraltar

In 1932, the governor of Gibraltar received instructions to build an airfield in the northern end of the peninsula. Plans for placing the airfield across the race course were drawn up and approved. It was begun in September 1934 and was ready to serve as an emergency landing field by March 1936. In October 1941, the decision was made to extend the runway over 1,600 meters into the sea. Much of the material used to extend the airfield came from tunneling into the Rock. By January 1942, about 1,000 meters were completed, and by 1943 the entire runway was finished and ready for the Allied invasion of North Africa.[3]

When the war broke out, the commander of the fortress had to prepare against an attack across the Spanish border and protect the harbor facilities at the same time. Between the beginning of the war and mid-1940, the defenses of Gibraltar were considerably strengthened with much of the work carried out by laborers from Spain. Everything from construction of new tunnels to setting up new batteries was done, but many new galleries and interior positions were added during the war.

3. Malta

Little could be done to improve the defenses of Malta after Italy entered the war. Coastal defenses were set up and old battery positions improved. Most of the defenses were concentrated on the southeast coast. Five airfields were used as the first line of defense and as bases for attacks on enemy shipping and naval units.

DESCRIPTION

1. Coast Defenses

The Fortifications and Works Directorate, a branch of the War Office, decided to concentrate its efforts on only a few of the numerous designs from the World War I era. The most common position on the coast was the pillbox, one of the best known of which was the six sided one.

Most of these bunkers were designed for light machine guns, but some took anti-tank guns ranging from 2-pd to 6-pd guns. Some of every type were placed on the coast, inland behind the beaches, or on the Stop Lines.

A variety of obstacles were placed on the beaches and inland. Anti-tank obstacles consisted of concrete cubes and cylinders, the more familiar concrete "pimples" (dragon's teeth), and iron rails. These barriers blocked beach exits, and, in some cases, lined possible landing areas. In 1941, more effective standards were established, such as the installation of obstacles in several lines and the placement of cubes at an angle. Old junk cars and similar obstructions had long since been removed and replaced by the new, more standard types.

Wire was strung along the beaches to deter infantry. A line of scaffolding was erected along the coast. Explosives, which were to be detonated by approaching craft, were attached to the scaffolding below the water line. The scaffolding was made of steel tubes, was about 3 meters high, and was deployed more quickly than other types of obstacles. More scaffolding was added higher up on the beaches. Since it was never put to the test, it is impossible to tell how it would have stood up but it seems that heavy bombardment would have easily disposed of it.

A typical well-defended beach included a line of concrete cubes interwoven with rolls of barbed wire along the high-tide line. A line of tubular scaffolding paralleled the concrete cubes about 10 to 15 meters to the front. Concrete pillboxes and anti-tank mine fields occupied key points along the beach such as the exits.[4]

In some places, a crude flame weapon may have been employed. The possibility of setting the sea afire was not considered a serious threat. Pipes carrying a flammable substance to a constricted point where it could puddle and be ignited were placed around possible landing sites. A type of fougasse weapon with a flammable substance akin to napalm was placed at a higher point where it could be ignited and hurled down onto narrow passages.

One of the first heavy artillery positions on the coast consisted of the two 14-inch naval guns installed at St.Margaret's-at-Cliffe, near Dover, in the late summer of 1940. They were manned by Royal Marines and named "Winnie" and "Pooh." Both were on barbette mountings, but only Winnie received an armored gun house.[5] In 1940, several old 9.2-inch railway guns and a huge 18-inch railway howitzer known as the "Boche Buster" were brought into the Dover area. "Boche Buster" did not have the range to fire across the Channel. Three new fixed batteries, which included a battery of three 6-inch guns overlooking Fan Bay, the Wanstone Battery, to the north, named after the nearby farm were installed in the area later. The Wanstone Battery consisting of two 15-inch Mk 1 ("Jane" and "Clem") with gun houses, originally destined for Singapore, was completed in September 1942. Just to the east of the Wanstone Battery and south of St. Margaret's-at-Cliffe, was a battery of four 9.2-inch Mk 15 guns, also ready in 1942.

The Royal Marines served three 13.5-inch Mk 5 railway guns from late 1940 until 1942, which operated in the Dover to Deal area.[6] The army added its own weapons to the defenses of Dover which included the Capel and Hougham batteries just west of Dover armed with naval 8-inch coast guns. These went into operation in 1942.

The Sea Forts, known as the Maunsell Forts after the civilian designer, were of two types: army and navy. The navy built both types. Their main purpose was to act as anti-aircraft units for stopping German mine laying aircraft and breaking up German bombing formations heading towards London. These forts also had the mission of deterring E-boat raids. The army fort consisted of several box like towers of steel comprising two levels and a roof on which their equipment was located. The tower was mounted on four concrete legs that rested on a concrete base. The lower level had the officers quarters, stores and latrine facilities. The upper level was the main barracks area for the troops. The fort's equipment and weapons were on the open deck space above this. Seven of these structures were placed close together and linked by steel bridges. The central tower was the control tower and four of the outer positions mounted the 3.7-inch guns, with one other position mounting Bofors guns. The towers with weapons formed a circle around the control position. One tower beyond these, and also linked by a bridge to one of the gun positions, served a searchlight. The entire garrison for this type fort was about 120 men.

The navy fort was mounted on two large concrete pillars which were hollow and placed on a barge shaped concrete cassion which rested on the sea floor. These pillars contained seven levels with the magazines and storage rooms on the two lower levels, and the crew area was on the next four levels. The top level of both pillars held the power generators. Above each of these pillars was a 3.7-inch anti-aircraft gun on the main deck, and above them was a deck with two Bofors guns. Between the guns of the main deck were the officers quarters, a kitchen, and the latrines for the garrison. Above this was the control room and radar installation.

Three army forts were set up near the entrance to the Thames, and four naval forts stood further out in the Thames Estuary to form a radar line. Three army forts also occupied positions off the Mersey Estuary leading to Liverpool on the west coast. The Humber Estuary was protected by Bull Sand Fort (1919) and Haile Sand

Fort (1918) built on sand spits. Bull Sand, armed with four 6-inch Mark VII guns, returned to full service in 1939 with two of its guns replaced by twin 6-pd weapons for anti-boat service. The military removed Haile Sand's old armament of two 4-inch guns in 1928, and in 1939 set up two 12-pd guns which in 1940 were replaced with twin 6-pd guns. Older Victorian forts received new armament for similar purposes on other inlets and British harbors.

2. The Stop Lines

The Stop Lines employed defenses similar to those of the beaches, except for scaffolding. They served as anti-tank barriers. The GHQ Line depended heavily on canals and natural features. It was a continuous line, but again the pillbox remained the main defensive position. The northern sections of the GHQ Line were not completed. The three major sections found in the Southern Command's area of the GHQ Line as identified by Henry Wills in his book *Pillboxes* were as follows:

Section	Length	Number of Pillboxes	AT Positions	Ditches (length)
Red	300 km	186	11	28 km
Blue	90 km	170	15	8 km
Green	145 km	319	0	32 km

These sections represent only a small part or the GHQ Line in the vicinity of Bristol to a point only about 50 km east of Bristol.

In addition, the numerous other Stop Lines between it and the coast included additional positions and anti-tank obstacles.

The steel rail obstacles included a type which formed a right angle. Some of the anti-tank ditches were concrete. In some cases the army built bridges to cross the anti-tank ditches so normal traffic could continue.

Over 200 pillboxes for 2-pd anti-tank guns and over 100 for 6-pd Hotchkiss guns were planned but many were not built. Many pillboxes were only bullet proof, and a number of bunkers were prefabricated. Some of the more unusual ones included cantilever roofs so as to give all round fields of fire. A retracting pillbox for five men was designed for airfields so as not to obstruct air operations. These were basically the main defenses of the island plus a few other unusual pillboxes that included one or two stories. In addition to these, almost 200 Alan-Williams steel turrets were ordered. These were steel domes which could mount a Bren or Lewis machine gun, or an anti-tank rifle.

With respect to camouflage, the British were quite resourceful. Some pillboxes were camouflaged to appear as kiosks on beaches, buildings in towns, and even signs and haystacks.

3. Gibraltar

The northern face of the rock had galleries cut into it by engineers in the eighteenth century and was improved to take modern weapons. The new chambers were cut wide enough to place Nissen huts in them or a more standard type of hut. Accommodations for electricity, drainage, and communication were part of each tunnel system. A blast trap was used to protect entrances. This was achieved by having the access to the main communications tunnel turn shortly before entering it so that any blast effect would be absorbed at the end of the tunnel entrance.

Over two dozen gun batteries occupied the Rock during the war, plus positions for Bofors anti-aircraft guns. The largest guns were 9.2-inch guns in six single gun batteries and one two gun battery. There was also a two gun battery of 9.2-inch howitzers. Several batteries of 6-inch guns and 3.7-inch anti-aircraft guns mostly in two gun positions, (some of the latter in four gun batteries), supported the larger weapons. Many of these were mounted high on the rock on both sides.

4. Malta

The British set up six battery positions along the main islands' vulnerable southeast coast. Except for beach defenses and the old forts which guarded Valletta and the southern ports of Marsa Scirocco and Birzebbuga, there were few other fixed defenses of significance.

WEAPONS AND EQUIPMENT

Rail Guns and Coast Artillery

	Range	Location & Number 1939-40
18-inch (457-mm) (RR) howitzer	100+ km	1 near Dover
15-inch (381-mm) gun	38.4 km	2 near Dover[7]
14-inch (356-mm) gun	43.2 km	2 near Dover
13.5-inch (RR) gun	36.5 km	3 near Dover
9.2-inch (234-mm) gun	33.5 km	21 Southern England, 8 Gibraltar
9.2-inch (RR) gun	20.6 km	- Southern England
9.2-inch (RR) howitzer	13.1 km	- Southern England

9.2-inch howitzer	15.1 km	2 Gibraltar
6-inch (152-mm) gun	12.8 km	41 England,
		8 Gibraltar
12 pd gun (76-mm)	7.3 km	31 (1939) English ports[8]
6 pd (57-mm) gun	4.7 km	- Great Britain,
		6 Malta

Main types of anti-aircraft weapons in use in 1940 for Great Britain, Gibraltar and Malta:
    3.7-inch Anti-Aircraft; 40-mm Bofors Anti-Aircraft
The Emergency Batteries included:
    6-inch guns, ancient 4.7-inch guns, 4-inch guns, 3-inch (12 pd) guns, and 3 pd guns totaling 510 pieces in October 1940 with most on pedestal mounts and gun shields produced after the emplacement of the weapons.
Typical Emergency Battery Program positions:
    Four 6-inch guns
    Fire control position
    Command Position
    Search light position
    Crew of about 140 men

Two batteries of 8-inch (203-mm) guns, with a range of 26.7 km, went into service near Dover in 1942. These weapons on barbette mounts had gun shields. A long range 13.5-inch gun named Bruce performed limited service in 1942. It was supposed to have a range of over 100 km, but it had problems similar to those of the old German Paris guns with regard to the wearing down of the bore with each shot.

WORLD WAR II

The Local Defence Volunteers organization formed before the Battle of Britain soon became the Home Guard. These poorly armed civilians set up the first roadblocks and interior defenses while watching the skies for paratroopers. After the evacuation from Dunkirk the military hastily prepared to defend the coast under the direction of General Ironside. With few heavy weapons left from the BEF, and much equipment lost, the new commander of the island's defenses, General Brooke, decided not to concentrate his forces on the beaches, but rely more upon the Stop Lines.

Across the Channel the Germans installed heavy guns to bombard the coast at Dover. The British responded with their own weapons which were not as heavily armored or as large a caliber. "Winnie," the first of two 14-inch guns, went into action in the late summer of 1940. The other heavy pieces joined in as they were installed. The dueling continued for much of the war. The final action came in support of the British 2nd Army as it cleared Calais with the Dover guns firing on the German Battery Todt in September 1944.

To invade Britain the RAF had to be defeated first. To insure a shorter supply line the Germans had selected the southeast coast for their invasion, Operation Sea Lion, to be preceded by the use of airborne units. This location would have limited the ability of heavy units of the Royal Navy to interfere with the invasion. The radar stations which ran along and near the coast were part of the defenses which the Germans overlooked. They made it possible for the RAF to win the battle of the skies and make the invasion impossible. If the Germans had been able to send over an airborne division it is doubtful the Home Guard could have stopped it, since regular army units on Crete a year later inflicted heavy casualties on a similar force, but failed to stop it.

The seaborne invasion force would have found a coastline with rather impressive obstacles, although anti-personnel mines were lacking. The heavy guns defending the Dover area did not become a real factor until after 1940. The lack of well equipped and armed troops would have allowed the Germans to establish a beachhead once the artillery batteries were neutralized.

The Germans planned for an assault on Gibraltar, Operation Felix, in 1941, but this required Franco's Spain to help. An amphibious operation was out of the question for the Axis forces. A ground assault against the peninsula would have neutralized the vital airfield and land batteries along the bay. This would have shut down the harbor area. But the British batteries could also have rained havoc on Spanish positions at Algeciras. The chances of actually storming and taking the Rock were not good and the tunnels held an unknown amount of supplies which may have allowed a lengthy siege. Only Axis air power might have made a decisive difference, but this is all speculative. Franco, who greatly desired possession of Gibraltar, was not willing to risk joining the Axis to partake in an operation which might prove an embarrassment so soon after winning his civil war.

The Axis powers tried to isolate the island of Malta early in the war. In July 1941 a battery of 57-mm coastal guns destroyed five Italian boats in two minutes during a human torpedo attack on Valletta harbor. In March 1942 the Germans and Italians planned an assault on Malta (Operation Herkules) with each using a parachute division. The attempt to strangle the island with air power had only been partially successful, but it continued to jeopardize Axis supply lines to North Africa.

Axis plans called for airborne forces to secure a bridgehead on the southern heights of the island from which to attack the airfields south of Valletta. The Italian navy was to carry two to three divisions for an amphibious landing on the southeast coast, while its heavy units bombarded the coastal batteries there. A diversionary naval attack was to be made at Marsa Scirocco. Events in North Africa moved too quickly after the fall of Tobruk and resulted in delaying the invasion. Soon the airborne forces were sent to reinforce Rommel's army at El Alamein and the invasion was canceled. The British lifeline was preserved and the Italian crippled.

Remains of a line of AT Cubes used here on a Stop Line and also on some beaches.
(Bernard Lowry)

Brick FW3/24 pillbox located at Weston Zoyland Airfield near Bridgewater, Somerset.
(John Hellis)

Typical FW3/24 pillbox located at Trebyen, Cornwall. (John Hellis)

Bunker for a 6 Pounder Hotchkiss AT Gun located on the Taunton Stop Line at Curry Mallet, near Taunton. (John Hellis)

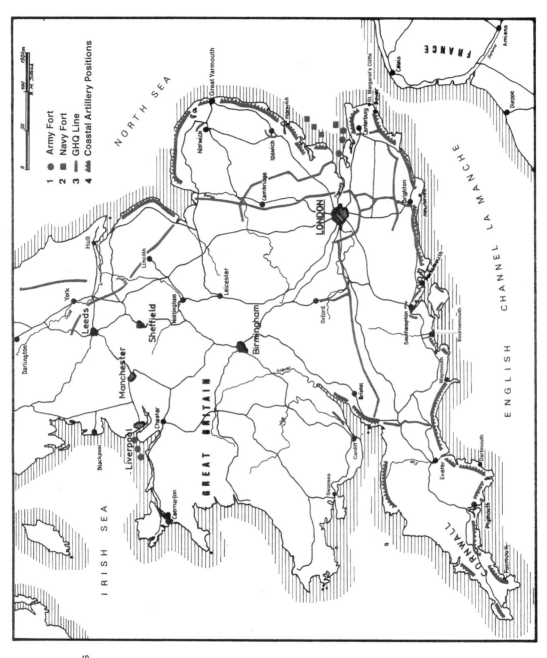

British Defenses: Sea Forts
1. Army Fort
2. Navy Fort,
Land and Coast Defenses
3. GHQ Line
4. Coastal Artillery Positions

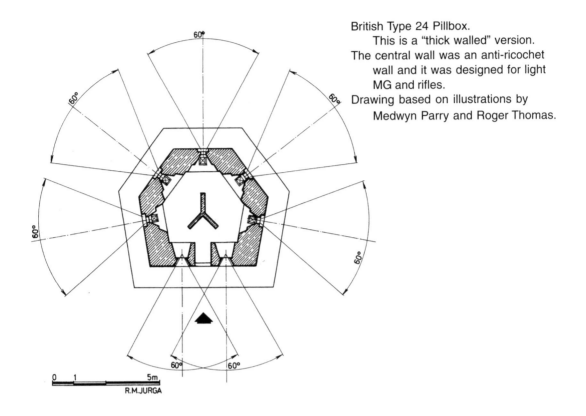

British Type 24 Pillbox.
This is a "thick walled" version.
The central wall was an anti-ricochet
wall and it was designed for light
MG and rifles.
Drawing based on illustrations by
Medwyn Parry and Roger Thomas.

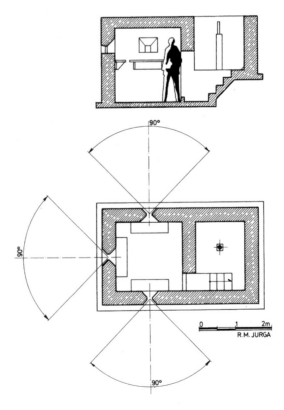

British Type 23 Pillbox.
The non-embrasured half was open and
mounted a light AA weapon.
Based on an illustration by Medwyn
Parry and Roger Thomas.

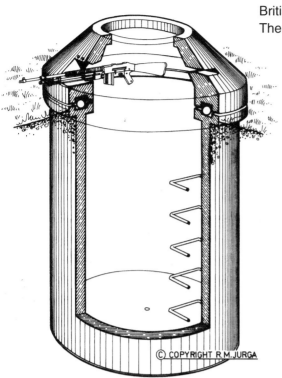

British TTET Turret for one man with a light MG. The turret revolved a full 360 degrees.

British prefabricated PICKETT-HAMILTON FORT. Used on airfields in 1940 so that if attacked the 2-man machine gun crew could raise the turret with the hydraulic jack.

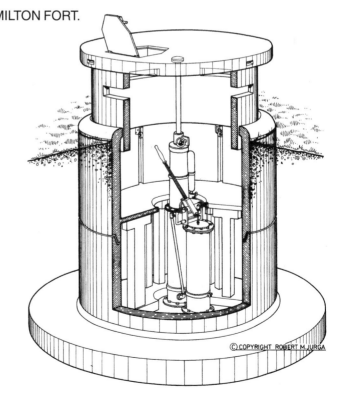

Malta

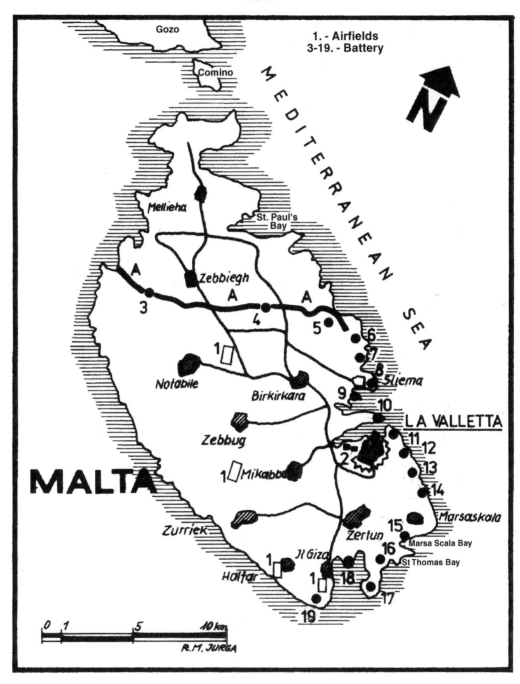

Plan of Gibraltar:

Underground system

a. William's Way
b. MacPherson's Chamber
c. Thomson's Switch
d. Orillon
e. Turnbull's Lane Shelter
f. Haye's Level
g. Fordham's Accommodation
h. Great North Road
i. Admiralty North-South Tunnel
j. Green Lane Magazine

k. Flat Bastion Hospital
l. Fosse Way
m. Admiralty Water and Oil Reservoirs
n. Arrow Street Chambers
o. Lord Airey's Tunnel
p. Fosse Way Magazine
r. Opper Sandy System, Dogleg Tunnel
s. Levant Accommodation
t. Vivey Quarry Shelter, Marble Arch
u. Harley St. Power's Drive
v. North Gorge Tunnel
w. New Tunnel, Little Bay Tunnel

x. Rock w.t.
y. Glen Rocky Distillery
z. Napier Tunnel Artillery
1. Bofors Gun
2. 2 x 3.7-inch guns
3. 4 x 3.7-inch guns
4. 2 x 4-inch guns
5. 2 x 6-inch guns
6. 6-inch gun
7. 9.2-inch gun
8. 2 x 9.2-inch guns

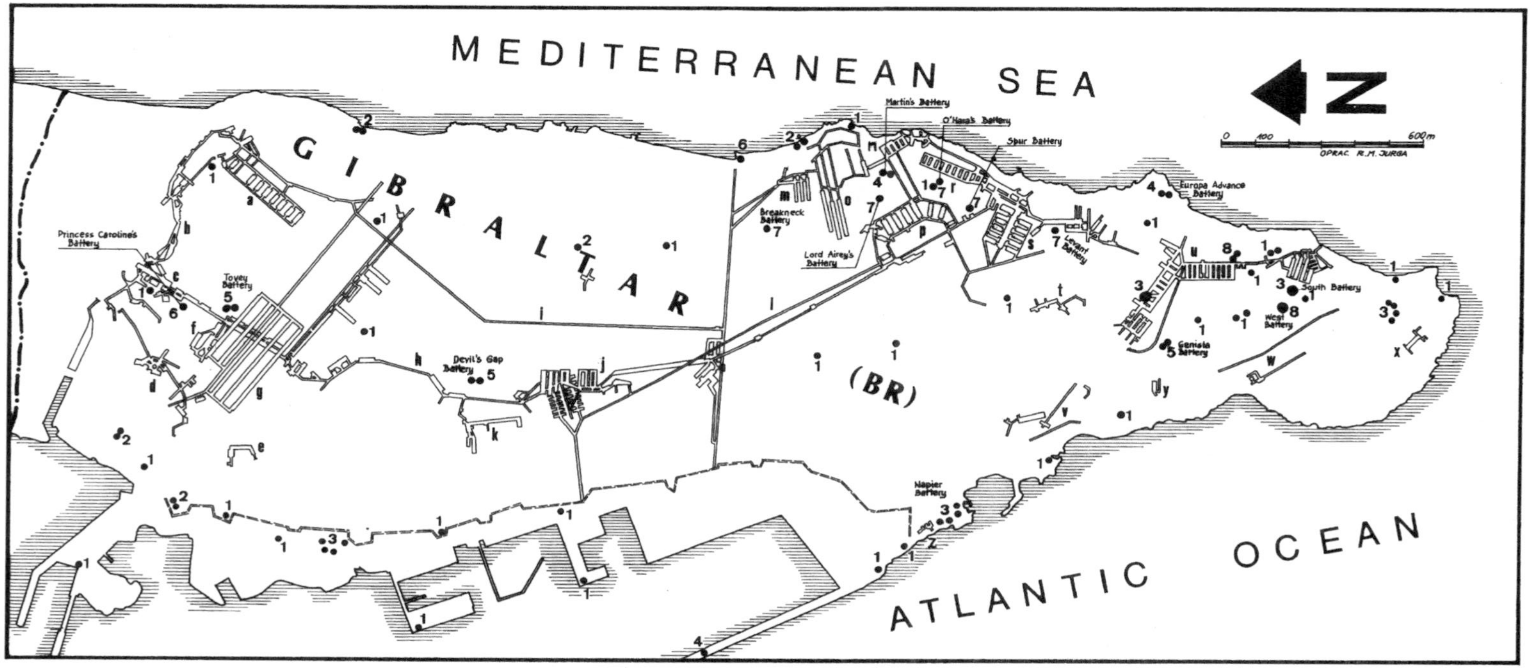

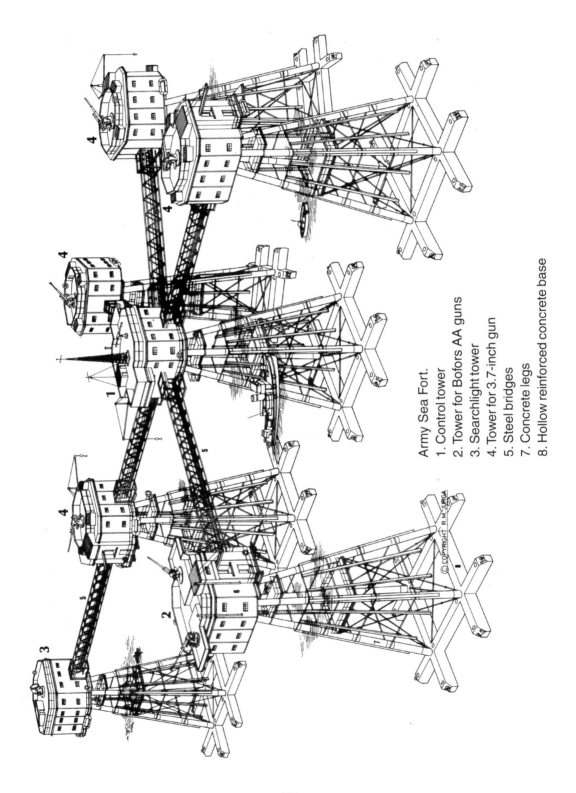

Army Sea Fort.
1. Control tower
2. Tower for Bofors AA guns
3. Searchlight tower
4. Tower for 3.7-inch gun
5. Steel bridges
7. Concrete legs
8. Hollow reinforced concrete base

© COPYRIGHT R.M.JURGA

Chapter 7

ITALY

BACKGROUND

Italy was another of Europe's relatively new states. Military and diplomatic maneuvering united most of the Italian peninsula in March 1861. The Sardinian king, when crowned King of Italy, united the Italian people for the first time since the fall of the Roman Empire. The addition of Venice in 1866 and Rome in 1870, largely completed Italian unification.

The timing of Italy's reunification was fortuitous with regard to defenses, because a new generation of fortifications arose throughout Europe after the Franco-Prussian War, particularly in the 1880s, when the "torpedo" or high explosive shell was perfected. Thus Italy had the opportunity to adopt the newest techniques and technology in the construction of the fortifications it needed to secure its borders. However, it seems that the Italian military engineers were not able to take full advantage of the window of opportunity offered to them by history. Most of the fortifications that were completed in Italy by the end of the century were not as modern as those built by most of their neighbors.

Italy had two problems with defense. The first was that she shared borders with France, Switzerland, and Austria-Hungary dominated by Europe's most rugged and imposing mountains, the Alps. Ironically, the barrier that offered great defensive potential for Italy also protected its neighbors from attack. In some areas the Alps formed a highly defendable barrier, while near the Austro-Hungarian border along the Adriatic, Italy only held the foothills while its neighbor controlled the heights. The situation was similar in the Austrian-occupied region of Trento.

The second problem was the excessive length of the Italian coastline. Italy felt a need to defend the Adriatic coastline against Austria, its enemy in the recent wars for reunification, which still held Trento and Trieste. The Triple Alliance contracted in 1882 failed to allay Italy's fear of its erstwhile foe. In addition, the Ligurian coast required defenses against France, which was no longer considered a friend due to colonial rivalry over Tunisia. So, caught between two hostile powers, the Italians thought it prudent to protect their entire coastline from naval raids.

In 1862, after ceding Savoy to France, the Italian government formed the *Commisione permanente di difesa* to study the problem of fortifying the Franco-Italian border and the coast. It took only a few years after the completion of the commission's work in 1871, for the government to approve the funds for construction of the new defenses. Some of these forts controlled the access routes through the Maritime, Cottian and Graian Alps. In 1875 another defense committee chose the 150-mm cannon to arm the land fortifications. The fortification armament for the remainder of the century consisted of 150-mm and 120-mm cannons and howitzers and 150-mm mortars. At the same time defensive positions were planned for the Austro-Hungarian border where their old adversary held the key terrain.

The heaviest concentration of fortifications was on the western approaches to Turin. The Fenestrelle and Assietta fortress complex, created before the end of the century, defended the Chisone Valley and the adjacent Susa Valley, blocking the main lines of advance from Briançon, France, to Turin through the Cottian Alps. This complex consisted of two rings of forts and was armed with 150-mm and 120-mm cannons and 150-mm howitzers and mortars. The defenses above the Assietta Pass, which overlooked both valleys, were completed in 1903. In the older as well as the newer forts, some of the artillery pieces were mounted on barbette carriages, in casemates, or in open positions. A few were mounted in turrets. The guns on barbette mounts of other open positions proved to be vulnerable during exercises carried out in the 1890s. The short term solution was to add armored shields to these weapons for the partial protection of the crew.

To the north of Fenestrelle and partially covered by its guns, was Susa, which consisted of several forts and batteries armed with 120-mm cannons, 57-mm guns, and mortars. These positions closed the Dora River Valley at the point where it merged with the Cenischia. Further down the valley, a pass was formed by the Doria Riparia that led to Turin. This pass was defended by several forts built between the 1870s and 1890s and armed with weapons ranging from 120-mm cannons and 150-mm howitzers to 57-mm guns. Only Fort Fenil was relatively modern, being the only one completed in the 1890s and mounting eight 120-mm guns in armored casemates along with two 90-mm and two 57-mm guns, and encircled by a deep moat. This position constituted the last line of defense on the route to Turin.

Heavily fortified advanced positions were also created near the border. At Bardonecchia access to the Fréjus Tunnel was controlled by a defensive position consisting of a caserne built in 1875. The area's defenses also included Fort Jafferau with eight 150-mm weapons in open emplacements atop the mountain of the same name at 2,775 meters elevation, which supported the positions below that guarded the tunnel and pass. This fort was later armed with the newer 149-mm guns. In addition, the two turrets of 120-mm guns, two batteries of 150-mm guns in barbettes, four 57-mm guns in turrets, and six 90-mm guns of Fort Bramafan covered the tunnel and pass at the confluence of the Cenischia and Dora rivers.

Further north, in the area of Moncenisio (Mount Cenis) near the border, fortifications stretched from Mt. Malamot across the pass to the slopes of Mt. Lamet. Three new forts had been built to help the older fort from the Napoleonic Era close the Moncenisio Pass. In 1897 two three-gun batteries were placed behind earth works near the top of Mt. Malamot at 2,913 meters, in the vicinity of a fortified caserne built six years earlier. This position dominated the southern half of Lake Moncenisio (Lake Mont Cenis).

At the beginning of the century, Fort Pramand was constructed near Salbertrand on Mt. Pramand (over 2,612 meters high) to close that section of the Dora Riparia River, between Susa and Cesena. Located southeast of Fort Jafferau, it was one of the first forts to be armed with 149-mm turret guns (four guns) early in the century. An additional 149-mm gun battery was located nearby.

Fort Chaberton, one of the most important forts of this region, was nearly finished by 1906. Located near Cesena, it was intended to close the approaches from Briançon. It was built on top of Mt. Chaberton at 3,130 meters above sea level, the highest elevation for any modern fort of the period. The fort was considered an autonomous unit for long-range fire. It mounted eight 149-mm guns installed on cement and brick towers shielded from the French by the crest of the mountain.

While the *Genio del Corpo* (Engineer Corps) handled the design and construction of the Italian forts, the artillery corps was responsible for their main armament. Early in the century the war minister and the artillery corps had wanted to use an Armstrong 152-mm gun in some of the forts, including Fort Chaberton. However, they finally opted for the Italian-built 149-mm/35 for financial reasons. The guns were installed at Fort Chaberton and a few other Alpine forts between 1904 and 1914.

Some of the older Italian forts were disarmed after 1911. Others were refurbished and modernized in preparation for a war with France and, for the most part, remained in service during World War II. After it joined the Triple Entente in 1915, Italy, which had concentrated its defensive efforts against France, found that its pre-war fortifications were no longer needed against its erstwhile enemy. Most of the artillery of these forts was removed and sent to the Austrian front.

After World War I, Italy ended up with new border lines that required new fortifications. After the Great War, one of the strongest networks of fortifications in

Italy stretched along the Italo-Austrian border for approximately 650 km. However, most of these defenses were former Austrian works that faced Italian territory.

Coastal defenses were also carefully considered by the Italians. In 1871 the government commission for defense selected the port of Genoa, the naval base of La Spezia, and Rome as the priority sites for coastal defenses. In 1882 the commission decided to install armored turrets with 400-mm Krupp guns at La Spezia, Taranto, and other ports. However, as in the case of the land defenses, when funds became scarce these plans had to be dropped.

When World War I began, La Spezia was armed with 300 pieces of artillery, over half of which were 240-mm to 320-mm weapons, that included landward defenses. Genoa was also heavily defended and included a main battery of 320-mm guns for coastal defense. During the war the emphasis shifted toward the Adriatic ports. Venice, which was well defended, included a battery of two 400-mm Krupp guns in turret, a battery of two 381-mm/40 guns in turret, a battery of six 321-mm guns, a battery of two 305-mm/50 cannons, four batteries of six 280-mm howitzers, and a battery of six 240-mm cannons. The port of Brindisi had two batteries of 381-mm/40 guns similar to those of Venice, one four-gun and one three-gun battery of 280-mm howitzers, and a battery of four 254-mm/45 cannons. Ancona had several heavy batteries that included 280-mm howitzers and 254-mm/45 cannons. A number of other ports had heavy defenses, but surprisingly Naples did not.

One of the most ambitious projects of the Great War era was the creation of the Ponti Rifugio for the protection of shipping along the west and south coast of Italy. This plan called for the installation of over 300 batteries of 57-mm to 152-mm guns along the coast. The Ponti Rifugio plan also proposed to draw its personnel from the army rather than the navy, which was largely in charge of protecting the Italian harbors.

MAJOR FORTIFICATIONS

The Vallo Alpino (The Alpine Wall)
Coast Defenses
Island Defenses

LOCATION

Over thirty-five percent of Italy is mountainous and more than forty percent is hilly. Its economic centers are concentrated on the plains, mainly in the north, where most of them are protected by the rugged terrain of the peninsula. The industrial region of Turin-Genoa-Milan is easily defensible.

1. The Vallo Alpino

The Vallo Alpino or Alpine Wall stretched along one of the greatest mountain barriers in Europe spanning about 1,850 km of the entire Italian land border with the remainder of Europe. It consisted of three fronts: Occidental (Western) that ran along the 487 km of the French border, Septentrional (Northern) following the 724 km of Swiss border, and Oriental (Eastern) facing 420 km of frontier with Austria and 220 km withYugoslavia. These fronts were further subdivided into sectors or *settori* and sub-sectors, that changed numerous times because they were based on the jurisdictions of *Guardia Alpina alla Frontiera* or G.A.F. (Frontier Alpine Guards) units.

In 1940 the sectors on the Occidental Front ran northward from the coast to the Swiss border, and were numbered I through X. They made up three major defended areas, the most important of which was the central, between Monginevro and Moncenisio.[1]

The Occidental Front included the Western Alpine region consisting of the Maritime Alps, the Cottian Alps, and the Graian Alps, which created a major barrier, even without fortifications, with only six major routes from France and three key mountain passes. The Maritime and the Cottian Alps had elevations averaging above 2,000 meters above sea level while the Graian Alps towered above the others averaging heights of more than 3,000 meters. In most cases these routes were set widely apart and all were difficult, even on the coast, because of the high, rugged mountains they traversed.

Part of this western region included the Pennine Alps, which like the Graian Alps, consisted of soaring heights and large, glacier covered sections. The Pennine Alps formed an almost impassable barrier between Italy and Switzerland, penetrated only by a couple of important but easily defended passes. Most of this region required no defenses, especially since no hostilities were expected on the part of the Swiss. During World War I Italy had set up positions in this area for fear of a German attack through Switzerland. These defenses remained serviceable after the war."

The Septentrional Front stretched along most of the Central Alps that included two major groups of mountains averaging elevations above 2,500 meters. The sections shared with Switzerland required little defensive work. The Oriental Front extended eastward toward the Adriatic Sea, along the remainder of the Alps.

The area that bordered with western Austria included the Dolomites and formed part of the Trentino region, ceded to Italy after the Great War. Its mountains averaged heights of more than 3,000 meters above sea level and it was virtually impassable. Access from Austria was only possible through a limited number of passes, the most important of which was the Brenner Pass. The remainder of the border with Austria was dominated by the Carnic Alps, with elevations above 1,500 meters and included only two crossing points.

Along the Yugoslav border the terrain was less forbidding, but no less mountainous. It included part of the Carnic and the Julian Alps. In this region Italy inherited the heavily fortified Carso Plateau, the Pola Peninsula, and parts of the Carnic and Julian Alps. This made the eastern border easy to defend and completed the Alpine Wall.

2. The Coast Defense

In most cases, the coastal terrain was favorable to defense even though it was not as ideal as the Alps. The rugged Ligurian coast, an extension of the Maritime Alps, was easy to defend. Only one major pass, the Cadibona Pass near Genoa, allowed access from the coast into the northern plains. Most of the Italian coast line in the west was easily defended because most of its beaches were located in large bays dominated by the hilly interior or rocky promontories. The east coast had more beach areas, but fewer seaports than the west coast. Any assault against a lightly defended sector, in most cases, could be checked by taking up positions in the Appennines that covered most of the peninsula. The natural barrier formed by the marshy coastline of Venice and the Po River Valley was no longer threatened after the change of borders, and the acquisition of bases along the eastern Adriatic.

3. Island Defenses

Sardinia, Sicily, Pantelleria, and the Italian occupied islands of the Dodecanese offered favorable defensive positions and allowed Italy to project its naval influence into the Mediterranean. Most were mountainous and served as bases from which the Italian army and navy could challenge any possible British threat and secure the route to the Italian Empire in North Africa.

However, the greatest drawback for the Italian armed forces was the extent of the coastline and land frontier, and the number of islands to be defended. Even though it was an industrial power, Italy did not have the resources to defend adequately its whole periphery.

HISTORY

After the Great War, the coast defenses were given less attention as Mussolini pursued his dreams of colonial expansion, investing in offensive weapons and units.

The plans for the defense of the peninsula during the Mussolini era involved primarily the creation of the Vallo Alpino, because relations with France, Austria, and Yugoslavia were becoming uncertain. The Vallo Alpino was conceived in 1930 when General Guidetti of the Genio, or corps of engineers, was put in charge of studying the situation.

The creation of the Vallo Alpino began with the renovation of many of the old Austrian forts for use as casernes or ammunition depots and the preparation of new border fortifications. On the French front, the forts of 1870s, 1880s, and World War I vintage with their high profiles, served better as casernes for Alpine units, than as active defenses. Nonetheless, some of them remained armed and were integrated into the defensive system. In the mid-1920s Fort Chaberton awaited the return of the artillery that had been transferred to the Austrian front during the Great War. It also received additional construction. Work on a cavern battery in the face of Mount Chaberton was begun but never completed.

New construction on the Vallo Alpino began in 1931 and continued for several years to keep up with the French Maginot Line. The Northern Front with Switzerland was untouched, although a number of defensive positions built during World War I remained in service.[2] Unbeknown to the general public for many years, fortifications went up on the Oriental Front.[3] Apparently little was done until late in 1939, well after Italy became Germany's ally, when a serious effort was made to build up the defenses against their Axis partner. Mussolini, apparently well aware of Hitler's ideas in *Mein Kampf*, wanted to ensure that no attempt would be made to place Trento, with its large Germanic population, in the Third Reich.

Work began slowly on the Eastern Front when Italian troops were sent to the Brenner Pass in 1934 in response to the attempted Nazi coup in Austria, and continued through 1942. In the spring of 1935, the American consul reported that the Austrian frontier was being fortified from Fortezza to Brnico, Dobbiacco, and Tarvisio. He also noted extensive work in the Adige Valley between Verona and the Brenner Pass where several lines or systems were being built and new positions were being cut into the mountains. The consul also observed new defenses on the Yugoslav border, which, according to Italian military sources, were very light and designed to support offensive operations. He opined that the work had been going on for years and that the military used only Italian laborers for security reasons. This may well be the reason so little is known about these works.

According to 1936 reports, the Brenner Pass was rigged with explosives wired to detonate when driven over by heavy vehicles. In the spring of 1940, the Swiss press reported the presence of twenty-eight forts in the Brenner Pass. Other observers counted as many as thirty-six to forty-two, despite the excellent camouflage. New roads were built and older ones were widened on all fronts, especially at Tarvisio, near the Austro-Italian border.

On the whole the Italian defenses were to consist of several lines of defense. The Occidental Front bordering France included two to three lines and the Oriental Front, facing Austria and Yugoslavia, three. The sector bordering Switzerland didn't progress beyond the planning stages but the old positions, blasted into the ground to form the Cardona Line during the Great War, remained serviceable. Thus, on paper at least, the defenses of the Alpine Wall were indeed as formidable as the Little Maginot Line of the Alps.

While Northern Italy was protected by the Alpine Wall from land invasion, the rest of the country needed protection from air and naval assault. To this end, more than a dozen key areas were selected in the early 1920s. In 1924 the military decided to fortify all major naval bases on the Mediterranean coast and certain strategic ports and economic centers extending from Genoa on the Riviera, to Maddalena on Sardinia, to Naples and Palermo in the south. These places were to receive heavy artillery ranging from 203-mm to 381-mm as well as numerous smaller weapons, including anti-aircraft guns.

Many emplacements from World War I remained in use until 1943. The battery of Amalfi (381-mm gun turret), one of the positions opened to military attachés in 1922, was equipped with such state of the art equipment as the latest fire control system for modern forts and the Braccialini goniostadiometer that was purported to give the range of targets up to 30 km.

In 1931 new plans were drawn to improve strategic island positions such as Leros. The first new battery in Italy after the end of the Great War was not set up until 1934 at Maddalena, Sardinia. It consisted of two gun turrets that mounted four 203-mm/45 guns each. In addition, a new type of installation was perfected with all its facilities beneath the concrete structure and armed with 381-mm/40 guns. The first of these batteries, completed at Augusta, Sicily, in 1939, included 381-mm guns. The second battery of this type mounted two 203-mm guns.

However, the limitations of the national industry, financial restraints, and various other problems did not always permit the fruition of Italy's ambitious defensive schemes. Thus the proposed twin turret batteries for the strategic island of Pantelleria that would have mounted 320-mm and 203-mm guns, were not even built.

During World War I five army coast artillery fortress regiments had occupied the key regions. Between the wars the number was reduced to three in the 1920s, and replaced by the Coastal Militia in 1935.[4] In 1938 the Coastal Militia became the Naval Artillery Militia and defended all the major naval bases on the peninsula and Pantelleria. Between 1941 and 1943 the army organized coastal brigades that eventually formed twenty-five coastal divisions.

DESCRIPTION

1. The Vallo Alpino

The Vallo Alpino consisted of three zones. The first was the *Zona di Sicurezza*, or Security Zone, whose mission was to prevent a surprise attack, impede an enemy advance, and allow the army time to mobilize. This zone included some strong points to stop the enemy as well as smaller outposts. The second was the *Zona di Resistenza*, or Resistance Zone, which had larger fortifications and whose mission was to continue resisting even after becoming isolated. It included casemates and other types of blocks for artillery, infantry, and observation with, usually, separate entrances. These large positions contained casernes with all the facilities for the garrison beneath the concrete structure. The third was the *Zona di Schieramento* or Marshalling Area where the artillery and other army units mobilized. This area normally included much of the anti-aircraft defenses.

The *Zone di Sicurezza* included well concealed *avamposti* (advance posts or outposts) made of concrete and armor. They replaced older *avamposti* from the last war and may have been stronger than many of the French avant-postes of the Little Maginot Line.

The *Zona di Resistenza*, the main defensive zone, contained several of the older forts, some of which served mainly as casernes and/or storage areas and others as active combat positions. On the Occidental Sector, forts like Jafferau and Chaberton, rearmed with 149-mm guns, served as advanced positions. On the Oriental Sector in Trentino, about twenty to thirty former Austrian forts were converted into casernes or ammunition depots. They were located in the *Zona di Resistenza* as well as the *Zona di Schieramento*.

All three main types of Italian fortification were found in the *Zona di Resistenza*. These works, known as opere, included Types A, B, and C. In Subsector IX/a (Moncenisio) of the Occidental Front, the fortifications extended from Mt. Malamot across the valley, reinforcing or replacing the older defenses from the last war. Fort Malamot's artillery was removed and replaced with 47-mm anti-tank guns in cloches, and lighter weapons. Subterranean works were also added to the fort. Additional work was done on sector IX/a after 1935 when Italy's Ethiopian adventure created more international friction. About thirty of the three types of opere were built during those last few years, and more were on the drawing board.

An army report of 1942 mentions the creation of defensive barriers consisting of various types of bunkers, probably including all three types of opere, that were to block a valley or passage through it. Also, obstacles like anti-tank ditches would supplement these positions. The report noted that in many places, especially on the front with Yugoslavia, many of these positions were not satisfactory because additional work needed to be done to further secure their flanks.

The largest type of positions, Opere A, normally required much excavation since they were built into the rock instead of exposed buildings like those associated with the casernes. They received the heaviest type of concrete protection to resist heavy artillery. The concrete thickness varied according to the amount of rock cover, but was generally no less than 3 meters of concrete in the areas where the rock cover was not sufficient. The high cost of construction limited the number of Opere A built and completed. Most consisted of five or more combat blocks linked by underground galleries and subterranean facilities with casernes, and other facilities that included a usine for generating power and a heating system. An armored chimney located outside of the opera served the electrical ventilation system and gas proof doors secured each entrance. Although individual positions could be isolated and resist for an extended period of time, they were not intended for long-term occupation. Like the French Maginot ouvrages, they provided basic life support systems with no luxuries. However, they were even more Spartan, only offering the security of being out of harm's way.

In many cases the Opera A consisted of more than one level but had no special equipment such as monte-charges for moving munitions up to the blocks or engines to pull the carts through the long galleries. Munitions and supplies were moved strictly by manpower.

The combat blocks received information from observers located in armored cloches. The armament for these blocks included machine guns and, in some cases, 47-mm anti-tank guns. They were usually located where they could effectively dominate an important town or road and were expertly concealed into the terrain.

A good example of a very large Opera A, also serving as a battery position, was #17 of Gravere, located at an elevation of 930 meters and consisting of fifteen combat blocks.[5] It occupied the upper part of a mountain and had two entrances leading to two separate galleries linked by several access tunnels. The interior included all the facilities necessary to support the 240 man garrison. This opera consisted of four artillery blocks that mounted a 75-mm gun each and three observation positions located near the top of the mountain. Two blocks for 47-mm anti-tank guns covered the eastern side of the opera, near the entrances. The other blocks of the opera held heavy or light machine guns and defended every side of the mountain. Opera #17 did not have diamond fossés because it overlooked a steep mountain side.

More common fortifications were the medium opere known as Type B with a maximum of four combat positions but the same amount of concrete protection as Type A. They housed smaller garrisons and contained even fewer interior facilities.

Some positions designated as battery positions, usually in caverns excavated into the face of a mountain, may also have been included in the count of Type A and B opere. They usually consisted of several artillery pieces mounted in individual blocks linked by a tunnel to a service area and entrance.

Opera #32 at Moncenisio belonging to Gruppo Gran Croce with two entrance blocks and three combat blocks, is a good representative of Type B opere. Most of its underground facilities were situated midway between the entrances and the combat blocks. Its combat block consisted of a small firing chamber for a single heavy weapon, flanked by a smaller position for a light weapon, such as an automatic rifle. The smaller position covered the facade of the bigger position with flanking fire. In front of the crenels was a diamond fossé similar to those used in France.

The most common fortifications were the small, Type C opere that consisted of only two combat positions for machine guns or AT guns. Their concrete protection was less than 2.5 meters thick. It was able to withstand the fire of small to medium caliber artillery. The interior facilities of these opera were decidedly limited.

Opera 15-bis of Gruppo Rivera Rivero, located near Lake Moncenisio, is a fine example of a large Type C. It was a large two-level casemate with the troop facilities on the lower floor. The entrance, located in a rear corner of the upper level, was protected by a caponier-like position with three crenels for an automatic weapon that fired across the entrance, to the front, and the opposite side. Another exit was located on the other side of the opera, just behind the front of the casemate and diagonally opposite of the entrance, and was covered by another caponier that formed part of the front of the casemate. Grenade launchers protected the facade overlooking the front. Small firing rooms for an anti-tank gun and two heavy machine guns gave frontal fires, and two other small crenels for automatic weapons covered the curved face of the block and the embrasures of the main weapons.

Type A and B Opere, like the ouvrages of the Maginot Line, were built to suit the terrain, and their features were so individual that it is difficult to classify them according to a common standard for size, type of weapons, and organization. What many had in common was the great number of one- or, in some cases, two-weapon combat blocks that occupied a minimal amount of space. Diamond fossés that protected crenels and entrances were also common, except in difficult terrain such as cliff faces.

Anti-tank obstacles like walls, ditches, and barbed wire, formed part of the defenses where necessary. Many opere included cloches designed either for observation or for weapons of a distinctly Italian style. Many observation cloches were reached by handrails or long stairways since there were no lifts.

The smaller Type C Opere conformed to no particular standard type but, like the larger works, were superbly camouflaged.

Financial restraints limited the use of armor so that entrance doors, crenel plates, turrets, and observatories had to be used sparingly. The opere were linked to each other with underground telephone cables, special light signals, and radios. However, the Italian forts were not as lavishly armed or equipped as their Maginot counterparts because of financial limitations.

The weapons used in the Vallo Alpino consisted of medium artillery ranging from 120-mm to 149-mm guns mostly installed in older forts. Some opere had mortars and even flame throwers in fixed positions. Plans were also made to employ poison gas in some valleys in the event of a successful enemy advance. In some cases additional large anti-tank ditches blocked access to the opere and in at least in one case, at Pont Ventoux, they completely closed off a valley.

The following is only a partial list of some Italian positions on the Occidental Front to serve as an example of their size and armament:

Moncenisio area with about 30 Type A and B Opere.
Gravera area covering Monte Morone and Susa had about 30 opere.

    Gruppo Corna Rossa with
        4 combat blocks -Machine guns and anti-tank guns.
    Opera #21 near Ospizio with
        6 combat blocks -Machine guns and small cannon.
    Opera #19 near Oiano della Vaccheria with
        5 combat blocks - One small caliber gun and a machine gun in each block.
    Opera #7 under Fort Combe extremely large Type A with
        several combat blocks - Two 75-mm guns, one 65-mm gun, six 47-mm
        AT guns, two 20-mm guns, eight heavy machine gun.
    Opera #10 near Gravere large Type A with
        9 combat blocks - four 81-mm mortars, three anti-tank guns,
        twelve heavy machine guns.
    Opera #116 at Cros du Rey

    Some old forts refurbished:
    Fort Bramafan - new machine gun positions and emplacements
        for two batteries of 149-mm guns.
    Fort Pramand - four 149-mm gun turrets.

This is only a small sample of the numerous positions on the Occidental Front. The positions described were in the sectors defending the passes at Monginevro (Montgenèvre), Fréjus, and Moncenisio (Mont Cenis). Smaller works covered the Petit St. Bernard Pass. Additional opere defended the passes of the Maritime Alps, including the key Tende Pass. Here a number of opere were carefully sited to control the terrain. In this area was the large opera of Balcone di Marta with a number of blocks including four with 75-mm guns that formed a cavern battery, and over 1,300 meters of tunnels with elevation between the highest and lowest level of over 100 meters.

The Oriental Front included about 50 Type A opere, many incomplete, approximately 160 Type B, and fifty artillery pieces. The armored forts of Montecchio, near the eastern shore of Lake Como at Colico, Il Canale near Tirano, and Venini, near Bormio were also in service. Montecchio—completed in 1915—and Il Canale had four turrets mounting 149-mm guns while Venini had four turrets with 120-mm guns.

In 1939, on the Occidental Front of the Alpine Wall, about 460 opere mounting 133 pieces of artillery were manned. At the same time, work continued on all fronts, including the border with the Reich. In some places civilian construction companies worked around the clock as Mussolini prepared to enter the war. By June 1940 the number of occupied forts grew to over 550.[6]

By 1942 the frontier with Germany was mostly protected by medium to heavy opere that were better armed than positions on the Western Front. The total number of opere on all fronts of the Alpine Wall by August 1942 increased to 1,475; another 450 were still under construction. In addition, about 700 defensive casernes and shelters were finished and another 60 were still being built. There were also plans to build another 1,400 opere, casernes, and shelters, two-thirds of which were to be erected on the German front.

The frontier was defended by the *Guardia alla Frontiera*, or Frontier Guard, that formed eleven commands along the Alpine border and garrisoned the opere. During World War II, the Occidental Front was divided in three sectors under the jurisdiction of three active army corps. The I Corps was responsible for Sectors VI, VII, VIII, IX, X, the II Corps for Sector II, III, and IV, the XV Corps for Sector I and V.

2. Coast Defenses

Between 1939 and 1943 the Italian coastal defenses consisted of a variety of battery positions, some of which formed the defenses of a few heavily fortified ports. Ports like Venice remained fortified even when the emphasis shifted to the western and southern coasts after 1915. The positions ranged from small shielded guns on barbette mounts, to huge batteries. The battery of Monte Moro, located east of Genoa, housed large 381-mm/40 Ansaldo guns that had been hauled up the mountain and installed in armored turrets. Its supporting facilities were inside the mountain. Battery Mameli di Pegli near Genoa included an armored rangefinder revolving on a circular concrete casemate used for observation. These new emplacements were added to the few older positions built late in the Great War.

During World War II the batteries of Amalfi (Venice), Brin and Bandiera (Brindisi), Opera A (Augusta), Monte Moro (Genoa), and Arenzano each consisted of a twin gun turret with 381/40 guns. The other large battery positions were not turret-mounted and consisted of 305-mm to 203-mm guns.

The main defenses were assured by the following numbers of batteries protecting the fortified port areas:

FORTIFIED AREA	NUMBER OF GUNS PER BATTERY				
	2 guns	3 guns	4 guns	5 guns	6 guns
Genoa	2 x 381-mm	3 x 152-mm			
La Spezia -			2 x 305-mm		
			1 x 152-mm	4 x 152-120*	
			1 x 120-mm		
Naples	1 x 190-mm	1 x 152-mm			
Straits of Messina			1 x 280-mm		2 x 280-mm
				1 x 152-120*	
Sicily					
Augusta/	1 x 381-mm	3 x 152-mm			
Syracuse	1 x 203-mm		4 x 152-120*		
Palermo			4 x 152-120*		
			2 x 120-mm		
Trapani			1 x 152-mm		
Taranto	1 x 152-mm		1 x 305-120**		
			4 x 152-mm	1 x 203-120*	
			4 x 120-mm	2 x 152-120*	
Brindisi	2 x 381-mm		1 x 152-mm		
		2 x 152-mm			
Venice	1 x 381-mm		3 x 152-mm		
	3 x 305-mm		2 x 120-mm		
Pola	1 x 190-mm		5 x 149-mm		
	1 x 152-mm				

+Example: 1 x 190-mm is one battery with two 190-mm guns at Naples.
*Four 152-mm or 203-mm guns and one 120-mm gun.
**Three 305-mm guns and one 120-mm gun.
Note: The 280-mm weapons are howitzers.

The above list does not include weapons smaller than 120-mm, nor the numerous anti-aircraft weapons. Like most Italian fortifications, these batteries were superbly camouflaged.

Armored trains continued to serve as mobile artillery. Along the Ligurian coastal front the navy operated four armored trains with four 120-mm guns each and one train with four 152-mm guns. Southern Italy and Sicily were covered by four armored trains with four 152-mm guns and two 76-mm guns, one train with six 102-mm guns, and one with four 76-mm guns.

3. Island Defenses

The large number of islands from the Eastern Mediterranean to Sardinia under Italy's control, offered convenient lookout points from which enemy ship traffic could be kept under surveillance, and bases from which the Italian navy could operate. Unfortunately, the cost of building fortifications and the expense of transporting building materials and weapons by sea made it impossible to defend all the available points. Thus only important islands were fortified. Sardinia was selected because it had to be protected because of its proximity to French Corsica, the islands of Elba and Pantelleria because they dominated key straits. The island defenses, like those on the mainland, were outfitted with a wide variety of weapons,including some of the heaviest and most modern. In addition, Sardinia, Elba, Pantelleria, and other islands included smaller weapons.

The following batteries were established before and during the war:

Batteries	2 guns	3 guns	4 guns	5 guns	6 guns
Sardinia					
Maddalena		1 x 305-mm	1 x 305-mm		
		2 x 152-mm		1 x 203-120+	
			1 x 152-120+		
				1 x 152-mm-120+	
		1 x 120-mm			1 x 152-120+
Cagliari			3 x 152-mm		
Elba			3 x 152-mm		
Pantelleria			3 x 152-mm	1 x 120-mm	
			2 x 120-mm		
Dodecanese					
Rhodes		3 x 152-mm			
		3 x 120-mm			
Leros		2 x 152-mm		1 x 152-120+	
			2 x 120-mm		

+Included one 120-mm gun.

In some cases plans for building batteries did not come to fruition. Thus the island of Leros was to be the site of Opera Z, a battery of 254-mm and 203-mm guns, that was not built. At Pantelleria construction of the planned heavy batteries proved to be impractical and the project was abandoned. The large defended base area in the Gulf of Naples that was to encompass the coastal islands of Ponza, Ischia, and Capri, did not materialize because the 305-mm guns were not installed.

Many gun positions, such as those built on Rhodes, included underground galleries, magazines, and other rooms, usually hewn into the rock and sometimes lined with bricks. Concrete observation towers for directing the guns were completed.

WEAPONS AND EQUIPMENT

Some of the artillery employed in the Alpine Wall included:

	Range
420-mm howitzer on concrete platform	17. km*
149-mm/12 Model 1914	6.5 km
149-mm/35 Model 1910	9.7 km
149-mm/40 Model 1935 (Armstrong-Montagna)	21.7 km
75-mm/27 Model 1906	6.6 km
57-mm/30 (naval)	2.1 km
47-mm/32 Model 1935	7. km
20-mm/65	1.8 km

*Only one which was received from Austria as reparations.

The Coast Artillery included:

381-mm/40 Model 1914	20.6 km
305-mm/50 Model 1912	18. km
305-mm/46 Model 1909	18. km
305-mm/17 Model 1914 Howitzer	12.6 km
280-mm/9 Model 1885 Howitzer	9. km
254-mm/45 Model 1924	24. km
203-mm/50 Model 1924	28. km
190-mm/39	18. km
152-mm/50 Model 1914	18.5 km
152-mm/40 Model 1891	12.5 km
120-mm/21	9. km
102-mm/45	17. km
90-mm/53	14. km

WORLD WAR II

The history of the Alpine Wall in World War II was rather brief. The military rushed to complete many of the opere before their entry into the war. During the short campaign in France, the French and Italians fired a few rounds against each other's fortifications with no significant effect.

The only major encounter took place between Fort Chaberton and some of the Maginot ouvrages and advanced posts. Since early in 1939 the citizens of Briançon had suffered from so called "Chabertonitis," a fear engendered by reports that the guns of Fort Chaberton looked "down their throats." When the battle started, the French were not able to respond to Chaberton's fire because the Maginot forts at

Briançon were not designed for frontal fire. However, a French battery of 280-mm mortars was soon moved into position under the cover of fog. As soon as the cloud cover lifted from the top of Mount Chaberton, the French let go a volley of huge bombs, smashing one turret after another until the Italian fort was effectively silenced.

The Italians continued working on the Alpine Wall through the war, especially along the old Austrian border. Their efforts were no secret, since they were even reported on in a U.S. Army handbook published in the spring of 1942. Needless to say, Hitler was not pleased with the continued construction in the region. The construction along the Swiss and German borders was soon called the "we-have-no-faith-line" by the press.

In August 1942, Chief-of-Staff General Vittorio Ambrosio reported to the High Command that although the northern border with Germany continued to be strengthened, the lack of materials was causing serious delays. He also pointed out that although plans were made to defend the Swiss frontier with fortified barriers placed on both sides of main roads, only at Sempione was work actually begun. In addition, he wrote, the fortifications of the entire Alpine Wall lacked anti-tank defenses and had inadequate close defense. Despite these problems, General Ambrosio remained convinced of his ability to seal the frontier with Germany.

Soon after Italy entered the war, a French naval squadron sallied forth to attack the fortified coastal areas along the Ligurian coast. The Italians were unable to stop it from bombarding Savona even with the help of the 120-mm guns of Armored Train Number 3. It took a squadron of torpedo boats to drive the French off. Another French attack at Arenzano was met by the 152-mm guns of Battery Mameli and two monitors defending Genoa. Neither side suffered any significant damage even though Battery Mameli managed to score one hit on a French destroyer.

In February 1941 a British squadron of two battleships out of Gibraltar bombarded Genoa. The Mameli battery went back into action, along with Armored Train Number 5 and the old monitors, but their fire was not effective. The result of the encounter was the construction of two new batteries: Battery 250 at Arenzano and Battery 251 at Monte Moro. Each of these batteries, completed in 1942, received a twin 381-mm gun turret.

In June 1943, the Allies bombarded the island of Pantelleria from the air, hitting most of its sixteen-gun batteries after a week of intensive bombing. Fifty-three of the eighty guns were damaged, and the 11,000 man garrison surrendered before the invasion took place.

The new coastal divisions began to prepare defensive positions along the coast before the invasion of Italy in 1943. After the surrender of Italy, the Germans took over the remaining Italian coastal fortifications, and Mussolini's loyal forces manned the battery positions with mixed German crews. The German labor organization,

Organization Todt, built new defenses along the coast that were dubbed the Ligurian Wall by the Germans.

No serious attempt was made to breach the Alpine Wall along the Occidental Sector during 1944-45 by the Free French and American forces. The Germans and some of the Fascist units occupied some of the Italian positions. When Italy surrendered, the locals stripped everything that could be carried off from some of the opere, except ammunition and guns. However, most of the fortifications were easily returned to service.

Through the entire war, the Alpine Wall successfully carried out its mission, since it was not attacked. As to whether or not it was a good investment can only be answered by the fact that it was widely believed in 1939 that the French had seriously considered a major ground offensive against northern Italy.

Alpine Front - SouthernTyrol. Bunker on route from Inn Valley with its protective earth covering stripped away. (Günther Reiss)

Alpine Front with France. Distinctive Italian cloche, camouflage removed, on fort overlooking Mt. Cenis Pass. (Karol Vasat)

Left: Alpine Front. Italian bunker with gun embrasure located in Mt. Cenis Pass. (Karol Vasat)
Below: Italian Coastal Position. German artillery casemates built 1943-1944 for Monte Morro battery.(Carlo Alfredo Clerici)

INSERT
Battery Ammiraglo Toscano, Opera M,
Two twin gun turrets at Taranto:
1. 203-mm twin gun turret
2. Magazine
3. Crew's Quarters
4. CO's Room
5. Plotting room

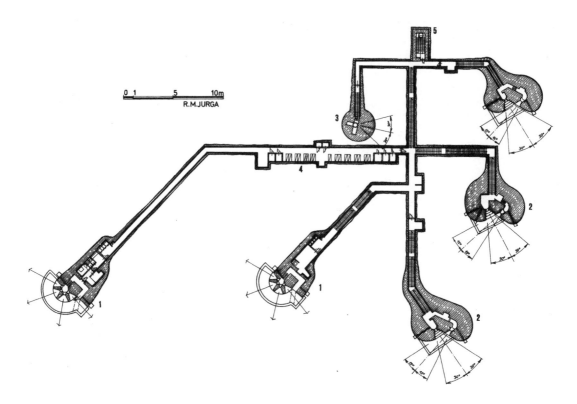

Bardonecchia Sector, Opera 116.
1. Entrance block with MG embrasures (main entrance is at far left and a short distance away were latrines and the kitchen outside the fort, but not shown here)
2. Blocks for AT Gun with embrasure covering facade and fosse
3. MG cloche
4. Caserne, WC, magazines
5. Observation block with cloche

Right hand Page:
Plans of Italian Alpine Forts.
Gravere Opera Grossa 17
Battery Monte Morone
Sette Fontane Bardonecchia
Valle Cenischia Opera 15bis
Melrnise Bardonecchia Opera 88
Piano S Nicolao Opera 32
Borgunovo Bardonecchia Opera 6
Melmise Bardonecchia Opera 87:
I- Entrance
IP- Main Entrance,
IS- Secondary Entrance
A - Heavy MG Position
AC- 47-mm AT gun Position,
P - Block for one 75-mm/26 gun
O - Observatory

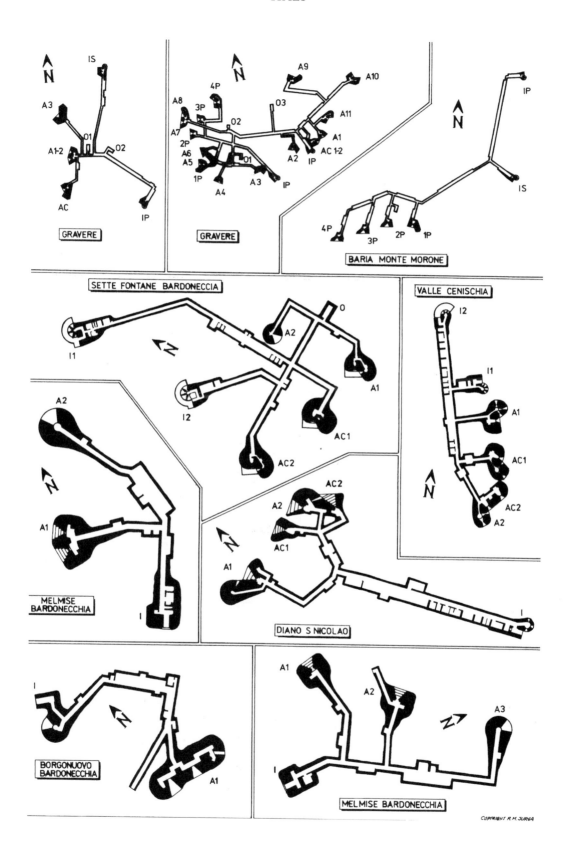

GRAVERE

GRAVERE

BARIA MONTE MORONE

SETTE FONTANE BARDONECCIA

VALLE CENISCHIA

MELMISE BARDONECCHIA

DIANO S NICOLAO

BORGONUOVO BARDONECCHIA

MELMISE BARDONECCHIA

COPYRIGHT R.M. JURGA

209

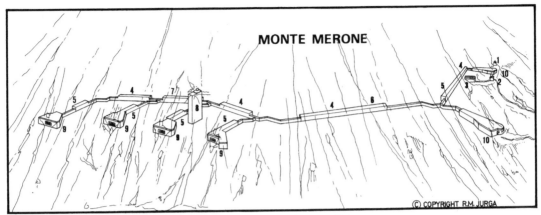

Battery Monte Morone, 3rd Line of Defense with 80 and 4 x 75/27-mm guns

1. Latrines
2. Kitchen
3. Water tank
4. Crew's quarters
5. Magazines
6. Commo Center and CP
7. Crew's room
8. Observation block with cloche
9. Combat blocks
10. Entrance blocks

Italian Position Number 15 in Alps.

1. Defended Entrance
2. Guard Room
3. Position for light MG to defend rear of block
4. Flanking position for light MG to defend front of block
5. Corridor
6. & 7. WC
8,9,10,11,12. Stairs
13. Magazine

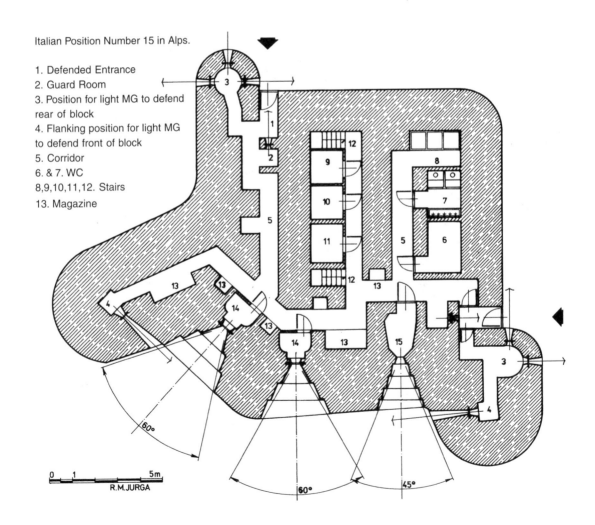

Chapter 8

SCANDINAVIA

BACKGROUND

Although culturally similar, the nations of Scandinavia were not politically united, especially in their common pursuit of neutrality. Except for Sweden, none of these countries had the economic base and manpower to set up extensive permanent fortifications and defend them. Thus, only Sweden managed to remain neutral after 1940.

The only Scandinavian nation with an overseas empire, Denmark, was fast declining as a colonial and military power. Although it still maintained its hold over Greenland, Iceland, and the Faeroe Islands, it had sold the Virgin Islands to the U.S. during World War I. Its fleet was too small to defend the empire, and its army was not large enough to protect the homeland itself.

In the early 1930s, a dispute over settlements in Greenland almost led Denmark to a ruinous war with Norway. Later in the 1930s, in an attempt to modernize its military services, the Danish government decided to update its coastal defenses, especially on the islands that were the key to the rest of the country. "

Norway, which had broken away from Denmark near the end of the Napoleonic Era to form a union with Sweden, became independent in 1905. After the secession, the two nations agreed upon a 20 km wide neutral strip inside the Norwegian border.

Unlike Denmark, Norway enjoyed an easily defendable topography so that its relatively small army was not too great a drawback. The coastline consisted of rugged terrain with sunken valleys known as fjords that led to the seaports that an invader must take to establish a foothold in the country. Many of the fjords leading to the ports were guarded by forts. The small Norwegian navy was based at Horten, in the south. Until 1934, the coastal defenses were entrusted to the army, which included the Fortress Artillery branch created in 1899. The permanent defenses of the naval bases came under the jurisdiction of the navy. In 1934 the navy took over the coast defenses, leaving the army only in charge of the forts facing Sweden.

Sweden reached its military apogee in the eighteenth century but its power waned after it lost Finland to Russia in 1809. It remained, nonetheless, the most populous and most industrialized of the Scandinavian nations. Sweden did little to improve its military position during World War I, except to refurbish its navy. Between the wars it became a major arms producer, which led to an improvement of its own army, despite the government's lack of concern until 1939. It wasn't until the early years of World War II that Sweden decided to build up its armed forces and permanent defenses.

Of the three Scandinavian countries, Norway had the smallest population with only 2.9 million inhabitants, but its geography worked in its favor as far as defense was concerned. Denmark was somewhat more populous, with 3.8 million subjects, but was geographically more vulnerable to invasions. Neither country fielded a significant army, and only Norway owned useful fortifications. Sweden, on the other hand, with its 6.4 million people, had a large population base to work with and significant industrial capacity.

MAJOR FORTIFICATIONS

Danish Coastal Defenses
Norwegian Coastal Defenses and Forts
Swedish Coastal Defenses and Fortress Boden

LOCATION

1. Danish Coastal Defenses

Denmark was a geographic nightmare as far as military defense was concerned. The areas that needed protection were the large Danish islands and Eastern Jutland, where the bulk of the population was concentrated. Jutland was defendable near the border, but its terrain was unfavorable to fixed defenses. A small invasion force would have been able to outflank any fortifications near the border by landing on the sandy beaches of the west coast. In addition, only the small port of Esbjerg, on the west coast of Jutland, offered a practical base of operation. The islands to the east of Jutland, home to at least half of the Danish population, included Sjaelland (Sealand) with the city of Copenhagen, Lolland, Flaster, and Fyn, and were virtually impossible to secure.

The best defensive strategy was to establish coastal batteries to control the narrow waterways between the islands in places like the channels of the Great Belt—between Fyn, Sjaelland, and Lolland—and Little Belt—between Fyn and Jutland. The advantage of using these islands was that they had a number of small ports suitable for military installations. The island of Bornholm in the Baltic, to the east of the main Danish islands, was of particular strategic importance. At the end of the last century, Denmark decided to concentrate most of its efforts on building a fortress ring around Copenhagen. By the 1930s, most of these coastal positions remained in service, but not all the land forts were finished.

2. Norwegian Coastal Defenses and Forts

The coastline of Norway, dominated by fjords, was easily defended against modern invasions. The Leads, a coastal waterway, provided a safe route for German shipping through neutral territory as long as Norway remained out of the war. The 21,200 km of jagged coast line could shelter naval ships, offering them many possibilities for raiding. However, the conquest of Norway required the acquisition of one or more ports, a hazardous undertaking, since even the old weapons of the 1880s represented a very real danger to vessels in the fjords.

Like most of Norway, the border with Sweden was mostly mountainous, with few routes into Sweden. After declaring independence from Sweden, Norway, which continued to fear an invasion from its erstwhile confederate, took measures to defend the main routes into its economic heart, southeast of Oslo and east of Trondheim.

The main defensive areas in Norway were found between Halden and Sarpsborg, on the southeastern coast, on the Glomma River in the area of Askim to the southeast of Oslo and north of Sarpsborg, and in the area of Kongsvinger. Their mission was to block the three main routes from Sweden to Oslo.

3. Swedish Coastal Defenses and Fortress Boden

Sweden's extensive coast line covered 7,600 km on the Gulf of Bothnia and the Baltic Sea. Its economic heart lay in the south, extending from the plains of the south-central coastal region to the Smaland highlands. The important mining center in the vicinity of Kiruna-Gällivare, in the north, relied heavily on the Norwegian port of Narvik for the export of its iron ore during the winter months. The key point on the rail line in this region and the invasion route from Finland (pre-1918 Russian border) was fortified at Boden. Numerous rivers flowed from the Kjolen Mountains to the Gulf of Bothnia, limiting the number of roads in the northern half of the country. These rivers created many elongated lakes, especially in the southern half of the country where the lakes and Smaland Highlands, afforded many easily defended positions. Mälmo and Götberg overlooked the vital passages between the Baltic and North Sea.

Like Norway, Sweden depended on its coastal ports for its security. The size of its population allowed it to have a military force of sufficient strength and in addition, the navy's excellent bases made it possible to keep an enemy at bay.

Because of their location on the Skagerrak, Kattegat, and Baltic, the three Scandinavian countries needed coastal defenses to deter aggression, especially on the Baltic islands of Denmark and Sweden. The Finnish Åland Islands were the key to the Gulf of Bothnia, while Danish Sjaelland and Bornholm, and Swedish Öland and Gotland occupied key points on the Baltic.

HISTORY

In 1920, Denmark abandoned its land defenses, retaining only a number of coastal forts and batteries until 1940. In November 1932, the Danish government passed a defense act to rearm the country. The navy was allowed to build several new vessels and modernize others to defend the coast that included two coast defense battleships with 150-mm guns. Many of the coastal batteries continued to mount the 355-mm, 170-mm, 120-mm, 75-mm guns, and 290-mm howitzers they had in 1918. Some of the weapons, such as 47-mm and 355-mm guns, were actually models from the 1880s. In short, little was done to replace the nation's artillery. The air force, on the other hand, was allowed to acquire some modern equipment to defend key places like the naval base at Copenhagen.

The only significant improvements to the batteries defending the fortress of Copenhagen took place in the 1930s when armored hoods were installed over the armored shields of many of the heavy guns. Before World War II, Denmark owned a total of ten battery positions, some located in forts. One battery dated from the 1890s and most mounted old weapons like the 120-mm cannons. In addition a small number of modern weapons were added after World War I.

Norway's situation was different because it built forts in 1905 to protect itself against a possible Swedish invasion before their secession. Three old border forts were modernized and six new ones were erected. They were armed with modern 120-mm, 105-mm, and 75-mm guns ordered from Schneider and placed in turrets or behind armored shields. The border areas of Ørje/Urskog and Kongsvinger received two new forts apiece. The older updated forts were located in the Halden area, near the coast. When the union between Norway and Sweden was dissolved later in 1905, the creation of the 20 km neutral zone forced Norway to disarm or destroy the forts that lay within it. Only the forts of Gullbekkåsen and Vardåsen in the Kongsvinger area had remained in service, and the treaty forbade their modernization. Forts Ørjekollen and Urskog were destroyed and their 105-mm guns placed in storage for future use. However, within a short period of time, new forts went up on the edge of the neutral zone.

In 1907, the Norwegian government ordered the construction of Fort Greåker and the Ravneberget Battery of the Sarpsborg Fortress behind the old Halden position, which were completed in 1910. Fort Greåker received the 120-mm gun turrets from one of the forts destroyed at Halden, and Battery Ravneberget two 105-mm Schneider cannons from old Fort Urskog. The other two guns of Fort Urskog were sent to the Forhlten coastal battery, located between Harstad and Narvik. However they were not yet mounted in 1940.

Two forts were built in central Norway along the border between 1908 and 1910 to cover the two routes leading from Sweden into Norway, east of Trondheim. The unusual Fort Verdal, built into a mountain, included guns mounted in caverns. The most famous of the Norwegian forts was Fort Hegra, guarding the route south of Verdal, directly east of Trondheim.[1] Its two batteries, only protected by armored shields, like the other inland forts, were set up to face east, against Sweden, a common problem with Norwegian border forts. Battery positions were also set up near the Glomma River, on the main road between Oslo and Stockholm. The construction of three more forts was authorized in 1910, but only the forts of Høytorp and Trøgstad were actually built. When they were completed at the end of World War I, they became part of the Fossum Fortress along with a number of blockhouses and galleries for machine guns that covered the bridges across the Glomma River at Fossum.

Most of Norway's effort was oriented towards coastal defense. The Norwegian coast line was divided into three Sea Defense Sectors to which fortress areas were attached in 1934 when the Coast Artillery was integrated into the navy.[2] Most of the major cities and assembly areas for the army's half dozen divisions were located in the Sea Defense Sectors.

Most of Norway's fortifications dated from the latter part of the nineteenth century. The famous Oscarsborg fortress on the Dröbak narrows was an old position completed in 1856 and modernized in the 1870s and 1890s. It guarded the approaches to Oslo on the Oslo Fjord. The old Carl Johans Vaern Navy Base at Horten was defended by two forts completed in 1859 and modernized in the 1870s. In 1890 the Norwegian government undertook a major effort of modernization when it ordered a three-gun battery of 280-mm Krupp cannons for Oscarsborg.

In 1891, a defense committee selected twenty-one areas to be fortified, but only the Oscarsborg Fortress, the Tønsberg Fortress defending the Melsomvik Naval Base, the Kristiansand Fortress, the Bergen Fortress, and the Agdenes Fortress guarding the approaches to Trondheim, were actually renovated. The government ordered weapons from Great Britain, France, and Belgium and Krupp naval guns for some of the batteries from Germany. Fortress Oscarsborg and Bergen also received a torpedo battery apiece. The one at Oscarsborg was below the water line and that at Fort Kvarven in Bergen was the standard above water unit.

Norway did not attempt to improve its coastal positions until the outbreak of World War I, when two new forts were built on the islands of Rauøy and Bolaerne at the mouth of the Oslo Fjord. Plans were made for a battery at Ofot Fjord, near Narvik in the far north. The new weapons were ordered from Bofors in Sweden and Bethlehem Steel in the U.S. However, by the time they were delivered, the war was over, so they went into storage. There followed another period of inactivity that lasted until the 1930s, when it was decided to improve the defenses of Oslo Fjord. At that time, the forts of Rauøy and Bolaerne were armed with 150-mm Bofors guns. Work also began on Fort Måkerøy that received two 305-mm Bofors coastal defense howitzers, and Fort Torårs likewise.

Meanwhile, new plans were drawn up for relocating the batteries of Kristiansand and Bergen, and adding batteries and forts at the latter. The two new forts at Bergen, still under construction when the war began, were slated to include a 150-mm gun battery.[3] Work on these positions was not completed by 1939 nor were the forts protecting the approaches to Narvik.

After World War I, Sweden found itself as the major power in Scandinavia thanks to its modest fleet of coastal defense ships, but it did not pursue a policy of expansion. Thus it failed to seize the opportunity to annex the Åland Islands during the civil war in Finland. Its army was reduced after the war but its navy was kept intact.

The town of Boden, near the Gulf of Bothnia, sat on the rail line connecting the iron mines of Gällivare to the port of Lulea. Soon Boden developed into one of the country's largest rail centers. Fortifications were built there before the turn of the century to protect the region and its iron mines. In addition, the decision to create the fortress zone at Boden was made in 1900 by the Swedish Parliament only six years after the railroad reached the town from Stockholm.

The blasting and excavation work for Fort Gammeläng on Mount Svedje, to the east of Boden, and four more large forts began in 1901. All were completed by 1912. Between 1901 and World War I, the army built and occupied more than twice as many smaller works in the intervals. The first gun was installed in 1906 and the first test shot was fired in 1907. Stone barracks for the fortress garrison of Boden were built between 1902 and 1912, replacing the original brick structures. The stone for their construction was quarried from the sites of the forts. More forts had been planned, but the increasing construction costs only allowed the first group to be built. If the large forts had not been built at the same time, some would have not been erected at all. Between the wars, the forts were modernized, receiving electricity, ventilation, heating, and communication lines.

Sweden spread misinformation about Boden in order to discourage foreign incursions from Finland—part of Russia before 1918—and Norway. Although it kept the defenses of the Boden area secret, it leaked enough information in the 1920s to convince potential enemies that the fortress ring consisted of at least four mountain forts located at Mjösjöbergt, Åberget, and Paglaberget. These forts were compared to the forts of Verdun and touted to be much stronger because they had been blasted into the granite rather than soft earth, and had enough protection to resist the type of bombardments witnessed in 1916. Foreign intelligence officers expressed the belief that they compared to the forts of Metz. It was claimed that their armament consisted of 210-mm mortars or possibly howitzers.

After the turn of the century, Sweden concentrated its defensive effort around designated coastal fortress areas at Vaxholm—which protected Stockholm—at Karlskrona in the southeast, at Helsingborg and the narrows between Sweden and Denmark, at Göteborg with Fort Oscar II on the Kattegat, and on the island of Götland. Many of the guns were mounted on barbette mounts and a few in turrets. However, a number of large caliber weapons, such as 305-mm and 240-mm, became outdated between the world wars or simply wore out. Additional up-to-date 210-mm guns, used on newer warships, were set up late in the 1930s on the islands of Götland and Karlskrona.

Between the wars Sweden became a major arms producer and concentrated at first on export rather than local consumption. The Bofors works signed an agreement to produce weapons for Germany and other nations. These contracts helped develop the Swedish arms industry to such an extent that by 1939 it was able to produce many of the weapons needed for home defense. In addition, after World War I, Krupp established the Landsverk company in Sweden which produced weapons for export.

The Swedish Defense Act of 1936 authorized a significant increase in spending for the armed forces. However, internal politics slowed military development until Germany became an apparent threat to Sweden's security. A number of new weapons were ordered from Bofors for coastal defense in 1936 and 1937. In addition, plans were drawn up between the wars to modernize the fortifications and modify work done or not completed during World War I. By 1939, four 210-mm guns and seven 150-mm guns for barbette mountings were delivered along with some 75-mm anti-aircraft guns and twelve 40-mm anti-aircraft guns. Bofors rebuilt six old 120-mm M.94 cannons and manufactured twelve new 150-mm M.40 guns for coast defense by 1940. The coast defense command not only decided to put some weapons in casemates and turrets, but also to use mobile guns. South of Boden, on the route to the iron ore mines, a coastal defense position was set up at Henso. After the German invasion of Norway, the Swedish defensive effort intensified. An armored train was sent to the border with Norway, near Narvik, to protect the route to the iron ore mines.

Between July and September 1939, the Swedish army completed 267 bunkers during the first phase of construction of the Per Albin line, today known as the Scandia Line. This was done against the wishes of Prime Minister Per Albin Hansson, its namesake! The line was built in four phases: the second phase, when another 124 bunkers were built, lasted from December 1939 to April 1940; the third phase, which continued from April to June 1940, saw the completion of another 527 bunkers; and finally the fourth phase, which extended from June until October 1940, saw the addition of 145 more bunkers. The line spanned the southern tip of Sweden from a point south of Halmstad to a point west of Karlskrona near Ronneby, covering over 350 km. Most of the bunkers were for machine guns, but some mounted anti-tank guns. The coast in this area was open to an invasion staged froom northern Germany or the nearby Danish islands of Sjaelland and Bornholm.

After the German invasion of Norway smaller defensive lines were set up at a dozen road sites on the Norwegian border. These included mostly machine gun bunkers and shelters using the rough terrain's defensive advantages.

When the war began, the Swedish navy consisted of three coastal battleships—which had been modernized before the war and given 11.14-inch guns—a few older coastal ships with 210-mm and 150-mm guns, and a light cruiser with 150-mm guns. Naval squadrons operated from bases at Stockholm, Göteborg, Karlskrona, Malmö, and Visby (island of Götland) that were close enough to support the coastal defenses in their area. However, with only nine modern coastal submarines and a few destroyers, the navy's ability to repel an invasion was limited. The Royal Coast Artillery fell under naval command for the defense of the key bases.

DESCRIPTION

1. Danish Coastal Defenses

The most interesting Danish fortifications were the island forts such as the Flak Fort at Saltholm island, Fort Dragør, and Fort Middelgrunds, protected by lagoons formed by jetties. Fort Dragør, at Copenhagen, and nearby Fort Taarbaek mounted mostly older models of heavy artillery. In fact, most of Denmark's ordnance was of World War I vintage or older, ranging from the 305-mm, 170-mm, and 120-mm gun batteries at Fort Middelgrund to the 355-mm gun battery at Fort Dragør. The Flak Fort, which had some of the newer weapons, housed 290-mm howitzers and 210-mm cannons from the World War I period. Most of the guns were mounted on barbette carriages and protected by armored shields and earthen ramparts. The ammunition and barracks areas were under concrete.

Though old, the guns of these coastal defense batteries could be quite effective in the narrow waters of Denmark.

DANISH BATTERIES IN 1933

Name	Number of Guns						
	47-mm	75-mm	120-mm	150-mm	170-mm	210-mm	290-mm
Fort Lynaes*		4*	2				
Fort Taarbaek			2				4H
Lynetten+	2	2		4			
Fort Middelgrund*	1	5*	6		12		(5 x 305-mm)
Flak Fort*	1	4*	4			6*	4
Fort Dragør*	1	3*	4*		4*		(4 x 355-mm)
Kongelund Battery*	2	4					4H
Mosede Battery *		4	6				
Borgsted Battery*			2				
Fort Masnedø			6	4			

*Weapons and positions still in service at this battery after World War II.
+Battery positions existing since 1894. H=howitzer. Items in parenthesis () are larger caliber guns in service.

Most of Denmark's coast defenses were clustered in the vicinity of Copenhagen. The Flak Fort was built just north of the island of Saltholm on the Øresund, the body of water separating Sealand from Sweden. The Kongelund Battery, on the southern end of the Copenhagen Fortress, was armed with four 150-mm Bofors guns in 1939 taken from the old coastal battleship Herluf Trolle.

2. Norwegian Coastal Defenses and Forts

The defenses of Oslo Fjord rank as the most important in Norway. Fortress Oscarsborg, located on the Kaholmen Islands and dating back to 1856, received its first "modern" piece of artillery, a breech loaded Krupp 305-mm gun, in 1879. The main battery of three 280-mm M.1889 guns was created in 1893. At the turn of the century, a torpedo battery of 450-mm Whitehead torpedoes was set up on North Kaholmen Island. This battery was cut into the rock and the tubes were underwater. The excavated central rock chamber included complete facilities including torpedo magazines, usine, rest area, etc. There were three fan shaped launching tunnels for torpedoes below this area. The torpedoes were lowered down a shaft into the position from which they were launched underwater on a platform that could traverse twenty degrees. They were not "fired" as in a standard torpedo tube, but moved on their own power through the tunnels.

The fortress also included four British Whitworth 280-mm M.1891 howitzers which formed a battery on Håøya Island, near the Kaholmen Islands. On Håøya

Island eight 120-mm guns formed the Lower Top Battery and two newer 120-mm guns M.99 the Upper Top Battery. Anti-aircraft guns were added during World War I. The battery positions, consisting of masonry and concrete defenses for the guns, lacked overhead protection against air-attacks.

NORWEGIAN BATTERIES AND MANUFACTURERS OF GUNS

Oscarsborg Fortress

Main batteries	3 x 280-mm Cannon (Krupp) L/40
	1 x 305-mm Cannon (Krupp) L/25
	4 x 57-mm Cannon (Finspong)
	2 x 57-mm Cannon (Cockerill)
	3 x 450-mm Torpedo Tubes (built 1901)
	Whitehead Model 5 Torpedo
	Length 5 meters, Diameter 450-mm,
	Warhead 118 kg TNT, Speed 29-31 knots
Håoya Batteries	2 x 120-mm Cannon (Armstrong) M.99
	8 x 120-mm Cannon (Palliser) M.91
	4 x 280-mm Howitzer (Whitworth) M.91
Nesset Battery	4 x 57-mm Cannon (Cockerill)
Kopås Battery	3 x 150-mm Cannon (Armstrong) M.99
Husvik Battery	2 x 57-mm Cannon (Cockerill)
Veisving Battery	2 x 40-mm AA Gun (Bofors)

Tønsberg Fortress

Fort Håøya	2 x 210-mm Cannon (Armstrong) M.00
	2 x 120-mm Cannon (Armstrong) M.95
	4 x 65-mm Cannon (Hotchkiss)

Oslofjord Fortress

Fort Rauøy	4 x 150-mm Cannon (Bofors) M.20*
	2 x 65-mm Cannons
	2 x 40-mm Bofors AA guns
Fort Bolaerne	3 x 150-mm Cannon (Bofors) M.20
	4 x 120-mm Cannon (Cockerill) L/44*
Fort Måkerøy	2 x 305-mm Howitzer (Bofors) M.16*
Fort Torås	2 x 150-mm Cannon (Bofors) M.20*

Formerly known as the Topdalsfjord Fortress, Kristiansand Fortress was built at the end of the last century. Its key points were Fort Odderöya and Gleodden Point, whose battery covered the Skagerak. Little was done to modify Kristiansand Fortress between the wars, although plans had been prepared to shift the batteries away from the town. The Main Battery consisted of 210-mm guns supported by three batteries of 150-mm guns (East, Center and West Batteries). The shore battery consisted of 65-mm cannons and a howitzer battery for support. Machine guns constituted the only air defenses. Kristiansand Fortress consisted of:

Fort Odderöya	2 x 210-mm Cannon (St. Chamond) M.02

	6 x 150-mm Cannon (Armstrong) M.02
	4 x 240-mm Howitzer (St. Chamond) L/16
	4 x 65-mm Cannon (Cockerill)
Gleodden Battery	3 x 150-mm Cannon (Armstrong) M.97
	2 x 65-mm Cannon (Hotchkiss)

The Bergen Fortress consisted of an inner and an outer ring, which were authorized in 1895 to replace the obsolete existing fortifications. The main forts and batteries occupied the inner ring that was located close to the city. The outer ring consisted of battery positions that protected the minefield blocking the approaches to Bergen. In 1940, the batteries of the outer ring were turned into small forts. In addition to the weapons listed below, some of the Bergen forts received field pieces in 1939. Fort Kvarven was equipped with two 110-cm searchlights and Hellen with one. The forts of the outer ring had a 90-cm and a 110-cm searchlight apiece.[4]

Bergen Fortress
    Inner Ring

Fort Kvarven	3 x 210-mm Cannon (St. Chamond) M.98
	3 x 240-mm Howitzer (St. Chamond) L/13
	3 x 57-mm Cannon (Cockerill)
	2 x 75-mm AA Guns M-16[5]
	3 x 450-mm Torpedo Tube*
Fort Hellen	2 x 210-mm Cannon (St. Chamond)
Sandviksfjell Battery	2 x 240-mm Cannon (St. Chamond) L/13
Lower Sandviksfjell Battery	2 x 65-mm Cannon (Cockerill)

    Outer Ring

Fort Lerøy	2 x 65-mm Cannon (Cockerill)**
Fort Herdla	2 x 65-mm Cannon (Cockerill)
Fort Faerøy	2 x 65-mm Cannon (Cockerill)
Fort Håøy	4 x 57-mm Cannon (Cockerill)

*These were normal torpedo tubes, for launching a torpedo above water, unlike those at Oscarsborg, and they were in a casemate.

**Fort Lerøy was supposed to receive a 120-mm gun battery with four old L/40 Schneider weapons from the old border forts, but the war prevented its installation.

The defenses of Trondheim Fjord centered on the Agdenes Fortress. The condition of the weapons in these forts was reported to be deplorable in 1940.

Agdenes Fortress (entrance to Trondheim Fjord)

Fort Brettingen	2 x 210-mm Cannon (Armstrong) M.00
	3 x 150-mm Cannon (Armstrong) M.97
	2 x 65-mm Cannon (Hotchkiss)
Fort Hysnes	2 x 210-mm Cannon (Armstrong) M.97
	2 x 150-mm Cannon (Armstrong) M.97
	3 x 65-mm Cannon (Hotchkiss)
Fort Hambaara	2 x 150-mm Cannon (Armstrong) M.97

Work was underway on a pair of forts on the entrance to the fjord leading to Narvik, but neither was ready in 1940.

All the frontier forts built after 1905 included subterranean casernes and magazines linked to the combat positions by tunnels. Many of the weapons were put in open positions and had only gun shields for protection.

The two main Norwegian forts on the Glommas Line were armed with a variety of weapons. In 1923 forts Høytorp and Trøgstad received two single 120-mm howitzer turrets that mounted a modified Cockerill field piece.6 They were given two additional 75-mm Cockerill guns in one-gun turrets apiece between 1934 and 1935 to augment the firepower of their two older Schneider-Canet 120-mm turret guns. The four 120-mm single-gun turrets were transferred to forts Høytorp and Trøgstad from the four forts of the old Fredriksten Fortress after World War I. At Fort Høytorp there were also four old Schneider 120-mm fortress howitzers in gun pits, eight 84-mm field guns, and lighter weapons. German 75-mm Rheinische guns were added to this arsenal between the wars. Fort Trøgstad had two turrets with modified 120-mm Rheinische howitzers.

Both Fort Høytorp and Trøgstad had measured about 400 meters in length and 300 meters at the widest part. Their artillery was clustered in different sections of the forts. At Høytorp all four gun turrets were grouped in a citadel-like position on the northeast side, protected by infantry and machine gun positions and barbed wire obstacles. On the south side of the fort was the 84-mm gun battery, and just north was the 120-mm howitzer battery.

Fort Trøgstad stood about 8 km to the north of Fort Høytorp and was oriented east-west instead of north-south. Its two-turret 120-mm gun battery was located in a citadel-like position on its east end, while the two turrets for 75-mm guns occupied a similar position on the west side. Between these two batteries stood the battery of 84-mm guns. Several infantry works ran along the northern side of the fort. Like Fort Høytorp, Fort Trøgstad was also surrounded by a barbed wire barrier and a fence that extended 50 meters to 200 meters beyond that.

Further north, Fort Hegra guarded the border with a battery of two 75-mm Schneider Cannons and a battery of four 105-mm Schneider guns that were installed in 1910. The 105-mm guns came from the Fort Ørjekollen when it was destroyed earlier in the century. Like most of the Norwegian forts, this hilltop fort occupied a strong position but lacked turrets and was oriented towards border defense. The mountain fort of Verdal mounted one 75-mm gun and two 84-mm guns in caverns.

The frontier forts of Vardåsen and Gullbekkåsen served little purpose, especially when Sweden ceased to pose a threat. In 1939, their two 120-mm guns were relocated to Bergen to form a battery at Fort Lerøy.

3. Swedish Coastal Defenses and Fortress Boden

The Swedish defenses, which consisted of a mixture of old and new works, were the most modern of the Scandinavian nations. Some positions like those at Vaxholm, and at Göteborg, were equipped with old 150-mm gun armored turrets. Fort Vastra Hastholms at Karlskrona, and Byviksfortet at Oscar-Fredriksborg (near Vaxholm), mounted 120-mm cannons. The obsolete 240-mm guns on barbette mounts at Fort Oscar II and at Oscar-Fredriksborg were modified and moved to coastal positions in the southeast, where their poor range was sufficient.

After September 1939, the Swedish government authorized the improvement of the coastal defenses. The main effort centered around five major commands: on the west coast at Göteborg, the south coast at Helsingborg, the southeast at Karlskrona, the Stockholm area, the north coast at Henso, and on the island of Götland. Every year new positions that included casemates and turrets were put into operation. Between 1940 and 1945, many mobile 150-mm gun batteries with new Bofors weapons were added.

Each of the major commands set up so-called barrier positions that defended the entrances to major fjords and key coastal sites and included individual batteries and forts. Some of the forts comprised more than one battery, old torpedo-batteries, and the more widely used mine fields. The gun batteries ranged from heavy artillery, of usually 240-mm, to medium weapons such as 120-mm. Some batteries consisted of light 57-mm guns and anti-aircraft artillery of various calibers. The total number of all types of coast-defense batteries was twenty-four in 1937 and rose to forty in 1939 and ninety in 1942. In 1939, fifteen batteries consisted of heavy guns (210-mm and larger). This number rose to twenty-one between 1942 and the end of the war. The number of medium weapons (120-mm to 150-mm) rose from fifty-seven in 1939 to seventy-nine in 1942. These numbers show that Sweden was not as vulnerable as its neighbors were in 1940.

Between 1940 and 1942 some of the major Swedish coast defense positions were divided into divisions whose main unit was either a major battery position, a fort, or a Spärren or barrier position. The Spärren could contain one or more batteries. The major coast defense positions were distributed as follows:

Fortress Zone	Batteries				Minefields
	57-mm	80-mm	120-mm	150-mm	
Stockholm-Fort Vaxholm					
Spärren Singö	2			1	2
Spärren Söderarm	3	1	1	1 +(210)	1
Spärren Arholma	2	2			1
Spärren Korsö	3	1		2	1

Spärren Längbäling	6	4			2
Spärren Mellsten	10			1	2
Battery Järflotta				+(240)	
Spärren Askö	3			1	1
Spärren Ängsholmen	3		1	1	1
Spärren Siarö	2			2	1
Spärren Djurönäs	1		1		1
Karlskrona					
Spärren Längören	1		1		
Spärren Östra					
Hästholmen	2		1		
Spärren Kungsholmen*	3		1	4+(240)	1
Ellenabbsfortet	1				
Spärren Djupasund	1				
Spärren Bollösund	1				
Battery Öppenskar				+(210)	
Battery Aspöberg				+(305)	
Battery Ryssjön				+(305)	
Spärren Västra					
Hästholmen**	1		1		1
Spärren Ronneby	2				
Helsingborg					
Battery Ystad			1		
Battery Trelleborg				1	
Battery Helsingbog				1	
Battery Viken	1				
Göteborg-Fort Oscar II					
Spärren Alfsborg#	2			1+(240)	1
Spärren Galtö	2		1		
Spärren Donsö	1				1
Spärren Styrsö				1	
Battery Torslanda				+(240)	
Spärren Björkö	1			1	2
Spärren Marstrand	3				1
Spärren Lysekil			+(105)		
Henso					
Spärren Dalmo	2			2	1
Spärren Sanna	2		1		1
Gotland Island					
Spärren Trelge	1			1	1
Spärren Bungenäs	3			1	1
Hultungs Battery				+(210)	
Spärren Slite	1			1	1

*Includes Fort Kungsholms

** Includes Fort Hästholmsfort with both batteries in turrets.

#Included a turret battery of 150-mm and 57-mm guns, and a 240-mm gun battery at Fort Oscar II.

In some of the coastal defense positions the weapons were mounted on barbette carriages, but most were in casemates and turrets. Every year stronger positions were created.

The Per Albin Line was mostly in the Helsingborg command and it consisted of bunkers with two to four machine guns covering one to two flanks. They were designated Ksp I, II, III, or IV (Ksp for machine gun, and the Roman numeral for the building phase). Bunkers designated PV had 37-mm Bofors anti-tank guns. Most positions had an observation cloche. Because of heavy concentration of defenses in this line, some bunkers were only 165 meters apart.

On the island of Götland the Tingstäde Fortress was the main center of resistance. It was located north of Visby and consisted of six small forts built between 1911 and 1916 which formed a semicircle around the town with the lake on the open side. Only one of these was an artillery fort, and during World war II its four old 84-mm gun turrets remained in operation. The fort's garrison was 300 men. The remainder of the fortress was defended by open concrete machine gun positions.

Sweden did not dedicate as much effort to its land borders as to the coast except for the Boden area. Five major forts and about a dozen smaller medium and light works formed the fortress ring that had a circumference of about 25 kilometers.[7] Its garrison consisted of about 25,000 men, both regulars and reservists. The artillery men occupied the forts and the infantrymen the intervals, and sometimes, cave-like shelters outside the forts. The large forts, located on mountains from which they took their names, included:

-Fort Rödberget at 120 meters, south of Boden on the west side of the river.
-Fort Gammelängsberget at 126 meters, east of Boden.
-Fort Mjösjöberget at 115 meters, just north of Gammelängsberget.
-Åberget at 98 meters on the opposite side of the river from Rödberget.
-Degerberget at 171 meters to the north of Boden.

These forts, blasted into the granite mountains, had encircling moats of a depth of over 6 meters and a width of 9 to 12 meters. The forts had one main entrance located above the fossé and, in some cases, more than one emergency exit in addition to the exits in some of the caponiers that protected the moats. The subterranean works consisted of three to five levels and a main gallery in the middle. The only tunnels below the main gallery passed beneath the fossé to access the caponiers. The tunnels were cut into the granite and were not lined with concrete, but in the rooms of the forts the walls were cemented. The roof of the forts consisted of 10 to 15 meters of granite mountainside. The forts included subterranean magazines, a caserne, a usine (power room) and other facilities at different levels.

Other features included telegraph and power line links that were buried up to a meter beneath the surface. The usine's two diesel engines provided electrical power to the fort. The air intakes were in the moat or on top of the fort. The garrisons, of up to 700 men, had sufficient resources for two months. In some of the forts supplies were delivered by trucks that drove through the entrances. In others they were unloaded at the outside gate because the entrances were too small for trucks. During the construction years, only horses and wagons could reach the building sites.

Every fort at Boden had light and heavy artillery. The light weapons were 84-mm weapons and mortars. They were probably manufactured by Bofors. The forts also mounted 84-mm howitzers, but the number varied with Fort Rödberget having seven and others less. Fort Mjösjöberget had eight 84-mm caponier guns while most others had two. An 84-mm gun with water cooled machine guns (Model M/36) occupied a position in each fort's entrance. Fort Rödberget had seven mortar pits on its surface, but this number varied in other forts. The total number of light weapons may have varied between the World Wars.

Each of Boden's forts mounted eight single gun artillery turrets. Laborers hauled the large 10-ton gun turret into the forts in four pieces. The armor thickness varied between 60 and 90 cm. The forts of Rödberget and Mjösjöberget each included four 150-mm howitzers in turrets. The range of these weapons was only 10 km. The other three forts, Åberget, Degerberget and Gammelängsberget, each had four 120-mm guns in turrets. These guns, probably Bofors M/99 models, had a longer range of 18 km. The remaining four turrets each had carried an 84-mm gun.

The forts of Boden each had one, possibly two observation cloches which could direct the fort's artillery. A single fixed searchlight position was also created, but later this was replaced with a larger mobile searchlight for use in detecting aircraft.

One of the medium works was the Mount Svedje Battery, built in 1913 on the same mountain as Fort Gammeläling. It consisted of an eastern and western battery. In 1917, a crew of twenty-five men served the four field guns of the western battery. In 1940 the number of guns grew to six. The eastern battery consisted of two guns. Four more guns were mounted above it. This medium-size fort had no caserne for the garrison, but included a wood burning stove for cooking and heating. The troops slept in the long entrance corridor that held about thirty men. Two fällbersskansen or "sausages" at the northern and southern ends of the fort consisted of infantry positions with rifle embrasures that held 111 soldiers to defend the southeastern flank and support the eastern battery. "Sausages" like these were built along roads leading up to the forts and were on the outside shoulder of the road.[8]

WEAPONS AND EQUIPMENT

A variety of weapons were employed in Scandinavia. Denmark and Norway used many foreign models, especially British and German. Sweden, on the other hand, produced many excellent weapons of its own.

COAST DEFENSE AND FORT WEAPONS:

Norwegian and Danish	Range
305-mm Howitzer M/16 (Bofors)	20,000 meters
280-mm Cannon L/40 M/89 (Krupp)	20,900 meters
240-mm Howitzer L/13 (St. Chamond)	7,000 meters
240-mm Howitzer L/16 (St. Chamond)	9,000 meters
210-mm L/46 Cannon (St. Chamond)	16,000 meters
210-mm L/44 M/97, M/00 (Armstrong)	10,000 meters
170-mm Cannon L/40 (Krupp)	27,200 meters
150-mm Cannon M/97, M/99 (Armstrong)	12,000 meters
150-mm Cannon L.50 M/20 (Bofors)	19.000 meters
120-mm Cannon L/44 (Armstrong)	10,000 meters
120-mm Cannon M/99 (Armstrong)	10,000 meters
120-mm Turret Cannon (Schneider)	12,000 meters
120-mm Cannon (Cockerill)	17,500 meters
120-mm Howitzer (Cockerill)	6,300 meters
105-mm Cannon M/1901 (Schneider-Canet)	11,300 meters
105-Fortress Cannon (Schneider)	7,000 meters*
84-mm Gun (Bofors)	?
84-mm Field Gun (Krupp)	5,000 meters
75-mm Turret Cannon L/50 (Cockerill)	10,500 meters
75-mm Turret Cannon L/30 Schneider)	?
75-mm Gun (Rheinische)	
(German Feldkanone 246 (n) or 01(n)	
65-mm QF Cannon L/43 (Hotchkiss)	5,000 meters
57-mm Model 1891 (Finspong)	5,700 meters
57-mm QF Cannon L/62.6 (Cockerill)	5,400 meters

*For land forts. Data on Swedish weapons used at Boden not available at this time.

Norwegian Turrets			
120-mm gun	Diameter	2.83 meters	
	Armor	110-mm roof	240-mm walls

WORLD WAR II

When Germany struck in April 1940, Denmark was unable to resist. Its army and coastal batteries offered virtually no opposition against overwhelming odds. If the Germans had been challenged by the Danish coastal batteries, the occupation of the main islands would have been costly. However, a German troop ship sailed right past the forts of Copenhagen and landed its cargo of assault troops unchallenged.

Norway had made some preparations since the war began by 1940 while try-ing to maintain its neutrality, but last-ditch efforts were of little avail. The key for-tress of Oscarsborg held fewer than 300 men. The other four forts of the Oslo Fjord Fortress were hardly better prepared. At Kristiansand there were only about 400 men despite the preparations made in 1939. The 65-mm guns of the shore battery were not even manned when the invasion began. The situation at Bergen and Trondheim was equally precarious. Narvik's defenses were almost non-existent. The Germans easily entered the fjord only to be challenged by a pair of old coastal de-fense ships that were quickly dispatched. German troops landed at the entrance of the fjord and quickly took the forts of Ramnes and Havnes, reporting later that they consisted only of a few partially completed bunkers. German planners, who had hoped to use these forts to protect the fjord from an Allied attack, concluded that they could not implement their objective.

The story of the German invasion of Oslo Fjord is well known. The flotilla first encountered the little guard ship *Pol III*, then sailed through the fog, past the guns of Fort Bolaerne, until it was challenged late in the evening of April 8, 1940, by Fort Rauøy. Unharmed, the invaders sailed up the fjord until, shortly after 4:00 AM, they came within firing range of Fortress Oscarsborg. Despite the fact that there were not enough Norwegian gunners to fire and reload the three 280-mm guns of the Main Battery, the German cruiser Blücher was hit by the first shots of the Main Battery and then by the 150-mm guns of Kopås Battery. After taking two hits from 280-mm rounds, thirteen from 150-mm rounds, and thirty from 57-mm rounds, the German warship sailed beyond the reach of the guns only to be struck by two torpe-does from the ancient Torpedo Battery. About one hour after the first salvo of the battle, the *Blücher* went down. It was the first major success achieved by coastal guns during the war and probably the only one by a coastal torpedo battery.

The Norwegian gunners at Oscarsborg next directed their fire against the cruiser *Lützow*, scoring three hits with 150-mm rounds and knocking out its forward gun turret before the Germans withdrew. Later, German troops landed further down the fjord and took the Husvik and Kopås Batteries before forcing Oscarsborg to surrender on the next day. Meanwhile, in the afternoon of April 9, Fort Rauøy was captured and the Germans turned its guns on Fort Bolaerne. On April 4, the re-maining forts surrendered even though most took no part in the battle.

The story was repeated at Kristiansand, where, on the morning of April 9, a 150-mm round struck the German cruiser *Karlsruhe* as it led an invasion force to within 6,000 meters of its landing site. After a brief exchange of fire with Fort Odderöya, the Germans retired and waited for air support. About an hour later, at 6:00 AM, a second German attempt was rebuffed again. The cruiser finally with-drew beyond the range of the coastal guns and began bombarding the town but missed the fort. An air attack detonated a magazine at the fort, then a third attempt was made at 10:00 AM. The Germans finally succeeded thanks to an error in judgment. Believing that they were French ships, the Norwegians allowed the vessels to land at the harbor, realizing too late that they carried German soldiers. With no supporting infantry, the Norwegian garrison had to surrender. Errors and confusion had prevented the Gleodden Battery from firing.

At Bergen, German troops landed at the entrance to By Fjord at 4:30 AM to take out the batteries of Kvarven guarding the passage. The cruiser *Koenigsberg* led the German squadron. At 5:15 AM the Norwegians opened fire, hitting the cruiser three times and a supporting ship once, as they sailed past the battery. The Sandviksfjell Battery fired on the cruiser *Köln*, but the German cruisers and aircraft forced it to give up. The defenders of Bergen surrendered late in the morning, but not before another German cruiser was disabled. Less heavily protected seaports such as Arendal, Egersund, and Stavanger fell quickly.

At Trondheim a German task force, led by the cruiser *Hipper*, slipped past the searchlight batteries of the forts of Brettignes and Hysnes. The guns of Fort Hysnes opened fire on the accompanying German destroyers, forcing the cruiser to fire back as three destroyers landed troops to attack the batteries. The Trondheim forts remained under Norwegian control on April 9 despite the loss of the city.

As the German invasion force moved inland toward Oslo, the forts of the Fossum Fortress went into action. Forts Trøgstad and Høytorp, like most of the frontier forts, had either no garrison or only a caretaker force. Nonetheless, they fired their 120-mm gun turrets on the Germans between April 13 and 15. They were forced to surrender after they expended all their ammunition.

The little fort of Hegra, on the road to Sweden from Trondheim, distinguished itself when Major Reidar Holtermann organized a motley force of Norwegian volunteers that quickly grew from fifty to two hundred men. Holtermann prepared the 75-mm and 150-mm guns and the snow-covered positions of the fort for battle. Despite the fact that the fort's guns could not be aimed at the railway to Sweden, the fort continued to resist, even after the Germans had cleared it with an armored train. One German attack was repelled as the garrison prepared to fight in the galleries. The main assault came on April 23, but failed. On April 25, the Germans simply gave up the idea of taking the fort, which finally surrendered on May 5.

The Norwegians demonstrated that obsolescent coastal defenses and forts were still effective in modern war. Had they been properly defended and prepared, they would have exacted a far heavier price from the Germans.

Sweden's many coastal positions and land forts were better prepared than Denmark's and Norway's. Surprisingly, on April 9, 1940, the Per Albin Line was not even manned and many of its positions had not even received their armament yet. The Swedes soon reacted. Although the Germans prepared an invasion plan for Sweden, their associated naval operations were less ambitious than those undertaken in Norway. They only scheduled a couple of landings in lightly defended areas because they had learned their lesson in Norway, where they had already lost a number of vessels.

In February 1943, the German commanders in Norway were instructed to prepare plans for the occupation of Sweden in the event of an Allied landing. The first of the two main invasion routes considered was east of Oslo, into southern Sweden and Stockholm. The other line of advance was from Trondheim to the Gulf of Bothnia, to prevent the allies from making contact with southern Sweden, assuming an Allied invasion force advanced from Narvik to Kiruna.

The Germans, who thought that two successive lines of defenses faced southern Norway, along Lake Vänern, planned to bypass them by moving across the border, to the northeast of Oslo and down the Klarälven River. They also believed that there was a line between Lake Vänern, via Filipstad, to Ludvika, Falun, and the sea and a fortified zone around Stockholm as far West as Västeräs and Avesta, forming a semicircle about 200 kilometers long.

Thanks to its efforts to strengthen the coastal defenses and the army after April 1940, Sweden saved itself from invasion. During 1941 the Germans pressured the Swedish government to allow troop trains to carry German units from Norway to Finland through Sweden. The forts of the Boden fortress kept their guns trained upon the German trains to prevent the type of surprise-operation that had distinguished the Germans earlier in the war. As the war progressed the Germans committed themselves elsewhere, making it impossible to undertake a major campaign against the improved defenses of Sweden.

280-mm gun of main Battery of Oscarsborg Fort. (Svein W. Olsen)

Frontal view of 280-mm gun "Moses" of Main Battery of Oscarsborg Fort. (Svein W. Olsen)

210-mm Gun Emplacement at Ft. Kvarven, Bergen. The German 150-mm SK L/45 replaced it. Note observation position to its right. (Svein W. Olsen)

Ft. Kvarven, Bergen. Torpedo Battery, similar to others used in Norway and Yugoslavia. These were old positions from the last century in many cases. (Svein W. Olsen)

Map of Norway, Sweden, Finland

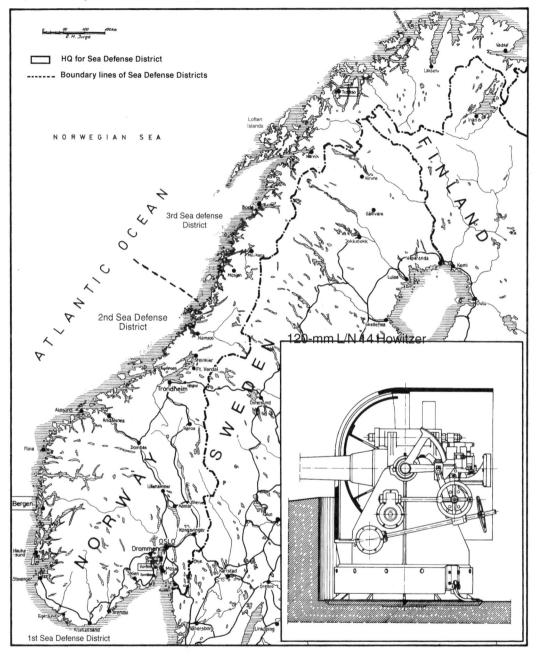

Example of fort at Boden.

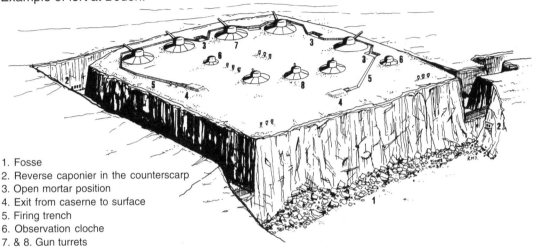

1. Fosse
2. Reverse caponier in the counterscarp
3. Open mortar position
4. Exit from caserne to surface
5. Firing trench
6. Observation cloche
7. & 8. Gun turrets

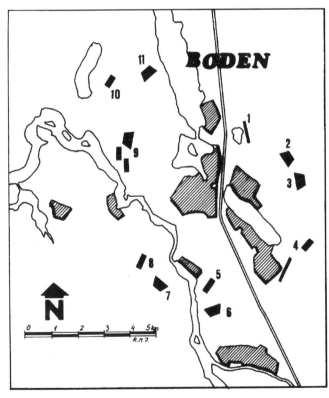

1. Defensive position Ovre Avan (Storvan)
2. Ft. Mjosjoberget
3. Ft. Gammelangsberget
4. Battery Fallberget
5. Battery Nord Aberget
6. Ft. Sud Aberget
7. Ft. Rodberget
8. Battery Slumpberget
9. Fort and batteries Pglaberget
10. Battery Leakersberget
11. Ft. Degerberget.

Right hand Page:
Fort Hoytorp.
Built 1910 and renovated 1930.
1. Guard room
2. Underground magazines
3. Latrines
4. Searchlight (40-cm) emplacement,
5. Heavy MG bunker
6. Wall with embrasures for rifles
7. Schneider turret with 120-mm gun
8. Cockeril turret with 75-mm guns
9. Open battery for 120-mm Schneider howitzers
10. Open battery for 8 x 84-mm Krupp guns,
11. Searchlight (75-cm) emplacement
12. Gas operated searchlight (60-cm) emplacement
13. Anti-infantry obstacles (barbed wire)
14. Underground corridor system

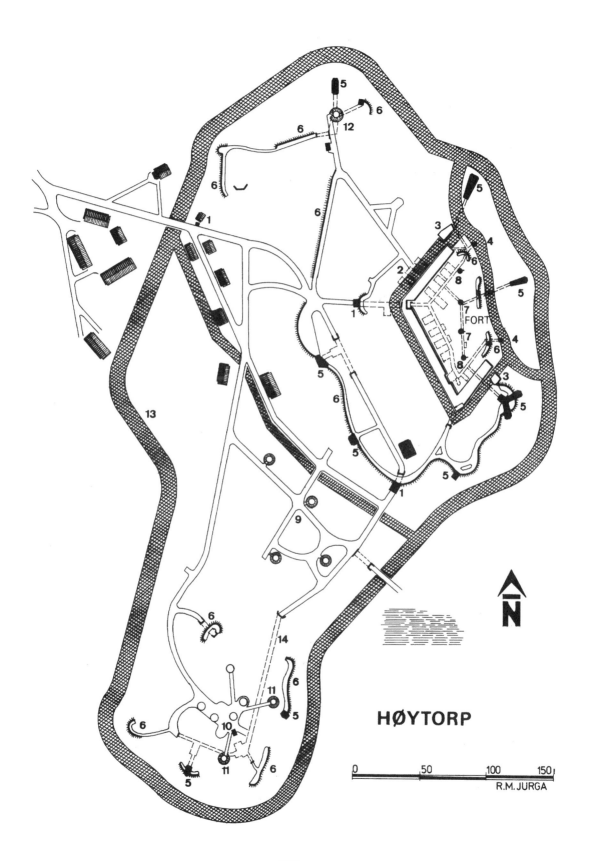

HØYTORP

0   50   100   150

R.M. JURGA

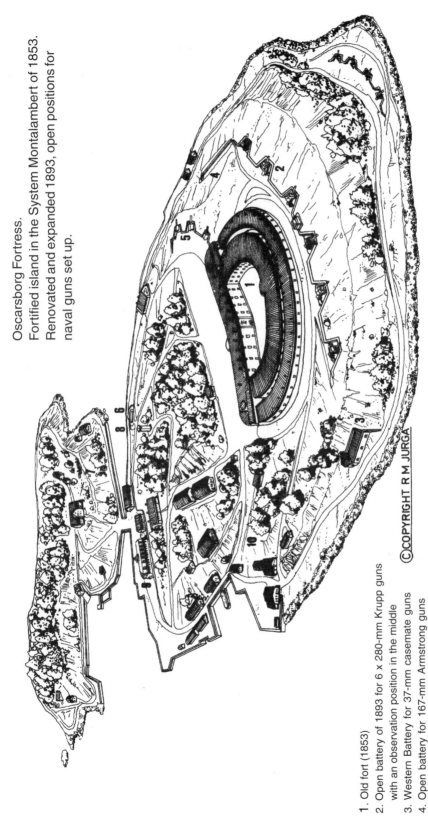

Oscarsborg Fortress.
Fortified island in the System Montalambert of 1853.
Renovated and expanded 1893, open positions for naval guns set up.

©COPYRIGHT R M JURGA

1. Old fort (1853)
2. Open battery of 1893 for 6 x 280-mm Krupp guns
   with an observation position in the middle
3. Western Battery for 37-mm casemate guns
4. Open battery for 167-mm Armstrong guns
5. Eastern Battery, for 3 x 267-mm Armstrong guns
6. Earthen redoubt
7. Two gun battery
8. Tower guard room
9. Barracks & military school
10. Barracks for gunners

Denmark

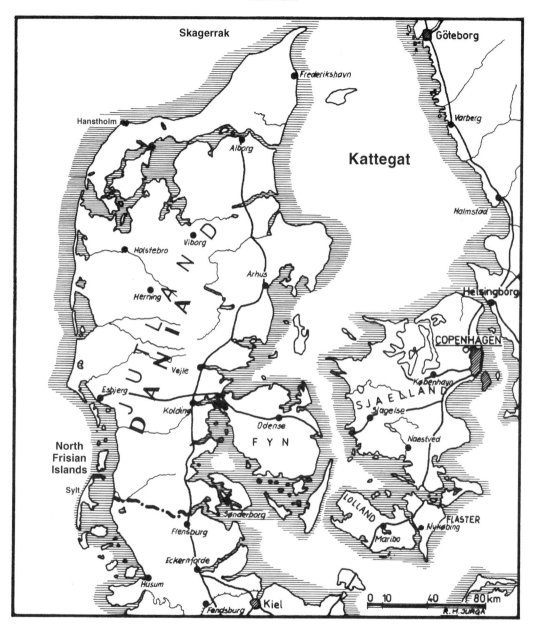

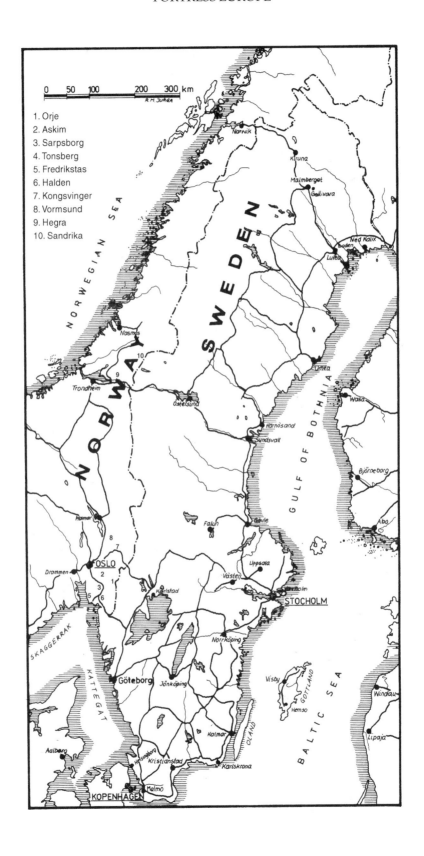

Chapter 9

CZECHOSLOVAKIA

BACKGROUND

Czechoslovakia's history as an independent nation began after World War I. During the nineteenth century its key components, Bohemia, Moravia and Slovakia, had been under the control of different empires. Bohemia, once called the "Cockpit of Europe" by Otto von Bismarck, had formed part of the Austro-Hungarian Empire. It had no modern fortress rings but many older fortifications dating from the Renaissance and earlier because other Austrian territories had shielded it in the last century.

When it gained its independence, Czechoslovakia found itself faced with hostile neighbors. Indeed, Germany and Austria felt that too much of their territory had been taken to create this new nation. Furthermore, in 1919 Czechoslovakia incurred the enmity of Poland when it seized its territory of Teschen (Cieszyn) at a time when the Poles were engaged in a life or death struggle with Soviet Russia. Finally, on the southern border, the Hungarians were trying to reclaim some Slovak territory, which, they felt, were rightfully theirs.

To hold its enemies at bay, in the 1920s Czechoslovakia formed a rather tenuous alliance, known as the Little Entente, with Yugoslavia and Rumania with the tacit support of France. This move succeeded in holding only Hungary at bay but failed to impress Germany, Austria, and Poland. By the 1930s, after the rise of Hitler, the Czechs, realizing that the mountainous border region was no longer sufficient to shield them from the two German states, decided that it was critical to create a defensive barrier.

The length of the Czech border made the creation of a continuous fortified barrier difficult. It consisted of approximately 1,100 km on the German side, 400 km on the Austrian, and 600 km with Hungary. The 200 km long Rumanian border did not necessitate defenses and the 700 km Polish border was easily defended for most of its length by the Carpathian Mountains. Thus the Czechs were faced with a Herculean task, especially with the onset of the Great Depression.

MAJOR FORTIFICATIONS

The Czech Maginot Line or Benes Line
The Slovak Defenses

LOCATION

The Germans gave these fortifications the name of Benes Line, but the Czechs referred to them as their own Maginot Line. Since heavy fortifications covered only a small stretch of this position, in the present work the term "Benes Line" will refer to the whole defensive system of Czechoslovakia, while the term "Czech Maginot Line" will refer to the defenses between Ostrava and Nachod.[1] To the west of Nachod lighter defensive works ran along the border, formed a semicircle around Pilzen, and continued eastward along the border to Bratislava.

The mountains running east from the Elbe River near Dresden, Germany, to Ostrava, commonly known as the Sudeten Mountains, consist of various ranges that include, from west to east, the Luzické Hory, Jizerské Hory, Krkonose, Orlické Hory, and Nizky Jeseník. The heaviest Czech fortifications were built on both sides of the Orlické Hory that extend from the vicinity of Nachod to Králiky. Some of the major positions were built from west of Nachod to the vicinity of Trutnov. The large defensive works actually began in the Krkonose, or Giant Mountains, known to the Germans as the Riesengebirge. A second, higher range of the Krkonose that began near Trutnov reached elevations of up to 1,600 meters along the German Silesian border, creating a formidable obstacle that required fewer defenses. There were few fortifications in the Nizky Jeseník range that rose to an altitude of about 700 meters to the east of the Krkonose. The more rugged Hruby Jeseník that ran north and parallel to the Nizky Jeseník, and reached elevations up to 1,400 meters, were lightly fortified. More heavily fortified works began where the Hruby Jeseník range ended, to the west of Opava, and continued to the vicinity of Ostrava, covering the Oder Gap.

There were only scattered light defenses in the western part of the Sudeten, in the Jizerské Hory and Luzické Hory. However, more continuous lines of light fortifications covered all the mountain passes to the west of the Elbe, where the Krusné

Hory or Ore Mountains (Erzgebirge in Germany) formed much of the border, particularly at the Bohemian Gate, a gorge created by the Elbe River where it enters Germany.

The western border with Germany, equally mountainous, was lightly fortified because the Cesky Les, or Bohemian Forest, created another formidable barrier. These lighter fortifications occupied the east side of a river valley that ran along part of the southwest border and the higher sections of the Bohemian Forest. The Sumava range formed part of the southwestern border with Germany and part of the Austrian border. Although not as high as the highest point in the Krkonose, the Sumava had larger expanses of territory at elevations above 1,500 meters. The Eisentein Pass, one of the few access points to the region, was easily defended.

A continuous line of light fortifications began at the point where the mountain barrier opened on the border with Austria, to the southwest of Brno on the Moravian border, and extended to Bratislava. Almost half of the southern Moravian border with Austria, known as the Moravian Gateway, was covered by heavier fortifications. However, there were no large forts like those found on the northern border. At Bratislava, in Slovakia, some heavy fortifications were built.

The southern border of Slovakia and Ruthenia opened into Hungarian territory, and was crossed by the primary trade routes that lead back to Hungary or west toward Moravia. Between Bratislava and Kosice this was mostly covered by light fortifications that defended the economic heart of Slovakia, which was vulnerable from the south. Scattered light defenses also covered some sectors near Uzhorod because this part of Ruthenia was also exposed to Hungary. On the other hand, the northern sections of Slovakia and Ruthenia were well protected from Poland by the great barrier of the Carpathian Mountains.

The economic heart of the country, which lay between Pilzen and Prague, was protected by a first line of light defenses that ran from north to south, to the west of Pilzen, and a second, similar line to the west of Prague. A pair of light defensive lines were planned to cover the hilly terrain of western Moravia in the Moravian Heights. A final line was to be built from a point west of Ostrava, through the foothills of the Carpathians, to the Austrian border in eastern Moravia. The terrain of the western half of Czechoslovakia was ideal for successive fortified lines and allowed the army to operate on interior lines.

HISTORY

The Little Entente offered the Czechs no security against German aggression in the 1930s, a fact that became apparent at the end of the 1920s, when the French army appeared to take a purely defensive posture. Foreign Minister Benes had already alerted his fellow Czechs that they must act, but his warnings went un-heeded until Hitler's war machine began to expand. By the time the Czechs took action, time was running out. Since their attempt to improve their relations with Poland, Hungary, and Austria met little success, they turned towards the Soviet Union in early 1935. However, this association proved to be just as problematical as the one with France because there was no direct land link between Czechoslo-vakia and the Soviet Union. Thus, realizing that they were virtually isolated, the Czechs finally decided to fortify their borders.

Thus in 1934, the Czechs sent a military mission to study the first completed sections of the Maginot Line. The French, on the other hand, sent General Belhague, one of the designers of the Maginot Line, to assist the Czechs with the construction of their heavy defenses. Other French military advisers soon followed. As a result of this technical support, the Czech forts and heavy casemates show a strong French influence.

General Ludvik Krejcí, the Czech chief of staff, prepared a ten-year plan that set the completion date of the fortifications for 1946. In the 1930s, General Jan Syrovy, his superior and the equivalent of commander-in-chief of the army, received the credit for conceiving the Czech Maginot Line. The planning stage took most of 1935 and the first work began in 1936, at the time the Germans reoccupied the Rhineland. Unlike the French, who focussed on fortifications, the Czechs also strove to mod-ernize their air and tank forces, expending their resources to acquire adequate num-bers of aircraft and tanks.

As they began the construction of the fortification, the Czechs established a better security system than the Belgians or the French because they refrained from using foreign construction companies or laborers from Germany. Their greatest se-curity problem was the Sudeten Germans, who inhabited the regions where most of the fortifications were to go up.

Because time was critical, the Czech military leaders decided that the heavi-est fortifications would be built from Trutnov to Ostrava to prevent a German army in Silesia from splitting the country in two. Successive defense lines from the western border to the foothills of the Carpathians would allow continued resis-tance if the enemy breached the outer defenses. The heavy defense line of the north, and the smaller one in the south, on the Moravian Gateway, would secure the flanks.

In 1936 the Type 36 light bunker was designed and it soon occupied the most forward defense line. This type of bunker was small, rather weak, and gave frontal fire but it was economical and easy to build. However, it could serve no more im-portant purpose than the French avant-poste. The larger Type 37 light bunkers fol-lowed, occupying the main defensive line. In most cases Type 37 bunkers formed one or two lines behind the line of heavy casemates.

The real Czech "Maginot Line," stretching from Trutnov to Ostrava, included a series of Maginot-like forts. Unfortunately, none were finished by the fall of 1938, although several were near completion, awaiting only their artillery weapons and turrets that had not yet been delivered from the factories. Work on other forts, which the Czech called "tvrz" or fortress had barely begun.[2] Thus the line was far from being fully operational.

Fort Dobrosov illustrates the trials and tribulations the Czechs had to face during the construction of their fortifications. The position was surveyed in April 1937 and building began in September 1937. Its estimated completion date was the fall of 1940. The construction proceeded smoothly and the labor force was increased from almost 500 to about 1,000 workers one year later. However, by the time of the 1938 Munich Conference, only three blocks of the original plan, which called for an entrance block and six combat blocks, neared completion. Two of these blocks were infantry blocks and the third was an artillery casemate that had no cannons yet. The subterranean galleries that should have spanned 1,750 meters and included additional underground facilities, were only roughly hewn and only partially completed. During the Munich Crisis only one infantry block was occupied by a garrison of twenty-five men. At that time five other forts begun earlier were still a year from completion. The Czech army, nonetheless, readied them for combat, despite the absence of artillery.

The annexation of Austria to Germany in March 1938 spurred the Czechs to build large defensive works in the south. These were not actually tvrzí, but rather medium and heavy individual casemate positions for infantry and artillery. Again, not all were completed by the fall of 1938. The final defense lines that were to stretch across Moravia from north to south never passed the planning stage by 1938. Yet, despite their small number, the completed Czech fortifications were an asset to be reckoned with since they had the advantage of easily defended terrain and the support of a relatively modern army.

The protection of the Czech borders was entrusted to Border Infantry Regiments and Border Defense Battalions in 1935. At the end of 1936, special higher commands were created to lead these troops. Late in 1936, when the Czechs maintained an army of merely 100,000 men, the government approved the creation of forty-two fortress battalions with a combined strength almost equal to the standing army's.

Eight Border Sector Commands, each of division strength, were deployed on the Bohemian and Moravian frontier and four on the Slovakian border. Each command included a fortress regiment and several border-defense battalions. Similar sized commands, known as Defensive Groups, manned the interior defenses, including those of Prague and Pilzen. These specialized formations were considered elite units like the Czech artillery and tank troops and the French fortress troops. Neither ethnic Germans nor political extremists were allowed to serve in these units.

The line of heavy fortifications in the region of Zamberk was occupied by two army corps: the II Corps and the IV Corps. The IV Corps covered all the positions between Zamberk and Ostrava and fell under the command of the Second Army. The II Corps guarded the area extending west, past Trutnov, and was under the First Army. Instead of using Fortified Sectors like the French, the Czechs established Engineer Group Commands or ZSVs that were subdivided into the equivalent of sub-sectors. Thus ZSV III comprised eight sub-sectors.

SECTOR (AND PREFIX)	TVRZÍ
IV Corps	
Border Defense Command 37	
ZSV II Moravaská Ostrava (MO)	Orel, Smolkov
Border Defense Command 36	
ZSV IV Opava (OP)	Sibenice, Vrch, Orlik
ZSV I Staré Mesto (STM)	Kronfelzov
II Corps	
Border Defense Command 35	
ZSV III Králiky (K)	Hurka, Bouda, Adam
ZSV X Rokytnice (R)	Bartosovice, Hanicka
ZSV V Nachod (N)	Skutina, Dobrosov
Border Defense Command 34	
ZSV VI Trutnov (T)	Jirova Hora, Poustka, Babí

DESCRIPTION

There is no denying a strong French influence on the Czech school of fortification. Indeed, many of the Czech structures are strongly reminiscent of the French "New Front" fortifications, especially the smaller ouvrages and the single mixed-entrance blocks.

First of all, the organization of the fortified fronts was strikingly similar to the Maginot Line's. Thus the heavy Czech fortifications that began west of Trutnov and ended near Ostrava spanned a distance of almost 200 km and included fifteen artillery tvrzí. This defensive line was obviously similar in length to the Maginot Line and had a similar number of artillery tvrzí only slightly smaller. In addition, as in the Maginot Line, the Czech artillery tvrzí were supported by interval casemates, heavy bunkers the Czechs called forts, which were quite similar to the French. However, a few of these interval casemates were more heavily armed than their French equivalents and were used as a substitute for the French petits ouvrages.

Most of the tvrzí were located in the II Corps area, which included the Orlické Hory and the Krkonose, where several forts were built on both sides of the ranges.

The forts in this area, clustered about 5 to 10 km apart, close enough to support each other as adequately as the French Maginot ouvrages. In addition, the forts of the Krkonose were positioned close enough to the border for their artillery to cover the approaches on the enemy side.

On the other hand, in the IV Corps area—between Zamberk and Ostrava—most of the tvrzí were more than 10 km apart, which did not allow for adequate mutual protection. Furthermore, few of the artillery pieces were able to reach the other side of the border.

The design of the Czech tvrzí also owed much to the French school even though there were significant differences between the two schools. For instance, the average Czech tvrz included six combat blocks instead of seven, had a single entrance block instead of two, and accommodated a garrison of about 525 men instead of 625 men. However, like the French, the Czechs designed three types of combat blocks for infantry, artillery, or observation. As in the Maginot Line, the tvrzí included one or more cloches per block, no more than one turret per block, and three guns per artillery casemate. However, the Czechs departed from the French model when they substituted the French 75-mm weapons with their own longer-range 100-mm guns mounted in twin gun turrets and three 105-mm howitzers in gun casemates.[3] In addition, the Czechs designed a special non-retracting turret for 120-mm mortars to take the place of the French 81-mm mortars. The machine gun turret was non-retracting, but, like the mortar turret, it had a low profile to reduce its vulnerability. Furthermore, having apparently learned from the French experience, the Czechs used a modified and improved cloche. They also used light weapons of Czech manufacture, similar to the French, in their casemates.

The Czech tvrzí from east to west were as follows:

TVRZÍ (GERMAN NAME)	BLOCKS
Orel	1 100-Tur, 1 120-Tur, 2 Obs, 1 Inf Cas
Smolkov (Harbiner Berg)	1 100-Tur, 1 105-Cas, 1 Obs, 1 AO
Sibenice (Galgenberg)	1 100-Tur, 2 105-Cas, 1 120-Tur, 3 Inf Cas, 2 Iso Inf Cas
Vrch	1 100-Tur, 1 120-Tur, 1 Obs, 1 Inf Cas
Orlík	1 100-Tur, 1 105-Cas, 1 MG Tur/Inf Cas
Kronfelzov	1 100-Tur, 1 105-Cas, 1 120-Tur, 3 Inf Cas
Hurka (Berghöhe)	1 100-Tur, 1 105-Cas, 1 MG Tur/Inf Cas, 1 Inf Cas, Iso AO
Bouda (Baudenkoppe)	100-Tur, 1 Obs, 2 Inf Cas
Adam (Adamsberg)	1 100-Tur, 2 105-Cas, 1 120-Tur, 1 MG Tur/Inf Cas, 2 Inf Cas, 3 Iso Inf Cas
Bartosovice	Plans for 4 blocks and entrance not completed
Hanicka (Herrenfeld)	1 100-Tur, 2 105-Cas, 3 Inf Cas, 1 Iso AO, 2 Iso Inf Cas
Skutina	1 100-Tur, 1 105-Cas, 1 120-Tur, 2 Inf Cas
Dobrosov	1 100-Tur, 2 105-Cas, 1 120-Tur, 2 Inf Cas
Jírová Hora	1 100-Tur, 2 105-Cas, 1 120-Tur, 4 Inf Cas
Poustka	1 100-Tur, 2 105-Cas, 1 120-Tur, 1 MG Tur/Inf Cas, 4 Inf Cas
Babí (Trautenbach)	2 100-Tur, 2 105-Cas, 2 120 tur, 1 MG Tur/Inf Cas, 3 Inf Cas, 1 Iso AO, 4 Iso Inf Cas

NOTES: AO=Artillery Observation, Obs=Observation and/or GFM cloches, Cas=Casemate, Tur=Turret, / = combination, Inf=Infantry, Iso=isolated positions, MG=Machine Gun, 120=120-mm Mortar, 105=100-mm Howitzer, 100=100-mm Gun.

The design of each of the above tvrzí included a single entrance block that was several hundred meters behind the combat blocks. Some casemate combat blocks had entrances similar to those of the French, which may only have been intended for exits.

The largest tvrz planned was Babí, the last on the western end of the line of heavy fortifications. Babí was designed with two 100-mm gun turret blocks and two 120-mm mortar turret blocks instead of the regulation one per fort and two 105-mm casemate blocks instead of the standard two. With ten combat and one entrance blocks, it was intended to be by far the largest of the Czech tvrzí. To the east of Babí, the neighboring forts of Poustka and Jírová Hora were the next largest with eight and nine combat blocks respectively. They had the same amount of artillery, except for the fact that Poustka/Jírová Hora had one less 100-mm gun turret block.

Reluctant to depend on any other country, the Czechs decided to themselves produce all the key components of their tvrzí such as weapons and armored parts. This decision caused delays because some of the artillery pieces had to be designed and tested before they could be produced in larger numbers. As a result, the 100-mm weapons were not ready for production until 1938.

The casemates were to be armed with 100-mm howitzers. Since the Czech turrets and armored cloches were not identical to the French, they had to be perfected and tested before they could enter the production lines. The cloches were the first major armored elements to be manufactured and installed. There were various types of cloches: observation cloches, light weapons cloches, and heavy machine gun cloches. The first cloches were installed in various tvrzí in 1938.

The Czechs needed more time to produce their artillery turrets but they ran out of it when the Munich Crisis took place. As it is, only the blueprints for artillery turrets remain. These turrets were to be powered electrically, requiring only a few seconds to move into the correct firing position. However, they could also be operated manually, but in this case their movement would require over a minute and a half. The steel walls and roofs were 175-mm to 450-mm thick for all turret types. The mortar turret was the most unusual because only its heavy roof was exposed to the surface and its pair of breech loaded mortars were mounted on a circular rotating piece in the middle of the roof.

The Czech classification system included six types of concrete protection. The first two types, identified by the Arabic Numerals 1 and 2, were found mainly in interval positions, the last four, identified by Roman Numerals I through IV, were used on heavier works. The Roman Numeral series was similar to the French, its heaviest type—Type IV—being 3.5 meters of reinforced concrete and designed to resist 420-mm rounds. The main difference between the French and the Czech concrete lay in the method of mixing and pouring. The Czech method apparently yielded a greater resistance than the French, but less than the German.

The Czech artillery casemate was quite similar to the French, and, as in the Maginot Line, each was modified to suit the terrain. Its armament consisted of three howitzers with a 45 degree field of fire each, a light machine gun position that covered the fossé, and, usually, two cloches. Adjacent to each gun room was an M-3 magazine. An emergency exit, located either on the upper or lower level, opened into the fossé and was defended by an interior blockhouse position. The subterranean gallery was accessed by two lifts and a stairway. The lower level included a rest area, called "ready room" by the Germans, storage rooms, filters, and a WC. At the lower level, under the gun positions, there were gas-proof chambers for expended shell casings that were conveyed there through a funnel behind the guns. The artillery casemates were served by approximately eighty-five men.

The Czech artillery turret block was also similar to the French. Below the turret and its forward armor were two levels. Here too the spent shell casings were ejected into a funnel and slid down a toboggan to a shell room in the subterranean gallery. The upper level included a munitions magazine, an M-3, and a control room. Below was the counterweight, filter room, and rest area. A stairway and lift gave access to the subterranean gallery. The artillery turret block required a garrison of about sixty men.

The mortar turret blocks were similar, but the turret did not need additional rooms at the lower level for controls and equipment. Below the turret was the first level that comprised the M-3 magazines and a rest area. The lower level included the filter rooms, WC, and storage areas. The mortar turret block was served by about forty men.

The infantry block varied in size and shape and included firing rooms for heavy and light machine guns and one or more anti-tank guns. In many tvrzí there was one infantry block with a turret for twin machine guns. Since the turret did not retract, it had a less complex mechanism that required less space. Normally, the infantry blocks consisted of two levels, like the other blocks. A fossé protected the space in front of the firing crenels. Some infantry blocks only had cloches for observation and/or machine guns. Isolated positions that were not linked to the tvrz by subterranean tunnels had their own usine.

The entrance blocks usually included a truck and troop entrance similar to a Maginot mixed entrance and came in three types. Babi, Poustka, Jírova Hora, Skutina, Adam, and Smolkov had level approaches. The tvrzí of Dobrosov, Bouda, and Hurka had inclined entrances to give sufficient depth for the main subterranean gallery. Finally, Hanicka, Sibenice, and Orel had the least desirable type of entrance that gave access to the main gallery by elevator. No information is available on the plans for the three remaining forts. Almost directly behind the heavy entrance gate was an armored portcullis that rose from the floor. At the point where the corridor leading from the main entrance to the interior curved, there was a second armored door covered by an interior crenel. This arrangement made it impossible for an artillery piece to fire directly at the armored door from the outside. The area between the two armored doors also served as a gas decontamination area. The garrison of the entrance block was housed on the level below the entrance. Normally the entrance was protected by one or two cloches located above it that allowed for all around defense.

The underground facilities were slightly different from the French. Whereas the French tended to place the caserne by the entrances along with the usine, M-1 magazine, and storage facilities, the Czechs put the caserne in a central location among the combat blocks, leaving the other facilities by the entrance. However, the distance between the entrance and combat areas in the Czech tvrzí was generally not as great as in the Maginot ouvrages, which might account for the difference. In addition, the Czech M-2 magazines also supplied the artillery blocks. In the M-1 magazine, the large cells opened directly onto the main gallery. Unlike the French, the Czechs created larger positions in their main gallery for placing explosives. Finally, like most French ouvrages, the Czech tvrzí had a secret emergency exit consisting of a shaft filled with earth and sand that could be cleared by dumping the fill in an adjacent chamber.

In addition to the nine tvrzí on its northern flank, the ZSV XI was also to have received a line of nine independent artillery blocks on its southern flank. Although none of these artillery blocks were actually laid down, the plans show that these positions would have been one-block forts designed as a combination artillery casemate and entrance block.

The entrance would have looked like most standard entrances with an anti-tank gun and a light machine gun position. The artillery position would have been similar to most artillery casemates with three guns firing to the flank, and a light machine gun position covering the fossé and exposed face of the casemate. The entrance and artillery position were to be fused together and two cloches would have provided all-around protection. Besides the standard two levels, the independent artillery blocks would have included a third level with about half the area of one of the other levels, and situated beneath the entrance.

The blueprints show an entrance side that measured about 20 meters across and presented only about 10 meters of exposed façade. The exposed section of the artillery side measured about 20 meters in length. The thickness of the reinforced concrete walls and roof is not known, but it is estimated as at least Type III.

Five special independent 120-mm mortar turret block positions similar to those of the tvrzí were planned for the support of the nine independent artillery blocks. Apparently no blueprints were drawn for these positions, but like most separate artillery positions, they would probably have required a usine, a filter room, and magazines.

The interval positions between the tvrzí were just as important in Czechoslovakia as in France. However, unlike the French positions, some of the Czech casemates included heavy weapons such as 90-mm mortars. The majority of interval positions were armed with the standard array of machine guns and one or two anti-tank guns. Most of the interval casemates consisted of two levels and included a usine, a filter room, and one to three cloches. Compared to the French, their designs were less standard.

The interval positions, be they casemates for the 90-mm mortars or casemates with a machine gun turret, were classified as heavy works and in many cases were similar to the blocks of the tvrzí. However, to avoid confusion, they will be referred to as interval casemates in the present work. They usually consisted of two levels and included most of the features of the standard infantry block of an tvrz: a usine, a filter room, munitions storage, crews quarters, and food storage. Most comprised one to three cloches and firing positions for anti-tank guns and/or heavy machine guns and lighter weapons. They also had the protective fossé in front of the main firing chambers and a gas decontamination area between the armored doors of the entrances. The casemates were connected to each other by underground telephone and telegraph cables. About 250 of these casemates were built and more were being planned. Over a third had Protection II which means that the roof was 2.0 meters thick, and the thickest wall (facing forward) was 2.25 meters thick. They could withstand a hit by a 280-mm round. Most of the other positions had Protection III and IV that could resist a 305-mm and 420-mm round respectively.

The lighter fortifications included two basic types of bunkers: Model 36 and Model 37. Found in all the defense lines, the simple Model 36 bunker usually occupied the forward positions along the border. It had no armored embrasures, no facilities for the crew, and no observation equipment. There were six variations on the basic model: types, A through F, but apparently only types A, B, C, and E were actually built. All fired forward and were exposed to the enemy's direct fire. At best, they could withstand 75-mm rounds since their walls and roof were usually less than .60 meters thick. The crew of one of these bunkers consisted of two to six men armed with a heavy or light machine gun, depending on the bunker type. Over 850 of these bunkers were completed by 1937.

The Model 37 light bunker was more important than Model 36. It was intended mainly for flanking fires and came in five basic types:

Type A—one embrasure firing to each flank or obliquely to partially cover forward area
or rear area depending on the model. Walls and roofs varying from .60 to 1.0 meter
in thickness (the first being able to resist 75-mm rounds and the last 105-mm rounds).*

Type B–one embrasure covering a flank and the other firing forward. Walls and roof varying
from .6 to 1.2 meters in thickness (the first being able to resist 155-mm rounds).
Type C–single embrasure for frontal fire. Walls and roof .5 meters thick.
Type D–single embrasure for flanking fire, built in pairs to cover each other and obstacles
between them. Walls and roof varying from .6 to 1.2 meters in thickness.
Type E–single embrasure for firing forward or obliquely. Walls and roof varying from .6 to
1.0 meter in thickness.
*They came in standard and reinforced types.

Model 37 was not very large, but had more facilities for the crew. It was designed for light and heavy machine guns, and included equipment for observation, such as sights and periscopes, and defensive features such as armored doors and embrasures.

An attempt was made to create an almost continuous line of anti-tank and anti-infantry obstacles that included the now famous steel hedgehog. The concrete hedgehog was used extensively, but, though economical, it was not as formidable as the steel version. The hedgehogs were usually emplaced in two to three rows. Steel rails embedded in concrete were also used in many cases with a line of steel hedgehogs. Usually wire was strung up between rows of steel rails and other obstacles and sometimes covered entire obstacles. In some places sizable anti-tank ditches with a concrete wall were built. Every tvrz and its component blocks and other positions as well were at least surrounded by wire obstacles. The main line of defense, consisting of casemates and tvrzí, included an almost continuous line of barbed wire anti-infantry barriers interrupted by roads barred by anti-tank obstacles.

Near the border most roads were blocked by concrete barriers built to form chicanes. In addition, preparations were made to block roads and close forest paths.

WEAPONS AND EQUIPMENT

Armament of the Czech Ouvrages		Maximum Range (meters)
100-mm Howitzer	(turret)	11,190
	(casemate)	11,190
120-mm Mortar (Mine Thrower)		7,500
47-mm Anti-Tank gun		5,880
50-mm Mortar		800
7.92-mm Heavy Machine Gun		3,200
7.92-mm Light Machine Gun (Bren Gun)		3,200
Other weapons used in fortifications		
76.5-mm Cannon		12,500
90-mm Mortar		4,500
Turrets	Diameter (meters)	Roof Thickness (mm)
Gun	4.0	400
Machine Gun	2.89	300

Mortar	2.50 (exposed area including forward armor rotating section about 1.16)	400
Cloches		
Infantry Type N	1.3	150-300
(Light machine gun and 50-mm mortar)		
Type D	1.3	200-300
(Heavy machine gun)		
Artillery Type P	1.3	200-300
(Artillery periscope)		
Cupolas (had no roof periscope like other Czech cloches)		
Type D	1.3	200-300
(Heavy machine gun)		
Type M	1.5	200-300
(Twin machine guns)		

The Czech protection classification system had two more categories than the French system. Most categories were identical to the French, but a comparison indicates that the Czech concrete was stronger.

Protection	Concrete Thickness	Resists weapons of
1	1.20 meters	155-mm
2	1.75 meters*	180-mm
I	1.75 meters	210-mm
II	2.25 meters	280-mm
III	2.75 meters	305-mm
IV	3.50 meters	420-mm

*Although the thickest wall is similar to that of Type I, other features were not.

WORLD WAR II

The incomplete Czech defenses were never tested in combat. Smolkov, Hurka, Bouda, Adam, and Hanicka, begun in 1936, were almost operational by 1938. The only work that remained to be done was the outfitting the combat blocks and the completion of the installation of the interior equipment. Although some cloches were actually installed, no turrets or artillery pieces had yet been delivered. At Orel, Skutina, Dobrosov, and Babí work began only in 1937 and at Sibenice, in early 1938. Thus none of these forts approached completion in the fall of 1938. However, in some of these tvrzí one or more blocks were ready for use. Construction had not even begun on the remaining tvrzí.

Bouda, one of the smallest tvrzí, was one of the few ready before Munich. It received all of its cloches and weapons by early August 1938, with the exception of the 100-mm gun turret. Smolkov, also minus its artillery, was the only tvrz completed in the area where the Germans planned one of their major assaults on the Czech flanks.

At mobilization the Czech First Army was deployed in the critical northern sectors, seven of its divisions in Northern Bohemia and four divisions of the Second Army in Northern Moravia. Most of the Benes Line fell under the command of these two armies, the Czech Maginot Line being under the Second Army. The southern sectors, under the command of the Fourth Army, were defended by a mechanized division, a motorized division, and six infantry divisions. Many of its heavy infantry casemates were still incomplete and independent artillery blocks remained unbuilt. The Third Army in Slovakia had two divisions and the partially completed defenses on the Hungarian border. A special strategic reserve of three mechanized divisions, a motorized division, and an infantry division was deployed mainly in Slovakia.

Given the type of terrain the Czechs had to defend and the size of the German army in the fall of 1938, they had a good chance of putting up an effective resistance. Despite their incomplete state, the existing fortifications could have presented a formidable barrier to the enemy. However, during the Munich Crisis of the fall of 1938, President Benes was informed by his military leaders that the country could not resist longer than three weeks without support from its allies. Thus Czechoslovakia surrendered its border regions, the Sudetenland, to Germany, leaving only the incomplete tvrz of Dobrosov in Czech hands. Early in 1939 the remainder of the country was occupied by the Germans.

German reports on the potential of the Czech defenses were contradictory. Some claimed that the fortifications were much stronger than expected, while others asserted that they would not have presented a serious problem. As it is, the question of the effectiveness of the multi-national Czech army and the Czech defenses is moot.

The Germans proceeded to use some of the Czech bunkers and tvrzí for testing their weapons' powers of penetration. They most certainly studied the design of the tvrzí, comparing it to the data they already had about the French Maginot Line. In the next few years the Germans stripped almost every heavy infantry casemate and tvrz block of its cloche, hauling off their loot for use in German defenses elsewhere. Many of the famous steel Czech hedgehogs also found their way to the Atlantic Wall. Early in 1945 the Germans used the heavy infantry casemates in the Opava-Ostrava area rather effectively against the Soviets. However, the war simply passed by most of the other Czech fortifications.

Tvrz Bouda. S-22a "Krok" - Entrance. 1 light and 1 heavy MG and two cloches (removed by Germans). Note similarity to French mixed entrance, and the protective fossé. (Karol Vasat)

Tvrz Dobrosov. N-S75 "Zeleny" - Artillery Block. One of the few blocks completed at this fort. 3 x 100-mm guns (never mounted) and 2 cloches. The exit is in the fossé near the second pole from the rear. The embrasure in the front of the picture covers the fossé. (Kaufmann)

Right: Tvrz Dobrosov. A section of the only partially completed galleries of the fort. (Kaufmann)

Below: Tvrz Babí. T-S73 - Infantry Block. Unusually large infantry positions with 4 cloches and two flanking firing chambers. The two flanking casemate positions can be seen. Each mounting a 47-mm gun. The four humps on the roof were positions for the cloche. Little else was completed at Babí. (Kaufmann)

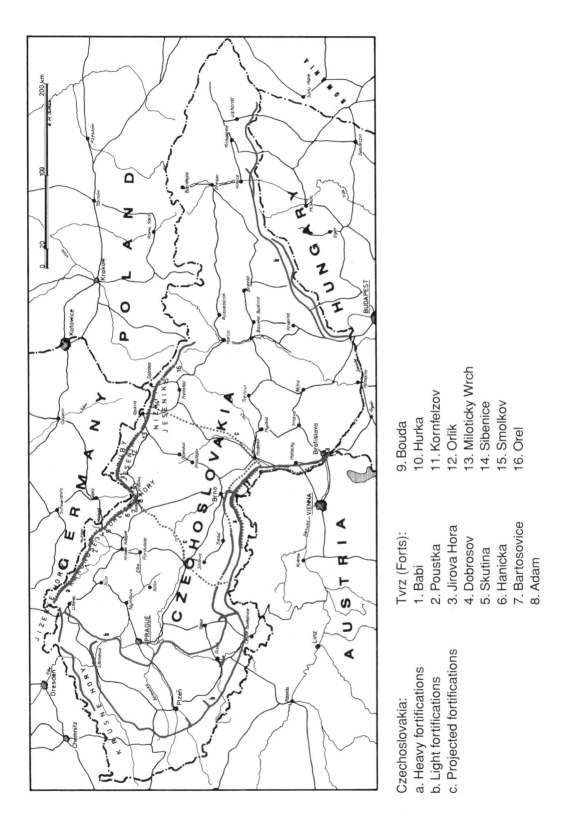

Czechoslovakia:

a. Heavy fortifications
b. Light fortifications
c. Projected fortifications

Tvrz (Forts):

1. Babi
2. Poustka
3. Jirova Hora
4. Dobrosov
5. Skutina
6. Hanicka
7. Bartosovice
8. Adam
9. Bouda
10. Hurka
11. Kornfelzov
12. Orlik
13. Miloticky Wrch
14. Sibenice
15. Smolkov
16. Orel

Czech Trvz Kornfelzov.
Block STM 14 for 2 x 100-mm howitzers in a turret.

1. F3V Turret for 2 x 100-mm Howtz
2. Ready Ammo
3. Magazine
4. Food stores and water tank
5. MG Cloche
6. Stores
7. Pantry
8. Bathroom
9. Toilet
10. Storage for spare parts
    of ventilation system
11. Ventilation system and
    filter room.

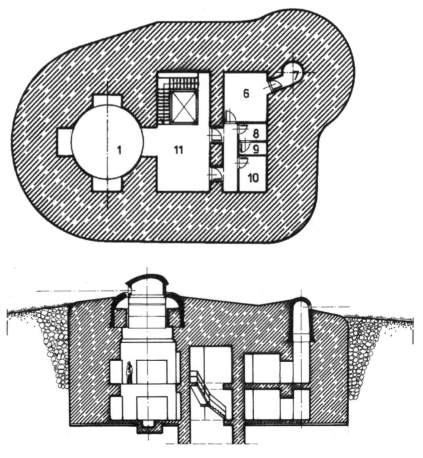

R.M. JURGA

Cross Section of block

Czech Trvz Kronfelzov.
Block STM 45, artillery casemate for 3 x 100-mm howitzers.

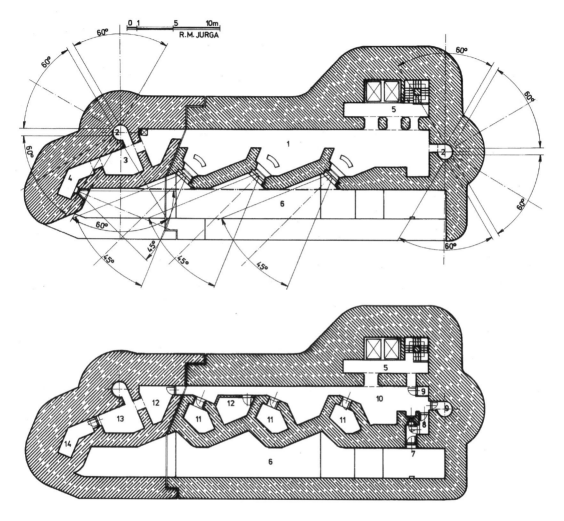

1. Firing positions for 3 x 100-mm fortress howitzers
2. Cloche for light MG
3. Water reservoir
4. Flanking light MG crenel
5. Elevators and stairs
6. Diamond fosse

7. Protected Exit
8. Gas Lock
9. WC
10, Corridor
11. Storage chamber for spent shells
12,13,14. Magazines

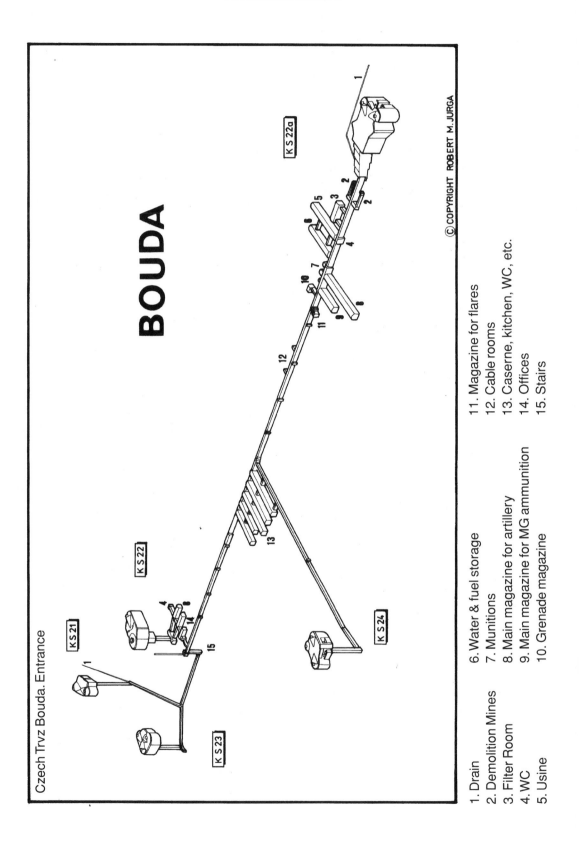

Czech Trvz Bouda. Entrance

BOUDA

1. Drain
2. Demolition Mines
3. Filter Room
4. WC
5. Usine

6. Water & fuel storage
7. Munitions
8. Main magazine for artillery
9. Main magazine for MG ammunition
10. Grenade magazine

11. Magazine for flares
12. Cable rooms
13. Caserne, kitchen, WC, etc.
14. Offices
15. Stairs

© COPYRIGHT ROBERT M. JURGA

Type 37 Czech Bunker.

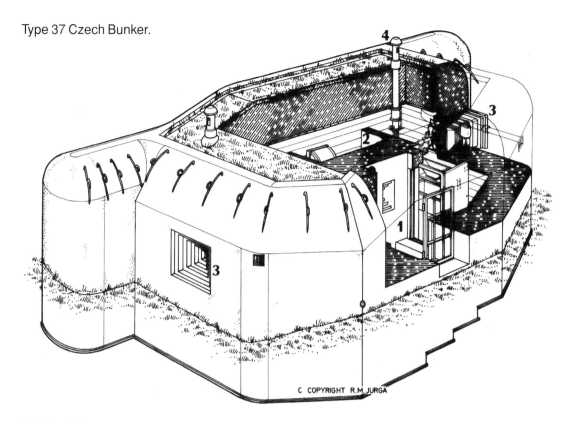

1. Defended entrance
2. Interior with hand ventilator
3. Heavy MG emplacement on fortress mounting behind armor plate
4. Periscope

Czech Casemate of Brezinka.

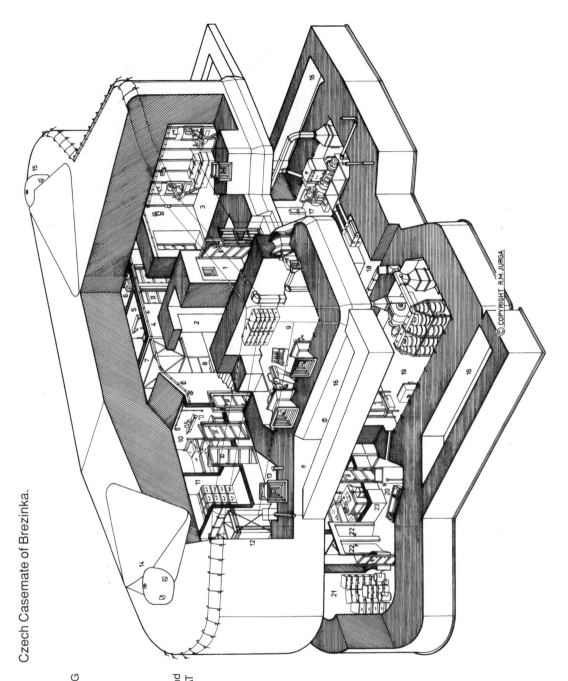

1. Defended entrance
2. Guard room
3. Firing room for 2 heavy MG
   and 1 light MG behind
   armor plate
4. Corridor
5. CO's room
6. Commo center
7. Water tank
8. Stairs
9. Firing room for 1 heavy and
   1 light MG and a 37-mm AT
   gun and MG combination
10. Crew's quarters
11. Magazine for AT shells
12. Magazine for MG ammo
13. Position for light MG in
    corridor
14. Cloche for heavy MG
15. Cloche for light MG
16. Diamond fosse
17. Usine
18. Store room
19. Filter room & ventilators
20. Wash room
21. Magazine for grenades
    and flares
22. WC
23. Crew's quarters.

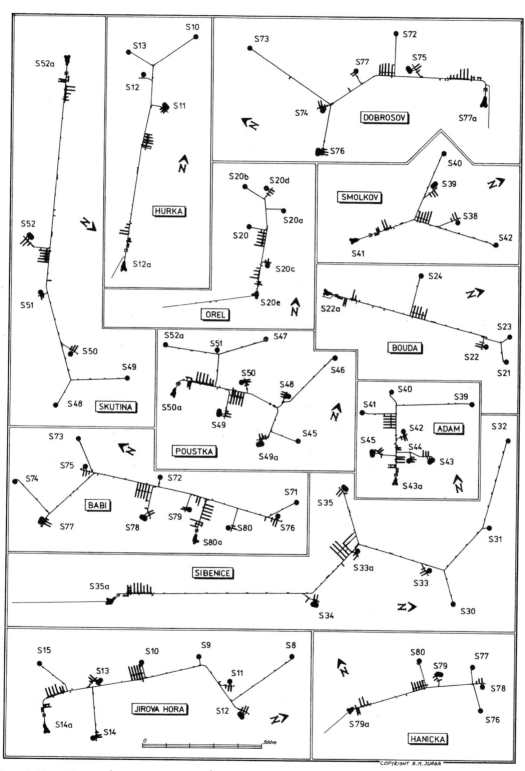

Czech Trvz Plans

Chapter 10

POLAND

BACKGROUND

After the eighteenth century partitions dismembered and obliterated the Polish state, a new Poland was formed in 1919 and inherited numerous German, Austrian, and Russian ring defenses built after 1870. The Germans had fortified Thorn, Poznan and Grudziadz, the Austrians Krakow and Przemysl, and the Russians Grodno, Warsaw, Modlin, and Brest-Litvosk. Some of these fortifications were still equipped with their original armament.

Due to its geographical position, Poland has been involved in many of the conflicts that have plagued Europe throughout the centuries, and its strategic and political doctrines have been determined by its neighbors, Russia and Germany among others. Between the world wars, Poland was sandwiched between Europe's most powerful Fascist and Communist nations. Its large plains seemed to be inviting invasion.

Since the war of independence had sapped its resources, Poland needed time to catch up with its neighbors both economically and militarily. Yet time was a luxury it did not have. The Polish government and the General Staff expected Germany to seek territorial acquisitions to compensate for its losses after the Great War. They knew that the Germans would not be content with the terms of the Treaty of Versailles concerning their eastern border, and that the Treaty of Locarno did not settle the question. The Polish leadership anticipated a demand for the annexation of territory to link East Prussia to the rest of Germany, and a general revision of the border line. In addition, it found the aspirations of the Soviet Union equally disquieting.

Poland tried to insure its security by signing a peace treaty with the Soviet Union on July 25, 1932, and another with Germany on January 26, 1934. In addition, it entered into mutual-aid agreements with France and England. However, Poland was fully conscious of the fact that these treaties were not a guarantee of its territorial integrity and that it needed to make military plans as well. Fully realizing that battling on two fronts simultaneously was a losing proposition but a very real possibility, Marshal Józef Pilsudski sought a viable answer to the Polish dilemma. The solution he came upon was to adopt the French defensive doctrine. However, the French solution was too expensive for Poland's slim resource. There simply were not enough funds to raise a wall of concrete and steel on the borders, so the Polish fortifications were a considerably more modest version of the Maginot Line.

MAJOR FORTIFICATIONS

Eastern Border
Western Border
Coast Defenses

LOCATION

The terrain of Poland's eastern frontier area extended from the rugged glaciated region adjacent to East Prussia to the great Pripet Marshes east of Brest-Litvosk. The marshes, interlaced with many water courses, were difficult to traverse for a modern army and divided the eastern part of Poland into two regions. Between these regions lay the Polish plains that gave the country its name, heavily forested in many places. In the northeast stood Vilno, a city contested with the Lithuanians, and in the southeast, Lwów (Lemberg), the only major city in the area and the nearby Polish oil fields. Also in the southeast, to the south of Lwów, began the foothills of the Carpathian Mountains. The Bug, which ran in a northerly direction, flowed at 150 km to 200 km from the border, constituting the only significant river barrier in the area. From a point near Lwów to Brest-Litvosk, it formed a large swampy flood plain before it turned to the northwest. The area to the east of the Bug was the most lightly populated region of Poland, except for the Lwów region. The watercourses flowing out of the Carpathians to join the Dniestr River, meet it on a very broad, swampy, flood plain that provided the security for Lwów to the south. The tributaries on both sides of the Dniestr also barred the approaches from that direction.

The southern border encompassed the Carpathians that extended into Slovakia, forming parallel ranges that presented a formidable obstacle to an aggressor from either direction. The old fortresses of Przemysl, Jaroslaw, and Krakow were strategically located in defensible positions to block an invasion coming out of Slovakia.

North of Warsaw and east towards Grodno, the Polish Plain merged with the morainic regions of East Prussia. The area was heavily forested with numerous lakes and marshes. The Narew River, a tributary of the Bug, also created a marshy flood plain that paralleled the East Prussian border. The Polish Plain, itself a product of glaciation, covered most of the country. Broken by few hills, it consisted mostly of low and level to rolling terrain with many open and wooded areas. It was ideal terrain for army maneuvers. The Vistula, sometimes called "Poland's Mississippi," presented a large, formidable obstacle. It is navigable from the San, one of its tributaries in the south, to its mouth. It was subject to flooding after heavy rains in the Carpathians, and when it overflowed onto its flood plain, it became one of the country's greatest defensive assets. Some fortress cities like Warsaw and Modlin sat on a high terrace overlooking the river, safe from inundation.

On the western frontier of Poland there were fewer natural defenses. Krakow in the southwest corner and the Carpathians and their foothills in the south created a strong barrier. Just to the west and northwest lay Black Silesia, Poland's industrial heart, that relied on the small hills in the area for defense. The Warta River, which flowed north to Poznan, did not form a major barrier even though its valley was marshy. Most of the border area facing Germany consisted of open plain with few obstacles beyond the moraines of Pomerania that constituted part of the Polish Corridor.

The most important element in Poland's favor was the lack of modern roads. Winter snows and heavy summer rains easily turned the old roads and the surrounding fields into a quagmire. This could be a serious advantage for an army that still depended heavily on the horse against a mechanized enemy. Unfortunately, Nature did not favor Poland in September of 1939.

HISTORY

After several visits to the French fortifications, the Polish military engineers returned to Poland full of new ideas and soon formulated new projects. As a result, the Polish fortifications exhibit a strong French influence. The first concrete fortifications in the new Poland went up between 1924 and 1925 on the Vilna Defensive Position. On July 29, 1929, the first tests on bunker resistance capacities were carried out at the testing grounds of Modlin.

The defensive preparations on the border with the Soviet Union began in 1926, when the General Inspectorate of the Armed Forces was established. The first plan of operations, formulated in 1928, comprised blueprints for a defensive line to protect eastern Poland. The mission of this line was to buy time for the field army to mobilize by defending the lines of communications, and by making the most of the surrounding terrain.

In 1934, Poland, which still considered the Soviet Union its greatest peril, concentrated all its attention on the eastern border. Nonetheless, the border with Germany was not neglected. Work began there in 1933, but only the Silesian border received heavy fortifications. Military planning changed as relations with Germany deteriorated during the second half of January 1939. The major building effort was then transferred from the eastern to the western front. Unfortunately, time ran out before the army could fully implement its plans.

In 1938, when Poland took advantage of Hitler's takeover of Czechoslovakia to occupy Zaolz, its military engineers came across the Czech fortifications. The Poles not only inventoried these defenses but, like the Germans in their "Protectorate," they used artillery pieces to test as many as 231 bunkers.

Operation "Direction West" (Kierunek Zachód) was formulated between 1928 and 1935 under the leadership of Marshal Józef Pilsuldski and the Chief of the Polish General Staff, Brigadier-General Janusz Gasiorowski. The latter saw to the installation, among other things, of a series of concrete company-size strong points equipped with heavy arms and artillery along the main communication lines leading to the heart of Poland. The mission of these strong points was to hold the enemy until the arrival of his heavy artillery. This delay would buy time for the army to prepare behind the lines. Edward Rydz-Smigly, heir to Pilsudski's policy and appointed as Marshal of Poland on November 10, 1936, was forced to juggle his limited resources between the eastern and western border and simultaneously attempt to modernize the army.

In February of 1939, when German aggression became increasingly likely, Marshall Rydz-Smigly advised Brigadier-General Waclaw Stachiewicz, Chief of the General Staff of the Polish Army, to implement plan "Direction West." The implementation was hastily carried out to meet the realities of the moment. The first line of defense was established, and the units were assigned to specific armies and commands. On March 3, 1939, the commanders of the armies received a portion of their instructions dealing specifically with their own sectors. They proceeded to plan the defensive lines with a deadline for the completion of the preliminary work set for May 31, 1939.

As a result of the shift in focus through the 1930s, the Polish defensive lines acquired a fragmented character, failing to become a continuous line of fortifications. The onset of the war on September 1, 1939, terminated the building effort.

DESCRIPTION

The schron was the basic building block of the Polish defenses and came in various types. One of the most common types of schron was the one-room machine gun shelter or bunker.[1] Its configuration was determined by its mission. The entrance of these small blockhouses was protected by a wall about a meter long or more. On the interior walls there were niches for a hand-operated fan, a coal-burning stove, and a supply of ammunition.

Another very common type of schron was a casemate that mounted machine guns firing to a flank. The weapons embrasures of these small casemates occupied side walls protected by concrete orillons (ears or wings). Some had one embrasure covering one flank and others an embrasure for each flank. The section facing the enemy was covered with earth and the entrances were similar to those of the block-houses. Due to their small size, these positions had no elaborate facilities. However, their low profiles were not easy targets for artillery fire. Some included an armored cloche for a machine gun that fired across the forefield. This cloche was more vulnerable to artillery than the remaining elements of the position, and for this reason it was separated from the rest of the bunker by an armored gas-proof hatch.

The basic combat position of the fortifications on the western borders was a schron with a machine gun embrasure on one or both flanks that sometimes included a cloche. An earlier, larger, structure included garages for a 37-mm anti-tank gun (Mle 1897), from which the gun was moved to a field position. In a few places there were anti-tank casemates that mounted this type of weapon in an armored embrasure that covered the flank.

After 1937, plans were made to build many positions consisting of armored casemates for 37-mm guns (Mle 37) mounted on an overhead rail. The large defensive positions such as the OWS (Fortified Region of Silesia), Wegierska Góra (Hungarian Hill), and Jastarnia, consisted of fifteen to twenty casemates that housed several types of weapons. They also included schrony with armored plates for heavy machine guns of the Browning 1930 type, similar embrasures for light machine guns, a grenade launcher, and a cloche or half cloche for combat and observation. The crew quarters were not comfortable and had no latrines or other facilities. The bunkers were linked by telephone lines. The larger ones were also outfitted with special horizontally placed steel pipes for light signals in case telephone communications were cut.

Schrony for anti-tank guns and field guns began to appear in 1939. Most served as flanking casemates and were larger than the other schrony. They were designed to shelter both 37-mm anti-tank guns and 75-mm field guns and were to include observation cloches, few of which were actually installed. By the time the war started, many positions were only partially finished.

Sector command bunkers, intended to shelter the command post of a sector, included an observation cloche with an artillery periscope, and a cupola that was separated from the rest of the shelter by a gas-proof hatch. These command bunkers included communication equipment and special tubes for light signals.

In addition to these positions, some of the older works such as the forts of Modlin were restored. New schrony were added at Modlin to extend the defenses of the position. The armament of the Modlin forts included a variety of weapons, some in revolving cupolas and others in open emplacements or casemates.

Various anti-tank and anti-infantry obstacles were used, including rows of steel rails, barbed wire, obstacles to close off roads, local demolitions, and devices for flooding wherever practical.

1. The Eastern Border

The fortifications on the eastern border rested on the Wilia, Niemen, Prepec, Stycz, Styr, Narew, Serwecz, Szczara, and Prut rivers. There were six sectors: Wilno (Vilna), Lida, Baranowicze, Polesie, Wolyn, and Podole. The main Soviet thrusts were expected to come from Belrus in the direction of Warsaw, Baranowicze, and Bialystok and from the Ukraine towards Wolyn. The largest fortifications were built in the Polesie Sector, which was considered to be the most important. It was the longest sector, covered the most difficult terrain, and lacked roads. The fortified line incorporated the water courses where a system of dams and weirs were created to impede the enemy's progress. Only 800 of the planned 1,400 water obstacles were actually built.

The fortifications projected in 1936 for the Polesie Sector were not completed. They were to have included six 75-mm guns and eight mortars and numerous heavy and light machine guns east of Chelm. Only four schrony were nearly completed, lacking only their interior fittings because the original plans had to be modified to meet the limitations imposed by a tight budget. Each schron consisted of two blocks, A and B ,and a linking tunnel, a rarity in Poland. The two blocks lay at different levels on the terrain. Only three tunnel systems were completed, including the one to the mortar casemate. Most of the blocks consisted of two to three levels, had D or E strength, and mounted a cloche. The largest schron was for four mortars, had C strength, and accommodated a crew of 26 men. All the positions had a complete set of facilities but no usine. Mines were to be added to the usual array of anti-tank obstacles. When the war began, these blocks were still incomplete and remained unoccupied.

The fortified sector of Baranowicze was supposed to receive positions with a revolving turret for a 37-mm or a 75-mm anti-tank gun. However, the armored elements were not yet mounted when the army suspended work on this sector in 1939.

2. The Western Border

Much of the work on the western border was done late in the 1930s except on the largest sector of permanent fortifications known as the Fortified Region of Silesia (*Obszar Warowny Slask* or OWS). It was built between 1933 and 1939 along a wide semi-circle encompassing Chorzów, Katowice, and Milków. The mission of the OWS was to secure the Central Industrial Region, the industrial heart of Poland located in Upper Silesia. This fortified region stretched for over 60 km and included 160 positions.

Since Upper Silesia was a highly industrialized area, most of the positions were located in urban settings. The line consisted of the defensive points (*punkty oporu* or PO) of Bobrowniki, Lagiewniki, Dabrowka, Godula, Nowy Bytom, Szyb Artura, Radoszow. The POs of Niezdara-Tapkowice and Kotulowiec were still in the planning stage by the time the war broke out. In 1939 new field fortifications for anti-tank guns were built to strengthen the OWS line. Their armament consisted of anti-tank guns.

In addition to the various types of blockhouses and casemates, the OWS included independent blockhouses or samodzielne schrony bojowe whose weapons covered all directions. It also comprised heavy flanking gun casemates or *ciezkie schrony tradytoryjne* armed with 75-mm guns to defend the area between POs and all roads in the environs. There were two of these gun casemates at Bobrowniki, Hill 305, that mounted two 75-mm field guns in individual gun rooms. The guns were placed on a rotating platform that allowed them to fire from two different directions. These casemates had complete facilities including a usine, filters, rest area, munitions room, and an observation cloche. Other schrony that housed the command post, machine guns, 37-mm (model 37) guns, and observation, supported the position.

Seven other positions and another fortified region, primarily made up of the coastal defenses, guarded the border with Germany. The Wizna Position, located near the confluence of the rivers Biebrza and Narwa, near the town of Wizna, faced the expected direction of attack from East Prussia. Built in 1939, it was a strong fortified position 9 km in length, whose framework was made up of eleven schrony armed with heavy machine guns, 75-mm guns, and cloches.

The Golancz Position was to rest on the lakes just to the north of Poznan. Originally in the region of Wagrowiec, Golancz was to consist of twenty schrony. In a note dated August 11, 1939, General Tadeusz Kutrzeba revised that number to twenty five. However, by September 1, 1939, only fifteen were actually built: nine casemates for a heavy machine gun (CKM) with frontal fire, three with a flanking CKM, two with CKMs covering each flank. All these structures had resistance Strength B.

The Prosna River Line in the region of Kalisz lay to the southeast of Poznan. The original plans called for twelve schrony but later changes raised this number to thirty-three. However, only nineteen were actually built: one for observation, five for CKM with frontal fire, eight for a CKM firing to a flank, and five with CKMs firing from embrasures on both flanks.

The Pszczyna Line, intended to support the OWS Line in the defense of Upper Silesia, was to extend from Czestochowa, through the Silesian defensive region of the Tarnów Mountains, to Chrzanów and Katowice. This line was to incorporate the Pszczyna, Bielsko Biala, Zywiec, and Rabka positions. Fifty-six schrony were originally planned for the area of Pszczyna. The building effort in the Pzsczyna Line was concentrated in the center of the area of operations of the Krakow Army. Fifty-six schrony were originally planned for the area of Pszczyna, on the terrain assigned to the 6th Infantry Division. However, when the order came to strengthen the areas of Rybnik and Zar, this number was dropped to twenty-four. By the time the war broke out, only fourteen schrony were actually built from a distance of 6 km from Pszczyna, to the forest north of it. Only initial excavations were done in the area south of Pszczyna in the direction of the village of Goczalkowice.

The remaining positions covered the northern front with Germany. In the Polish Corridor, which fell under the command of the Pomorze Army, preparations were made to cover an attack from two directions: from East Prussia towards Torun and Wloclawek and from West Pomerania towards Gdansk and Bydgoszcz. The defense plans for the Pomorze Army included the construction of a fortified line supported by field positions in the Bydgoszcz Bridgehead. In the region under the jurisdiction of the 9th Infantry Division, near the town of Koronów, the Koronów Lake Position was supposed to rest on the lakes in the area. Only thirteen schrony of the thirty originally planned were completed by September 1, 1939. Two of these had not yet been covered with the protective layer of earth. Fifteen more schrony were in various stages of construction, most only in the initial stage.

The Modlin Army defended the Mlawa Position, the regions of Lidzbark Welski, Mlawa, Krzynowloga Mala, and the main line that rested on the Vistula and Narew rivers. It was assigned the task of slowing down the enemy advancing from Eastern Prussia toward Warsaw, Nidzica, and Modlin. A defensive line was planned for the vicinity of Mlawa which was occupied by the 20th Infantry Division, and blocked the most direct approach from East Prussia to Warsaw. Of the ninety-three schrony— mostly casemates—projected for the Mlawa Line, only forty neared completion or were finished when the war broke out. Others were in the early stages of construction.

3. The Coast Defenses

The small Polish coastline fell under the jurisdiction of the Fortified Region of Hel. The focus of interest in this area was the Hel Peninsula, which defended the seaport and naval base of Gdynia, Poland's "window on the world." Between 1933 and 1935, Second Lieutenant Heliodor Laskowski directed the construction of a four-gun coastal battery armed with long-range 152.4 mm Bofors guns. In addition, there were three two-gun batteries mounting 75-mm guns on barbette mounts including munition magazines, casernes, storage rooms, and so on. Four large shelters for torpedoes and artillery munition were also built to meet the needs of the navy. Another battery, similar to Laskowski's, and a battery for 320-mm guns, were also planned, but funds ran out before these guns could be acquired.

The Military Transit Depot at Westerplatte, in Danzig (Gdansk) was guarded by five concrete blockhouses that served as sentry posts and had 0.30 meter thick walls. Three machine guns were mounted on the roof.

In 1939 the peninsula was blockaded from inland with the defensive strong point of "Jastarnia." Plans for this position called for seven *objetkty*, bunkers or casemates, in three successive lines. However, there was only enough time to complete three large and one small casemate, and pour the foundations of the remaining three.

These positions were characteristic of the Polish school of fortification. They were rather small, well integrated into the terrain, tied to each other with a carefully planned field of fire, and supported by field fortifications. Gun emplacements giving flanking interlocking fires were also characteristic of this school. Earth covered the front walls of the casemates for camouflage and protection. Frontal defense was assured mainly by heavy machine guns placed in cloches embedded in the roofs. Each casemate was to mount one or two cloches that, unfortunately, were not completed in time for the war. The schrony built next to the railroad also held 37-mm anti-tank guns.

WEAPONS AND EQUIPMENT

RESISTANCE STRENGTH

Schron Type	Resistance Type	Resists (mm)	Concrete thickness (meters):		
			Roof	Exterior	Interior
Reinforced Concrete	A	75 to 105	.80	1.00	.40
	B	105 to 155	1.00	1.20	.40
Concrete	A	75 to 105	1.10	1.40	.55
	B	105 to 155	1.40	1.70	.55

WEAPONS USED IN OR TO SUPPORT FORTIFICATIONS:

	Range in meters	
152-mm Model 1930 Bofors	26,600	Coast Artillery
120-mm Model 78/09/31 Schneider	12,400	Support at Modlin

75-mm Model 1897 Schneider	11,200	
75-mm Model 02/29	10,700	Fortress artillery platoons
37-mm Model 36 and 37 Bofors	7,100	Mounted in Bunkers

HEAVY MACHINE GUNS
7.92 Model 30 Browning 1917 water-cooled MG
7.92 Model 14 Hotchkiss
7.92 Model 08 Maxim

WORLD WAR II

The German battleship *Schleswig-Holstein* fired the first salvo of the war by opening fire on the Military Transit Depot at Westerplatte in Danzig (Gdansk). The Poles riposted with two 37-mm guns, a 75-mm gun and small arms from the five sentry-post bunkers. After seven days of determined combat, isolated, without hope of reinforcement, its ammunition depleted, the 182 man garrison surrendered on September 7. In the Hel Peninsula, the Polish forces determinedly repelled all German attacks from land, sea, and air. Forty-six German aircraft were shot down and a destroyer damaged. The small units of the Polish fleet that had remained behind when the few destroyers and submarines escaped to Great Britain, took part in the defense. The German forces, blocked by field obstacles, was unable to reach the Jastarnia defensive point. The Hel Fortified Region did not surrender until October 2, 1939, when its garrison ran out of ammunition, food, and medical supplies.

In 1939 the Polish Army had virtually given up its effort to defend its eastern territories as the German threat loomed in the west. It rushed instead to complete the fortifications in the areas most threatened by the Germans. The units originally earmarked for Baranowicze, Wolyn, and Polesie in the east were integrated into the Modlin, Pomorze, and Krakow Armies in the west. Thus when the war broke out, the eastern fortified border sectors did not take part in the action, except in a few isolated places.

On the OWS, engagements with the Germans began a few days prior to the invasion, when bands of Freikorps, sent to create a diversion and gather intelligence, stumbled into the Polish fortifications by accident and exchanged fire with the garrisons. When the war officially started, the Germans avoided the OWS, leaving the Freikorps to operate in the area. Nonetheless, the OWS line managed to hold up the conquest of Upper Silesia for three whole days.

The Wizna Position, strengthened by troops from Operation Group Narew, included elements from field fortress units. The crews of this position consisted of

720 men, who fought from September 7 to 9 against the German 10th Panzer Division and the Fortress Brigade Lotzen, which they held up for two days until Heinz Guderian's panzer group entered the battle. The commander of the position, Captain W. Raginis, refusing to accept surrender, committed suicide by blowing himself up in the command bunker.

Early in the campaign the Poznan Army became isolated. The 26th Infantry Division abandoned the Golancz Position without a fight on the night of September 3-4 because other events left it exposed on a flank. The 25th Infantry Division also evacuated the Prosna River Line Position without a fight.

Further to the south, the Krakow Army was engaged by the 5th Panzer Division, which advanced through the area south of Pszczyna in the direction of the village of Goczalkowice where the schrony were still in the initial stage of construction. The 6th Infantry Division was forced to abandon the defenses on the Pszczyna Position to the north that it had put into service.

Near the former Czech border, at Wegierska Górka, in the Beskidy Mountains on the Sola River, a 4 km long position blocked the pass. It included five schrony, four of which were on the valley walls and mounted 37-mm or 75-mm guns. A command post was located among the schrony, near the river. None of these positions (twelve were planned) were fully completed. The troops had to set up their machine guns on sandbags in the wells intended for cloches on the casemates mounting the two 75-mm guns. The garrison, which included members of the 151st Fortress Company and a company from the National Guard Battalion Zywiec, fought fiercely under the command of Captain Tadeusz Semik. It surrendered on September 3, in the face of German air strikes and flamethrower attacks. Thus Hungarian Hill became known as "The Westerplatte of the South."

On the Warta Line, the Germans engaged the 10th Infantry Division on September 4. By midnight of September 5, after bloody encounters with the German Eighth Army, the Poles withdrew towards Szadek-Lutomiersk.

The Pomorze Army in the Polish Corridor was overwhelmed by the German Fourth Army and Guderian's attached panzer group early in the campaign. The Koronów Lake Position was abandoned without a struggle when the Germans attacked the interval separating it from the neighboring Drozdzenica-Piastoszyn Position.

The 20th Infantry Division of the Modlin Army effectively defended the Mlawa Position for three days, after which it abandoned the fortifications on the order of the Commander in Chief of the Armed Forces to avoid being surrounded. In this area both the complete and incomplete casemates of the line had been occupied and put to use, giving the Germans the impression that they had come across a formidable obstacle.

In his entry dated September 1, 1939, German historian General Nikolaus von

Vormann wrote that: "to the north of Mlawa the corps ran into a known enemy fortified position defended on both sides by swamps, and it was not able to break through, despite the use of tanks and Stukas. The units of the corps withdrew, having sustained heavy losses."

The Germans would again engage troops of the Modlin Army at the old forts of Modlin, which were not taken until the end of the campaign. In fact, the town of Modlin was one of the last to surrender.

Polish Fortified Group in Black Silesia. An artillery casemate on Hill 310 at Bobrowniki for 2 x 75-mm guns and which each have two embrasures so they can fire in two directions and 2 MGs. Walls up to 1.5 meters. Note observation cloche in center. (Kaufmann)

Guns of Hel coast defense. The arrow points to one of the coastal defense guns of Hel in 1939. The gun to the right of it was a 120-mm Bofors gun mounted on a minesweeper that defended the harbor. The other guns are post-war Soviet weapons used at Hel. (Kaufmann)

Mlawa Position. This line of fortifications consisted of small casemates like this one which had firing chambers on one or both sides and the entrance to the rear. The concrete had not completely set on most when the war began. The wooden frame which had not yet been removed can still be seen around the embrasure. (Kaufmann)

Polish Fortified Group. Observation cloche on another position of the group on Hill 310 at Bobrowniki. (Kaufmann)

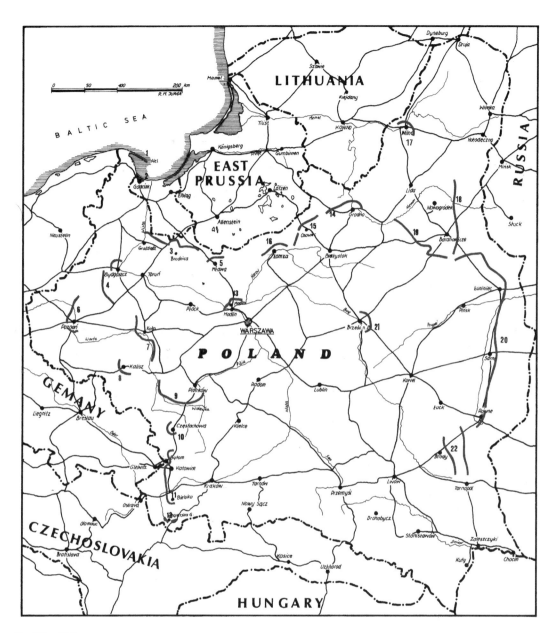

Fortified Lines:

1. Fortified Region of Hel
2. Transit Depot of Westerplatte at Free City of Danzig
3. Grudziadz-Brodnica Line
4. Bydgszcz Position
5. Mlawa Position
6. Poznan Position
7. Position Kolo
8. Sector Kalisz
9. Warta-Widawka Line
10. Position Czestochowa
11. Fortified District of Silesia
12. Veskidy Ring, includes Wegierska Gorka (Hungarian Hill) and Przyborow
13. Modlin Sector
14. Grodno Sector
15. Osowiec Position
16. Lomza Sector
17. Vilna Sector
18 & 19. Baranowicze Sector
20. Polesie Sector
21. Brzesc Sector
22. Wolyn Sector

Polish heavy bunker of Wedrowiec built on Hungarian Hill Position in Western Beskidy Mountains in summer of 1939.

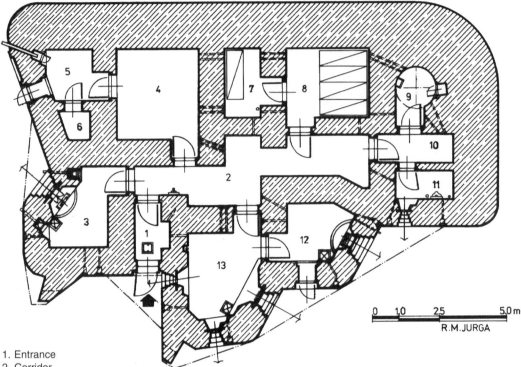

1. Entrance
2. Corridor
3. Firing room for Heavy MG on fortress mounting with two grenade throwing pipes in wall
4. Crew quarters
5. Store room with emergency exit and pipes for signal lights aimed at command block
6. Magazine
7. COs quarters
8. Crews quarters
9. MG cloche (not installed in 1939)
10. Telephone
11. WC with embrasure for light MG
12. Firing room for heavy MG with emergency exit
13. Firing room for 47-mm Bofors Fortress AT Gun with two crenels for light MG.

Polish heavy bunker in Silesia near Tapkowice built in summer of 1939.

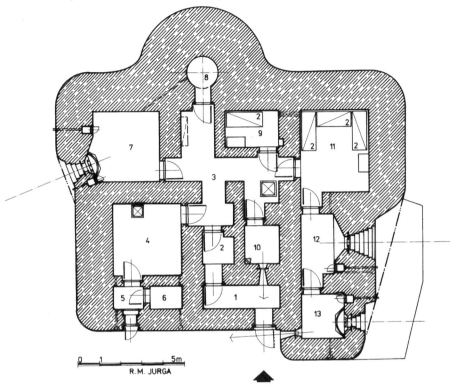

R.M. JURGA

1. Defended entrance
2. Gas Lock
3. corridor
4. Usine & ventilation room
5. Magazine & emergency exit
6. Grenade and ammo magazine
7. Firing room for heavy MG on fortress mounting with two grenade
   launching tubes (called grenade throwers)
8. MG Cloche
9. CP
10. WC
11. Crews Quarters
12. Firing room for Bofors 47-mm Fortress AT gun and
    grenade throwers
13. Firing room for heavy MG, light MG defending
    entrance and grenade thrower

Polish heavy bunker in Silesia near Laziska built in 1939.
One of 10 positions built with garage for AT gun.

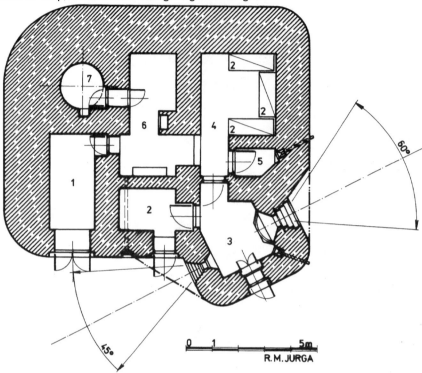

1. Garage for 37-mm Bofors AT gun
2. Entrance with air filters
3. Firing room for heavy MG on fortress mounting with grenade
   thrower, light MG covering entrance and emergency exit
4. Crews quarters
5. WC with grenade thrower
6. CP
7. MG cloche

Fortified Group of Vegierska Gorka (Hungarian Hill), the "Westerplatte of the South".

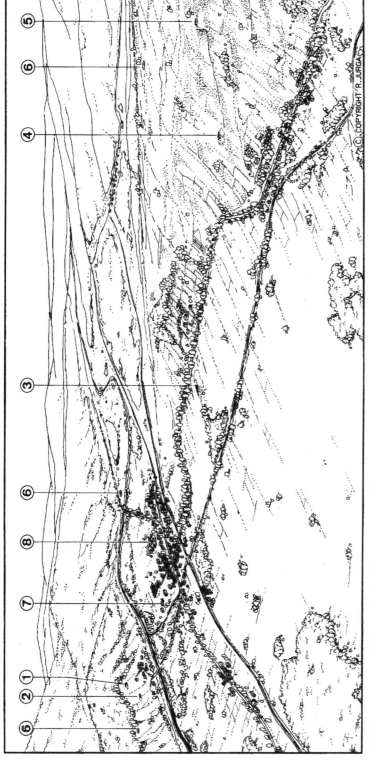

1. Artillery casemate Waligora for 2 x 75-mm gun and MG
2. Bunker Wloczega with embrasrues for Bofors 37-mm AT gun, and MG
3. Heavy bunker Wedrowiec - a command bunker with embrasures for Bofors 37-mm AT gun and heavy MG
4. Bunker Wawoz with embrasures for 37-mm AT gun and heavy MG
5. Bunker with embrasures for heavy MG
6. Excavation for building a bunker in 1939
7. Foundation of a bunker in 1939
8. Barracks

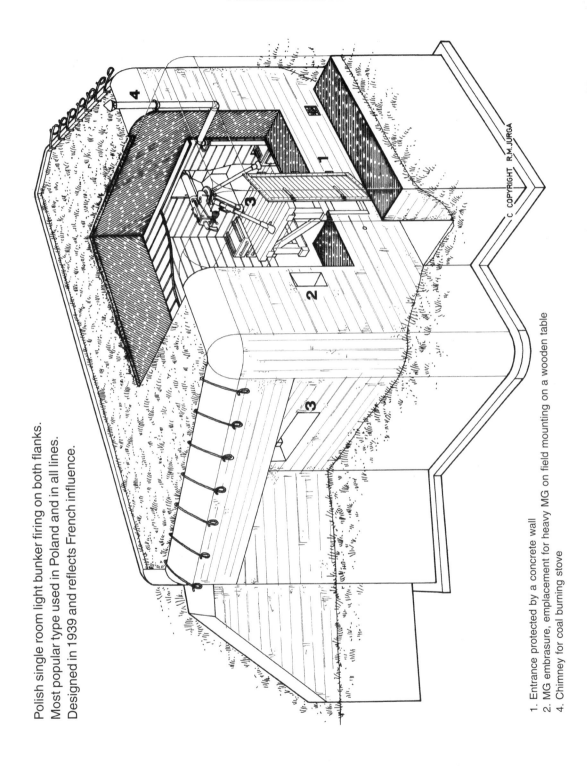

Polish single room light bunker firing on both flanks.
Most popular type used in Poland and in all lines.
Designed in 1939 and reflects French influence.

1. Entrance protected by a concrete wall
2. MG embrasure, emplacement for heavy MG on field mounting on a wooden table
4. Chimney for coal burning stove

C COPYRIGHT R.M.JURGA

Chapter 11

YUGOSLAVIA

BACKGROUND

Created as the Kingdom of the Serbs, Croats, and Slovenes at the end of the Great War, this nation of Southern Slavs proved to be a hotbed of trouble in one of the most backward parts of Europe. In 1929, Yugoslavia included approximately 4 million Serbs, 2.7 million Croats, 1.4 million Slovenes, and about 4 million members of other ethnic groups teetering on the brink of civil war.[1] At that time the government changed and the country was renamed Yugoslavia.

Known as the Kingdom of Illyria and a haven for pirates in Roman times, the Yugoslav kingdom had been for centuries an arena for the struggle between Turks and Europeans. It was also the target of Hungarian and Venetian expansion. Most of its major defenses before World War I had been built to protect the ports of the Dalmatian Coast.

Soon after attaining independence, Yugoslavia lost Fiume to a paramilitary force led by Italian nationalist Gabriele d'Annunzio in 1919. The Treaty of Rapallo of 1920 made the city a free port, but Italy maintained de facto control. The treaty also allowed Italy to take control of the port of Zara and several Adriatic and coastal islands. Yugoslavia could do little to prevent this, especially since it was preoccupied with Hungarian ambitions. In 1921 Yugoslavia, Rumania, and Czechoslovakia created the Little Entente with the aim of containing Hungary, their common foe. France, who promoted the entente, offered military advice to Czechoslovakia and Yugoslavia. However, in the 1930s only Czechoslovakia was able to take advantage of France's technological support because it had the required industrial base. Yugoslavia, which had an agrarian economy, could not make the most of France's offer. Fortunately for Yugoslavia, its two hostile neighbors were located on its northwestern and northern border so that its defensive efforts could be concentrated in that direction and along the coast.

MAJOR FORTIFICATIONS

Italian Front
German Front
Hungarian Front
Coastal Defenses

LOCATION

Yugoslavia's topography was favorable to defense because the country was large and mountainous. Its most productive agricultural region was located on the Pannonian Plain, in Croatia, and northern Serbia. The Danube and two of its tributaries, the Sava and Drava, which drained this area, formed part of the defenses against Hungary. Spring runoff swelled these rivers so much that they became as wide as the Mississippi for weeks. The Danube served as a major transportation artery not only for Yugoslavia, but for most of Central Europe.

Belgrade, on the Danube, lay at the edge of the Pannonian Plain and the Samadija region, a very hilly and easily defended section of central Serbia. The southern part of Serbia was the mountainous Kosovo region crossed by the Morava River, another tributary of the Danube, and the Vardar River, which flowed into the Aegean. Both rivers formed a corridor into Greece called the Morava-Vardar Depression, one of the most important land routes from northern to southern Yugoslavia. The region was easily defended against Bulgaria and Greece.

The Dinaric Alps, a part of the Eastern Alpine system, were the nation's highest and most rugged mountains. At average altitudes of 2,500 meters above sea level, they were not as high as the Western Alps but still presented a major obstacle for a modern army. The coastal range fell off steeply into the Adriatic, creating many islands and a rough coastline with deep harbors. Other ranges of the Dinaric Alps sloped eastward into the Karst Plateau, which formed a large part of the country. Forests covered most of the less fertile regions. The cavernous limestone formations of the plateau literally swallowed up many rivers and streams and resembled, in many respects, the Carro Plateau in northeastern Italy, offering the defender all the advantages.

1. The Italian Front

Yugoslavia's border with Italy extended for about 290 km. The Julian Alps commanded the main front, aiding in the defense. The easily defended karst topography dominated the region. The front was divided into five sectors. The 2nd sector began at Susak, on the coast and ran northward, to the vicinity of Cabar. The 5th Sector began at Cabar and followed the border to the vicinity of Rakek. The 1st sector stretched between Rakek and Vrhnka, protecting the main road from Ljubljana to Trieste. The 3rd Sector continued on to Skofjalloka, covering Ljubljana. The 4th Sector extended northward to the vicinity of Bohinjska Bistrica and there turned eastward to Trzic[2]. These defenses occupied Slovenia and protected Ljubljana and Zabreg, separated by the Sava River and dominated by mountains.

2. The German (former Austrian) Front

The border with the German Reich was almost totally dominated by the Alps, cut by only a couple of passes and the Mura River valley. The 6th Sector covered this area from Dravograd to the Mura. Only the Mura and Drava valleys could be considered major invasion routes, but the rivers and the rugged terrain were serious obstacles.

3. The Hungarian Front

The Drava River formed part of the boundary between Yugoslavia and Hungary. To the south, the Kalnik Mountains, the Bilo Gora Range, and the Papuk Range constituted a major obstacle. On the Hungarian side of the border, the hilly and mountainous Barany region protected the Drava River between the Austrian border and Valpovov. The 7th Sector began at Valpovov and covered the gap between the Drava and Danube Rivers. The 9th Sector extended from the Danube along the Hungarian border to the Rumanian border. The 10th Sector, located to the rear of the 9th sector, stretched between the Danube, near Batina where the 9th Sector began, along the King Peter Canal to the Tisa River. The 10th Sector was the only one located behind another sector. The reason for the concentration of defenses in this area was that it was part of the Great Hungarian Plain that covered most of Hungary east of the Danube and offered the most direct route to Belgrade, the economic and industrial heart of Yugoslavia.

4. Coastal Defenses

Yugoslavia had to defend a number of islands that protected the entrances to the bays of the main ports such as Kotor (Cattaro), Dubrovnik, Sibenik, and Split. The islands at Korcula and Zara, whose mountainous terrain gave the defender all the advantages, were among the most important to be fortified. Yugoslav positions ringed the Italian enclave at Zara.

HISTORY

The Little Entente proved to be an inadequate check on Hungary after it allied itself to Fascist Italy. In response, Yugoslavia created fortification staffs charged with the development of defenses in an individual area. The first staff was set up at Ljubljana, which was threatened by Italy.

However, it was not until the 1930s that Yugoslavia made a serious effort to defend its borders. In the mid-1930s, the situation in Central Europe became increasingly precarious as Hitler and Mussolini confronted each other for the first time in 1934 and later embraced each other as allies. As Germany openly violated the Versailles Treaty, the Western Powers vacillated and continued building their own fortifications to ward off German aggression. Eastern Europe was vulnerable since Czechoslovakia and Poland could not settle their differences and present a common front to the growing threat. The Little Entente teetered on the verge of collapse.

In 1937, faced with such an uncertain future, Yugoslavia caught the fortification building fever that was sweeping Europe. In January 1937, at the suggestion of French military advisers, a Yugoslav army commission went to Czechoslovakia to study methods of fortification.

Between 1935 and 1939, twelve fortress staffs numbering 15,000 men, went into operation. Five were stationed on the Italian border, one on the Austrian border, and six on the Hungarian border. Additional staffs handled the coastal defenses. Before the war broke out, these staffs grew to over 40,000 men. By 1941, they had erected twelve heavy positions and 4,000 concrete emplacements of various sizes. Yugoslav troops were assigned the task of building defenses after the invasion of Poland. The army called up reservists for several weeks of training, turning them into a construction labor force.

The numbering of the various defensive sectors appears to indicate their priority. The most important fortifications went up west of Ljubljana while the next most important sector was the 2nd Sector at Susak, also facing Italy. Only limited work was done on the border region of Hungary until early in 1939, a year after the annexation of Austria to the Reich. After the German occupation of the rump of Czechoslovakia, Yugoslavia redoubled its efforts, particularly since it felt increasingly isolated. Rumania had proved a poor ally for Czechoslovakia during the 1938 crisis, and by 1939 Yugoslavia had no allies or neighbors it could rely on.

Yugoslavia also attempted to fortify the border region with Hungary, fearing that the Germans would violate its territory on their way to an attack on Rumania. In addition, Hungary could not be trusted not to annex the area with a large concentration of ethnic Hungarians. Thus Yugoslavia hastily threw up field fortifications in the last months of 1939.

In 1939, the Yugoslavs set up four defensive lines between the Tisa and Danube rivers. The first stretched along the border and included anti-tank obstacles, and the second between Sombor and Senta, which became strong points with trenches between them. The King Peter Canal served as an 18 meter wide anti-tank obstacle for the third line. The fourth line had the strongest positions and a number of bridgehead positions at key towns were established.

According to an American observer, the terrain between the first and fourth lines was not adequate for defensive positions against a modern army. Other American intelligence reports revealed that a number of the Yugoslav casemates and blockhouses reflected a definite French influence.

Like most of the other nations, Yugoslavia placed its faith in anti-tank obstacles. Some of the permanent fortifications observed in the fall of 1939 were concrete machine gun and anti-tank bunkers while other positions also included underground works. Casemates for 105-mm weapons and some heavy bunkers were completed in the vicinity of Trata, but they were not armed yet.

In the 6th Sector, the only significant work was at Maribor. Here, an outpost line was placed on the Mura River, a main line behind the Drava River, and the bridgeheads at Putj and Maribor on the north side of the river. The Yugoslav army relied heavily on the natural obstacles here and in most other sectors. Between the 4th and 6th Sectors was the Austrian front where an outpost line was placed in the Alps to block the Drava Valley near Dravograd, the Seeberg Pass (1218 meters), the Libel Pass (1310 meters), and the Sava Valley. The work on the former Austrian frontier did not begin until the spring of 1939 for fear of German retaliation. The main fortifications were of light and medium type.

The only permanent works completed in any significant number were on the Italian front in the 1st to the 5th Sectors. Reportedly, a French engineer officer had directed the work since 1938. Before 1936 the Yugoslavs ran their positions along crest lines as a result of lack of experience. After the Yugoslav engineers visited the Czech fortifications the plans were changed, and with the aid of French engineers, the new defenses were sighted on forward slopes with the crests used only for observation posts and assembly positions for counter-attacks.

On the Italian Front where the Yugoslavs expended their greatest effort, they found that they did not have the finances or time to create a truly modern position. They had prepared plans for the construction of several French-style ouvrages, but changed them to more modest positions with fewer combat blocks. The design of the planned forts shows that the Yugoslavs apparently received technical advice from the Czechs for creating more economical positions. Roads in this area were improved and widened to help the defenders.

The outpost line ran close to the Italian border with the main line close behind it. The strongest positions included the casemates and artillery positions between Vrhnika (1st Sector) and Zelezniki (4th Sector) which covered Ljubljana. Emphasis had moved to the 2nd Sector near Susak for fear of an Italian assault flanking the Sava River line. The 2nd Sector was almost continuous except for a gap occupied by mountain troops.

By 1940, the Yugoslavs had to prepare additional fortifications for the Banat area as German troops moved into Rumania. Planning went ahead for fortifications near the Iron Gate. Meanwhile some light defenses were completed on the Bulgarian front to close the Vardar Valley.

The outpost or advanced post line contained bunkers for the Frontier Guards. These small positions held a couple of automatic rifles and a squad in peacetime. Anti-tank obstacles were usually found about a kilometer to the rear of this line.

Only the 1st, 2nd and 3rd Sectors included the largest and best equipped positions in Yugoslavia. Work progressed on six forts (Czech type ouvrages or tvrz) in the 1st and 3rd Sectors, but none were finished in time to meet the Axis invasion. The army prepared plans for other interior lines such as one covering Zagreb to the coast, another using the Glina and Czama Rivers behind this line, and finally one behind these following the Ilova and Una rivers. All of these blocked the Sava Valley, but the army only had time to do a small amount of work on these positions. Even less was achieved on one last position along the Drina River west of Belgrade. One post-war estimate from a Polish source claimed that by 1941 only one fourth of all the planned fortifications were actually completed.

Lack of time and money prevented Yugoslavia from preparing adequate defenses. On the other hand, the modifications and renovations were not sufficient. The Czechs were the main source of armor, including cloches. The heavy cloches were shipped on special rail cars through Rumania from Czechoslovakia to avoid problems with the Hungarians. When Czechoslovakia fell to the Germans, the Yugoslavs had to rely on the more expedient solution of using concrete cupolas instead of steel ones. The Yugoslavs perfected the use of concrete cupolas, although their value was limited. The only item not in short supply was limestone for cement. The Yugoslavs combined French and Czech techniques with their own. One interesting method they used was making walls of two layers of concrete. The outer layer contained a spiral grid to resist projectiles.

Seventy-two companies of *Granicari* (Frontier Guards), organized into battalions, defended the frontiers. The peacetime army deployed three brigades and four independent battalions with sixteen batteries to defend the Italian, German, and Hungarian borders. One brigade with five batteries (24 guns), and an independent battalion with one battery (4 guns), for a total of 6,500 men, defended the Italian Front. Another brigade of 2,200 men including three batteries (16 guns) covered the German border. The third brigade with five batteries (30 guns), and an independent battalion with two batteries (12 guns) totaling 6,400 men occupied the Hungarian Front. On mobilization these units expanded to about 50,000 men with 160 guns in forty batteries. The border defenses were intended to delay the enemy for up to three weeks while the army mobilized.

The Sixth Army was assigned to the coast defenses with naval units. It consisted of a motorized brigade and an independent regiment which on mobilization expanded into a division and brigade respectively. The division was headquartered at Split. Boka Kotor (Cattaro) and Sibenik held coastal defense commands. Although intelligence reports indicated that many coastal sectors were defended, they may have included batteries of obsolete weapons. As late as April 1940 only Kotor and Sibenik had permanent defenses and the others lacked coast artillery and anti-aircraft guns. Split was next in line for armament when it became available. Fortifications for lighter weapons may have been completed by this time in most of these other ports.

DESCRIPTION

The French type ouvrages were not completed and only a small number of large concrete positions were built. Most of these were on the Italian front or the coast. Few bunkers had received their armor and thus lacked armored embrasures and cloches. The most effective work done was on the camouflage of the positions and the creation of some anti-tank obstacles. Because of this only a few examples of positions can be given.

Of the seven ouvrages designed for the Italian front, plans of one, Fort Tri Kralja, are available. The original 1937 document shows fourteen infantry, one artillery and two entrance blocks designed to withstand artillery of up to 305-mm. The layout does not follow the typical French pattern except for the caserne being located to the rear. This fort was to occupy the upper part of a mountain with its combat blocks at elevations ranging from 740 meters to 870 meters. Each block, except for three, were to have cloches. German reports indicate some were to be concrete instead of steel. The entrances appear to have been designed similar to those of the French ouvrages, one for men and another for munitions. Another plan for an entrance shows a mixed entrance with many similarities to those used by the Czechs. The artillery casemates fired to the flank like those of the French, and had two large magazines below. The fort was divided into four combat sections with one on each side of the mountain. The main gallery was to run from the caserne to the four blocks of the combat section on the west side of the mountain. Another main gallery ran from the northern section of the block to the southern group, and the two galleries intersected in the middle of the fort. Plans for the ouvrage changed by 1938, and by 1940 only two small infantry blocks had been built on the west side of the mountain and about 500 meters of galleries and a light caserne excavated.

Plans for 1941 show another ouvrage named Goli Vrh with two infantry casemates designed like those of the French, although one had a concrete turret. Another plan from 1940 of the ouvrage of Strmica reveals that the caserne area had features more reminiscent of the Czechs. Fort Strmica had also been designed in 1937 as a fort with an entrance block and six combat blocks on a mountain 625 meters high. By 1941 it was reduced in scale to a simple entrance and three small combat blocks for machine guns. It still included most of the planned galleries, amounting to over 300 meters, but the caserne was reduced in scale. It included the standard features found in most Maginot ouvrages from communications room to filter rooms. These ouvrages were to rely on heavy machine guns and, where necessary, a few anti-tank guns. They were not designed for close defense and did not have fossés or other features used by the French and Czechs possibly because of their locations which may not have been easily accessible.

Other heavy works for the Italian front included a two-level observation block with a cloche and 2.5 meters of concrete protection. An impressive position completed on the same front was a two-level double casemate for machine guns with an underground entrance in a fossé and a concrete turret. The turret's roof was 1.0 meter thick.

The Yugoslavs planned to have a few heavy machine gun casemates with steel cloches similar to those of the French. The most interesting work appears to be a combination of the French artillery block and the Czech independent artillery block. It was a casemate for four 105-mm howitzers. Unlike the French guns, these were field pieces and given a 60 degree firing angle. This two-level position had a protective fossé in front of it, and at least one of these casemates was nearly completed at Trata on the Italian front.

The medium works could be for both frontal or flanking fire or all around defense, and were supposed to have armored crenel covers. Some of these were similar to those of the French. They had two levels and more than a single chamber. They were much larger than the light positions, which were mainly for machine guns and normally had only a single chamber.

Along with their unusual concrete turrets, the Yugoslavs also created a unique armored position in concrete. It consisted of a turret-like steel structure which had its weapons embrasure lowered by a lever system. When lowered into the concrete the armored back end of the structure raised up to seal the position. One of these positions was found at Radmannsdorf where the concrete structure had two of these machine gun turrets and a periscope observation position between them.

The Yugoslavs created an interesting, if not effective, variety of positions and accessories. With regard to obstacles, they used the standard array, from pyramidal concrete blocks to iron rails in three to five rows. Apparently these rails were not sunk in concrete, but instead just buried in the ground reducing their effectiveness. One example of an antitank ditch had a concrete wall (the counter scarp or outside wall) 3.5 meters high with the ditch almost 8.0 meters wide.

Sibenik, the best defended port, apparently lacked land defenses to ward off an assault from Zara. It had fourteen coastal batteries, including one with two 280-mm howitzers near the old fortress, and three batteries of 47-mm naval guns (four guns per battery) guarding the narrows. A battery of two 150-mm naval guns was in a commanding positions on Prvic Island. Two batteries of old 120-mm naval guns were southeast of the city. A battery of four 47-mm naval guns was on the northwest end of the island of Zlarin, and a battery of two 150-mm naval guns covered the coast near Zecevo. On the island of Zirje there was a battery of two 150-mm naval guns, and supporting it on the island of Kakan was a battery of two 190-mm naval guns and an army battery of four 100-mm guns. Finally, another battery of four 47-mm naval guns on Logorun Island mounted its own searchlights. Additional searchlights were on Zlarin Island. To complete the defenses a boom closed the narrows leading into the harbor. An underground depot was built for ammunition and mines. All communications with the island positions were made by visual signals.

Kotor (Cattaro) was the main naval base and was even more heavily protected then the others, but many of its weapons were old and unsatisfactory. It included eighteen coastal and anti-aircraft batteries. These included two single weapon 300-mm mobile howitzer batteries with prepared positions. These were old Austrian guns. A battery of four 120-mm naval guns stood on a promontory on the west side of the gulf. Other batteries included 210-mm and 150-mm naval guns, and 47-mm and 70-mm guns. The 70-mm guns were taken from Austrian torpedo boats. One of these batteries had two new Skoda 150-mm naval guns and was on the peninsula of Molunat. The Yugoslavs converted two batteries of 90-mm naval guns into anti-aircraft weapons.

At Kotor was Battery Molunat with two 150-mm L/40 naval guns on concrete platforms. Its supporting munitions and ready rooms were in the mountain. Each gun position had a gallery of from 25 to 50 meters in length leading to it. Below each gun was a ready room, and beneath that a munitions room with a lift which was protected by a concrete cover on the surface. At the third and lowest level was the command room.

On the other side of the channel leading to Kotor was Battery Kozmac with two 240-mm L/40 Skoda guns in a turret at an elevation of 500 meters. Its entrance was at about 90 meters above sea level with a tunnel that ran several hundred meters to the underground facilities. It also included a battery of three torpedo launchers. These coast defenses were some of the most impressive works made by the Yugoslavs.

In addition to these positions, the Yugoslavs established an outpost line of observation and signal stations on the coast which held a garrison of about platoon strength and sometimes included 37-mm guns. These were located at Susak and on the islands of Krk, Rab, Silba, Mulat, Dugi Otok, Uljan, Murter, Zirije, Hvar, Vis, Korcula and at Sibenik, Movar, Split, Dubrovnik, Sveti-Ilya, Oboswik and Budva.

WEAPONS AND EQUIPMENT

The Yugoslavs had three main types of fortifications. They were rated as heavy, medium, and light. The latter were basically reinforced field fortifications.

	Type	Roof	Walls - Front (in meters)	Rear	Resists Weapons of
Heavy	IV	2.00-2.75	2.00-2.75		420-mm
	III	1.70	1.70		305-mm
Medium	II	1.50	1.50	1.00	220-mm
	I	1.00-1.25	1.0	.60-.80	150-mm
Light	-	.20-.50	.30-.50		splinter proof[3]

The main types of artillery used were as follows:

Weapon	Range (in meters)
305-mm M.16 Skoda Mortar	12,300
149-mm M.15/28 Skoda Cannon	23,800*
338 155-mm M.17 Howitzer	11,200
120-mm M.78 Cannon	10,900
105-mm M.36 Skoda Cannon	18,100*
100-mm M.14/19 Skoda Field Howt	9,800*
80-mm M.5/8 Field Gun	9,300
75-mm M.7 Field Gun	7,300
75-mm M.28 Skoda Mountain Gun	8,700*
47-mm Skoda Anti-tank Gun	4,000*
37-mm Skoda Anti-tank Gun	3,000*
Coast Artillery	
240-mm L/40 Naval Gun	17,800
240-mm M.98 Mortar	6,500
210-mm M.80 Mortar	7,300

210-mm M.73 Mortar	5,000
190-mm L/42 Naval Gun	13,000
156-mm L/50 Coast Gun	17,000
155-mm M.77 Cannon	10,300
150-mm L/35 Naval Gun	10,300
150-mm L/40 Naval Gun	10,600
120-mm L/35 Naval Gun	10,000
105-mm L/45 Naval Gun	13,700

*These were some of the more modern weapons.

WORLD WAR II

By 1941 Yugoslavia found itself in a precarious position when Italy engaged Albania and German troops moved into Hungary, Rumania, and Bulgaria. A diplomatic arrangement with the Germans was rendered meaningless when a coup deposed Yugoslavia's regent, putting the young Yugoslav king in power. Hitler, already concerned about the war between Greece and Italy, wanted to resolve the problem. The situation in Yugoslavia convinced him that the solution included the conquest of Yugoslavia.

The Yugoslav army hoped to defend all its frontiers and keep a route open through the Vardar Valley to link up with the Allies through Greece. However, the German blitzkrieg began on April 16, 1941, as Yugoslavia continued to mobilize. The advanced positions had no depth and could not check the Axis advance. A three-pronged attack coming down the Drava Valley from western Hungary, across the Rumanian border towards Belgrade, and down the Marava Valley from Bulgaria, bypassed most of the Yugoslav defenses and converged on the capital.

The defection of Croatia actually did not make the hopeless situation any worse. The Italian army prepared to invade with German assistance a few days after the Yugoslavs were on the verge of collapse. The incomplete fortifications contributed little to the defense of the country and may have caused the Yugoslav army to become too dispersed in an attempt to hold on to the defenses of the northern half of the country.

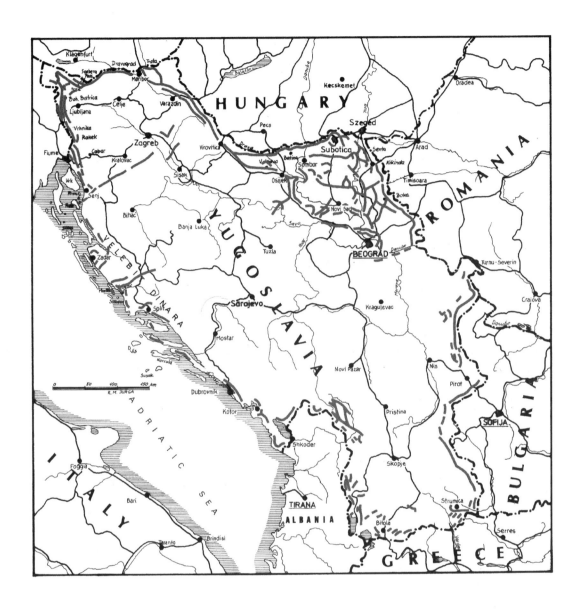

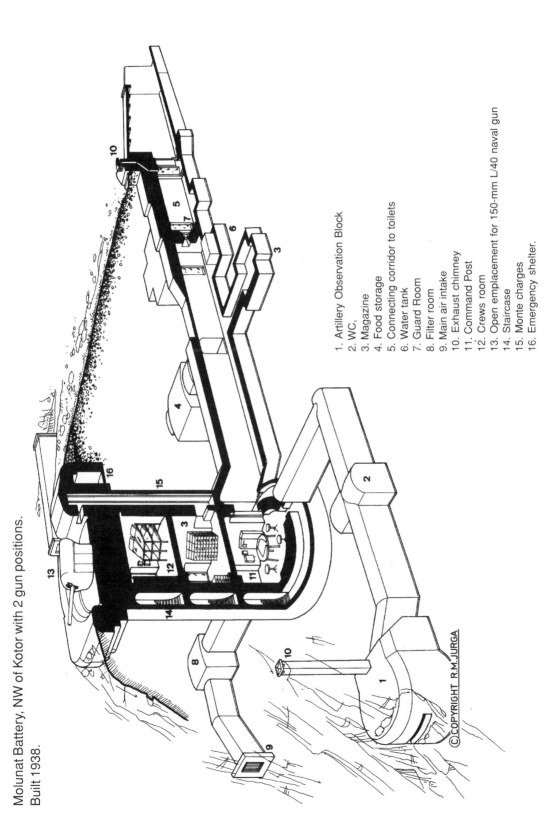

Molunat Battery, NW of Kotor with 2 gun positions.
Built 1938.

1. Artillery Observation Block
2. WC,
3. Magazine
4. Food storage
5. Connecting corridor to toilets
6. Water tank
7. Guard Room
8. Filter room
9. Main air intake
10. Exhaust chimney
11. Command Post
12. Crews room
13. Open emplacement for 150-mm L/40 naval gun
14. Staircase
15. Monte charges
16. Emergency shelter.

©COPYRIGHT R.M.JURGA

Yugoslav two level position for 3 MG and an AT gun near Zaier-Tal on Italian border.

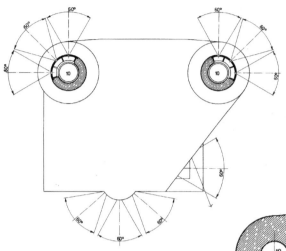

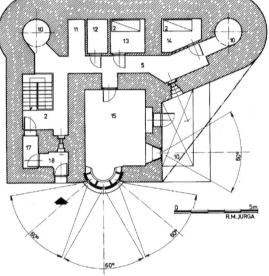

1. Crews Quarters
2. Staircase
3. Magazine
4. Grenade magazine
5. corridor with rifle crenel on upper level
6. Storage room for engineer materials
7. kitchen
8. Drinking water reservoir
9. WC
10. Reinforced concrete cloche for heavy MG
11. Storage room

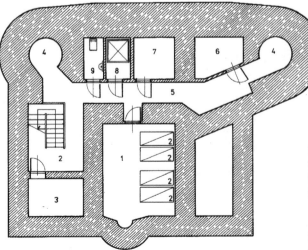

12. Commo center
13. COs room
14. NCOs room
15. Combat room with concrete half cloche for heavy MG and position for 47-mm Czech AT gun, and emergency exit
16. Diamond fosse
17. Gas air lock
18. Defended entrance corridor.

Yugoslav Artillery Casemate for 4 x 105-mm Howitzer.
Delivers flanking fire to cover road to Zirovsti Vhr near Trata.

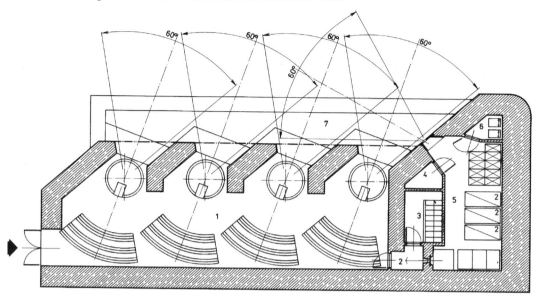

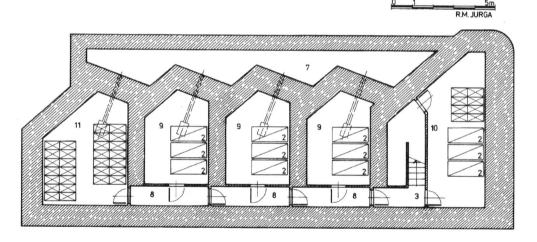

1. Firing chambers
2. Gas Lock with defensive crenel
3. Staircase
4. Telephone commo
5. Crews quarters, ammo, water tanks
6. WC

7. Diamond fosse
8. Corridor
9. crews quarters
10. crews quarters, magazine
11. Main magazine

Yugoslav two level block for all around defense near Radmannsdorf.
Access through a well into lower level.
Two half-armored half-cloche and two embrasures with armored plates.

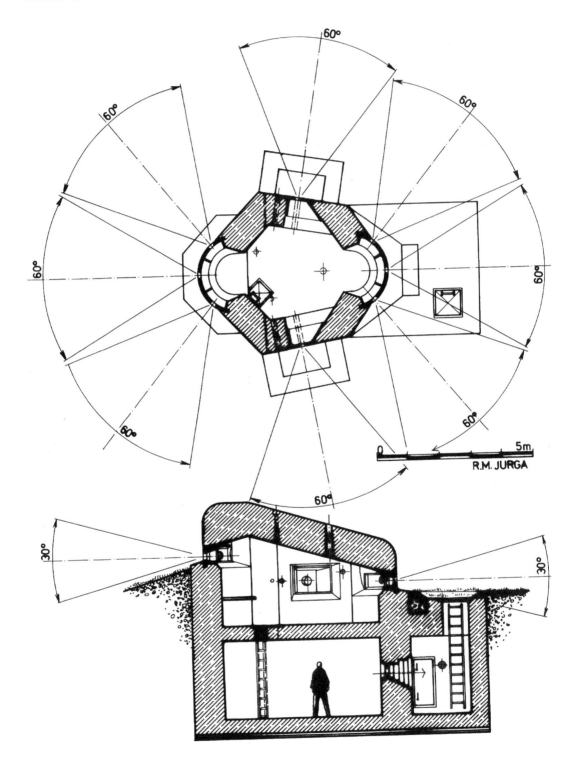

R.M. JURGA

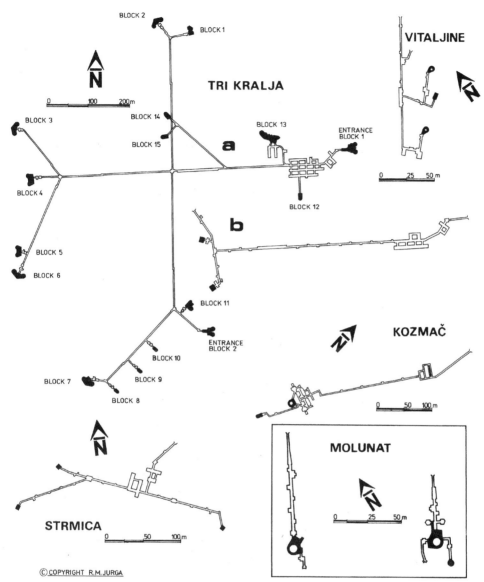

Plans of Yugoslav forts.

Tri Kralja (Plan A)

    Plans from 1937 as coastal fort with 14 combat blocks

    1 artillery block

    2 entrance blocks

    Entrance Block 1 - cloche for heavy MG

    Entrance Block 2 - cloche for heavy MG

    Block 1, 7, 11 - cloche for heavy MG, 2 heavy MG in casemate

    Block 2, 3, 4, 6, - 3 cloche for heavy MG, Block 2 cloche for heavy MG

    Block 8, 9, 10, - naval gun behind armor plate,

    Block 12, 14, 15 - cloche for light MG

    Block 13 - 2 cloche for heavy MG, 3 guns in casemates for flanking fires.

Tri Kralja (Plan B, as completed in 1940) two infantry blocks, subterranean caserne.

Vitaljine built on western front.

    A battery on the Adriatic Sea consisting of two open positions for 150-mm L/40 naval guns and a obsv & fire direction position. Subterranean works about 10 meters below with two entrances.

Strmica was a battery on the western front and in 1941 only 3 modified blocks for heavy MGs built of 7 planned in 1937. Entrance block not built.

Kozmac was one of the heaviest naval batteries completed.

    It consisted of one firing position for a 240-mm L/40 Skoda guns in a twin turret and an observation position. Underground included caserne and magazines next to combat position. The entrance defended by a guard room.

Molunat battery 12 krn NW of Kotor on peninsula.

    Two independent positions for naval guns of 150-mm L/40 in armored shields and gun position #2 had an observation block.

Yugoslav Disappearing Cupola for a Hvy MG.

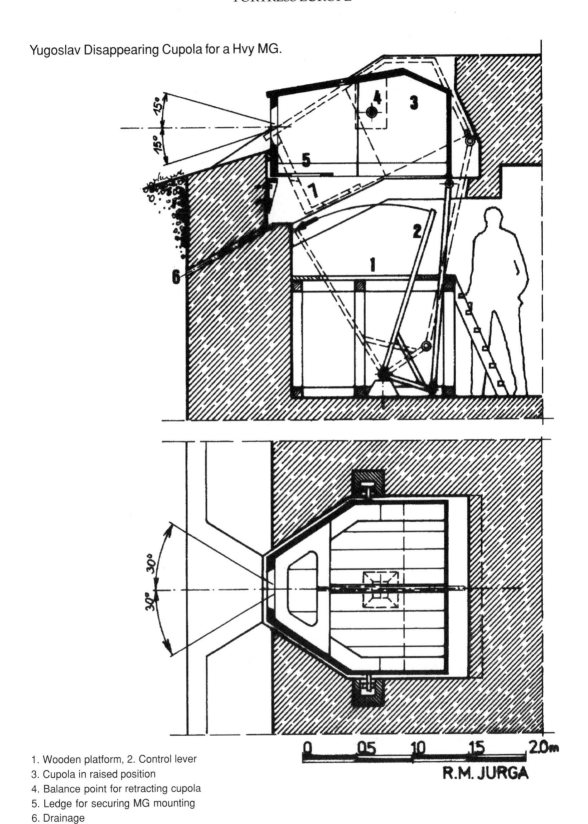

R.M. JURGA

1. Wooden platform, 2. Control lever
3. Cupola in raised position
4. Balance point for retracting cupola
5. Ledge for securing MG mounting
6. Drainage
7. Cupola in retracted position

Chapter 12

THE BALKANS

BACKGROUND

The Balkans became known as "The Powder Keg" of Europe after the upheavals that took place there in the early part of the twentieth century. Yugoslavia, which is treated in the previous chapter, was largely part of the Austro-Hungarian Empire with the exception of Serbia. The remainder of the Balkans began to break away from their Ottoman Turkish overlords during the nineteenth century. Serbia was virtually independent after the first quarter of the century, while Greece, with the help of the great European naval powers, won full independence in the 1820s. In the late 1870s Rumania and Bulgaria became free of Turkish domination.

The Balkan Wars began in 1912 when Bulgaria, Serbia, and Greece declared war on Turkey to free Macedonia. Before long Turkey lost most of its European possessions and the Bulgarians stood at the gates of Constantinople. However, Greece, Serbia, and Bulgaria argued over how to divide up Macedonia and the new nation of Albania was created on the Adriatic. After the peace talks, a Turkish revolt caused the war to continue until the spring of 1913. Then in May 1913 the Bulgarians decided to settle their disagreements with their neighbors through force of arms, launching the Second Balkan War. The Bulgarian offensive ground to a halt after two months. Meanwhile, Turkey rejoined the fight in July and Rumania shortly after, when it invaded Bulgaria.

By the time the conflict ended, the political map of the Balkans had changed significantly. Greece was awarded many of the Turkish Aegean islands, including Crete. Bulgaria, which acquired virtually no new territories, wanted retribution. Serbia and Greece divided Macedonia between themselves. Turkey reestablished its presence in the southeast corner of Europe by holding on to the Bosphorus and Dardenelles. Turkey and Bulgaria aligned themselves with the Germans in World War I while Rumania later found itself on the side of the Entente and the defeated Serbia.

After the Great War, the newly created Yugoslavia became the largest of the Balkan nations. Rumania allied itself with Yugoslavia and Czechoslovakia in the Little Entente to keep Hungary from trying to regain former territories of the Austro-Hungarian Empire. Bulgaria remained distrustful of its neighbors, refusing to relinquish its claims to the lands it had lost. Greece tried to take advantage of the newly formed Turkish Republic by seizing parts of Ionia, but Turkey firmly held on to its borders. The small, mountainous country of Albania remained a tempting target for Italian expansion.

The cessation of hostilities brought only an uneasy peace to the Balkan nations. Greece had to contend with Italy in the Aegean and the Adriatic, and keep a wary eye on its Macedonian frontier at the same time. Rumania faced even more serious problems, sandwiched as it was between the Soviet Union and Hungary, both of whom coveted parts of its territory. The dissolution of the Little Entente and the fall of Czechoslovakia left Rumania in a very precarious position.

In the Balkans, Hungary and Bulgaria, which sought to expand and reclaim their alleged "lost lands," erected few, if any, significant fortifications. Yugoslavia, Rumania, Greece, and Turkey, on the other hand, set up or planned major defensive barriers in order to safeguard their existing borders and ensure their neutrality.

MAJOR FORTIFICATION

Metaxas Line and the Greek Fortifications
The Carol Lines and Rumanian Fortifications
The Turkish Straits

LOCATION

1. Metaxas Line and Greek Fortifications

The Metaxas Line covered much of the Macedonian and Thracian borders with Bulgaria where the terrain was mostly mountainous, intersected by a few river valleys that formed the main communications routes. In 1938, Greece's entire frontier region with Albania and Turkey was mountainous and underdeveloped, and few roads allowed travel from one country to the other.

The border with Bulgaria, which stretched over 490 km, was no further than 75 km from the Aegean Sea at any point. It was crossed by only five roads, the most important of which ran near the Yugoslav border and followed the Struma Valley.

The other four were so small they were seldom shown on maps and were of poor quality, especially on the Bulgarian side. One of these routes followed the Nestos River, while the one furthest to the east passed through a border pass through the Rhodope Mountains, which dominated most of the Bulgarian frontier with Greece.

The Metaxas Line was divided into sectors, the most westerly of which was the Krusia Sector that passed through the mountains of the same name. It ran from the Aksios (Vardar) River valley eastward along the border to the valley of the Struma, covering part of the Yugoslav border. The Struma Sector dominated the Struma Valley, extending eastward into the mountains where it joined with the Neverokopion Sector. This sector spanned the area between Achladochorion and the Nestos River. The Nestos Sector followed the River Nestos to the Aegean and concentrated on the town of Echinos. The last sector, which was not actually linked to the Metaxas Line, began at Komotine and covered the city of Alexandropolis in eastern Thrace for which it was named. Between these last two sectors individual fortifications blocked the Makaza Pass through the Rhodope Mountains.

Another sector where land fortifications were planned, was along the Albanian border, one of the most rugged parts of the country. The only other fortifications of any significance consisted of coast defenses guarding several major harbors on the mainland and a number of Aegean islands. The most important of these defenses were the positions that protected Athens and its port, Piraeus, and Thessaloniki, the northern key to the Metaxas Line.

2. The Carol Lines and Rumanian Fortifications

The province of Bessarabia was separated from the Soviet Union by the Dniestr River, which served as its main defensive feature. It included the agricultural regions of Moldavia along the Dniestr, and Bukovina along the Prut. These two regions were hilly, particularly the forested area of Bukovina, located in the foothills of the Carpathians.

One of Rumania's defensive lines of the inter-war period was called the *Eastern Carol Line* by western sources, which did not specify whether it was located on the Dniestr or the Prut. In fact, the Dniestr constituted the main line of defense against the Soviet Union in Bessarabia. However, when the political climate deteriorated in the late 1930s, additional fortifications were erected on the Prut River and, after the fall of Poland, in the north, near Cernauti. In addition, roads were improved to facilitate the defense of this region.

Some of Rumania's most important defenses faced Hungary, protecting its resources and agriculturally rich plains and foothills from Hungary. The advanced line, extending from Arad, to Oradea, and Satumare, covered the entire Hungarian border facing the Transylvanian Alps. The forward position at Oradea covered the gap between Oradea and Cluj and the Transylvanian Plateau. The main line ran from Zalu to Ciucea, about 60 km northwest of Cluj.

Another defensive line, known as the *Western Carol Line*, was built in the south, to the west of Deva, to block the approach through the Muresh River valley from Arad. Finally, Rumania also planned a line to cover the coastal plain between Constanza, Lake Oltina and the Danube. These defenses, called the *Southern Carol Line* in the west, were meant to protect this rich agricultural region, with few natural barriers, from Bulgaria.

3. The Turkish Straits

Turkish Thrace allowed Turkey to retain its domination of the Straits of Bosphorus and Dardenelles, these vital straits controlled access from the Black Sea to the Aegean and Mediterranean. In contrast to the remainder of the Balkans, this region of Turkey was relatively open to invasion, except for one group of mountains in the north. Both straits, formed by peninsulas on the European side, were easily defended, as was demonstrated at Gallipoli in 1915. Most of Turkey's defenses consisted of coastal positions that controlled the Straits.

HISTORY

1. The Metaxas Line and Greek Fortifications

Until 1936, Greece had done little to improve its coastal and land defenses due, in part, to internal political problems. Finally, animosity toward Bulgaria prompted Greece to fortify its border with that country. The Greek Commander in Chief, General Hazipides, who planned the fortified line in 1936, intended to delay the enemy long enough for the Greek armed forces to complete mobilization. However, General Alexandros Papagos, who replaced him in 1937, decided to adopt the French defensive philosophy of the time. In other words, instead of building fortifications that merely delayed the enemy, he opted for a major fortified line that would prevent an invasion altogether. Thus he ordered the creation of stronger defenses, and later demanded further strengthening of the completed line. He even envisioned the line as a starting point for an offensive against Bulgaria. Greece's dictator, General Ioannis Metaxas, assured the army that the government would procure the necessary funds for the project. Soon the line, initially called the *Ochiromeni Topthesia* or Fortified Line or the *Nestos Line*, was named "Metaxas Line" after the dictator.

The Greeks worked on their fortifications for almost two years. They built field positions on the Albanian front, to the east and southeast of Goritza, in anticipation of an Italian invasion from that quarter. When the Italians occupied Albania in 1939, Greece reconsidered its plans, deciding to add fortifications on the Italian front as soon as the Metaxas Line was finished. However, this plan never materialized because the Metaxas Line was still incomplete by 1941.

The Balkan Alliance of September 2, 1934, with Turkey, Yugoslavia, and Rumania, left Greece feeling secure enough to leave its borders undefended against its allies. Greece concentrated its efforts on the Metaxas Line because Bulgaria, claiming ethnic links, had designs upon eastern Macedonia and Thrace, which would give it access to the Aegean.

The Greek Ministry of Defense, which was responsible for the security of the frontier, founded the Commission of Fortifications in charge of preparing the instructions and guidelines for the defenses. This commission was further divided into subordinate commissions consisting of officers from various branches. These smaller commissions, somewhat similar to the Czechs's, worked on the various fortified sectors of the Metaxas Line, surveying the terrain and selecting the building sites. Another engineer organization, based in Salonica, also subdivided into five sub-groups, did the technical planning.

Between 1936 and 1941, civilian companies were entrusted with the construction of the fortifications. The concrete was produced locally from limestone quarries and pebbles from beach areas. From Thera, now believed the island which the story of Atlantis is based on, ships carried volcanic material which was used to increase the strength of the concrete by about 30 percent.

Meanwhile the military prepared a defense plan that only called for delaying action in Thrace. The positions on the eastern sector, manned by an army corps, covered the seaport of Alexandropolis. The defenses on the Metaxas Line, on the other hand, protected Macedonia and ran from the Kerkíni Mountains west of the Struma Valley towards Porto Lagos near the mouth of the Nestos, but did not reach that seaport.

According to the 1938 plan, the Greek forces were to use the Metaxas Line along the Nestos River as a jumping off point for an offensive against Bulgarian contingents moving against Aleandropolis. The Greeks optimistically hoped that Turkey would strike Bulgaria from the other flank.

The work on coastal defenses also began in 1936 with the creation of the Superior Coast Defense Command based in Athens under the command of a rear admiral. In the spring of 1938 there were harbor defenses built in the Athens-Piraeus area, the Gulf of Patras, the Gulf of Corinth, and the Gulf of Amvrakia. There were also plans for harbor defenses at Thessaloniki, the Strait of Evrippu (Egrippos Channel), and the Gulf of Evia (Talanta Channel), which separated the island of Euboea from the mainland.

In 1937 a group of German specialists led by Admiral Kinzel went to Greece to help in the preparation of the Greek coast defenses. The group was given access to information on the organization, sites, and design of the emplacements. It left Greece a year later, but one or more members returned periodically to Greece to give additional advice.

In 1938, the Superior Coast Defense Command was subdivided into several Harbor Defense Commands that included: Western Greece (HQ at Patras), Crete (HQ at Canea), Southern Aegean (HQ at Piraeus), Northern Aegean (HQ at Thessaloniki), Euboea (HQ at Chalkis), and East Islands (HQ at Chois). A Coast Defense School was in the planning.

The war with Italy in 1940 forced the Greeks to shift the bulk of the army to the Albanian front. In 1941, two divisions faced the border with Yugoslavia. Only three divisions defended the Metaxas Line, two east of the Struma River, with the Nestos and Evors brigades in east (Thrace). In reserve was a motorized division west of the Struma. The Greek Second Army with only about 70,000 men, including the garrisons of the Metaxas Line and border companies, defended the Bulgarian front. The Germans estimated Metaxas Line required 150,000 men, and the lack of these troops reduced its effectiveness. The fact that in January 1941 General Alexander Papagos, the C-in-C of the Army, insisted that the British must send nine divisons to support his forces on the Bulgarian and Yugoslav borders seem to verify this.

2. The Carol Lines and Rumanian Fortifications

In the early 1930s, the Rumanian defenses facing the Soviet Union were limited in size and scale as well as being outdated. Some areas of Bessarabia had no fortifications at all. In 1932 a group of Polish officers on an inspection tour reported that the highways had been greatly improved but that more work was necessary, and that the fortifications of the region were inadequate to thwart a Soviet attack. They also noted that the Rumanians planned to defend Bessarabia on the Dniestr River.

In September 1939, the defenses of Bessarabia and Bukovina were still insignificant. However, after the fall of Poland, Bulgaria engaged 100,000 civilians to build the Eastern Carol Line, which was ready by the spring of 1940. It is still not clear if the main defenses were on the west bank of the Dniestr or the Prut. According to the media, King Carol had shifted his forces from the Prut to the Dniestr during the Finnish Winter War in order to build new defenses. Apparently the king believed that the Soviets would not attack because they were tied down in Finland.

The situation on the border with Hungary was somewhat different. Alarmed by the events of 1937, Romania hurried to build a defensive line, recruiting the civilian population to help with the work. Although every defensive line in Rumania was named after King Carol II, this line built on the border with Hungary can lay claim to being the original Carol Line, since it was the first to be built. Like most of the European fortified lines, it was often compared with the Maginot Line. Indeed American intelligence officers, who estimated that it would not be ready until the summer of 1940, claimed that it would be as strong as the Maginot Line. In reality, the Carol Line had little in common with Maginot Line.

After the partition of Czechoslovakia and Poland, the Western Carol Line was extended to the north and northeast, facing territory newly annexed by Germany and the Soviet Union. This extension was given the name of the Eastern Carol Line in 1939

Rumors started circulating about a third Carol Line that was to defend the Dobruja region against Bulgaria and protect the Constanza-Bucharest rail line. The Danube, a major water barrier, covered most of the border west of this projected line.

In the event, the various Carol Lines proved of little military value to Rumania because Germany negotiated the surrender of northern Transylvania, with most of the Western Carol Line, to Hungary in 1940. Bulgaria, on the other hand, was given South Dobrogea, which ended any further plans to defend that area successfully. The year brought more bad news when the Soviets occupied Northern Bukovina and Bessarabia, taking away the last of Rumania's defenses. The Rumanian dictator, General Ion Antonescu, ordered the preparation of a new line of fortifications between the Danube and the Carpathian Mountains, and along most of the Siret River, over a distance of 80 km. This new line was called the FNB Line because it ran from Focsani to Namoloasa and Braila. In 1942, Antonescu ordered the reinforcement of the line. Thus by 1944 the FNB Line included about 3,000 concrete positions and 60 km of anti-tank ditches.

3. The Turkish Straits

The Montreux Convention of 1936, which revised the 1923 Treaty of Lausanne, allowed Turkey to remilitarize the Straits and gave it the right to regulate the passage of warships during war and peacetime alike. No sooner was the treaty signed than the Turkish Parliament authorized funds for the rearmament of the positions on the Straits. Turkish troops reoccupied the area surrounding the Straits and military zones were set up.

Turkey does not appear to have invested any time and money on fortifications, but rather on weapons, mostly mobile weapons. In 1936, Turkey placed orders for guns, anti-aircraft guns, anti-tank guns, and prime movers with the Czech Skoda Company and the German Krupp Works. The first of these weapons were unloaded at the docks of Istanbul in December 1936. In 1937, it was reported that Turkey was attempting to purchase a number of 340-mm railway guns from the Skoda Works to defend the Dardanelles. In addition, it ordered ten 13.5-inch and two 15-inch guns from Great Britain for the defense of the Dardanelles. However, these guns, which were expected in early June, were not delivered because the British found their own need for these weapons superseded Turkey's.

DESCRIPTION

1. The Metaxas Line and Greek Fortifications

Before the war, the main criticism of the Metaxas Line was that it lacked depth. The American military attaché, LTC E. Villaret, disagreed with this point of view as he wrote in 1938 that despite its shallowness, "it is probably strong enough to hold at the only points at which it can be attacked because the poor communications make any overwhelming concentration of force against these points practically impossible." He neglected to mention, however, that many of the positions were located at almost inaccessible sites that dominated key communication routes.

Villaret claimed that the Metaxas Line, with its reinforced concrete positions that included "sunken batteries," machine gun bunkers, and underground shelters, was patterned after the Maginot Line. Actually, its many small combat positions placed at strategic points in the rugged terrain and its anti-tank and wire obstacles, were more reminiscent of the French Alpine defenses. The Greek combat blocks were small and often had subterranean facilities linked by a tunnel system. As in the Maginot Line, strong points similar to the ouvrages served as the main defensive points on the Metaxas Line and were supported by secondary positions.

The Metaxas Line was about 350 km long and, according to the Germans, included approximately 1,200 combat positions, about 700 of which were part of the forts. Assuming these numbers are correct, a high percentage of positions formed strong points or forts akin to the French ouvrages or the German Werkgruppen. The blocks of the Greek strong points were generally smaller, but covered an area of similar size.

The forts, concentrated at key points on the Metaxas Line, relied on the difficult terrain for defense. Many were integrated into command groups similar to the French fortified sectors. Some sectors consisted mostly of light positions and others of a combination of heavy and light positions. A group usually consisted of three strong points but could include as few as two or as many as five. All the forts in a group were given the name of the group to which they belonged. There was a total of eight groups that included twenty-nine of the forty-one forts built. The remainder of the forts, including the important fort of Nimfea guarding the Pass of Makaza and Fort Chinos (Eshinos) to the west of it, were independent positions. The most important forts were located as follows, from west to east:

Struma Sector: forts of Popotlevitsa (Popotlivica), Istebei, Kelkagia (Kelkaja)(3)*, Paliouriotes (Paljuriones), Rupel (Usita)(5)*, Karatas (3)*, and Kali ()*.

Nevrokopion Sector: forts of Persek, Babasora, Malianga (4)*, Perithori, Partalouska, Dasavli, Pisse (identified by the Germans as Ochiron-Lisse), Pyramidoeides, Kastillo (3)*, Ajos Nikolaos ()* and Bartiseva ()*±.

Nestos Sector: fort of ChinosAlexandropolos Sector: fort of Nimfea

*Positions noted were groups of forts with number in ( ). Those which have a ( ) without a number represent the ones at which there was no data available regarding the number of forts, but these three groups totaled eleven forts.

±The last three forts may actually have only been two. Kastillo was probably the German name for Bolax (Wolax). What the Germans identified as Ajos Nikolaos and Bartiseva may have actually been together as Lisse, all on the western valley of the Nestos River.

One additional fort named Beles was on the west end of the line north of Lake Kerentis atop the Kerníki Mountains near the point where the borders of Yugoslavia, Bulgaria and Greece meet. It was beyond support of the other forts of the Struma Sector.

The Rupel (Usita) group, the largest, numbered 1,200 men, Kelkagia 600, and Malinga 500. The garrisons of independent forts varied in number. Forts Paljuriones and Pisse (Ochiron-Lisse) held 500 men apiece, which was more than the individual forts of the Kelkagia and Malinga groups. In contrast, the smaller forts of Perithori and Poptlevitsa had garrisons of 200 men. Partalouska had 125 men and Dasavli as few men as 80.

The basin in the Nevrokopion section was encircled by fortifications such as the fort of Pisse (Ochiron-Lisse) that occupied an isolated conical peak. Fort Pisse (Ochiron-Lisse) and three others in the sector were covered by a large anti-tank ditch. Like most of the Greek fortifications, they were difficult to spot from the Bulgarian frontier. According to a 1941 German report on the main positions:

> The nearly completed works Usita and Paljuriones constituted the main defenses.... Field-type fortifications replaced a few missing bunkers at the southern front of the Usita works. Each work of the Usita group was staggered, from east to west, 20 meters above the next work. The western part also dominated the outpost area of the Paljuriones works. These works flanked the Kelkaya Group. The Kelkaya group, in turn, rose 700 meters above the Paljuriones works. A continuous anti-tank trench ran in front of the northern edge of the Usita and Paljuriones works, and on the northwestern rim of the Kelkaja works. The Istebei and Popotlivica fortifications were situated only 200 meters from the border. The Istebei works were completed; reinforced obstacles protected them against surprise attacks. Popotlivica was not yet half finished and presented only a linear fortification facing northwest (from *German Attacks on Fortified Positions*).

A Greek fort usually consisted of as many as twenty combat blocks or as few as a dozen or less. The blocks might be classified as small infantry casemates. They were mostly uni-functional, rather small, and devoid of cloches or turrets. However, according to a German report, there were blocks with an armored cloche. Most held machine guns, but some mounted mortars or searchlights. Anti-tank gun casemates guarded the more easily accessible approaches. Some of these casemates housed two mortars or anti-tank guns. Most blocks also served as observation positions, although there were special observation blocks. Some forts included a howitzer casemate and anti-aircraft gun blocks and, apparently, a few positions mounted 75-mm and 77-mm guns.

Fort Istebei is an example of a very large Greek fort with 400 men. It was entirely surrounded with barbed wire and had two entrance blocks and a large tunnel complex that covered an area of about 250 x 300 meters. The entrance blocks of most forts were usually rather simple structures usually lacking external defenses. Istebei's subterranean system included concrete-lined tunnels 1.0 to 1.4 meters wide and 2.4 meters high. The tunnels were generally about 15 meters below the surface and in some forts they ran for a few hundred meters, but in the larger ones like Istebei there were over 4 km of galleries. Since they were small, these tunnels were not curved, but formed sharp angles to create interior defensive positions. Interior defenses were reported to have been present in most of the major forts and these included air locks, blockhouses, and mined sections of the tunnels. Many of the tunnels ended in a block that served as a sally port. These well hidden exits were intended for use against enemy troops on the fort and also as an entry for a relief force. The underground facilities, located near the center of Fort Istebei and close to its entrance, consisted of command centers, a caserne, a usine, ventilation equipment, food stores, and an infirmary. The magazines were situated near the combat positions. Surprisingly, these small tunnels also included a narrow-gauge track for manually operated wagons that hauled artillery ammunition.

Although no large anti-tank ditch appears around the mountain top position of Istebei, some forts like the large one of Rupel had an anti-tank ditch running around their front.

Fort Istebei consisted of twenty-eight combat blocks, mostly for machine guns. A couple of these positions had light mortars in addition to machine guns. Two of the Istebei blocks housed 81-mm mortars. Mortar blocks in the Metaxas Line usually had an open firing position similar to the famous Axis "Tobrucks" with an armoured lid to cover the position. One block near the entrances mounted a howitzer and another, that stood nearby, anti-aircraft guns. The anti-aircraft blocks consisted of a light revolving cupola which opened by splitting into two halves. These positions mounted 20-mm machine guns. The specialized positions included three observation blocks and a machine gun casemate with a searchlight. One block in an isolated position with no underground connection was used for observation, and included machine guns and an anti-tank weapon.

Fort Istebei's interval positions held various types of weapons of German and French origin, most of which were already considered obsolete. Some of the smaller were forts like Pisse (Ochiron-Lisse) which consisted of three machine gun, three artillery and one anti-tank gun casemate.

The group located along the Struma Valley, a typical group position, is described in a 1942 German document. It consisted of three forts identified as A, B, and C. Fort A had twelve machine gun casemates, two observation positions, and a casemate with anti-tank guns. Fort C stood to its rear, and consisted of twelve machine gun positions, a mortar blocks, and two observation positions. Fort B, also behind Fort A, comprised twenty-five machine gun casemates, four artillery casemates, four mortar positions, eleven observation positions , and one anti-tank emplacement. The 1942 document does not identify the group, but it may well have been either the Karatas or Kali Group.[1]

In the intervals between forts were some 500 of the remaining combat blocks, which are the equivalent of French casemates or blockhouses with facilities. They included machine gun and artillery casemates, which, in some cases, occupied isolated positions. Some of these blocks were made of stone. Many artillery positions were located to the rear of the line.

There were three types of concrete thickness for the Greek fortifications that could resist 105-mm, 155-mm, or 220-mm shells. The highest category, used in most of the machine gun and anti-tank gun casemates, could also resist a 300 kg bomb. Depending on the type of positions, the roof thickness varied from 0.6 to 2.0 meters. The walls were usually between 1.0 to 1.5 meters thick with a standard of about 1.2 meters.

The obstacles not only included barbed wire and anti-tank ditches, but also anti-tank rails and concrete pyramids similar to the German "Dragon's Teeth." They blocked the approaches to strong points. In places, several rows of concrete anti-tank obstacles alternated with a couple of lines of anti-tank rails. Many anti-tank ditches were water-filled.

The army garrisoned the coastal defenses, except for the naval bases. Some of these positions built by Metaxas during the 1930s included concrete shelters and even gun turrets. The Greek coastal defenses of Athens-Piraeus included the positions on the islands of Fleve, Psitalia, and Salamis. A naval arsenal protected by three batteries of 88-mm anti-aircraft guns was located on Salamis. A battery of 150-mm guns stood at Punta, on the southeast end of the island. Psitalia Island had two batteries of 150-mm guns and three of 76-mm anti-aircraft guns positioned to protect Piraeus harbor. At Cape Tourla, on Aegina Island to the south of Salamis, there were two batteries of 305-mm guns, one of 150-mm guns, and anti-aircraft gun batteries. Near Perdica, on the same island, stood another 305-mm gun battery and an anti-aircraft gun battery. Fleve Island mounted a battery of 305-mm guns, two batteries of either 120-mm or 150-mm guns, and two anti-aircraft gun batteries[2].

Cape Papas, west of Patra, was home to four 305-mm guns in two batteries, two of which were emplaced by the end of 1938. Two more batteries of 305-mm guns were located near Cape Scropha, opposite Cape Papas. In addition, Cape Papas and Cape Scropha held four gun batteries of 75-mm anti-aircraft guns and 47-mm guns. At Cape Rion, on the Gulf of Corinth, there were machine gun bunkers and a pair of 76-mm and 47-mm gun batteries. In addition, a submarine net stretched from Cape Rion to Anirion. Fortifications also covered a naval base in the Gulf of Amvrakia.

Two fortified groups were built on the coast of the North Aegean. The 1st Group, East, at Cape Karabournu consisted of pre-war installations with a battery of four 270-mm Krupp guns in two twin gun turrets and a similar battery with 240-mm Krupp guns. It also had an ancient battery of three 190-mm guns that may have been deactivated in 1938, during the installation of a 305-mm gun battery. The 2nd Group, West, at the mouth of the Vardar River, consisted of old, pre-World War I installations that included a battery of four 100-mm guns and another of anti-aircraft guns.

The coastal defense positions were equipped with artillery weapons, all of which, except the anti-aircraft guns, were mounted in armored turrets linked by underground concreted tunnels that held the magazines. The heavy and medium caliber artillery, which came from the obsolete battleships *Lemnos* (ex-U.S.S. *Idaho*) and *Kilkis* (ex-U.S.S. *Mississippi*), consisted of:

8 - 12-inch (305-mm) guns
16 - 8-inch (203-mm) guns
16 - 7-inch (178-mm) guns

The following weapons came from other ships:

16 - 3-inch (76-mm) guns
9 - 273-mm guns
15 - 152-mm guns

The anti-aircraft guns, which were mounted so they could also cover the minefield and engage small vessels, included 47-mm, 76-mm, and 88-mm guns of recent German manufacture.

2. The Carol Lines and Rumanian Fortifications

Few details are available on the Rumanian fortifications besides their lightest works. It is known that, in some places such as Bessarabia, old forts were reinforced and put back into use wherever they were available.

By 1938, trenches were dug and underground shelters and over sixty concrete machine-gun bunkers built, mainly in the river valleys along the Hungarian front. The bunkers mounted two machine guns. The purchase of 600 units consisting of machine guns and 47-mm anti-tank guns from the Czechs at the end of 1938, seems to indicate that additional bunkers were being built to accommodate them. Apparently, the Czechs helped the Rumanians design their new positions, which were designed for their own weapons. Supporting positions included emplacements for four batteries of 150-mm Skoda guns. They were located on both sides of the main highways and camouflaged with latticed blinders to conceal them from motorists. Permanent guards helped pinpoint their location.

It is likely that other fortifications were built in Bessarabia and in the south along the same pattern. Apparently the new bunkers were larger than the older models. A permanent garrison of three special fortress detachments was drawn from three infantry divisions.

3. The Turkish Straits

Turkey set up a coastal defense system on the peninsula on the northern side of the Dardanelles. In 1939 it included three batteries of old Russian 8-inch howitzers, five batteries of 6-inch guns, and an assortment of smaller weapons. On the Asiatic side, there were two 210-mm Skodas in the vicinity of Çanakkale. There were also five batteries of 6-inch guns and three of 6-inch howitzers. A number of concrete emplacements were located on the coast between Kimkale and Guilpinar.

WEAPONS AND EQUIPMENT

GREECE

Coastal Defense:	RANGE (METERS)
305-mm naval guns	20,000+
88-mm AA Gun (Krupp)	10,600 (vertical)
76-mm AA Gun (Krupp)	11,400 (vertical)
47-mm AA Gun (Krupp)	5,185 (vertical)

(The 76-mm and 47-mm guns were probably Skoda and not Krupp since the latter did not produce that caliber of weapon.)

Metaxas Line fortifications:

155-mm Howitzer (Schneider)	17,800
105-mm Mountain Howitzer (Skoda)	9,800
88-mm AA Gun (Rheinmetall)	10,600 (vertical)
80-mm AA Gun (Bofors)	
85-mm Howitzer (Schneider)	15,150
81-mm Brandt-Stokes Mortar*	5,000
75-mm Mountain Cannon (Schneider-Daglis)*	9,025
65-mm Mountain Cannon (Schneider)	6,500
47-mm AT Gun (Skoda)*	4,000
37-mm AT Gun (Rheinmetall)**	7,000
37-mm AA Gun (Rheinmetall)	2,000 (vertical)
20-mm AA MG (Rheinmetall)*	2,200 (vertical)
7.92-mm MG (Rheinmetall)	
7.85-mm MG	
7.65-mm MG (Hotchkiss)	

(The 155-mm was the army's heaviest artillery. Many modern weapons were ordered from abroad but never delivered. The old 75-mm Schneider-Daglis Cannon became a mainstay of the defenses. Only about 100 artillery pieces supported the Metaxas Line since most of the army's 3,000 pieces faced the Italians.)

Rumania

47-mm AT guns	4,000
150-mm Skoda guns Mle 1927 (1928?)	23,900

Turkish

8-inch Russian howitzers	
6-inch guns and howitzers	
210-mm Skoda Kanonu M-52*	33,000

*Weapons used in blockhouses of Metaxas Line.
**Twenty-four of these were used in the forts.

WORLD WAR II

1. Greece

The Italian invasion across the Albanian border forced Greece to alter its defensive plans in 1940. Greek divisions were shifted to the Albanian front—defended only by light field fortifications—to contain and drive back the Italian forces. When Germany attacked Greece and Yugoslavia in April 1941, the Greek forces were off balance and the Metaxas Line was still incomplete. The British contribution was not enough to support the Metaxas Line, and they wanted the Greeks to defend a more central position on rugged slopes. This was where the British took up position. The Greeks were left on their own. However, the Axis powers lacked sufficient knowledge of the composition of the Greek fortifications to develop advanced plans for their elimination partially because of their location and excellent camouflage. The Germans soon found that they could not bypass the key routes and the strong points protecting them. In the end German superiority in weapons and numbers allowed them to force their way through.

The German 2nd Panzer Division, two mountain divisions, and three infantry divisions faced three Greek divisions in the Struma sector, the only place where the Greek fortifications were clearly visible from Bulgaria. On April 6, after eliminating minor resistance on the border, the German 50th Division ran into the isolated Nimfea group east of the Metaxas Line. Its surprise attack on Nimfea failed, but on the evening of April 7, after a bombardment of an hour and a half, German troops infiltrated the Greek lines, attacking from three directions. After losing several bunkers in close combat, the 400-man garrison surrendered that night. To the west, the partially completed fort of Echinos lasted three days before its garrison withdrew.

Meanwhile, the German 72nd Division advanced on the Nevrokopion Basin, but intense fire prevented it from bringing forward the artillery. On the afternoon of April 7 the field fortifications in front of Fort Malianga were captured. Two subsequent attacks on Fort Malianga failed and even an attempt to bypass the fort was foiled by the defenders. Only a few outposts of Malianga had fallen by April 9.

A German battalion was driven back by Fort Perithori and took heavy losses in a second attack on that strong point on April 6. German 88-mm anti-aircraft guns destroyed two bunkers, but Greek artillery drove them off on April 6. Early in the morning of April 7, the German battalion from the 266th Regiment managed to penetrate the position, but after eliminating several bunkers, it was driven out by the Greeks.

The German 266th Regiment was also repulsed in an attempt to capture the fortified mountain position east of Pisse (Ochiron). Two attacks on April 7 inflicted heavy losses on the Germans who found it impossible to climb the steep slopes below the bunkers. The 105th Regiment succeeded in taking the fortifications on the ridge of Kresti after heavy fighting. However, Greek counter attacks on April 8 almost recaptured the ridge.

Also in the eastern sector, German troops forced their way into one of the three tunnels of Pyromidoides. The garrison no longer capable of mounting a counterattack, detonated the mines in the tunnel sealing it off and continued to resist until the armistice. On the western sector of the Metaxas Line the 125th Regiment, a veteran from operations on the Maginot Line, was reinforced during its attack on the Struma positions. Its path was barred by the almost completed forts of Rupel (Usita) and Paljuriones, the completed Istebei group, and the half-finished fortifications of Poptlevitsa about 200 meters from the border. On April 6, artillery and air attack heralded the beginning of the attack, which failed. The Struma River could not be crossed. The Germans also suffered heavy losses in three fruitless attacks on Fort Usita on April 6. The German attacks continued to fail until April 9.

The 5th Mountain Division succeeded in taking a couple of positions in a surprise attack on April 6. Dive-bomber attacks on Hill 1941 at Rupesco (probably refers to Rupel), Istebei, and Popotlevitsa failed. The Rupesco position held out against the German mountain troops until April 9 when Popotlevitsa also surrendered after heavy fighting.

Another German mountain battalion attacked Istebei's western slope before the fall of Popotlevitsa, reached the heights, and eliminated a few of the bunkers early in the afternoon. However the remaining bunkers continued to resist, inflicting heavy casualties on the attackers, who had to be relieved by another battalion on the afternoon of April 7. A German assault team blasted through a cloche and attempted to enter the tunnels, but was repulsed by the Greeks. Finally the defenders surrendered after the ventilation system was damaged by explosives and they were overcome by smoke.

On April 6, a battalion of the 100th Mountain Infantry Regiment attacked the fort of Kelkaja, but was repulsed by the flanking fire from Istebei. That afternoon, using infiltration tactics, the Germans reached the fort but had to take the bunkers one by one. On the morning of April 7, they located the main entrance. But first they had to demolish parts of the fort, use flame-throwers against it, and finally damage the ventilation system before the garrison would surrender. The central part of the fort was taken later that day. The next day, the Greeks evacuated the southeastern part of the fort before the Germans attacked, even though most of the positions were still intact. From here the German 125th Regiment joined the mountain troops in the attack on the western sector of Paljuriones.

Further east, the 6th Mountain Division broke through the Krusia Sector by April 8 after crossing what the Greeks believed an impassable 2100 meter high snow covered mountain range, while the 2nd Panzer Division continued to envelop the Metaxas Line.

The forts of the Nevrokopion Sector held out until ordered by the Greek high command to surrender. The Struma Sector fought to the bitter end and its forts were eliminated one by one. The Germans attacked twenty-four forts and managed to take only five in their brief campaign.

The Germans best summarized the results of the victory over the Greeks by stating that their enemy was numerically inferior and lacked the troops to eliminate penetrations despite their tough determined resistance.[3]

2. Rumania

Rumania lost all of its pre-war defenses to territorial annexations in 1940. Its only remaining defenses, the FNB Line, went into action in August 1944 against the

Soviets. It was Rumania's last ditch effort before its government collapsed and defected to the Allies.

3. Turkey

Turkey's defenses were more impressive on paper than in reality. In actuality it had no effective defenses against the Soviets or the British and French in the 1930s. Its army was relatively weak compared to other military forces and not capable of mobile defense. Thus Turkey found itself negotiating with the Axis during the war because its lack of major fortifications could not provide security. Nonetheless, the rugged terrain of the country should have made defense relatively easy beyond the Straits.

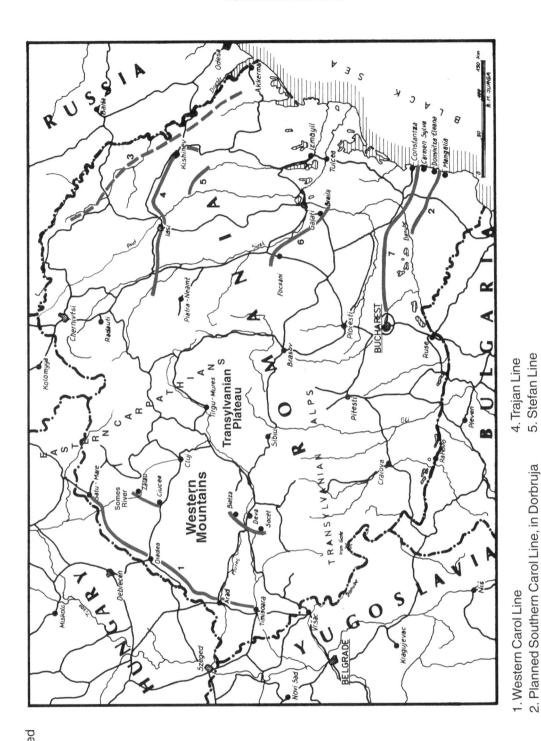

Rumanian Fortified
Lines

1. Western Carol Line
2. Planned Southern Carol Line, in Dorbruja
3. Eastern Carol Line
4. Trajan Line
5. Stefan Line
6. F-N-B Line (1941-1944), R-R Line (Bucharest-Constanza)

Example of a Rumanian bunker for heavy MG.

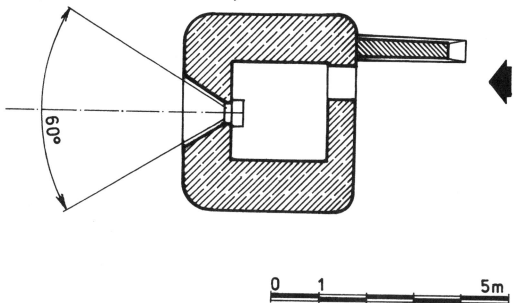

60°

0 1 5m

R.M. JURGA

Drawing of Greek Fortified Position

1. Proposed Greek defense line on Albanian frontier
2. Belasica-Krusia Line
3. Strymon Line
4. Nverokopjon Line
5. Nestos Strong Point
6. Fortified Group Echinos
7. Fortified Group Nimfea
8. Defense Ring of Alexandroplis
9. Aliakmon Line
#2-#7 are the Metaxas Line.

Metaxas Line (Greece) - Several Fortified Groups

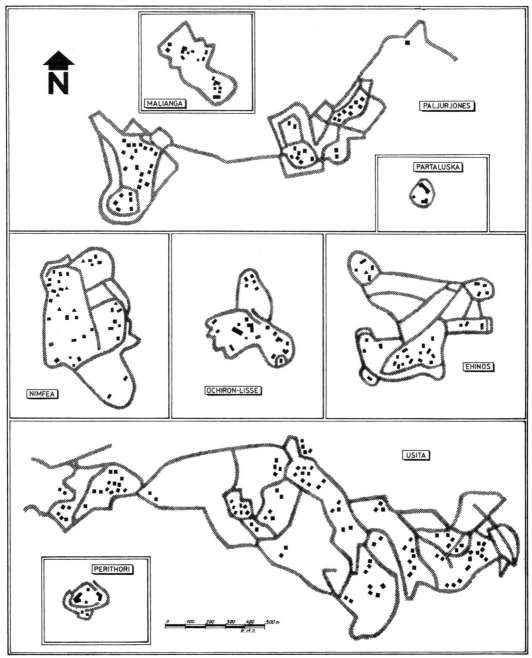

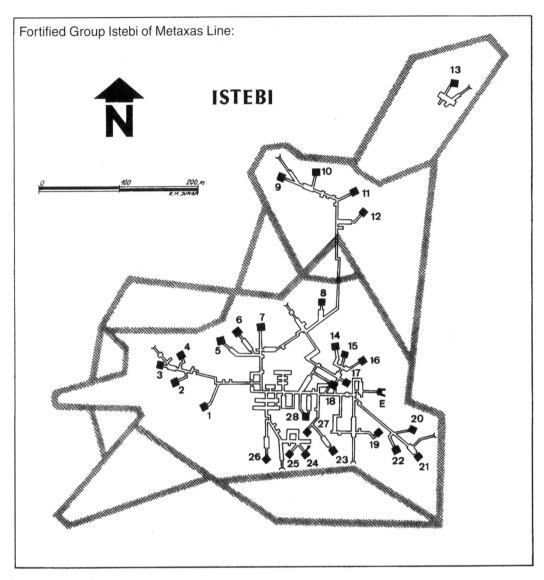

Fortified Group Istebi of Metaxas Line:

ISTEBI

Block E- Entrance

1, 3, 5, 6, 8, 10, 12, 14, 16, 17, 18, 20, 21, 22, 23, 26, and 28 for Heavy MG.

2. Heavy MG and Searchlight

4, 7, 15, 27. Obsv Cupola

9, 11. Heavy MG and Light Mortar

13. Heavy MG, AT Gun and Obsv Cloche

19. Howitzer

24, 25. Heavy Mortar.

Greek Strong Point Block for AA Gun.

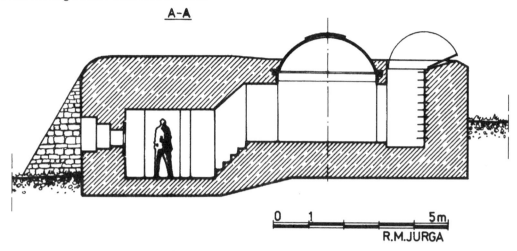

A-A

0   1   5m
R.M.JURGA

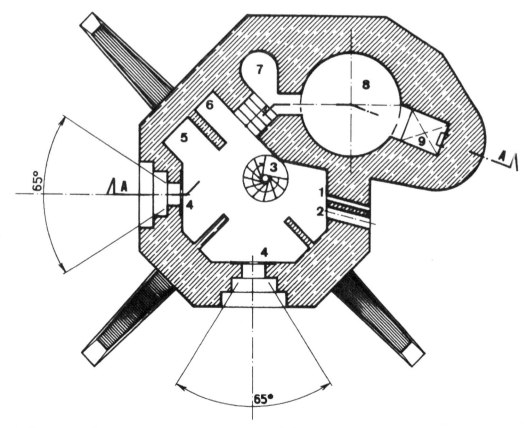

65°

65°

1. Observation slit
2. Pipe for signal light to communicate
3. Access stairs to underground
4. Heavy MG Position with armored plate
5. Magazine for MG

6. Commo center
7. AA magazine ammo
8. AA guns under a light revolving armor turret
9. Emergency exit

323

Strong Point Block linked to underground system and mounts 81-mm in cupola.

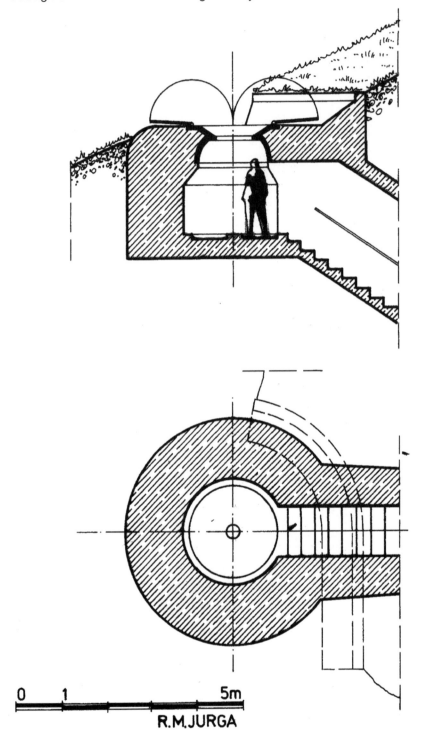

0   1   5m

R.M.JURGA

Nestos Defensive Position for Heavy MG.

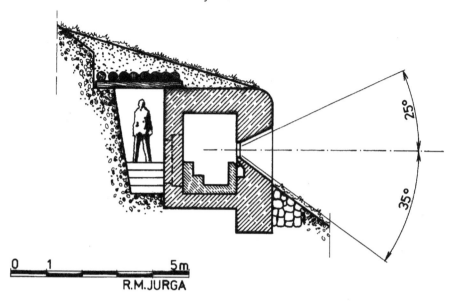

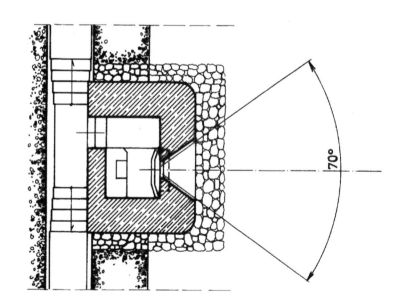

R.M.JURGA

Greek Bunker for 75-mm field gun and observation.

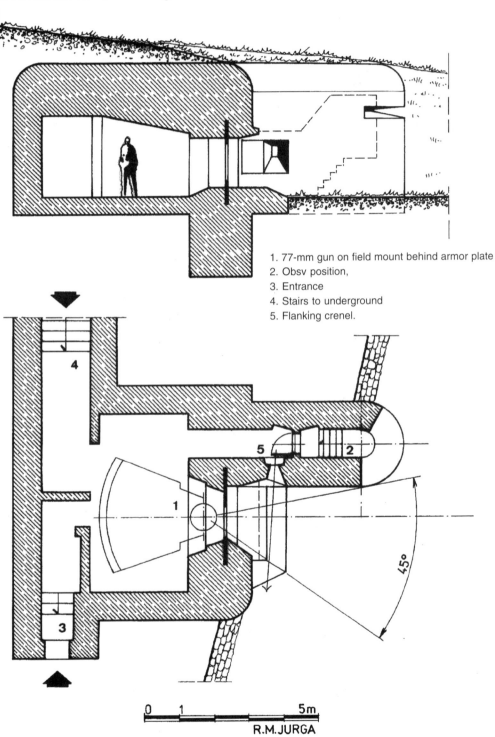

1. 77-mm gun on field mount behind armor plate
2. Obsv position,
3. Entrance
4. Stairs to underground
5. Flanking crenel.

0 1   5m

R.M.JURGA

Greek position for two rifle grenade launchers.

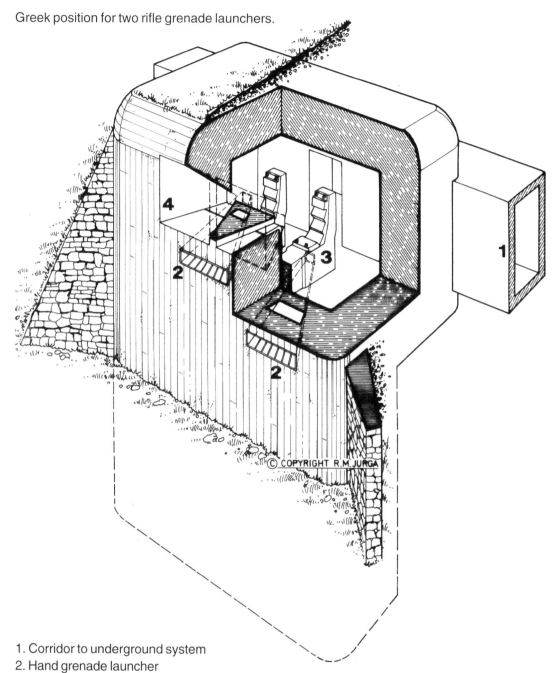

1. Corridor to underground system
2. Hand grenade launcher
3. Concrete wood covered ledge for supporting rifle located in four firing positions

Chapter 13

FINLAND

BACKGROUND

Sandwiched between Germanic and Slavic cultural areas, the Finns have been caught in a tug of war between the Swedes and Russians for centuries, probably faring better under Swedish than Russian rule. They spent the majority of the nineteenth century under the domination of Russia and many of them, including Carl Gustav E. Mannerheim, served in the Russian army during World War I. When the Russian Civil War tore the Empire asunder, both Red and White forces fought to dominate Finland in late 1917. The arrival of German troops brought victory to the White forces of Mannerheim and soon the bloody struggle ended, leaving the Finns independent at last. Although Finland was the state with the largest land area to achieve independence from Russia, its population barely consisted of a couple of million people.

When it gained its independence, Finland inherited old and abandoned Russian equipment and naval vessels from the Russians. However, they shortly received some aid from the French, who sent them aircraft and Renault FT-17 tanks. The fact that the Soviet Union recognized Finland's independence by signing the Treaty of Tartu in October of 1920 did not reassure the Finns. So, during the 1920s they attempted to build some form of defensive system against future Soviet aggression. They concentrated most of the work on the Karelian Isthmus and on the coast defenses in southern Finland.

The creation of a barrier across the Karelian Isthmus was a new enterprise for the Finns since few places in their homeland, besides Viipuri, had been fortified over the centuries. The new government of Finland forced Mannerheim, an opponent of democratic ideals, to retire, and spent almost a decade attempting to protect the country from a possible Soviet invasion. In addition to coastal defenses, the Finns fortified the landward approaches from the Soviet Union on the Karelian Isthmus, the most direct invasion route. Here the terrain consisted of forests, lakes, and marshes, and was crisscrossed by an adequate road system.

The only route to the north, the new Arctic Highway linking Petsamo and its nickel mines to Oulu, traversed one of the most desolate areas of Finland in the Arctic Circle. It was about 10 meters wide, and probably graveled but nonetheless it presented a tempting invasion route for Soviet troops coming out of Murmansk. However, it was not secured with fortifications because the Finns did not have enough resources to defend their Arctic outpost. In this area the determination of the Finnish soldier would effectively have to replace fixed defenses.

MAJOR FORTIFICATIONS

Mannerheim Line
Salpa Line
Coast Defenses

LOCATION

1. Mannerheim Line

The Mannerheim Line stretched approximately 130 km across the Karelian Isthmus, which consisted of some hills and rocky areas between Viipuri and the prewar border. Birch forests, interspersed with open fields covered large parts of the isthmus. There were also small swampy areas that ranged from a couple of hundred meters to 2 km in length and had few, if any, trees and a great deal of moss.

The Mannerheim Line included an intermediate position and the Back Line or Stop Line further to the rear. The main line ran from the Gulf of Finland to Lake Ladoga about 20 to 50 km behind the border, taking advantage of the numerous watercourses and wooded areas, and followed the Kuolemajärvi (Death's Lake)-Muolaa-Sakkola-Taipale route. According to some experts, it consisted of a western and eastern section.

The Western Section stretched about 54 km from the Gulf of Finland to Vuoksi and consisted of two lines 3 to 5 km apart. The Eastern Section extended from Vuoksi to Lake Ladoga, a distance of about 46 km, following the Vuoksi River, which would channel any invasion force. The area around the town of Summa was one of the key points to controlling the isthmus. The defended sectors covered all possible lines of advance along the isthmus but did not form a continuous line of bunkers and trenches. Many of the positions blocked roads, covered river fords, or occupied the spaces between small lakes that dominated the central part of the isthmus.

Lake Ladoga's shoreline was rocky for most of its length, and was most vulnerable in winter when the lake froze, allowing troops and vehicles to cross it. The Karelian Isthmus was mainly low-lying terrain south of Viipuri to the Soviet border with clay-like soil and occupied by much farmland between the forested areas.

2. Salpa Line

Theoretically, the Salpa Line covered the border with the Soviet Union from the Gulf of Finland west of the Karelian Isthmus and to the north of Lake Ladoga. In practice, however, its main positions lay west of the Karelian Isthmus. The heavily forested area along the Soviet border, from north of Lake Ladoga to the Arctic circle, consisted of less than 500 km of hard-surfaced roads and required hardly any defenses. Beyond the isthmus, in the heavily glaciated and wooded lake region of the southern half of Finland, the road system became more extensive, giving the Finns the advantage of interior lines. The terrain of the Karelian Isthmus, on the other hand, offered many advantages to the defender.

North of Viipuri, the land was more hilly than the isthmus and included more birch forest, fewer fields, more rocky areas, and about the same expanse of swamps. The line began near the coast, entering an area of numerous swamps and lakes.

In the south, the Salpa Line actually consisted of several lines although there is some question on whether they should all be lumped together under the same appellation. The first line, an advance position for delaying the enemy, began on the coast about 25 km west of Ristiniemi (southwest of Viipuri). Between this first line and Hamina were other lines that extended to the northeast and north and ended about 20 km southwest of Nuijamaa (south of Lappeenranta). The main line was set up almost directly behind the first line. About 30 km north of the coast it veered to the northwest towards Kivijärvi, at a distance of over 20 km behind the delaying line. In the summer of 1940 a new main line was set up about 20 km east of Hamina and on the coast, running from Sydänkylä northward to Kivijärvi. This new line was preceded by another advance position located about 5 km in front of it.

The remainder of the Salpa Line was not a continuous line of bunkers stretching north from the vicinity of Lappeenranta. The central section of the line ran along the lakes northward to Lake Pielis (Pielisjärvi). These lakes created an almost continuous barrier, at which the Finns set up positions at a number of key points, including islands. The line of concrete bunkers ended in the vicinity of Joensuu (northwest of Lake Ladoga). To the north of Pielisjärvi, the "Wilderness" served as the defense.

3. Coast Defenses

The Finnish Navy and Coast Artillery put the old Russian forts, except for Ino, back into operation. Much of the coastline consisted of rocky promontories separated by beaches, and, in some cases, swamps. In addition, there were numerous islands just off the shore. The Lake Ladoga side was rocky while the coastline on the Gulf of Finland had a low elevation and was covered by sandy beaches near Viipuri. Coast defense positions were set up on many islands adjacent to the Karelian Isthmus. In addition, an attempt was made to space out sufficiently the new gun positions along the coast. The preferred distance was a minimum of about 500 meters. Where possible, the gun battery positions were placed far enough inland to be out of the direct line of fire of naval vessels. Observation positions, on the other hand, occupied well camouflaged sites near the coast.

HISTORY

During the 1920s the Finnish armed forces were reorganized because many units, which had been indoctrinated in the old Russian system, had to be retrained. Many officers were schooled by the Germans. Furthermore, adjustments had to be made to much of the military and naval equipment, which was Russian. Finland's government and military establishment, who were certain that any future threat would come from the east, oriented all their planning and preparations in that direction.

However, the Mannerheim Line was the creation of both Finnish and Soviet propaganda. The Finns tried to fend off aggression through misinformation and exaggeration concerning their defenses. The Soviets, on the other hand, found it expedient to blame their initial failure and exaggerated their victory by inflating the importance of the obstacle they had to overcome. In reality, the Mannerheim Line was no Maginot Line, nor even an obstacle as formidable as the German West Wall.

The construction of the Mannerheim Line began between 1920 and 1921 when many of its positions known as *korsu* or dugouts–wooden bunkers in Finnish—were built. These wooden structures sometimes included machine gun positions and were covered with earth and stones.

The permanent structures, known as *bunkkeri*, could be constructed of either concrete or stone, above or below the ground. A large number of weak concrete bunkers were built during the 1920s. It was not until 1931, during the second building phase, that construction began on concrete bunkers of sufficient strength to resist at least 150-mm (6-inch) guns. The first of these heavier bunkers were not completed until 1932. The bunkers rarely mounted weapons heavier than a machine gun and were not intended to serve as the main fighting positions. Indeed, the Finns preferred to fight outside the bunkers.

Trenches like those made famous at Verdant became a key defensive element. Anti-tank obstacles were also set up. However, the army had virtually no anti-tank guns before the Winter War and only a small force of ineffective tanks. The strength of the line did not lie in its concrete emplacements, but in the soldiers who defended it. Unlike the Maginot Line or West Wall, the fortifications played a minor role compared to their defenders.

Security was not tight around the Finnish fortifications. Before the war, civilians were not denied access to the fortified areas, which, more often than not, were surrounded by private property. Before the war the work on the defenses was done by troops, reservists, and special construction units that were disbanded once the war started. After the war began, the work force was reorganized, but the recruitment of workers turned out to be a slow process. During the Winter War of 1939-1940 Belgian engineers assisted in building some new and smaller bunkers. Despite this effort, however, Finland was practically defenseless at the end of the war.

Only a week after the armistice concluded the Winter War, the Finnish commander-in-chief authorized work on a new and more heavily fortified position between the Gulf of Finland and Lake Kivi (Kivijärvi), which was given the name of Klamila-Luumäki Line (Luumäki Line) and was renamed Salpa Line, or Lock of Finland (Suomen Salpa) by Marshal Mannerheim on July 10, 1944. This line was built with the cooperation of 900 Swedish volunteers, who arrived during the Winter War and went to work about 18 km north of the coast.[1] Over half of the Swedish workers left for home by June and were replaced by Finns in September, which brought the number of workers up to 5,000. Additional work teams formed that summer, and by the spring of 1941, 30,000 men and 2,000 female volunteers labored on the new line, supported by soldiers.

The first construction phase on the Salpa Line ended in June 1941, when the Continuation War (as the Finns called World War II) broke out. It was followed by the next phase that lasted until September 1944, although some artillery positions were not set up on Lake Saimaa until December 1944. The line slowly worked its way northward, encompassing a larger area.

In June 1944, during the Continuation War, when the Finns reoccupied some of their former territory the line was readied for action as the Soviet threat increased and casualties mounted. Instead of extending the original line, the army leadership decided to shorten it in order to reduce the number of troops needed to defend it. The right flank was moved forward to a position running Virolahti-Häkälänjärvi-Tyllinjärvi. With 35,000 men on the job, construction progressed rapidly. The majority of the men worked on the Salpa Line between the Gulf and Lake Saimaa. By October 1944 the work was largely done and troops took up positions.

The Salpa Line involved a much greater effort than the Mannerheim Line. While the Mannerheim Line consisted of about 300 positions according to the Soviets, a number that probably included every korsu and bunker, the Salpa Line comprised closer to 3,000 positions.

In addition to the fortified line, the Finns salvaged and upgraded what they could of the old Russian arsenal on their territory. In 1918 the Finns quickly took over the Russian installations, putting them back into service wherever possible and building new ones. Not all of the Russian fortifications were viable however. For instance, Fortress Ino, only about 30 km distant from the first of the forts protecting the approaches to Leningrad, had to be abandoned because the retreating Russians had blown it up in May 1918. What remained of the fortress was destroyed by the Finns in accordance with the Treaty of Tartu. Nonetheless, the Finns managed to salvage one of the four 12-inch guns in twin turrets, four gun barrels, and sections of a turret. They also recovered two of the fort's eight 152-mm guns, four 8-inch gun barrels, and other sundry material. Little of value remained from the fort's four 11-inch howitzers, eight 10-inch guns and four 9-inch guns. The 12-inch gun was modified to increase its range from 30 km to perhaps over 40 km.[2]

In 1918 the Finnish coast defense forces also inherited the unfinished Fort Mäkiluoto which had been badly damaged by the Russians. The armament, which had included two twin gun 14-inch Vickers-built turrets, probably intended for Borodino Class battleships, was also damaged.

The Finns also inherited Fort Kuivasaari, protecting Helsinki's outer coastal defenses, which had been turned into a base by the Russians in 1896 and further fortified in 1911. Fort Kuivasaari was renovated at a time when the Russians had decided to extend their coastal defenses along the southern coast of Finland as far as Turku and the Årland islands, to control the approaches to Petrograd (Leningrad) on both sides of the Gulf of Finland. The fort had a four-gun 254-mm battery and was almost completed when the war began. In 1918, when German troops arrived to support the White forces, the Reds evacuated the fort, leaving it intact. In the 1920s, Finnish troops trained there with the fort's remaining guns.

One of the most important coastal positions Finland inherited from Russia was the fortress of Hanko (Hangö in Germanic) and its associated island forts. The Russians had intended mounting 305-mm (12-inch) guns and other heavy artillery pieces at Hanko, but did not have time to do so. One of the most important of the island forts was Russarö with six 9.2-inch (234-mm) guns, three of which were put back into operation, and four 75-mm guns. Batteries of 203-mm (8-inch) or 152-mm (6-inch) guns were located on three other islands. In addition there were two mobile batteries with seven 152-mm British Mk VII guns.

In 1923 the Inspector of Coast Defense, General K. E. Kivekäs, took control of the defense of the Finnish coast, which included all naval ports, coastal artillery units, and naval bases. In 1927, further reorganization placed the coastal artillery and the coastal fleet under a single commander. To man the coastal defenses, including those of Lake Ladoga, three artillery regiments, and an independent coast artillery battalion were formed by the army. In addition, two new anti-aircraft batteries were placed under the control of the navy.

Coastal artillery positions also protected the main naval bases at Helsinki and Pansio, near Turku. Early in the 1930s the government decided to erect a twin gun turret at Fort Mäkiluoto and at Fort Kuivasaari. At Fort Mäkiluoto the foundation of one of the demolished twin 14-inch gun turrets was used to set up a new 12-inch gun turret. The turret at Fort Kuivasaari became operational in 1935. However, between 1939 and 1940 the fort's four 254-mm (M-1895) guns were transferred to other coastal forts. In 1940 the base of Hanko and its associated islands was manned by the Finnish Hanko Coast Artillery Brigade.

In addition to the artillery, Finland started developing a navy whose main role was to defend the coast and support both ends of the Mannerheim Line. In 1923 a plan to be implemented in 1924 for building up the navy's 1,300 man force, included the acquisition of three coastal defense ships (3,900 ton displacement), two destroyers, two mine layers, six submarines, thirty coastal motor boats, and a couple of support ships. At the time, the navy only consisted of a few motor torpedo boats and a number of mine sweepers and mine layers. In the 1930s, the navy received the two coastal defense ships armed with four 254-mm (10-inch) guns in two turrets, completed at Turku. Several other vessels, including submarines and coastal defense craft, were built in Finland before the war. By 1939 the Finnish navy approached a strength of 4,000 men, without counting the coast artillery. A small fleet of twenty vessels operated on Lake Ladoga. In addition, a small submarine was especially designed to patrol the lake, but it was not used.

In 1940 the Soviets took over the Hanko area as a result of the peace terms of the Winter War, but the Finns removed the 9.2-inch guns. The Soviets once again planned to set up 12-inch guns on the island fort of Russarö (about 5 km south of the tip of the Hanko peninsula), but the largest weapons there were two gun batteries with 130-mm coastal defense guns. On the mainland they did employ a battery of three railway guns 305-mm (12-inch). In 1941, when the Finnish army recaptured the base during the Continuation War (as Germany's ally), they were able to put back into service some of the weapons including one of the 305-mm railway guns. They also repaired five 130-mm pieces.

DESCRIPTION

1. The Mannerheim Line

The Mannerheim Line mostly covered the main lines of advance from Russia across the Karelian Isthmus. The area between it and the border was the zone of destruction that was intended to delay the enemy. In fact, it was not a continuous line of bunkers and man-made barriers. Instead its main fighting positions consisted of wood-lined trenches protected by obstacles in front. These obstacles, which were not well covered, consisted of concrete and stone dragon's teeth. The stone version was the most inexpensive of the two.

The exact number of bunkers and fortified positions the Finns built, remains a matter of speculation. Mannerheim's count of sixty-six strong points of two or more bunkers each does not agree with General H. Öhquist, his subordinate, who commanded the II Corps in the Karelian Isthmus. According to William Trotter (See *A Frozen Hell*), Öhquist's number was higher because he counted strong points that included mostly weak, older structures.

The Western Section of the line consisted of mostly machine gun bunkers. The Eastern Section included about half a dozen artillery positions and about one fifth of the machine gun bunkers as in the other section. An important artillery strongpoint secured the right flank at Koivisto and another the flank of Lake Ladoga at Taipale.

One of the most common positions was the *korsut* or wooden bunker that varied in size and shape, and was not able to withstand heavy artillery fire. The main works were concrete bunkers mounting machine guns. The newer ones could resist 152-mm weapons while the largest bunker housed a squad of men and held four machine guns. A few positions were designed for field guns up to 75-mm. Since most fighting was done in trenches outside the bunkers, the lack of heavy weapons positions did not matter much. The majority of the bunkers were vulnerable because their weapons fired forward, but there were some that used flanking fire.

There were several types of bunkers, each designed to fit its location. Most bunkers had accommodations for the troops, but some only had a firing chamber. An unusual type of bunker, designed but not built, was to have been dug into the ground, its roof flush with the surface. It would have been outfitted with a small lift to carry a heavy machine gun to the firing position, its barrel pointing upwards. Once elevated, the weapon would fire across the roof of the bunker.

At Muolaa at least one bunker mounted a 75-mm naval gun. Its 2.0 meter thick roof was able to withstand hits from weapons smaller than 200-mm. It consisted of a gun room, munitions storage, ready room, and protected entrance way, and measured about 7 meters on its longest sides. Another bunker at Vuoksen Lauttaniemen housed four field guns, two firing on either side. It included crew quarters and its maximum width was only about 6 meters.

Between 1920 and 1924, 182 concrete positions were built in the Karelian Isthmus, 168 of which were erected in the main line, 144 in the vicinity of Taipale. The remaining fourteen positions occupied the Jänis Line and a rearward position. Most of these positions were concrete machine gun bunkers.

New types of bunkers were designed in the 1930s, 101 of which were built between 1936 and 1939. In addition, forty of the old bunkers were overhauled and eleven were modernized. In some cases, the exposed firing position of the older machine gun bunkers was concreted over and covered with earth. The bunkers were transformed into troop shelters. In some of the modernized bunkers underground facilities and/or additional chambers and protection were added. Among the newer constructions were more standardized machine gun bunkers, some with a cloche, an observation bunker with a cloche, shelters for an infantry squad with protected entrances, and a bunker for a battalion command post of about the same size as the troop shelter. The largest bunkers, mainly the shelters and command posts and a few types of machine gun bunkers, were usually no longer than about 10 meters.

Two of the most famous bunkers near Summa, known as the Million Mark Bunker and the Poppius Bunker, were linked to two other bunkers by underground tunnels. The firing rooms of Poppius held a single machine gun. Million Mark Bunker, located not far from it, had two larger combat positions, one of which had two heavy and one light machine gun and a searchlight. The other position had one less heavy machine gun. It also had three cloches, one of which was in a central position on the tunnel, in an observation block. In both bunkers the accommodations for the garrison were located in the tunnel.

In the fall of 1939, the Mannerheim Line consisted of twenty-nine sectors. Its bunkers were given an identification number consisting of a prefix derived from the abbreviation of the name of their sector, and a number designation. Each sector included fortified groups of one or more concrete bunkers or korsut, wire obstacles, and gun positions, and trenches. Of a total of 150 concrete machine gun bunkers, only 13 mounted two machine guns and 7 three machine guns. The remainder were single weapon bunkers. Slightly over 100 of these bunkers were built in the 1920s and only 7 were renovated in the 1930s. That means that slightly over 50 could be considered of sufficient strength to resist enemy fire. Only 8 gun bunkers and 9 command bunkers were built in the 1920s and none were added after that. Of a total of 41 troop shelters, only 12 were new and 3 were renovated bunkers.

Trenches, obstacles and camouflage also played an important part in the Finnish defenses. Thus six concrete trenches no more than 100 meters long were built in the 1920s along with a large number of korsut and wood-lined trenches. In addition, stone obstacles in the form of boulders weighing up to 3,000 kg, were laid in two rows in an attempt to stop tanks. Barbed wire was nailed to trees and stakes driven into the ground. However, this type of obstacle was not covered by fire from the bunkers and was mostly intended to warn of an enemy approach. The Finns also took advantage of wooded areas with great skill. For instance, they built observation posts in the trees, either below tree top level or above. Wooden towers allowed a good view above the tree tops. They also expertly camouflaged the defensive positions.

The Finns used no minefields in the Mannerheim Line even though they did manufacture their own anti-tank mines. The M-36 mine was similar to the German Teller mine and the M-39 mine was more cylindrical. In 1939, Finnish army depots produced 5,000 such mines. During the Winter War soldiers and depots produced 13,000 of the M/S-39, a wooden box mine with 8 kg of explosive, which was deployed as enemy vehicles approached, and was not placed permanently in any type of defensive mine field.

The Finns also produced anti-personnel mines. Among these was an anti-personnel mine with 1 to 5 kg of explosive that could be ignited by pressure or trip wire. The troops in the field produced their own "tube mine" consisting of a can filled with explosive and detonated like regular land mines. Again, these were used as booby traps rather than in mine fields.

Until 1941 only two types of cloche were used in Finland. One was small, with an inner radius of 40 cm. The other, was larger, with an inner radius of 55 cm, weighed 9 tons. It served as an observation cupola. Both cloche types were one-man positions with a maximum armor thickness of about 17 cm, able to resist shells from 8-inch guns. They had observation slits and an interior rotating ring with two slits— one for a submachine gun and the other for observation—that could be turned to any crenel or rotated so as to block all openings. These cloches were made at the Finnish Karhalan Konepaja or Karhala Machine Works.

The Forward Position, located in front of the Mannerheim Line and adjacent to the Neutral Zone, was manned by the Border Guards and local troops. This position did not constitute a part of the Mannerheim Line, but served to delay the enemy in conjunction with the Demolitions Zone. Both the Neutral Zone and the Demolition Zone consisted mainly of field fortifications.

The intermediate position and Back Line, on the other hand, had no permanent concrete structures. All their bunkers, built during the Winter War, were even smaller than the earlier works.

2. The Salpa Line

This new line included bunkers generally smaller and stronger than those of the Mannerheim Line. Most machine gun bunkers no longer fired forward, but to the flanks. They were also more skillfully adapted to the terrain than before, and many were built into the rock. Although the line was not completed, the number of works finished in the first construction phase (spring 1940 to summer 1941) and the second phase (June to October 1944) was substantial. The permanent structures included:

Positions for an artillery weapon	16
Anti-tank gun positions	52
Shelters for 10 to 60 men	125
Ball bunkers for 10 men	254
Tunnel positions	10
Machine gun positions	295

This was a total of 802 positions including fire control bunkers and other types not listed. In addition to these positions the Salpa Line comprised about 350 km of trenches, 49 Russian tank turrets armed with machine guns, 1,250 covered machine gun positions, 720 troop shelters, 500 artillery positions, and 400 fire control (observation) positions. The line also contained boulders averaging 3,000 kg in weight, placed in four rows of 200 km instead of the more conventional concrete dragon's teeth. These stone obstacles were heavier than those used in two rows built during the Winter War.

The machine gun bunkers varied in size. One of the larger types held twenty men and an observation cloche, and had machine gun embrasures covering the flank and the "L" shaped entrance. This type measured about 14 meters by 9 meters and had a concrete thickness of just under 2 meters. Initially, the machine guns were mounted on a makeshift wooden frame, but this was later replaced with a metal one.

The anti-tank gun bunkers housed a 45-mm weapon and normally also included an observation cloche that was almost three times thicker than those used in the Mannerheim Line.

The "Ball Bunker" was created by excavating a site and using a large rubber ball as a form for the concrete inner walls. When the concrete dried and the frame was removed, the roof of the shelter was spherical. It was then covered with earth and was accessed from a trench. This type of shelter held about ten men.

Most of the bunkers in the Salpa Line had a higher resistance than those of the Mannerheim Line and their cloches were much stronger. These new bunkers were classified according to their ability to withstand bombs. Thus the first class or heaviest bunkers had a roof thick enough to withstand a 1,000 kg bomb.

Normally, the men in the bunker communicated with those in the cloche through a voice tube. However, in the artillery control positions they used a telephone.

In addition to the concrete bunkers, the Salpa Line contained a large number of *korsu* or wooden bunkers. About fifty turrets from captured Soviet tanks armed with machine guns were installed in 1943 and later.

Like the Mannerheim Line, the Salpa Line also contained a variety of obstacles but no wood-lined anti-tank ditches. During 1943 the stone dragon's teeth were tested with captured Soviet tanks. An experimental section of concrete dragon's teeth was placed in the Karelian Isthmus in 1943. It consisted of four rows, each looking like a large concrete coffin with a ridge down the center and one end raised. However, these obstacles were not installed in the Salpa Line.

Fields of anti-tank and anti-personnel mines were also to be included in the Salpa Line. The first mines were laid in the spring of 1941, but they were removed in the summer. In 1944 no mines were laid out because the engineer units in charge of their installation were at the front.

After the Winter War, the majority of the new bunkers were outfitted with a steel sheet, steel netting or 2-inch wooden planks, to line their ceilings. A tube passing through the concrete next to the door carried a telephone line to the trenches. The walls and the ceilings of the machine gun firing rooms were lined with sound absorbing material. The machine gun crews were issued masks linked to hand operated fans to prevent suffocation. In 1943 the rear wall of the bunker was made thin enough to be easily broken from the inside and provide an escape route for the crew.

The permanent bunkers were heated with wood-burning stoves that were also used for cooking. In addition, hand-cranked fans created a slight over-pressure in the event of a gas attack. The bunkers were linked to the outside by telephone or radios with their antennas placed inside concrete.

3. Coast Defenses

The army coastal defense force not only protected the coastline from invasion, but supported operations on the landward side. Several important coastal forts and batteries occupied key positions. Forts Mäkiluoto and Kuivasaari were the only two actually resembling forts.[3]

In 1939 some of the key support positions for the Mannerheim Line and Finnish forces on the Karelian Isthmus were:

Lake Ladoga flank:

Mantsi	2 x 152-mm guns
Konevitsa	4 x 152-mm and 2 x 75-mm guns
Taipale	2 x 120-mm guns

There were 16 other positions with 20 x 152-mm guns, 4 x 120-mm guns and 4 x 75-mm guns, most in two gun batteries. Gulf of Finland flank (Viipuri Sector):

Ristiniemi	2 x 305-mm and 2 x 76-mm guns

Saarenpää	3 x 254-mm and 2 x 152-mm guns
Tiurinsaari	2 x 152-mm guns

There were also four other positions with 20 x 152-mm guns. Along the Finnish coastline were six other sites with gun batteries. These coastal forts included:

Kuivasaari (Helsinki Sector)	2 x 305-mm guns
Mäkiluoto (Helsinki Sector)	2 x 305-mm, 2 x 203-mm and 2 x 75-mm guns
Russarö (Hanko Sector)	6 x 234-mm, 1 x 152-mm and 6 x 75-mm guns
Orö (Turku Sector)	2 x 305-mm and 4 x 152-mm guns

There were twenty-nine other forts with 20 x 254-mm, 4 x 203-mm, 57 x 152-mm, 2 x 120-mm, 12 x 87-mm and 4 x 75-mm guns.

Some of these coastal defenses, such as Fort Russarö, were located on islands. Others, such as Battery Tiurinsaari and three other batteries, were on the Karelian's west coast. Others still, such as Battery Konevitsa and three other batteries, guarded Lake Ladoga. Petsamo on the Arctic coast had a battery of two 87-mm guns, but these weapons were so old that they did not even have a recoil mechanism.

During the Continuation War, new coastal defense positions were created, including twenty-five on Lake Ladoga that mounted weapons ranging from 75-mm to 152-mm guns. Additional coastal defense positions became operational by 1944. Their main weapons included 155-mm, 152-mm, 120-mm weapons, and a few larger guns.

One interesting fact has recently come to light. The Finns had made arrangements with the Estonians so they could coordinate the actions of Fort Mäkiluoto with the batteries at Naissaari to effectively close the Gulf of Finland with artillery fire in 1939. When the Soviets forced Estonia into their camp, this effective barrier was eliminated.

WEAPONS AND EQUIPMENT

The Finns produced most of their own weapons, including foreign models of aircraft. The Tampella company at Tampere manufactured 40-mm Bofors anti-aircraft guns, the 37-mm anti-tank guns, and field guns. The Valmet Company built foreign aircraft under license. Most of the small arms, except pistols, were made in Finland. Finnish industry also produced such items as the cloches for bunkers and small warships. Some items such as tanks, naval mines, and aircraft had to be imported. Most of the heavy coastal guns were old Russian models.

The weapons used included:

*305-mm (12-inch) naval guns	47,000 meters w/improved ammo
*305-mm RR guns	50,000+ meters
*254-mm/45 D (10-inch) guns	27,500 meters

234-mm (9.2-inch Bethlehem Steel)	?
*203-mm/45 C guns	25,000 meters
*203-mm/50 V	28,000 meters
152-mm guns	16,200 meters
152-mm (British Mk VII)	?
*120-mm/45 C guns	18,800 meters
*120-mm/50 V guns	18,500 meters
*120-mm/50 V2 guns	16,500 meters
*120-mm/45 A guns	13,500 meters
105-mm field gun (M-1913 Schneider)	11,040
4.5-inch (105-mm) field gun	6,440 meters
87-mm guns	?
76-mm field gun (M.02)	11,040 meters
75-mm field gun (M-1916)	4,400 meters
37-mm Bofors AT gun	?
81-mm mortar (built under French license)	
7.92-mm Browning Automatic Rifle- 1918 model	
7.92-mm Lahti Model 26/32 light machine gun	
9-mm Suomi M-31 submachine gun	

*The ranges for these weapons were compiled during the war by Finnish Naval HQ for ideal conditions.

WORLD WAR II

When the Winter War began in November 1939, the Finns quickly mobilized their few divisions and prepared to resist the Soviet invasion. The Army of Karelia, which comprised the majority of the army divisions, took up positions to defend the isthmus. Two of the coastal artillery regiments garrisoned the batteries of the Karelian isthmus: the 2nd Regiment on the west coast and the 3rd Regiment on the Lake Ladoga coast.

Despite the fact that the Finns had only about one hundred 37-mm anti-tank guns and a similar number of 40-mm anti-aircraft guns, they managed to halt the Red Army, which was poorly prepared for this type of war. Further north, the Soviet divisions penetrated the "Wilderness" regions, only to be cut off, isolated, and destroyed later in January. Outnumbered and outgunned, the small garrison of Petsamo was forced to withdraw in the first days of the war.

The Red Navy took part in the action early in the war when, on December 1, 1939, the heavy cruiser *Kirov* and two destroyers approached Fort Russarö. The Finnish artillery commenced firing at a range of 23 km, hitting one of the destroyers and forcing the Soviets to flee. On December 14, two destroyers and aircraft attacked Fort Utö, located off the southwest coast, but the fort's 152-mm guns sank one of the destroyers and drove off the other. The last Soviet naval offensive came on December 18, when the battleships *October Revolution* and its escort, subjected Fort Saarenpää on Koivisto, the western flank of the Mannerheim Line, to heavy bombardment. At first the guns of the fort were unable to respond, and the warship began to inflict damage with its 12-inch guns. However, one of the fort's guns was finally returned to action and, after several near misses, forced the enemy to withdraw. The next day the battleship Marat and its escort started bombarding Saarenpää, leveling many of the fort's surface structures. However, the Finnish gunners finally managed to score a critical hit on the battleship, forcing it to retire.

The Finnish border units had withdrawn into the Mannerheim Line by December 6. During the following days, battle raged around the fortified positions at Taipale and Summa. The older bunkers from the 1920s generally collapsed under the weight of the Soviet artillery barrages, but the newer ones stood up reasonably well. However, since the Finns seldom fought from the bunkers, their destruction had little impact on the battle. Heavy fighting took place around the Summa area beginning on December 17. Two days later a Soviet force of 100 tanks lost 20 of its vehicles to the Finns so the battle was called off on the third. On December 25 the Soviets launched a second major attack on Taipale, but again were unable to achieve a major success.

In January, the Soviet forces settled in to fight a trench war in the isthmus. The bunkers near Summa, particularly the Million Mark Bunker and the Poppius Bunker, resisted heroically, inflicting heavy casualties among the Soviets. As a result they became key objectives for the Soviet offensive of February.

In February and March the Finnish forces finally buckled under the Soviet steamroller. The stone dragon's teeth proved easy to drive over in the snow. In addition the coastal waters of the Gulf and Lake Ladoga had frozen, so that the Soviets were able to attack across the ice in an attempt to outflank the Mannerheim Line. However, the Finnish coastal batteries fired their large shells into the ice, literally breaking the ice under the Soviets' feet, inflicting heavy losses and, in one case, sinking tanks.

Nonetheless, the Soviets continued their relentless advance, using heavy guns to destroy many of the remaining bunkers of the line. In those bunkers that withstood the bombardment, the crews died from the concussion.

The Million Mark and Poppius bunkers, once more under attack, became the scene of heavy fighting and hand to hand combat. Mannerheim was forced to pull back to the intermediate line by the middle of February, and to the Back Line on February 27. The Finns sued for peace by the end of the month, but the Soviet troops continued to smash through the Back Line, near Viipuri early in March.

The Finns, left with no more resources to continue the fight, could only stand by as the Russians tore up their front. The Finnish army took heavy casualties, losing about a third of its infantry. The Soviet guns of over 200-mm caliber proved to be the undoing of the fortifications of the Mannerheim Line.

Now the victor, Stalin dictated the peace terms, taking what he had demanded before the war, but withholding compensation. Hanko and Fort Russarö became Soviet bases. Most of the Karelian Isthmus, including Viipuri, the second largest Finnish city, the Finnish Arctic coast, and Petsamo with its nickel mines, became Soviet territory.

With no other recourse, the Finns allied themselves with the Axis, and embarked on the Continuation War in June 1941. They recovered all their lost territories, including the isthmus and Hanko, and advanced no further. By that time, the Salpa Line was already in progress. However, the retreating Soviet forces destroyed most of what was left of the Mannerheim Line. The Finns set up new installations, including on Lake Ladoga.

As the German Eastern Front began to collapse in 1944, Mannerheim hastened the work on the Salpa Line and some advanced positions to conserve manpower. In the latter part of 1944 Finland found itself in yet another conflict with the Soviet Union. Finnish forces began to take increasing casualties as the Soviets advanced. Knowing the Finns would resist against the odds, as they had done during the Winter War, and apparently not anxious to test the new Salpa Line, the Soviets allowed their war with Finland to end. The new fortifications may well have saved Finland from the type of brutal occupation that the nations of Eastern Europe would soon have to endure.

When the war was over the Finns had to remove the 12-inch gun turret from Fort Kuivasaari, which fired only once during the war to harass the Russian troops evacuating Hanko in 1941. It was returned and restored to its position in 1960. The army still maintains many of the bunkers of the Salpa Line.

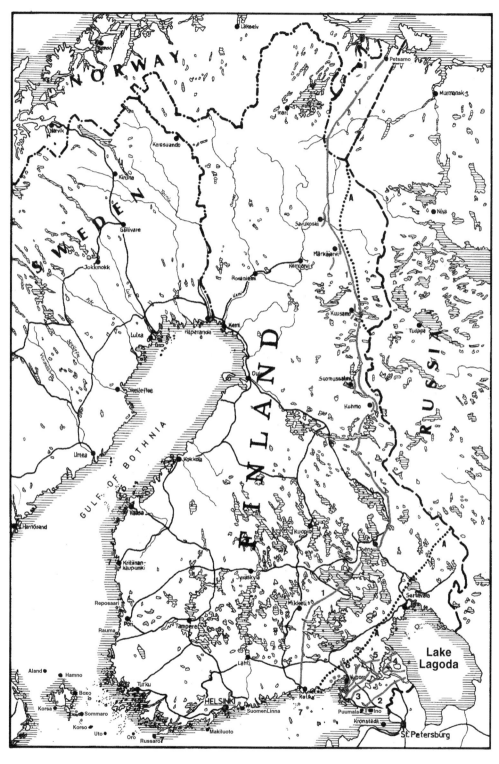

A. Finno-Soviet Border 1940   4. V Line   7. Coastal batteries
2. Salpa Line, Mannerheim Line   5. T Line
3. Main Line   6. Sain Canal Position

Model Finnish Bunker.

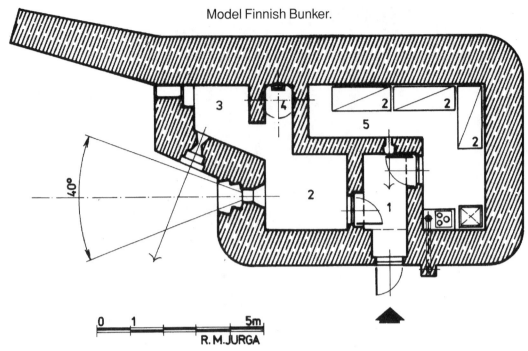

```
0   1              5m
       R.M.JURGA
```

1. Defended entrance
2. Heavy MG
3. Light MG and search light
4. Obsv Cloche
5. Crew's Quarters

Standard Finnish Bunker for flanking fires.

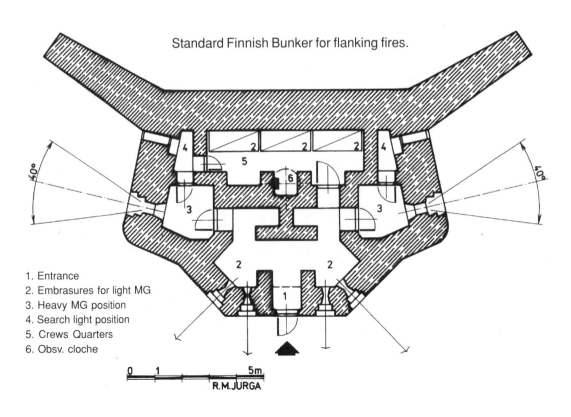

1. Entrance
2. Embrasures for light MG
3. Heavy MG position
4. Search light position
5. Crews Quarters
6. Obsv. cloche

```
0   1           5m
      R.M.JURGA
```

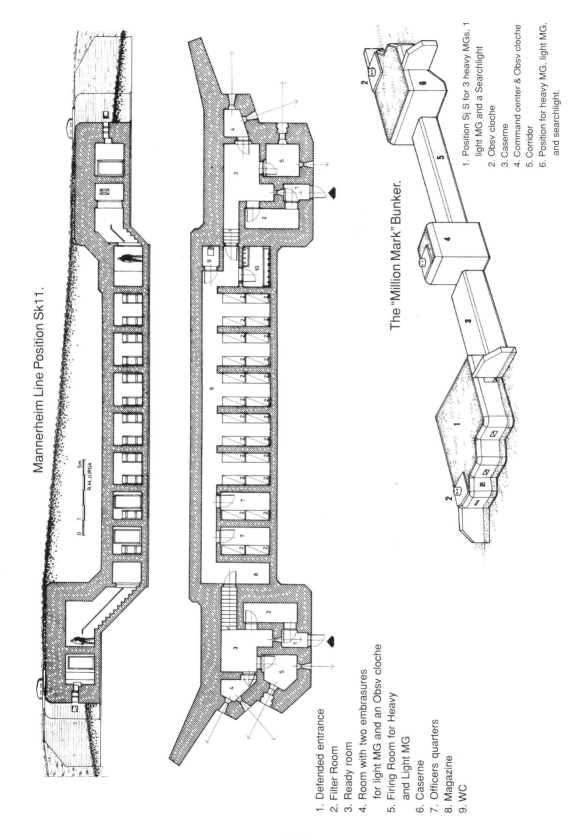

Mannerheim Line Position Sk11.

R.M. JURGA

0   1   5m

The "Million Mark" Bunker.

1. Defended entrance
2. Filter Room
3. Ready room
4. Room with two embrasures for light MG and an Obsv cloche
5. Firing Room for Heavy and Light MG
6. Caserne
7. Officers quarters
8. Magazine
9. WC

1. Position Sj S for 3 heavy MGs, 1 light MG and a Searchlight
2. Obsv cloche
3. Caserne
4. Command center & Obsv cloche
5. Corridor
6. Position for heavy MG, light MG, and searchlight.

Map of Mannerheim Line showing sectors

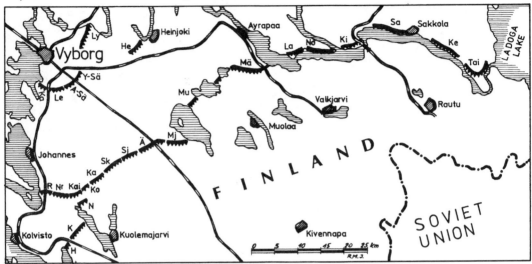

Map of Hanko sector.

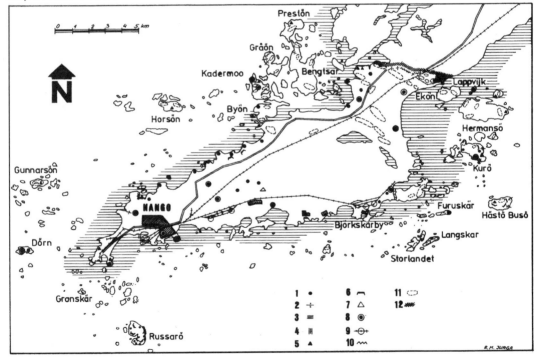

1. Searchlight
2. Heavy MG
3. Position for torpedo boats
4. Position for U-Boats
5. Obsv position
6. Gun battery

7. Radar Emplacement
8. AA battery
9. Firing position for RR gun
10. Trenches
11. Fortification construction area
12. Barbed wire obstacle

Chapter 14

SOVIET FORTIFICATIONS

BACKGROUND

The Russian army was no stranger to fortifications, especially after the defense of Sevastapol during the Crimean War, and the unsuccessful defense of Port Arthur in the Russo-Japanese War half a century later. By 1914 the Russians had erected relatively modern fortifications along their borders and coastlines, including the Gulf of Finland and the Polish shores. When Poland regained its independence, reclaiming some of its former territories in the east, and Finland and the Baltic States broke away, the Soviet Union lost many of these fortifications. Only Kronstadt and the associated forts protecting Leningrad gave the Soviet Union a last "Window on the Baltic." However, the Red Army managed to hang on to the Ukraine despite its unsuccessful bid for independence, thus retaining control over the Black Sea defenses. As a result of these changes, the Soviet Union's western frontier stood open to invasion, and northwestern Russia south of the Baltic remained without defenses.

MAJOR FORTIFICATION

The Stalin Line
The Border Defenses or Molotov Line
The Coast Defenses [1]

LOCATION

The general layout of the terrain of the Soviet Union in itself constituted a formidable defensive feature, consisting of large rivers, extensive forests, swamps, and sandy regions criss-crossed by a poor road system. The railroad system, which had carried over 80% of all Soviet traffic in 1937 according to the July 1941 issue of *Time* magazine, was the key form of transportation in this area. The railroads gave the Soviet Union a tremendous defensive advantage because their non-standard broad-gauge rail lines differed from the standard gauge used in Germany and most European nations. An invading army would be forced to change the gauge of the tracks or capture enough rolling stock and locomotives to support its own operations inside the Soviet Union.

In the territories they occupied in 1939, the Soviets converted the standard gauge railroads to the Russian broad gauge. This required Soviet engineers to have one rail moved approximately 9-cm outward on each of nine rail lines in occupied Poland. One additional railroad, by agreement, remained standard gauge. This line ran from Przemysl to Lvov and on to Rumania through Cernauti, so Germany could have a direct rail link to Rumanian oil.[2] The Russian rivers also formed substantial obstacles because they were large and difficult to ford. However, since most of them had a higher west bank than eastern bank, they put the Russian defenders at a disadvantage, giving the enemy the commanding position. Fortunately, most of the rivers had swampy banks on both sides, which effectively hindered assaults and bridging operations. In addition, bridges had to span most of the river's flood plain to avoid being destroyed by spring floods or winter ice floes. For instance, one bridge over the Desna spanned about 600 meters even though the river was only 100 meters wide and the Volkhov, south of Leningrad, was a swamp flowing through a marshy wilderness of woods and brush. The Dnepr[3] River, which became the main defensive line in 1941, was up to 200 meters wide and even wider in the Zhlobin area where the Germans encountered considerable problems. Its swift current added to the problems caused by its swampy banks that became quickly impassable in a rain. So, naturally, the Soviets concentrated their defenses on existing bridges.

Great forests almost encircled the Pripet Marshes along the post-1939 border, continued northward to Minsk on the Dnepr. On the east bank of the Dnepr they extended southward, to a point north of Kiev. Other massive forests stood south of the swampy area near Leningrad in the Valdai Hills, and between Smolensk and Moscow, making an effective barrier against invading armies. In addition, the Pripet Marshes were treacherous since they dried out under the hot summer sun, but quickly became a muddy mire as soon as it rained. The Soviets took advantage of all of these natural features when they revised their defensive plans early in 1941, reserving these areas for partisan operations in support of the main line of defense on the Dnepr.

The farmlands of the steppes of the Ukraine south of the Pripet Marshes remained largely devoid of forests, but were cut by major rivers such as the Dnepr and Dniestr. In the far north, on the Finnish border, Nature provided great expanses of taiga and barren tundra as barrier.

1. The Stalin Line

The Stalin Line passed through four Military Districts (MD): Leningrad,[4] Western, Kiev, and Odessa. It included the thirteen original *ukreplinnyje rajony* (UR or fortified districts) begun in 1928: Kingissepp, Pskov (Pleskau), Polotsk, Minsk, Mozyr,Korosten, Kiev, Novogrod-Volynski (Zwiahel), Letichev, Mogilev-Podolski, Rybnitsa, Tiraspol. Some sources consider the Karelia UR part of the Stalin Line, or the thirteenth UR, but others do not include it because it faced Finland. Each of these URs covered 50 to 150 km and included a forward position of obstacles and outposts with a depth of up to 12 km, and a main line about 4 km deep. Each UR, its flanks secured by natural obstacles whenever possible, was intended to dominate an approach route.

The URs of the Leningrad MD covered the approaches to the city and included the Baltic coastal defenses. The district was heavily wooded, mostly marshy and interlaced with numerous watercourses and many lakes such as Lake Ilmen, Pskov and Peipus. The URs of the Western MD occupied Belarus, forming a salient around Minsk, and resting on the Pripet Marshes. The dense woods of this district around the Pripet Marshes, and the great marsh, served as an effective barrier against modern invaders. They guarded the approaches to the Smolensk-Moscow Land Bridge, the main route to Moscow from the west, which passed between the upper courses and head waters of the Dvina and Dnepr Rivers. The URs of Kiev MD occupied the western part of the Ukraine and closed the gap between the Pripet Marshes and the Dniestr River. Here the terrain was more open than in the north. Finally, the URs of the Odessa MD rested along the Dniestr all the way to the Black Sea. The river formed the most effective natural barrier facing the Rumanian border. As the river neared the Black Sea and began to meander, its valley widened, forming a large marshy area.

In 1938, the Soviets began to fill the gaps in the line with the eight new URs. The URs of Ostrov and Sebezh in the Leningrad Special Military District (SMD), closed the gap between the old URs of Pskov and Polotsk along the Latvian border. The new UR of Slutsk extended the defenses of the Minsk UR southward. The other five URs advanced the main defenses in the Ukraine west of the Letichev UR to the Polish border, and included the URs of Shepetovka, Staro Konstantinov, Ostropol, and Kaments-Podolski. This gave the Stalin Line a total of twenty-one URs in 1938.

2. The Border Defenses or Molotov Line

The border of 1939-1940 required new defensive positions, which led to the creation of additional military districts and the expansion of older ones. The term "special," which had already been applied to the border districts in July 1938, was also assigned to the military districts on the new border. Since the Czech Crisis, this designation was added to indicate that more than normal defensive measures would be undertaken in such districts. The Kiev SMD and the Belarus (changed to Western in July 1940) SMD each were occupied by an army group. The Baltic SMD was created after the occupation of Lithuania, Latvia, and Estonia in the summer of 1940.[5] The Western SMD and Kiev SMD were expanded westward into Polish occupied territory. The Odessa SMD took over the Bessarabian territory annexed from Rumania in 1940, but there was no time to prepare new URs in it.

New URs were organized in all these special districts, except in Bessarabia, to cover the new border with Germany. Curiously, the Niemen River, a dominant feature near the border of East Prussia in the Baltic district, was not fortified. Instead, the fortifications were placed almost on top of the border. The same happened in other frontier sectors, but this does not mean that additional positions were not sited to the rear, in more defensible sites. A salient around Bialystok in the expanded Western SMD, extended to the Pripet Marshes. Only the Bug River along the southern shoulder of the salient formed an easily defensible position in this mostly level and wooded terrain. The expanded district of Kiev included the foothills of the Carpathians to protect the frontier with Hungary. Its northern sector used the Pripet Marshes and Bug Rivers to help the URs to close the frontier. Between the Bug and the Hungarian border, the Soviets found few natural defenses and had to set up URs to close the gap.

3. The Coast Defenses

As a result of the occupation of the Baltic States, the coastal defenses stretched out along the Baltic from Leningrad to East Prussia, forming the Leningrad and Baltic districts. The Russo-Finnish (Winter) War gave the Soviet Union additional Baltic bases, including Hangö (Hanko). The coast of the Black Sea was defended mainly by the special military district at Odessa, and defenses at Sevastopol and a few other bases.

HISTORY

The headline, "STALIN CREATES A 'LINE OF MAGINOT' IN THE U.S.S.R.," must have created quite a stir when it appeared on December 9, 1936, in *Sevodnya* (*Today*), a news publication produced in Riga, Latvia. The story was released by a Warsaw-based English correspondent for the *Daily Express*, so it could travel quickly across the continent. The article stated that, at a meeting of the Soviet Congress, Joseph Stalin had submitted the new program for armament whose "first part provides for the construction of a 3,000 km line of fortifications along the western and eastern frontiers of the USSR, similar to the famous 'Line of Maginot'." Stalin also called for the creation of a 3,000,000 man "shock" army in two years and the tripling of the air force. He added further that a Commissar for War Industry would be appointed and placed under the authority of Voroshilov, the Commissar of Defense. In addition, as key to future Soviet defense plans, war industry plants would be transferred from exposed areas in the west to the interior. Finally, concluded Stalin, the Soviets would begin building a fortification line within the next fortnight.

Admittedly, the work on the Soviet defenses was no secret since listening posts in the Baltic states had reported on them for years. The American military attaché who received the *Sevodnya* article was not certain whether Stalin meant to strengthen the existing fortifications or create a new line altogether.

During the Russian Civil War, the Red forces created fortified areas or URs that consisted mainly of field fortifications used both for defense and as bases for offensive operations. Early in the 1920s Fedor Golenkin, a former Russian general, proposed the creation of URs to cover the frontier while the army mobilized. The Military Engineering Inspectorate drew up the plans for a major set of fortifications late in the 1920s. The plan was similar to those of the Civil War and the ideas of Golenkin, in that certain areas would be covered by small positions and obstacles. The army established the first thirteen URs between 1924 and 1938, and initially began to work on the Polotsk and Karelian URs in 1928. By 1938, almost two years after the Estonian article, they had established eight new URs in the west.[6] Work stopped on eleven of thirteen URs by 1940.

A group of seven engineers was responsible for creating the defenses, employing rather antiquated concepts and methodologies. General Nikolai Petin, Inspector of Engineers in 1930 and Chief of Engineers in 1934, was responsible for much of the work until his execution during the 1937 purge. Mikhail N. Tukhachevsky, Director of Armaments since 1931, who helped formulate the role of the fortifications, wrote in 1934 that air power would impede the forward movement of forces and that it would be a mistake to commit large forces to the defense of the frontier. It would be necessary, he claimed, to develop defense in depth instead of a linear defense. The fortified regions on the frontier were to act as shields, covering the concentration of the next echelon of armies which would smash the enemy's flanks. Interestingly, the French, who were building the Maginot Line at the time, would have agreed with much of his doctrine. Mikhail V. Frunze, Commissar for Military and Naval Affairs, had stated earlier that "no war, be it highly maneuverable, would ever be waged without fortified zones. The carrying out of maneuver requires to some extent the existence of fortified zones that can be used as a base of operations"(Excerpt from Fugate *Thunder on the Dnepr*).

The actual work on the fortifications in the early 1930s did not yield satisfactory results. Robert Tarleton, who wrote a brief history of the Stalin Line, stated that there was a severe shortage of military engineers at the beginning of the decade due to the purges and that, in many cases, civilians took charge of the work. As a result, many positions that were nearing completion were left unfinished because the civilians did not know how to install the equipment and armament. In addition, work was desultory, since the workers were not greatly inspired by the Marxist work ethic. It wasn't until later in the decade that the situation changed.

In the summer of 1939, reports that the Russians had intensified the work on their fortifications filtered to the west. Meanwhile, more trenches were dug, anti-tank obstacles erected, and artillery emplacements created. It was also reported that a double line of fortifications was under construction along the border with the Baltic states. Other rumors indicated that the defenses along the border formed a non-continuous line, being mostly concentrated at critical points. Reportedly, new and more elaborate positions were also being created. At this time the Soviets were finally able to stop the information leaks, so that intelligence on Soviet fortifications became scant.

The actual work on the positions was carried out by the Military Labor Directorate, which formed labor directorates known as UNRs. Construction of each UR was under the control of a single UNR which directed all construction units and could also call upon the UR's assigned engineer and rifle battalions as a source of labor when necessary.

The occupation of Poland in 1939 soon led the high command to reconsider its position. During the autumn the army attempted unsuccessfully to build a line of field positions along the new border before the onset of winter. The Main Military Council decided to abandon the Stalin Line and move the defenses to the new border. Meanwhile, work ceased on all but one of the eight new URs created on the Stalin Line since 1938. It continued only on the Kaments-Podolski UR situated on the Dniestr River border with Rumania. On the other unfinished URs the construction crews packed up their equipment and moved westward, to the border positions of 1940. However, the army did not begin any substantial work on the border defenses until the summer of 1940, as Soviet troops occupied the Rumanian territory of Bessarabia and Bukovina in late June 1940. On June 26 Marshal S.K. Timoshenko, Defense Commissar, directed that the Western SMD and Kiev SMD begin the construction ordered a year earlier.

The new URs created from 1940-41 included: Murmansk, Sortavala, Keksholm, Vyborg, Hanko (Hangö), Telshiai (Titovo), and Shiauliai (Szauliansk). UNRs set up the URs of Kaunas (Kovno), Alytus, Grodno, Osovets, Zambruv, Brest, Kovel, Vladimir-Volynski, Strumilova, Rava-Russkaia, Przemysl, Verknne-Prut, and Nizhne-Prut running along the new border with Germany. Initial work began on the new URs of Chernovsty (Cernauti), Odessa and Danube, but only plans were prepared for the UR of Kishinev (Chisinau) in Bessarabia and Beltsevo. The defensive positions followed the border, and by 1940 there were about 4,500 fortified positions known as DFS (*dolgovriemienniye fortifikatsyonnyie sooruzenia* or permanent fortified lines). Many of the individual bunkers were weak, lightly armed, and fired forwards. Most lacked internal equipment such as a power supply, filters, and the like, by the time of the German invasion.

The engineers had completed 3,196 positions on the Stalin Line before 1938 in the thirteen original sectors, but few were of value because most were small and lightly armed. According to one estimate, only 10% of these fortifications had anti-tank guns. Barely one thousand new combat positions were built on the Stalin line—or half of the projected number—between 1938-39. Their design had been improved to include flanking fire, but many bunkers still lacked a ventilation system, a usine, and many other key components. The armament, in most instances, consisted of a combination heavy machine gun and a 45-mm anti-tank gun.

There were special artillery positions for 76-mm guns, and, in some cases, some of the fortifications of the older URs were refitted for these weapons. In some sites with concentrations of combat positions, underground tunnels linked the combat areas with support facilities to create a fortified position that could be classified as a fort. Of the structures completed by 1939 and early 1940 on the Stalin Line, only 409 received fortress artillery, the remainder mounted heavy machine guns.

By the mid-1930s these fortifications became known to the outside world as the Stalin Line. Gradually eleven of the thirteen original pre-1938 URs were eliminated, and by late 1940 the line was reduced to a mere shell. The weapons and equipment of most of the positions was sent either to the new border positions, or into long term storage. According to some reports, thousands of emplacements were blown up, covered with earth, given to collective farms for storage, or left under guard. The truth is that the army probably did not have much time to waste demolishing thousands of bunkers, nor is it likely that many of these positions actually provided enough storage space for agricultural needs. Many of the larger positions were preserved, but inspection reports indicate that they were overgrown with vegetation and that their equipment had deteriorated.

The Poles later called the Soviet defenses on the new border the Molotov Line. Russian workers labored on its construction on the actual border, literally in sight of the enemy. By 1941 the number of URs on the new border was increased to nine. Surveys for three new URs in Bukovina and Bessarabia were carried out in the spring of 1941, but resources were not committed for their construction until much later.

Large numbers of civilian laborers began to work on the Molotov Line in earnest in 1940. The local population was rounded up mainly to dig anti-tank ditches and set up other obstacles. In the meantime the authorities attempted to impose security around the building sites. The new Baltic SMD, Western SMD and Kiev SMD were given priority, receiving up to 140,000 civilian laborers. In some cases, like the Bialystok salient, soldiers set to work on the defenses. The construction units of the old Stalin Line were also moved forward to the Molotov Line.

Soviet industry could not meet the demands for raw materials needed for construction, so most work was not completed by the summer of 1941. In fact, only 25% of the positions of the Molotov Line were actually completed by the time of the German invasion in June 1941. A number of these positions were designed to hold field weapons and, according to some sources, almost a thousand held artillery. The remainder of the 2,300 combat shelters were armed with machine guns. Even though the Russians were good at creating defensive obstacles, they failed to install sufficient minefields on the Molotov Line. This was probably due to the fact that the military engineers did not have enough equipment and mines available to do the job properly.

According to Soviet military doctrine, the best defense was offense. For this reason troops were massed near the frontier while work continued on the fortifications during 1940. In January 1941 the top military leaders of the Soviet Union such as D. G. Pavlov the Russian tank expert, Georgi K. Zhukov the commander of the Kiev SMD, and Defense Commissar Timoshenko took part in a series of war games. These exercises proved that Pavlov and his supporters' doctrine of first strike could lead to disaster. Stalin, already alerted to the planned German invasion, apparently accepted Zhukov's and Timoshenko's idea of using a deep battlefield and preparing to meet the enemy with counter thrusts. Zhukov, who became the Chief of the General Staff, decided to reopen part of the Stalin Line and even add some new positions.

There is some evidence to indicate that work may have started on a deeper line of defenses that began as far east as Mozhaisk on the road to Moscow and included other sections along the Desna River to the Dnepr[7]. The Mozhaisk Line, according to the official history, was begun by order of the Military Council on July 18, 1941 and was to include three main defensive areas consisting of two lines between 30 to 60 km apart. The line's concrete bunkers usually took a single machine gun or anti-tank gun, and many were of a simpler construction. The line was still not completed by October. The Soviets claimed that 296 blockhouses and 535 bunkers were built with 170 km of anti-tank ditches, and this was supposedly only 40% of the emplacements planned.

German intelligence maps show a "Leningrad Line" running from the coast southwards to Krasnogvardeysk. According to a German document entitled *Russian Combat Methods in World War II*, a post-war report made for the U.S. Army, the line, which was very strong in this area, consisted of many earth and concrete bunkers "with built-in guns and other heavy weapons." In addition, there were "concrete pillboxes with hand operated disappearing armored cupolas for artillery and machine guns." Furthermore, an anti-tank ditch over 6 meters wide, 4 meters deep, and several kilometers long was strengthened with bunkers at every bend and two more anti-tank ditches behind it. According to German sources, this position had been prepared long before the Nazi troops ran into it in September 1941. It may have been part of Zhukov's plans for a deeper defense line which included the positions previously mentioned as in front of Moscow. It is obvious that Stalin certainly had not intended the Leningrad Line, with its anti-tank ditches and obstacles, to be a deterrent to a Finnish amphibious or flanking invasion, especially since Finland did not have the tanks and troops necessary for such an operation.

Pavlov, commanding the troops on the border and on the fledgling Molotov Line, did not realize that they were to be sacrificed. Zhukov, retrenched in his own position, did not allow the transfer of additional artillery from the Stalin Line to the border defenses. In late February 1941, at a meeting of the Supreme Military Council of the Red Army he had argued against the transfer of the weapons and the equipment to the border defenses, the artillery in particular. Stalin settled the argument in favor of Zhukov, and the artillery remained in its old positions of the Stalin Line despite claims to the contrary. On April 8 Zhukov directed six of the seven new URs in the Western SMD and Kiev SMD to be activated within two weeks of the outbreak of war even if none were completed. The installations were readied for combat even though most could not be fully equipped because of shortages of equipment and personnel. At the same time Zhukov ordered the quick arming of the border positions and the installation of armored doors on the bunkers to make them defendable. He realized that there was little time left, and that the border positions near completion had to be ready even without the equipment necessary for prolonged resistance, otherwise they would be of no value at all.

A July 1941 American intelligence report included a map showing the Soviet fortifications running from the Pruth River and along the entire border to the Baltic, incorrectly identifying all the defenses as temporary field fortifications. On the map, the line from Leningrad to the Dnestr, that is the Stalin Line, was identified as the first line of permanent defenses. Most interestingly, a second line was shown behind the Stalin Line consisting of some of the older URs of the pre-1938 Stalin Line in the Ukraine and along the Dnepr sweeping eastward from Novoskolniki, through the Valdai Hills, to the Volga. It was labeled as the second general line of permanent fortifications and may actually represent concrete evidence of Zhukov's defensive strategy.

The Soviet Union began strengthening its fortifications along the Baltic Sea in the summer of 1939, setting up new batteries and defenses, and modernizing several positions. The Baltic Coastal Command was headquartered at Kronstadt. The forts were concentrated in three areas: Sestoretsk-Izhora on the south side of the Gulf of Finland, the Krasnaya Gorka-Shepelevo area, and the Kopore-Luga area.

The key area of fortifications on Kotlin Island centered at Kronstadt, the "Malta of the North," guarded the approaches to Leningrad.

As a result of the Finnish War, the Soviet Union obtained a lease at Hangö where they set up a base. In the Baltic States, old forts were restored and new positions were replaced. The Soviet occupation of Estonia also brought an end to 1939 Finnish and Estonian plans to close the Gulf of Finland by using heavy 305-mm gun batteries at Aegna and at a planned site at Maissaari, and at Forts Mäkiluoto and Kulvassari.[8] Both Estonian batteries had been completed in 1917 and destroyed after the war. Aegna was restored to service in the 1920s and work continued on the Maissaari site through the 1930s.

In February 1941, the Soviets began to build the concrete coastal defenses in the Baltic States on the islands of Ösel, Dagö, and Moon to guard the entrance to the Gulf of Riga and other important points in the newly occupied territories. Batteries of 132-mm guns with gun shields were set up on concrete positions, and coastal defenses were also established on the approaches to Tallinn (Reval) and nearby islands. In the far north, the coastal batteries at the ports of Archangel and Murmansk, were separated by a large stretch of inhospitable coastline.

In the south the Black Sea fortress of Sevastopol was well defended. Two large 305-mm gun turreted batteries of Maxim Gorky I and II were begun between 1912 and 1917 and completed between 1928 and 1934. New positions were added to strengthen the old defenses of Sevastopol. A fortified base was set up at the mouth of the Dnepr and the port of Odessa received several coastal batteries.

Robert Tarleton believes the Stalin Line was not ready for combat. The Kiev SMD was the strongest at about 80% strength and with 650 of its positions still in existence in the URs of Korosten and Novogrod-Volynski in June 1941. Further north, only 70 unarmed bunkers in the Ostrov UR, and 75 in the Sebezh UR of the Baltic SMD were ready. According to German estimates, 120,000 border troops were positioned between the North Sea and Black Sea, in the summer of 1941, 12,000 of which were in the Karelia and Leningrad districts, 15,000 in the Baltic district, 24,000 in the Western SMD, 20,000 in the Kiev district, and 12,000 on the Rumanian border, in the Odessa district. Their mission was to guard and man the border defenses in the event of war. There was also a major shortage of officers and NCOs, which amounted to 50% in some cases. Soviet sources indicate that the URs of Polotsk, Minsk and Mozyr in the Western SMD were manned by approximately two machine gun battalions in June 1941. The Kiev SMD had two machine gun battalions and five caponier artillery platoons in the UR of Korosten. The Novogrod-Volynski UR (Zwiahel) had a machine gun battalion and ten caponier artillery platoons. The units assigned to the URs, also referred to as UR units, normally included two to four machine gun battalions and smaller artillery caponier units. It appears that many of the URs of the Stalin Line were at about

30% strength. Its normal garrison was supposed to be twenty-five machine gun battalions for the thirteen URs. Apparently, few if any of these UR units had been deployed on the Molotov Line.

DESCRIPTION

1. The Stalin Line

The Stalin Line covered 1,835 km and included over 3,000 positions, twice the length of the Maginot Line but with less than half the number of combat structures. While the French built 7.7 positions per kilometer, the Soviets built only 1.7.

Although the URs had some depth, most were designed for independent operation and were not meant to coordinate with neighboring URs. The core of the defensive structure of each UR consisted of a number of strong points consisting of fifteen to twenty (or more) independent combat positions and covering up to 1.5 km of front and a similar depth. A group of strongpoints formed what was referred to as a Battalion Defense Area since a machine gun battalion along with smaller artillery units was normally assigned to it. This defense area covered a sector of up to 10 km and a depth of 6 km. The number of Battalion Defense Areas varied; the UR of Polotsk had at least six and the UR of Minsk appears to have had five large battalion areas, but several of these were divided into two sections. The new UR of Slutsk had six.

The heaviest works consisted of forts that occupied key positions. These forts had underground works and supported several combat blocks in a set-up somewhat reminiscent of French, Czech, and Swiss works. One of these Soviet subterranean forts, Fort A or Hulsk about 10 km south of Zwiahel, was built early in the 1930s and exhibited some of the weaknesses typical of pre-1938 positions. Blocks 101 and 102 had three embrasures each for a heavy machine gun, Blocks 100 and 104 were machine gun casemates with two embrasures giving flanking fire, Block 98 was a single-embrasure bunker while Blocks 98, 101, and 102 gave frontal fires across the Slucz River. However, none of these blocks effectively covered the others. The artillery consisted of two 76.2-mm field guns in Block 99 and Block 103. Both the artillery casemates firing to the flank were similar to the French style, but were apparently not as well designed. The Russians called these casemates "half caponiers" when they fired to one flank and "caponiers" when they covered two flanks. Block 103 supported machine gun position 105 located on a bend of the river, further downstream. The other casemate supported a couple of DOTs (bunkers), and was within range of one of them. Nonetheless, there was a lack of sufficient mutual support and the rear of the fort was left unprotected. Field fortifications filled the intervals.

The combat blocks were rather small. Casemate 100 had an emergency exit and an interior about 1.3 meters wide and 3.6 meters long. Its outer wall was 1.5 meters thick. Blocks 101 and 102 also had emergency exits and a firing room with one crenel, and a main firing room with two crenels. Even though they faced the enemy, the walls were only 1.5 meters thick, which was satisfactory for small independent positions, but below the norm for blocks of most west European forts. Artillery Block 103 was larger, with a width of 9.8 meters and a length of 12.4 meters. Its two gun embrasures were staggered along the narrowest part that also included a small entrance. The gun rooms were 3 x 3 meters and a munitions room was located to the rear of the block. The walls and roof, 1.5 meters and 1.0 meter thick respectively, where even thinner than in the machine gun positions, where the roof was 1.1 to 1.5 meters thick.

Fort A occupied a hill and its blocks were connected to an underground tunnel through vertical shafts. Its simple, centrally located entrance, stood about 50 to 100 meters behind the main cluster of blocks, and was accessed from a ditch by a flight of stairs. The underground gallery, about 515 meters long, lay about 11 meters below the surface and was lined with concrete panels. It branched out to link all the positions except Block 99. The gallery was 1.05 meters wide and 2.15 meters high and the rooms opening off it had a width of 1.85 meters and a height of 2.45 meters. Several machine gun positions placed at corners in the gallery, protected the interior.

There were several munitions and filter rooms in the tunnel system. There was also a usine and a filter room with ventilators by the entrance. In addition, the 130 man garrison was provided with gas masks.

Among the few other examples of these Soviet forts is Fort Serebritsa which was also built into a hill in the Mogilev-Podolski UR, a sector along the Dniestr that remained active after the border advanced to the Pruth. The fort's gallery was 905 meters long and was reached through two entrance blocks. The fort included two triple-embrasure machine gun blocks (470 and 471) and a pair of gun casemates, each mounting two 76.2-mm guns (469, 472). These positions overlooked the river and both machine gun blocks fired forward.

Some of the other large fortified positions included independent gun casemates, a number of which had their own underground works. These casemates were generally larger than those of the above mentioned forts and were built in 1938 with the new URs, and added to the old URs. They were not however very common in the old URs.

By 1938, most of the older combat structures had become obsolete while the newer ones might have been satisfactory if enough had been completed. Their concrete thickness and the amount of reinforcing steel rods had been increased, and the quality of the cement had also been improved. Anti-ricochet devices for crenels, standard on most western fortifications, were introduced and similar protective arrangements were planned for the entrances.

Soviet permanent fortifications were classified according to the following categories:[9]

Light - resists infantry weapons
Reinforced - resists 76-mm guns and 122-mm howitzers
Medium - resists 152-mm howitzers and 100 kg. bombs
Semi-Heavy - resists 200-mm projectiles and 500 kg. bombs
Heavy - resists 305-mm projectiles and 1,000 kg bombs

This demonstrates that the strength of the Soviet works were on a par with many in the west, but the overall designs still lagged behind. The Soviet positions, even more spartan than the crudest shelters in the west, usually lacked the basic necessities.

The fortified positions of the Stalin and Molotov Lines included at least six types: (1) positions for machine guns firing to the front, although later models were planned for 45-mm AT guns; (2) casemates for flanking fire, called half-caponiers, holding light and heavy machine guns and AT guns (later models were to include cloches); (3) blockhouse for all-around defense;[10] (4) artillery blocks, also called half caponiers, in single (two embrasures) and double models (four embrasures); (5) command posts and observation positions; and (6) forts or *ukrelennyie gruppy* usually with smaller combat blocks and subterranean facilities.

Some machine gun and artillery casemates included a fossé in front of the weapons position, but it is difficult to determine if these were used in both the Stalin Line and Molotov Lines. If they were used in the Stalin Line, the engineers probably did not design them until after 1937.

A rare description of one of the independent artillery blocks or caponiers is to be found in *Small Unit Actions During the German Campaign in Russia*, a US Army report prepared by German officers. The block that was described was located behind the Dniestr in the Mogilev-Podolski UR that only fired to the flanks and covered two river crossing positions. Built into a steep bluff, it mounted a pair of 76.2-mm guns on each flank, had walls about one meter thick, and was excellently camouflaged. One of its machine guns, located in a concrete embrasure high above the entrance, fired forward. Its garrison numbered about sixty men. There were two underground levels, a usine, and a ventilation system. The position lacked entrenchments and wire obstacles around it. This may well have been typical of many other positions on the Stalin Line in 1941.

Work on the Stalin Line was abandoned before most improvements could be implemented, and it would be incorrect to assume that these fortifications were of the same quality as those in the west. Nonetheless, many of the Soviet positions proved to be strong enough to impede German progress when they became operational.

The Germans counted 142 completed casemates and gun positions, 248 anti-tank casemates and bunkers, 2,572 machine gun casemates and bunkers. The majority of the bunkers probably provided frontal fire.

2. The Molotov Line

The border defenses were probably the most modern positions built by the Soviets, who were only able to complete and arm a small percentage. The URs on the border had a greater depth than those of the Stalin Line and included a main defensive line of permanent fortifications backed by a rear line of field works. The main line covered from 6 to 10 km of front, had a depth of up to 10 km, and was organized around cores of up to five strong points forming a new type of fort. The strong points consisted of about fifteen to twenty permanent combat blocks. Almost half of the border positions were to be armed with anti-tank guns. In addition to these strong points, the Russians planned to build a number of artillery casemates for two 76.2-mm guns. However, by the summer of 1941, few of the URs were completed.

When completed, these large works were to include their own usine, gas protection, filters, heaters, stoves and other equipment to make them self supporting. The new works also had better drainage systems and decontamination facilities while periscopes, radio equipment, and underground telephone communications were also planned.

Although turrets for 75-mm and 76-mm guns were begun, none were ready in time for the war. It is claimed that in the rush to complete the line, the army brought in heavy weapons from the coastal defenses. In a small number of bunkers, cloches were installed.

According to a German war-time report, 68 artillery casemates and positions, 460 anti-tank gun casemates and bunkers, and 542 machine gun casemates and bunkers were completed in the four military districts on the border. More defenses were added to the old fortress of Brest-Litvosk and the border defenses were strengthened with anti-tank ditches, wire obstacles, and many types of anti-tank obstacles."

Some of the anti-tank obstacles included heavy wooden posts sunk into the ground at an angle in two rows, boulder obstacles similar to those used by the Finns, Czech hedgehogs and a Russian version of "dragon's teeth." Anti-tank ditches were also used.

Other new positions were prepared further inside the border after the German invasion. It appears that the ground work for these new positions was prepared before that. Along the Dnepr and east of Smolensk, field fortifications quickly went up soon after the invasion and a permanent line, the Mozhaisk Line, begun about 100 km west of Moscow. This line included small concrete and log bunkers built with concrete front walls and foundations, and log rear walls. In some of these bunkers the logs formed cribs that held rocks that increased the strength of the wall and may have been even stronger than the concrete wall with the weapons embrasure. This building method may have been adopted to expedite construction in the face of the rapid enemy advance.

3. The Coast Defenses

Kronstadt, the main naval base on the Baltic stood on Kotlin Island, 20 km west of Leningrad, on the mouth of the Neva River. A number of forts and batteries on the island, on the sea, and on the mainland to the east and west encircled the base. Since 1893 the main forts had included the Rif Fort on the west end of the island with its two armored turrets mounting two 12-inch Model 52 guns each, a four gun battery of electrically loaded 10-inch Model 00 guns, two batteries with two 6-inch Model Canet guns on each flank, and a 75-mm anti-aircraft gun battery. Fort Shants (Schanz) mounted eight batteries, including two batteries of four relatively modern 120-mm Vickers guns each, and two batteries of six obsolete Model 1877 9-inch guns. It also had sixteen obsolete 11-inch Model 77 and Model 88 mortars. A number of gun batteries with older weapons dating from 1877 to 1915 remained in service in many of the positions, along with 6-inch Model Canet gun batteries. The Demidov Battery on the southwestern part of the island consisted of six obsolete 9-inch Model 77 mortars and six 6-inch Canet guns. Forts Number 1 through 7 blocked the passage between Kotlin Island and the mainland to the east, and included mostly batteries of 75-mm and 76-mm naval and anti-aircraft guns. The old 3-inch gun batteries of these forts were removed during the 1930s. Fort No. 4 had a two gun battery of 120-mm Vickers guns. A number of the forts also had 150-cm searchlights. In addition, a stockpile of sea mines was maintained at several of the forts. The large number of anti-aircraft batteries primarily protected the fleet.

In January 1941, Fort Pervomaiski ("May First"), northeast of Kotlin Island and just off the mainland, was armed with five ancient 11-inch guns that were supposedly replaced by modern weapons, and also twelve 6-inch guns and six 130-mm guns. It also had two twin gun turrets mounting Vickers 8-inch guns. Fort Krasnoarmeiski ("Red Army"), another island fort just off the north coast of Kotlin, was similarly armed.

On the mainland, in the Yhinmäki-Shepelevo area, stood several heavily armed coastal forts. One of these, Fort Krasnoflotski ("Red Fleet"), had two turrets mounting two 12-inch guns each, four single 12-inch gun turrets, a battery of old 10-inch Model 00 guns, and three 120-mm Vickers guns. Further west, Fort Bukharin mounted three 6-inch Canet guns and four 120-mm guns. Not far away, Fort Pulkovo had two turrets mounting two 8-inch guns each. Shepeleov, the last fort in this sector, had at least two turrets mounting 14-inch guns and four 120-mm Vickers guns.

A prototype of a 406.4-mm gun at Leningrad's naval proving grounds took an active part in the defense of the city in 1941. Floating Battery Tallinn was actually the unfinished German cruiser *Lützow*, which mounted three German 203-mm guns. One of the coastal positions is purported to have mounted a three gun battery of 14-inch (355.6-mm) guns installed in the 1930s.

On the Finnish coast, the Hangö peninsula, taken as part of the peace terms of the Winter War, provided a dominant defensive position for the Soviets. The Soviet navy planned to arm Fort Russarö near Hangö with 12-inch guns in 1941. The fort had batteries of 130-mm (or possibly 152-mm guns). The defenses at Hangö also included batteries of 152-mm and 234-mm guns. Many other positions were still under construction at the time of the German invasion.

The Soviets also took over the old fortifications in Estonia, including Fort Aegna with its four 12-inch gun and several 6-inch and 130-mm guns and Fort Suurop with its four 234-mm guns. The Soviets were working on four 12-inch gun positions in 1941 at Fort Naissaari on the island of the same name, which already had eight 6-inch guns. Fort Aegna and Naissaari guarded the approaches to Tallinn (Reval). The Russians also set up 14-inch, 180-mm guns, and four 6-inch rail guns at Fort Paldiski. Eighteen other forts and batteries were built or improved and they were armed with 130-mm, 180-mm, 203-mm and 12-inch guns. All these positions received additional anti-aircraft defenses.

The Soviets set up six positions in Latvia. According to intelligence reports, they moved tubes for twenty-eight heavy guns, probably of 12-inch caliber, into Latvia in August 1940. Several old forts, including Fort Dünamunde, defended the mouth of the Dvina River north of Riga. In the Gulf of Riga the Soviets set up installations such as concrete emplacements for weapons and munitions storage and improved other facilities on the islands of Ösel, Dagö, Moon, and Worms. They also installed a new 185-mm battery on Ösel, two twin gun turrets for 185-mm guns at Sörve, and batteries of 132-mm and 185-mm guns with gun shields on the south side of the island. They also took over the old battery of the port of Libau at the western side of Latvia and turned it into a stronger position by adding a battery of four 132-mm guns.[11]

In the far north, coastal batteries mounting 305-mm, 240-mm, 155-mm and 100-mm guns defended Murmansk, and batteries that included 210-mm and 150-mm guns covered the approaches to Archangel.

On the Black Sea, there were several major strong points in the early 1930s. One of these, Odessa, received a 152-mm gun battery with observation bunkers and searchlight, a couple of batteries of 185-mm cannons with observatories, armored positions, and a battery of 203-mm guns. Further east, on the mouth of the Dnepr, was the fortified naval base at Otschakov, which included a couple of batteries of 203-mm guns with searchlights and other smaller artillery batteries.

Finally, the fortress of Sevastopol on the Crimea with its ring of forts and coastal batteries covered a circumference of about 10 to 12 km. Six heavy coastal batteries, two located north of Severnaja Bay, reinforced other coastal positions such as three old coastal forts on the north side of the position and three on the south side. Coastal Battery Shiskov, completed in 1912, mounted four 120-mm guns on pivots mounted on concrete platforms. Naval Battery Mamaschai (Coast Battery #10), completed in 1930 and one of the newer positions, mounted four 203-mm guns with gun shields on an open concrete platform similar to most of the other coastal batteries. Coast Battery #18, completed in 1917, and Coast Battery #19, completed in 1924, mounted four 152-mm guns each, and Coast Battery #3, two 130-mm guns. Fourteen new or reconditioned old forts, most of them north of the bay, and 3,600 concrete and earthen positions supported by about 350 km of trenches and thousands of land mines, completed the fortress in early 1942. Trenches and tunnels linked many of the positions. In the Sapun Mountains, at the base of the peninsula where Sevastapol was located, natural and man-made caves in the high, almost perpendicular, bluffs of the Tshornaya River were turned into formidable defenses.

In addition, the Maxim Gorky I and II (Coast Batteries #26 and #25), each had a pair of gun turrets: the first with twin gun turrets located east of Ljabimorka (north of the bay) and the second with a set of similar turrets situated on the south-western end of the peninsula where Sevastopol stood. Battery Strelitzka mounted six 254-mm guns. Fort Stalin and Fort Lenin included a battery of four 76.2 anti-aircraft guns. Other forts, such as Fort Volga, served as infantry positions. Finally, the old strong point of Malakoff was turned into an artillery and infantry position with two 130-mm guns with shields. Besides the normal anti-infantry and anti-tank obstacles, the Soviets employed a "flame ditch," a concrete lined ditch where fuel funneled through a pipe was ignited, creating a fire barrier.

Although it was not actually a coastal defense sector, the isthmus linking the Crimea to the mainland was defended by the Perekop Line, consisting of permanent works forming two continuous lines. In the low lying treeless plain, every rise over 10 meters dominated the area. The 15 km wide northern belt included the outpost of Perekop. The main defensive area, the 400 year old Tartar Trench, cut through the isthmus and served as a moat supported by two dams. The ditch was about 9.0 meters deep, 20 meters wide and was filled with water. The southern position, which crossed the isthmus taking advantage of the local lakes and canals, was supported further to the south by the Tshetarlyk River. Numerous bunkers covered barriers of steel anti-tank rail obstacles, tank traps, and mine fields. Unlike many of the positions on the border, these were already camouflaged and difficult to detect.

WEAPONS AND EQUIPMENT

POSITIONS COMPLETED ON OLD URS OF STALIN LINE IN 1939:*

	Gun Casemates & Positions	AT Casemate & Positions	MG Casemate & Positions	Command & Shelter
MD Leningrad				
Kingissepp	4 (0)	16 (0)	10 (1)	0
Pskov	11 (1)	11 (7)	72 (5)	6 (7)
MD Western				
Polotsk	0	9 (7)	196 (7)	5 (20)
Minsk	33 (0)	114 (30)	401 (11)	32 (3)
Mozyr	6 (0)	0	256 (0)	2 (0)
MD Kiev Korosten	8 (10)	0	206 (0)	0
Kiev	3 (0)	21 (0)	184 (0)	12 (0)
Novogrod-V	16 (2)	53 (7)	138 (22)	5 (3)
Letichev	22 (53)	0 (9)	336 (23)	36 (0)
MD Odessa Mogilev-P	18 (0)	13 (0)	264 (0)	8 (0)
Rybnitsa	4 (0)	0	250 (0)	6 (0)
Tiraspol	17 (0)	11 (0)	259 (0)	22 (0)

*These statistics come from the German Denkschrift on the Russian fortifications, compiled in 1942. The numbers represent the number of positions that were ready for operation; those in parenthesis were still under construction or incomplete.

Coast Artillery:	Range (meters)
355.6-mm (14")	31,000
305-mm (12")	24,600 to 42,000
234-mm	24,000
203-mm (8") (German)	33,500
181-mm*152-mm (6")	14,000 to 18,000
130-mm* (5.1")	19,600 to 25,400
105-mm and 152-mm (old weapons)	15,000 to 18,000
75-mm (3") (French Canet)	8,000

*These may be the weapons identified as 185-mm and 132-mm weapons by Germans.

Fortifications	
152-mm Howitzer 1938	12,400
122-mm Howitzer 1938	12,100
107-mm Cannon 1940 M-60	17,450
76.2-mm Cannon 1936	13,500
45-mm Anti-Tank 1932, 1937	4,670 to 8,800
120-mm 1938	5,700 to 6,000
82-mm Mortar 1936	3,100
50-mm Mortar 1940	800

7.62-mm Heavy Machine Gun (Maxim 1910)
7.62-mm Light Machine Gun (Degtiarev 1928)
*Sources are inconsistent with regard to the figures and the type of shell used

According to German documents, the so-called 76.2-mm Fortress Cannon on a special ball mount in a gun casemate, replaced the older 76.2-mm gun used in fortifications and had a faster rate of fire. The mount included a funnel that carried the used shell into the fossé in front of the gun position. The older gun positions on the Stalin Line did not have this type of funnel, but included an embrasure cover that dropped in front of the gun.

The mortars and most of the artillery were placed in field fortifications made of earth and logs. Many of these positions were probably not prepared until after the invasion in 1941.

In addition to these weapons, there were also small flame throwers, static weapons buried into the ground with only their nozzles exposed and ignited electrically or by trip wire. They were placed in front of the defensive position or among the obstacles. According to German sources, the Soviets used a 1941 design, which means that it is not likely that they were in the Stalin Line. However, they may have been placed in other positions such as the Minsk to Moscow highway or the Mozhaisk Line.

WORLD WAR II

The Germans, who invaded the Soviet Union on June 22, 1941, were not fully aware of the defensive positions that faced them. They estimated that 40% were completed, but had no drawings showing exact locations or composition of Russian installations, except for those located right on the border.

The staff of the German 8th and 29th Divisions had little knowledge of the condition or existence of Russian fortifications behind the Popily and Niemen Rivers. They planned to deal with any fortifications they encountered with massed artillery bombardment from twenty-nine heavy batteries, including eleven 210-mm mortar batteries.

The Germans easily overran the first bunkers, which were empty, poorly camouflaged, exposed in open terrain, and devoid of obstacles. The Germans smashed the bunker embrasures with anti-tank guns and destroyed many with flame throwers and demolition charges. The 8th Division quickly overcame most opposition on its front with these methods. Grodno fell on June 23 after all the bunkers in front of it had been eliminated. The 28th Division simply bypassed many Russian fortifications at Dorgun on the first day and moved to the Niemen. This division was later ordered to take the strongest border defenses in the area, the Sopockinie fortifications, which it had previously bypassed. After bitter fighting, Sopockinie was taken on June 24. Troops in a three-level bunker resisted for seven hours in the face of the German troops and engineers who detonated several hundred kilograms of explosives. The Germans attributed their success to insufficient Soviet troops in the area and to the incomplete state of the defenses, which lacked obstacles, minefields, and camouflage.

The old fortress of Brest-Litovsk, located on four islands with wide moats and old walls, was put back into service by the Russians soon after they occupied it in 1939. The German 45th Division attacked it, supported by huge 210-mm howitzers and two 600-mm mortars. After a river assault, the German troops encircled it, but it took them seven days of intense fighting to take the citadel, since they had underestimated the strength of the old works.

Further to the south, the Germans attacked the Sokal defenses on the Bug River where the Soviets had completed and camouflaged many of the bunkers. On the first day, the Germans methodically eliminated each position, leaving an engineer battalion behind to complete the work the next day. On June 25 twenty two- and three-level bunkers, which were still incomplete, went back into action. Even though they lacked camouflage, they managed to resist for a considerable time. One of the bunkers with a cloche proved particularly difficult to disable. The Germans used demolition charges to eliminate many of them. The procedure required engineers to advance under cover of flame-throwers and place demolition charges in the ventilation shafts, blasting the entrances.

The URs of Kiev gave stiff resistance from July to August 1941 with the city of Kiev holding off several assaults until August. Further north on other parts of the Stalin Line, many of the URs such as Slutsk, were little more than skeletons, of little use to the Soviets despite Zhukov's pre-invasion efforts.

The defenses on the Dniestr extended up to 10 km in depth. Along the east bank of the Dniestr the Germans encountered elements of the old Stalin Line. The defenses near the river lacked an outpost line. Two- and three-embrasure light bunkers for machine guns and a few gun emplacements, stood 400 to 2,000 meters apart in the Yampol sector (UR of Novogrod-Volynski) and were reinforced by field fortifications.

Elements of the German Eleventh Army in pursuit of Soviet troops retreating from the Pruth River, encountered these works in mid-July. Two infantry divisions attacked across the defended river crossings on July 18 at Cosauti and General Poetash. The Germans successfully forced a crossing at both points. Assault engineers eliminated the bunkers at Porohy with the use of flame-throwers and pole charges placed against the embrasures. Heavy explosive charges reduced the remaining bunkers. Russian troops continued to fight desperately even when outflanked and in a hopeless position, not knowing that the high command had already sacrificed them before the invasion began. German reports indicate that the Soviets reoccupied abandoned positions in places where local resistance was strong. In some instances, however, the troops turned out to be raw recruits forced to defend bunkers unfamiliar to them and they surrendered quickly.

A heavily fortified area of the Stalin Line at Dubossary, containing many bunkers, artillery batteries, and other supporting positions, finally fell at the end of July. German engineers and infantrymen, supported by anti-tank and anti-aircraft weapons, engaged in close combat, finally overcoming Soviet resistance.

In September, the Germans penetrated the position they called the Leningrad Line and struggled on. The Mozhaisk Line, the defenses in front of Moscow, was still incomplete and fell quickly in October. For the most part, the Soviets failed to use effectively the fortifications between the border and Moscow, partly because most were incomplete and not fully manned. Odessa, which had only field fortifications and no permanent landward fortifications, resisted until November 1941.

After the Germans overran the Perekop Line on the isthmus leading into the Crimea in October 1941, it was only a matter of time before Sevastopol fell. It held out for twenty-eight days in a battle that ended in July 1942. At Sevastopol the Germans deployed their super heavy artillery, including the 800-mm rail gun Dora, to destroy key points like Maxim Gorky I. On June 6, heavy German guns and mortars fired on Maxim Gorky I and scored direct hits that destroyed one of the gun turrets and damaged the other. Additional artillery fire and air bombardment failed to eliminate the Maxim Gorky damaged turret, which was finally put out of action by assault engineers on June 17. The battle for the battery continued as the Russians fought from its battered positions until July 1. The 800-mm monster rail gun inflicted little damage beside landing three rounds on Fort Stalin on June 5, and fifteen rounds on Fort Molotov on the next day. German heavy artillery concentrated on Fort Stalin on June 11-12. The four 76.2-mm guns of the fort had special shelters and remained in action until June 13 when an infantry assault finally took the fort. By early July, the Germans had fired over a million rounds. They had taken over 3,500 fortified positions, 7 armored forts, 38 bunkers built into the rock, 118 bunkers of reinforced concrete, and another 740 built of earth and stone. On July 4, after taking the Sapun positions, and the final assault that took Maxim Gorky II, the campaign against the last major pre-war fortified position came to a close. Soviet methods of fortifications began to change as the war progressed.

Map labels:

Hanko, Tallin, Leningrad, 1, Kingisepp, 2, Lake Peipus, Lake Ilmen, Novgord, Demyansk, Dago, Osel, Sorve, Pskov, 3, 14, Ventpils, Riga, Rzhev, MOSKWA, Lipaja, Daugapils, Moskva, 5, Polosk, 4, Zap. Dvina, Vyasma, Oka, Kaluga, Smolensk, Kaunas, Nieman River, Vilna, Orsha, Suvalki, 6, Mogilev, Bryansk, Minsk, B, Grodno, C, Bialystok, 7, Slutsk, GERMANY, The Pripet Marshes, A, Pripet, Mosyr, 15, Desna, Brest, 8, Kovel, WARSZAWA, Volodymyr Wol., Korosten, 9, Wisła, Zwiahel, Zhytomyr, Rava Ruska, Starokostantiv, 10, Kiev, 16, Przemyśl, Lvov, Kremenchug, Kharkiv, Letichev, Dnepr, RUSSIA, 11, Kamenec Podol., Mogilev, 12, HUNGARY, Dnestr, Bessarabia, Oradea, Nikolajev, Tiraspol, Ochakiv, Perekop, 13, Odessa, Prut, BLACK SEA, Crimea, RUMANIA, Sevastopol

Scale: 0 50 100 200 300 km, R. M. JURGA

A. Molotov Line 1939-1941
B. Stalin Line 1930-1939; Fortified Districts (URs):
1. Leningrad UR
2. Kingisepp UR

3. Pskov UR
4. Polozk UR
5. Daugapils Bridgehead
6. Minsk UR
7. Slutsk UR

8. Mosyr UR
9. Korosten UR
10. Novograd-Volynsk (Zwiahel) UR
11. Letichev UR
12. Mogilev-Podolsk UR

13. Tiraspol UR
14. Rybnitsa UR
15. Bryansk Line
16. Mozhaisk Line

Stalin Line Fortified Position of Zwiahel. Artillery Casemate #103 for Flanking Fires.

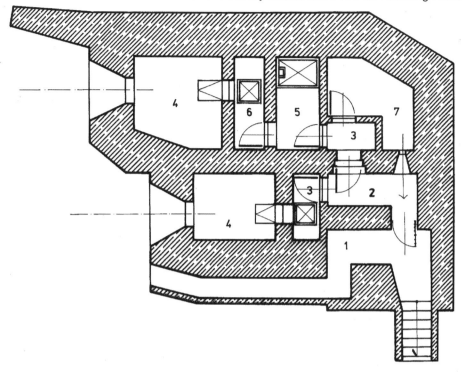

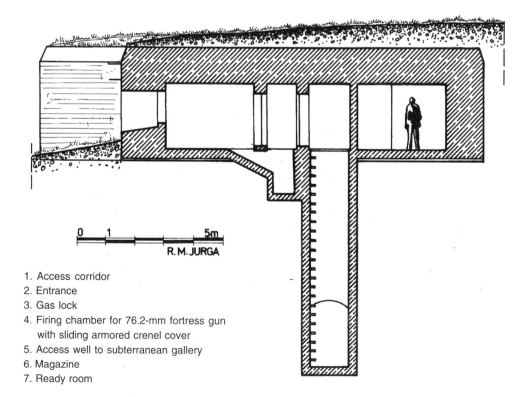

R. M. JURGA

1. Access corridor
2. Entrance
3. Gas lock
4. Firing chamber for 76.2-mm fortress gun
   with sliding armored crenel cover
5. Access well to subterranean gallery
6. Magazine
7. Ready room

Stalin Line Fortified Position of Zwiahel.
Block #102.

Stalin Line Fortified Position of Zwiahel.
Block #100 for 2 heavy MGs.

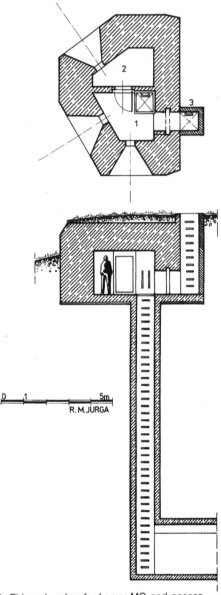

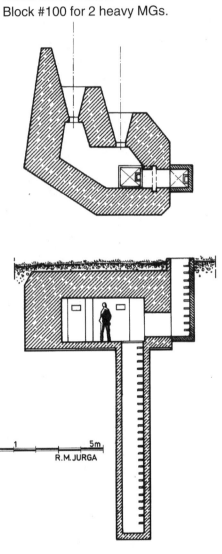

1. Firing chamber for heavy MG and access
   well to underground
2. Heavy MG
3. Guardroom

Stalin Line Fortified Position of Zwiahel.
Block #101.
Same armament as Block #102.

Stalin Line Fortified Position of Zwiahel.
Block #104 for MG.

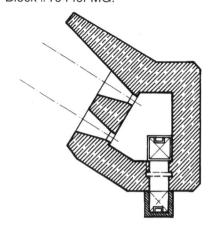

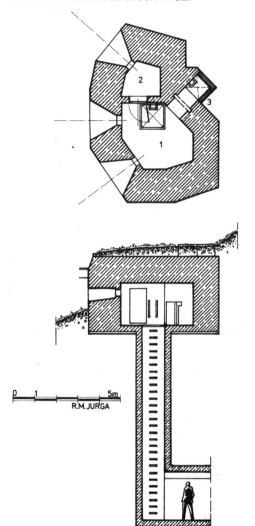

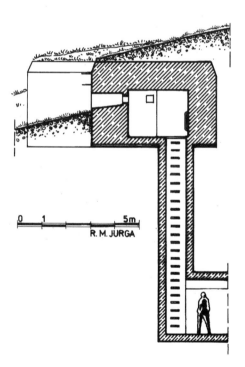

R.M. JURGA

R. M. JURGA

Stalin Line Fortified Position of Zwiahel.
Entrance Block "A."

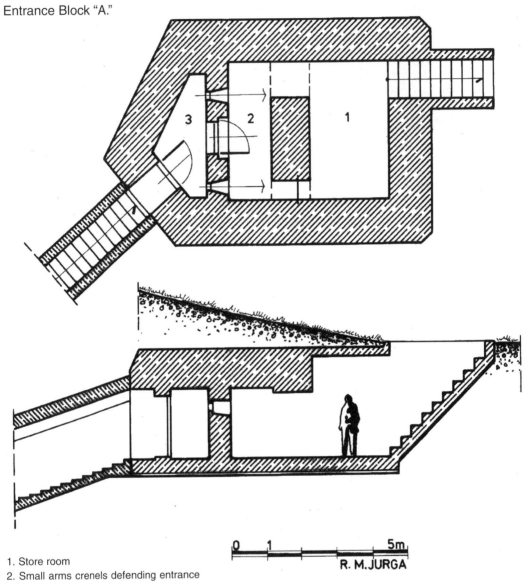

1. Store room
2. Small arms crenels defending entrance
3. Guardroom

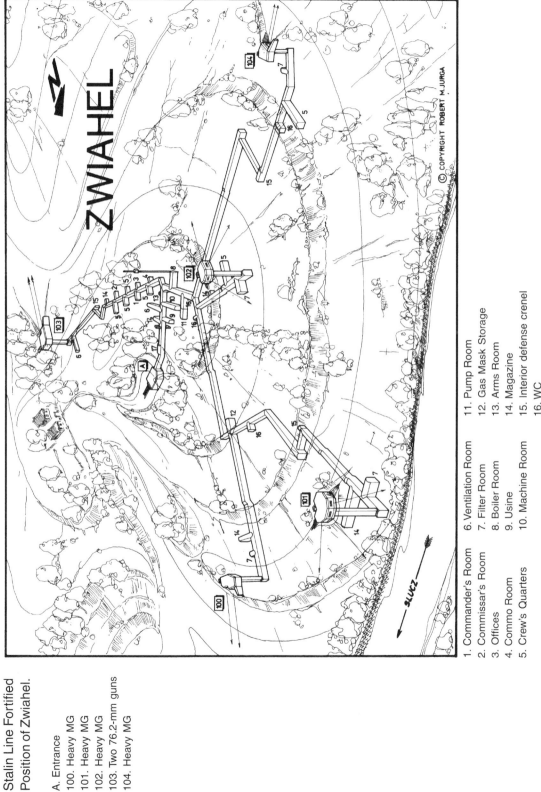

ZWIAHEL

© COPYRIGHT ROBERT M.JURGA

SLUCZ

Stalin Line Fortified
Position of Zwiahel.

A. Entrance
100. Heavy MG
101. Heavy MG
102. Heavy MG
103. Two 76.2-mm guns
104. Heavy MG

1. Commander's Room
2. Commissar's Room
3. Offices
4. Commo Room
5. Crew's Quarters
6. Ventilation Room
7. Filter Room
8. Boiler Room
9. Usine
10. Machine Room
11. Pump Room
12. Gas Mask Storage
13. Arms Room
14. Magazine
15. Interior defense crenel
16. WC
17. Showers

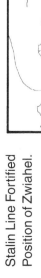

Molotov Line.
Casemate for flanking fire and part of Strong Point 330 near Brusno built in 1940.

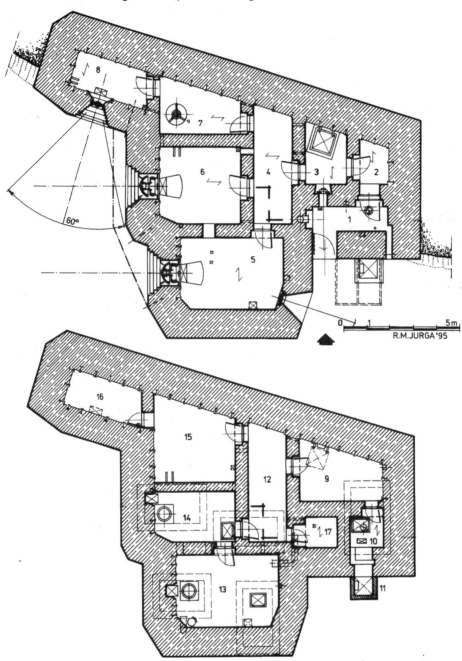

R.M. JURGA '95

1. Defended Entrance
2. Gas Lock
3. Corridor & access hatch to lower level
4. Corridor
5. Firing Chamber for 76.2-mm fortress gun and light MG
6. Firing Chamber for a 76.2 mm fortress gun
7. Command post with periscope
8. Heavy MG position
9. Corridor
10. Toilets with septic tank
11. Emergency exit
12. Crew area
13. Usine
14. Filter and ventilator room
15. Crew's quarters
16. Commander's room
17. Magazine

Molotov Line.
Double Casemate for flanking fire and part of Strong Point 330 near Brusno.

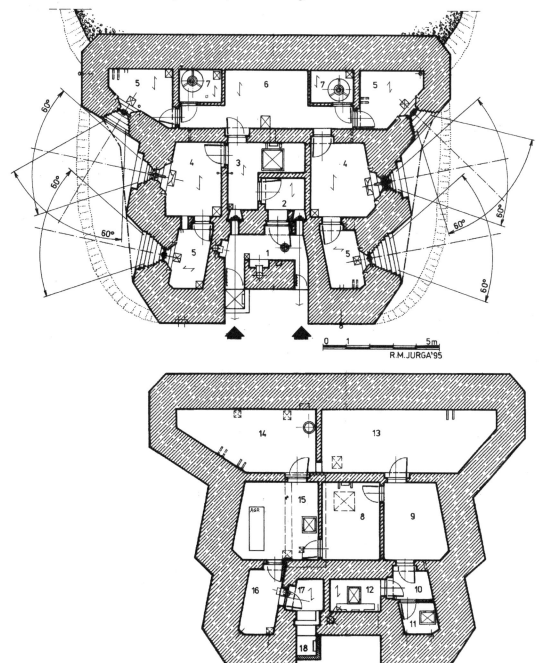

R.M.JURGA'95

1. Defended entrance and air intake
2. Gas lock
3. Corridor with trap door access to lower level
4. Firing room for 45-mm AT gun and heavy MG
5. Firing room for heavy MG
6. Crew's quarters
7. Obsv. post with periscope
8. Corridor
9. Crew room
10. Ante-room
11. Drinking water tank
12. WC with septic tank
13. Crew's quarters
14. Ventilation and filter room
15. Usine
16. Magazine
17. Store room
18. Emergency exit

Molotov Line.
Bunker of Strong Point 330.

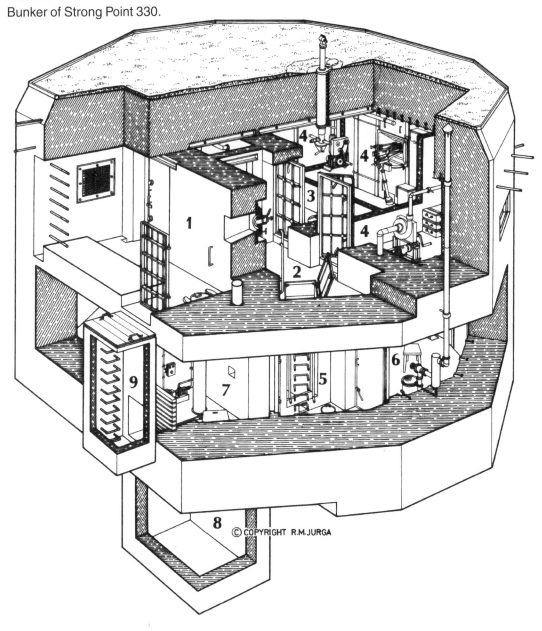

1. Defended entrance
2. Corridor & trap door access to lower level
3. CP with periscope
4. Heavy MG on fortress mount
5. Corridor
6. Crew area
7. Pump room
8. Tank
9. Emergency Exit

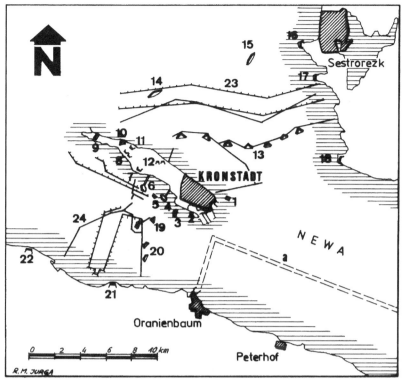

Kronstadt

1. Ammunition magazine
2. Naval Port
3. Ft. Kronslot
4. Ft. Peter
5. Ft. Alexander
6. Ft. Todteleben
7. Battery Todteleben
8. Battery Demidow
9. Ft. Riff
10. Ft. Schanz
11. Battery Michael
12. AAA batteries
13. Seven northern forts
14. Ft. Krasnoarmieiski
15. Ft. Perwomaiski
16. Battery Sestrorezk
17. Battery Finski
18. Battery Lissinoss
19. Ft. Paul
20. Southern forts
21. Battery Mala Ishora
22. Battery Mnoga Ishora
23. Underwater obstacle-wall
24. Underwater obstacle-poles

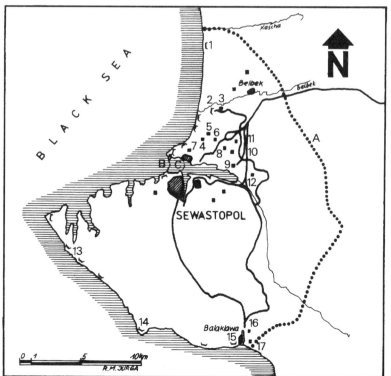

Sevastapol

A. UR of Sevastapol
B. Net obstacle
C. Log obstacle
1. Battery Mamoschoi
2. Battery Maxim Gorki I
3. Bastion I
4. Fort Tsheka
5. Fort Molotov
6. Fort GPU
7. Fort Lenin
8. Fort Volga
9. Fort Donet - ammo magazine
10. Fort Ural
11. Fort Stalin
12. Old Fort
13. Battery Maxim Gorki II
14. Battery Fiolent
15. Battery Balaclava North
16 Battery Balaclava South

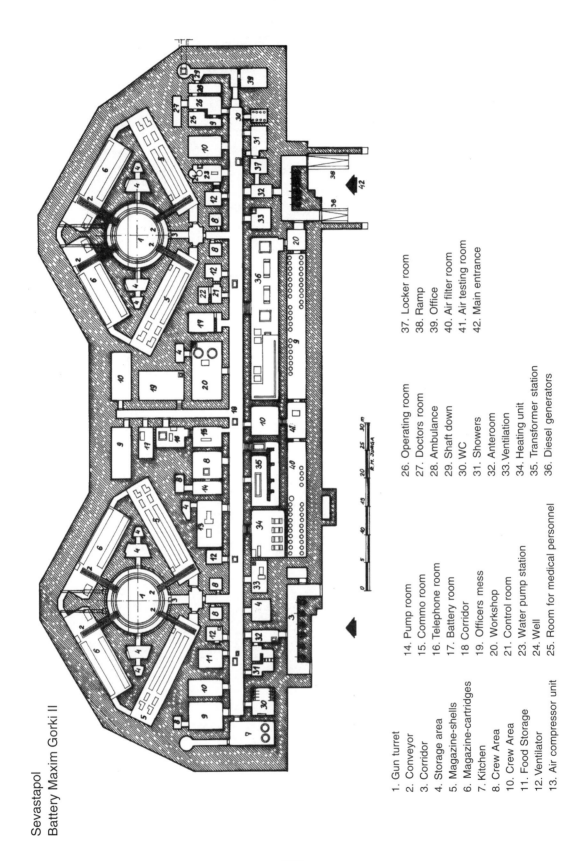

Sevastapol
Battery Maxim Gorki II

1. Gun turret
2. Conveyor
3. Corridor
4. Storage area
5. Magazine-shells
6. Magazine-cartridges
7. Kitchen
8. Crew Area
10. Crew Area
11. Food Storage
12. Ventilator
13. Air compressor unit
14. Pump room
15. Commo room
16. Telephone room
17. Battery room
18. Corridor
19. Officers mess
20. Workshop
21. Control room
23. Water pump station
24. Well
25. Room for medical personnel
26. Operating room
27. Doctors room
28. Ambulance
29. Shaft down
30. WC
31. Showers
32. Anteroom
33. Ventilation
34. Heating unit
35. Transformer station
36. Diesel generators
37. Locker room
38. Ramp
39. Office
40. Air filter room
41. Air testing room
42. Main entrance

Chapter 15

ATLANTIC WALL

BACKGROUND

"Enemy forces that have succeeded in landing must be destroyed or thrown into the sea by immediate counterattacks." Führer Directive No. 40, March 23, 1942.

Hitler's directive of March 23, 1942, marked the official birth of the Atlantic Wall even though the actual work had started much earlier. Unfortunately, since Hitler had no clear concept of defense, a rift arose between those German military leaders who advocated mobile defense and counter attacks to drive the allies back into the sea, and those who preferred a static defense system designed to prevent enemy disembarkation in the first place which would commit most field units to the coast. Eventually the proponents of the static defense concept prevailed, and the Atlantic Wall became reality.

One of the most ambitious coastal defense systems ever undertaken, the Atlantic Wall was built in an astoundingly short period of time. It extended for over 2,600 km from North Cape in the Arctic Circle to the Spanish border. Later it was expanded toward Petsamo in Finland. The Mediterranean, which included the coastal defenses of France, Italy, and Greece, could be considered, in a manner of speaking as an extension of the Atlantic Wall.

The German coastal defense system began with the creation of the Army Coastal Artillery in 1940, with its new coast artillery battalions (HKAA). The mission of the Army Coastal Artillery was to support the Navy Coastal Artillery, which could not expand sufficiently to meet the demands of such a long front. The Wehrmacht began to devote its full attention to coastal defense in 1942. However, in the following years, construction workers and equipment were diverted to work on other defensive lines such as the Gothic Line in northern Italy and the Panther Line in the

Soviet Union. In addition, the East Wall had to be resurrected and reinforced late in the war. However, most of the land positions built by the Germans were overshadowed by the Atlantic Wall, which attracted the world's attention thanks to propaganda and the epic battle for Normandy.

FORTIFICATIONS

Norwegian Coast
French Coast from St. Malo to Zeebruge
French Coast from Spanish border to St. Malo
Dutch, German and Danish Coasts
French Mediterranean Coast

LOCATION

1. Norwegian Coast

Norway's coastline was the longest of all the territories occupied by the Germans. The mountainous terrain and lack of roads, hindered the movement by land of reinforcements from one point to another. Only the entrances to the fjords and the major cities on the fjords that also served as ports offered potential invasion sites. As a result of this peculiar topography, every important fjord had to be defended but the remainder of the mountainous coastline was left almost unprotected.

2. Belgian and French Coast to St. Malo

The stretch of coastline between Brittany and Belgium was considered the most likely place for an Allied invasion because of its proximity to Great Britain. Its varied topography favored defense in some areas and offense in others. The area between Zeebruge in Belgium and Le Tréport in France, dominated by sandy beaches and dunes, was unfavorable to deep-sea shipping and the logistic support necessary for amphibious landing. The only breaks in this low coastline occurred at river mouths and near Cap Gris Nez where the beaches turned into cliffs. The littoral between Tréport and Carentan in France, consisted of cliffs cut by valleys opening onto beach areas. Along the eastern Cotentin Peninsula there was little relief behind the coast, which gave easy access to the interior. However, the lowlands of the peninsula were easily flooded. The northern part of the Cotentin, on the other hand, was dominated by cliffs that gave way, on the western side, to smaller beaches that extended, with some breaks, up to St. Malo in Brittany.

Some of the most important French ports on this front were Cherbourg, Le Havre, and Rouen, a major inland port. In Belgium, Antwerp had to be defended since it was the gateway to the interior. In addition, the Atlantic Wall encompassed several smaller Channel ports that had to be defended as well. Naturally, the Germans took advantage of the pre-existing fortifications erected by the French. An invader faced the difficult proposition of winning control of the mouth of the Seine to take Rouen and the mouth of the Schelde to capture Antwerp.

3. French Coast from St. Malo to Bayonne

The front between St. Malo and Bayonne included the Brittany Peninsula, dominated by hills punctuated by a few potential invasion beaches and several easily defended ports. Further south, on the Bay of Biscay, numerous open beaches gave way to low hills. In a few areas the cliffs reached the shoreline. Some of the key ports of this front were the naval bases of Brest and Lorient, already well protected, and the ports of St. Nazaire and La Rochelle-La Pallice. The major inland port of Bordeaux could not be put in use without control of the mouth of the Gironde.

4. The Dutch, German and Danish Coasts

The sandy beaches and dunes of Flanders continued along the shores of the Netherlands. The low lands behind them, including the islands of the Schelde, were easily flooded, negating any advantage of a seaborne assault. The major port of Rotterdam was useless without control of the mouth of the Rhine, while Amsterdam could not be put in service without control of both sides of the Great Dike on the Zuider Zee.

The Frisian coast of the Netherlands extended into north-western Germany, where it was masked by many large islands. The only major ports in the area were located in Germany and were difficult to capture because of their location and the protection of the off-shore islands.

The Danish coastline offered few ports on the lowlands of western Jutland. Its beaches faced shallow waters, unfavorable to the logistical support necessary for amphibious invasions. Operations against northwest Germany or Denmark would be limited to action against individual islands and offered few advantages.

5. French Mediterranean Coast

The Mediterranean coast of France was not, strictly speaking, part of the Atlantic Wall and is sometimes referred to as the Southern Wall. The area west of the Rhône included no major ports, but consisted of many low beaches difficult to defend. To the east of the Rhône, the port of Marseilles and the major naval base of Toulon were well protected by the terrain, and had been heavily fortified by the French. Most of the remainder of this coast presented a rugged appearance devoid of beaches. However, it also included a few stretches of long beaches opening into the hinterland.

The eastern portion of this coast formed the French Riviera, famous for its beaches dominated by the Maritime Alps. It extended into the Italian Riviera where the number of good invasion sites rapidly diminished.

HISTORY

After the fall of France in June 1940, the Germans moved to the coast in preparation for the invasion of England. While the Wehrmacht worked on plans for the next offensive, the first positions of the Atlantic Wall were being established. The Germans took over the French coastal defenses and moved heavy artillery to the coast, in the region of the Pas de Calais.

The mission of the heavy and medium gun batteries brought to the coast, was to protect Axis shipping in the channel and perform long-range bombardment. The medium batteries consisted of 150-mm guns and railway weapons like the navy's Gneisenau Battery that had four guns with armored shields. The heavy batteries included large railway guns with calibers of 210-mm, 240-mm, and 280-mm.

When the invasion was indefinitely postponed, the Germans began to work on permanent artillery positions. The first large concrete "Dome Bunkers" for a heavy rail gun, began to go up in September 1940. By the end of 1941, seven concrete battery positions were completed in France, one in the Netherlands, and four in Norway. These were Battery Graf Spee (4 x 280-mm guns) at Brest, Battery Hamburg (4 x 240-mm guns) and Battery Brommy (4 x 150-mm guns) at Cherbourg, Battery Friedrich August (4 x 305-mm guns) at La Trésorie, Battery Schleswig Holstein (3 x 406-mm guns) at Sangatte, Battery Oldenburg (2 x 240-mm guns) at Calais, Battery Kurfürst (4 x 280-mm guns) and Battery Prinz Heinrich (2 x 280-mm guns) at Framzelle, and Battery Tirpitz (3 x 280-mm guns) at Hoek van Holland. Most of these batteries had been brought from the northwestern German sities at Sylt, Nordemey, Borkum, Wangerooge, and Kiel. Battery Kurfürst and Prinz Heinrich came from Pillau, Battery Brommy from Memel, and Battery Schleswig Holstein(renamed Lindemann in 1942) from Hela on the Baltic. In addition, Norway received Battery Skagerrak (4 x 240-mm guns), Battery Goeben (4 x 280-mm guns), Battery Grosser Kurfürst (4 x 280-mm guns), Battery Yorck (4 x 170-mm guns), and Battery Goeben (3 x 170-mm guns).

The Norwegian defenses were given priority in 1941 in order to secure the Reich's northern flank before the beginning of the Russian Campaign. The rugged terrain restricted the number and location of air bases, making a defense based on large-scale air attacks impractical. Large stretches of the coastline could only be watched by occasional patrols. However, these isolated areas did not provide a good foothold for any force larger than a raiding party.

Almost all the construction material for the fortifications in Norway was shipped from Germany, which limited the number of concrete positions that could be built, especially when construction had to be speeded up. To save on construction materials, the Wehrmacht had to adapt many caves along the coastline to accommodate artillery positions. The Wehrmacht also borrowed the idea of using large rocks as anti-tank obstacles from the Finns.

In France, in the meantime, a series of Allied commando raids between 1940 and 1942 exposed the weaknesses of the Atlantic Wall. The 1941 raid on St. Nazaire in particular disturbed Hitler, who ordered his engineers to complete the submarine pens and protect more efficiently those still under construction. After all, the U-boats were the only remaining weapons that would allow him to take the war to the enemy after 1941, since the Luftwaffe was fully engaged in the East. That is why Hitler was anxious to secure the U-boat bases not only with massive concrete pens, but other defenses as well.

When the army groups withdrew from France between the fall of 1940 and the spring of 1941 in preparation for the invasion of the Soviet Union, only the newly formed Army Group D remained. Its commander, Field Marshal Erwin Witzleben, also assumed the position of Commander-in-Chief West (OBW) after Field Marshal Gerd von Rundstedt moved Army Group A to the East. As OBW, Witzleben was responsible for the defense of the French and Belgian coasts and came directly under the High Command of the Armed Forces (OKW). A newly appointed Inspector of Land Fortresses in the West was attached to OB West and his headquarters were moved from Metz to Paris in the same year. The High Command of the Army (OKH) was removed from the chain of command in the West and took control of the Eastern Front. The Armed Forces Command Netherlands had authority in Dutch territory, but fell under OBW's tactical command in the event of an invasion. Denmark and Norway were placed under separate commands.

While the Wehrmacht command in the West was in the throes of reorganization, the construction of battery positions proceeded and the heavy batteries at the Pas de Calais exchanged fire with British artillery in the Dover area. Plans were drawn for the defense of key areas of the coast, but by the end of 1941 only the ports had any significant defenses.

The first major German defensive projects on the Atlantic Wall were set in motion on the occupied British Channel Islands. The reinforced 319th Infantry Division, which eventually reached a strength of about 40,000 men, set up positions on the islands in mid-1941. Men from the office of the Inspector of Land Fortresses in the West had already surveyed the sites by that time. In October Hitler decreed that the islands must be turned into "impregnable fortresses." The Todt Organization (OT) arrived soon afterwards to begin the construction. The OT offices, fixed at St. Malo on the mainland, devoted their full attention to the defenses of the islands until October 1943.

Many of the older fortifications on the islands were incorporated into the new defenses, after being reinforced with concrete. OT built over 8 km of concrete anti-tank walls wherever there were no pre-existing granite walls along the beaches. It also installed the famous Mirus Battery of 305-mm guns on the island of Guernsey. However, it did not get around to placing a 380-mm battery on the key island of Jersey so other batteries had to assume the task of sealing the channel between there and the Cotentin Peninsula. As priority until 1943 was given to the submarine pens in France the OKH assigned no construction battalions to OBW General Witzleben, who had to borrow workers from the navy to build his land defenses. Before the end of 1941 Witzleben directed his army, corps, and division commands to carry out reconnaissance for suitable coastal positions and begin construction. By this time many of the old French coastal positions were put back into service.

Major construction on the Atlantic Wall began in 1942, after Wilhelm Keitel, Chief of the Wehrmacht High Command, called for the construction of a "West Wall" extending from the Arctic to the Atlantic. In that year the building regulations for concrete defensive positions had become standardized and many of the designs found successful on the West Wall were incorporated into the new coastal defenses. Field Marshal Gerd von Rundstedt returned to active duty, replacing Witzleben as OBW in March 1942.

As in the case of the East and West Walls, Hitler was not able to resist the temptation of adding his own personal touch to the Atlantic Wall. Thus in August 1942 he outlined the framework of the Atlantic Wall in Directive Number 40. He also exhorted his compatriots to show "fanatic" energy in the defensive effort and ordered the creation of strong points for thirty to seventy men armed with machine guns and anti-tank weapons. The new positions were to be able to withstand heavy bombardment and have inter-locking fires. The Führer further contemplated the completion of 15,000 concrete positions to be defended by 300,000 men. However, Fritz Todt, head of the OT, expressed doubts about his ability to complete more than 6,000 positions before the end of the spring of 1943. Hitler ordered Todt to concentrate his efforts on the submarine pens first, then the ports, the Channel Islands, and finally the open beaches.

The German High Command theorized that no invasion could succeed if seaports were not taken to lend logistical support. Their reasoning was based on historical precedent and was further supported by the Allied invasions of North Africa in late 1942 and Sicily and Italy in 1943. They never imagined that the Allies would build their own mobile harbors, the Mulberries.

In October 1943, Hitler ordered secondary defenses to be set up within 15 km of the beaches. However, these plans were not given priority, even though their purpose was to back up the front line positions and prevent a breakout. Meanwhile, work continued on fifteen fortress areas in Norway, which further depleted the available resources for the French coast.

The port strategy and existence of beaches convenient for invasion, caused the Germans to funnel their energies into the fifteenth Army's sectors between the Seine and the Schelde, which offered the most direct route to the Ruhr. Only late in the construction effort did the Normandy coast, defended by the seventh Army, receive much attention.[1]

In July 1942, OBW selected the fifteen Defense Sectors that were designated as fortresses by Hitler, along with the Channel Islands. They included:

Netherlands: Den Helder, Ijmuiden, Hoek van Holland and Vlissingen on Walcheren Island.
France: Dunkirk, Calais, Boulogne, Le Havre, Cherbourg, St. Malo, Brest, Lorient, St. Nazaire, La Rochelle-La Pallice, and Royan at the mouth of the Gironde.

More concrete was poured on the Atlantic Wall positions in 1940 than in 1941. However, the amount of concrete used between January and July 1942 was more than triple the amount used in the two previous years combined, topping over 700,000 cubic meters. The consumption rose to over 200,000 cubic meters per month in June 1942 and did not drop below that until June 1944. The peak month was April 1943 with over 760,000 cubic meters used, gradually dropping down to just over 200,000 cubic meters at the end of the year and rising back up in April 1944. The bulk of the German coastal defenses were built between the spring of 1943 and D-Day.

Starting in 1943, the German fortification effort began to face serious setbacks. Between 1943 and 1944, many of the workers engaged in building fortifications were sent to Germany and other occupied territories to repair the damage inflicted by the Allied air campaign. In addition, preparations were made in 1943 to defend the Mediterranean coast, which further drained the Reich's resources. However, despite these problems, Field Marshal Erwin Rommel pushed forward construction plans for 1944 and achieved maximum results after taking over Army Group B.

Before Rommel's take-over, most of the work had been concentrated on the *Festungsbereich* or fortress areas. When Rommel took over in 1943, the controversy over strategy was reopened. According to the previous policy, the German forces were committed to form a large tactical and strategic reserve whose mission was to counter-attack and drive any invasion force back into the sea. However, based on his past experiences in Africa, Rommel concluded that Allied air power would make such a strategy impossible. He decided, therefore, that every effort should be made to defend the shoreline and to transform the intermediate areas between Defense Sectors into positions more substantial than mere outpost lines.

OBW Rundstedt tried to find a middle ground between Rommel's ideas and those of his opponents like General Geyr von Schewppenburg of Panzer Group West. Thus Rommel was allowed to proceed with the construction of the Atlantic Wall even though he was prevented from pushing all available units as close as possible to the beaches. Rommel ordered his forces to lay down millions of mines, more than tripling the number placed before 1944, and set up thousands of obstacles at possible landing sites. He also closed the vulnerable gaps between fortress areas.

Every significant coastal port was fortified. The ports of Ijmuiden, Hoek van Holland, Dunkirk, Calais, Le Havre, Cherbourg, St. Malo, Brest, Lorient, St. Nazaire, and La Rochelle-La Pallice and the Channel Islands were declared fortresses by March 1944. Small fishing harbors were defended but not heavily fortified.

Even though French citizens were barred from the construction sites, information leaked out, including a German map showing the major positions. In addition, Allied reconnaissance flights detected many of the defensive structures. However, bombing had little effect on the great submarine pens until the huge block-buster bombs came into use.

In 1943 a new offensive element made its debut on the Atlantic Wall: the V-1 missiles. Their launch sites, consisting mainly of concrete installations, were strung out from the Channel Islands to the Calais area. In 1944 V-2 missile sites were added to the V-1 rocket bases. Some of these locations, like the complex at Wizernes which was built into a hill, were quite impressive. The only site for the secret V-3 long-range gun was in Minoyecques, not far from Wizernes in the Calais area, and was not finished in time for D-Day.

By May 1944, the OT had completed another 5,000 concrete structures on the French coast, including in southern France. These positions were in addition to 8,500 existing structures on the Atlantic and Channel coasts. The fifteenth Army occupied the most heavily defended sectors located between the Seine estuary and the Dutch border. It had more than twice the number of heavy and medium artillery pieces of the seventh Army, which held the much longer coastline of Normandy and Brittany.

On the home front, the defenses of the German Bight or Helgoland Bay, were not built until late 1944. Some gun batteries had been shifted from Germany to France between 1940 and 1941.

In the Eastern Mediterranean, the Germans set up some coastal defenses on the Greek mainland. In addition, OKW sent officers of the Fortress Engineers and Coastal Defense Staff South to advise the Bulgarians on coast defense, and the Italians on the fortification of the Aegean Islands. After Italy surrendered in September 1943, the Germans occupied many of their coastal fortifications.

In June 1944, the Atlantic Wall was still incomplete. Troops and civilian workers were still toiling over many of the obstacles. In addition, only 6.5 million of the projected 40 million mines had been laid. By the spring of 1944, OKW and OBW had completed only 10,500 of the 15,000 fortified installations Hitler had ordered (not including Norway). According to Colin Partridge, almost 6,000 smaller positions were also completed. This number included over 3,700 Tobrucks and 780 tank-gun platforms and bunkers.

Thus in 1944, the critical areas of the Atlantic Wall presented a formidable challenge indeed. Any assault directed at the defenses of the major or minor ports would have been tantamount to suicide, which is why the Allies did not seriously consider such a move. It is true that emergency plans such Plan Rankin A through C called for airborne troops and other units to capture Le Havre, but they were only to be set in motion in the event of a German collapse, when resistance would be minimal.

DESCRIPTION

The German-Norwegian coastal fortifications covered the coasts of Norway and Denmark. In Norway, the Germans defended fjord entrances and associated islands. The inner rims of the fjords were lightly fortified or guarded by field works. Strong points protected bases and blocked access routes to the interior; Narvik, Lofoten, Langoy, Tromso, Bodo were designated as fortresses in the northern sector; Mo, Vega, Rorvik, Trondheim, Kristiansund, Alesund, and Solund in central Norway; and Stavanger, Fleekefjord, Kristiansand, Arendal, Tønsberg, and Oslo in southern Norway. The defenses of Narvik were given priority over all the others in the north. Bergen, the key air and naval base of southern Norway, was second to Narvik in importance. The third most important base was Trondheim, with its sub pens.

The Norwegian defenses included 225 batteries with over a thousand medium and heavy pieces of which 42 guns were 240-mm or larger. In the area of Narvik the Germans set up batteries at Trondenes and Engeloy to protect the ore route from Sweden. The Danish coast had 70 batteries with 293 guns. The largest two batteries mounted 380-mm guns and were found near Oksby and north of Esbjerg. Construction of field fortifications on the coastal dunes required large quantities of material.

In addition to the gun batteries, the Norwegian defenses included fifteen torpedo batteries of various calibers that used single, double, triple and quadruple trainable launchers. The old fixed launchers of Fort Kvarven and Oscarsborg were part of the total. Two of these were near Narvik, one at Namsos and the rest south of Agdenes (near Trondheim). Except for those at Narvik, most were housed in concrete bunkers or sheds. The Danish sectors also included torpedo batteries.

The German Bight included the pre-war fortifications on the North and East Frisian Islands and the defenses of Heligoland that comprised twenty-two batteries, including twelve guns over 240-mm.

Along the Dutch, Belgian and French coasts the Germans concentrated their main defenses around the fortress areas. In these sectors the Atlantic Wall included 343 batteries with 1,348 guns of 150-mm or more. Between North Cape and Bayonne on the Spanish border there was a total of 700 coastal batteries belonging to the army or the navy. In a few places torpedo batteries existed, the most significant being at Vlissingen (Flushing) on the Dutch coast, and in a large bunker west of Brest, France. In the spring of 1944, the Germans planned to create about 200 torpedo batteries in Western Europe with the new wire guided T10 Spinne torpedoes. They would have been placed in concrete splinter-proof sheds, but only one battery was set up at Ostend before the Allied invasion.

Toulon, Marseilles, and Sète became the core of the German defenses on the French Mediterranean coast. However, their defenses were far from complete by the summer of 1944.

Parts of the Atlantic Wall were classified as *Verteidigungsbereich* or Defense Areas. A typical area in 1943 consisted of several kilometers of coastline with both perimeter and strongpoint defenses. The perimeter defenses comprised barriers such as anti-tank ditches, walls, trenches on land and minefields out to sea. The strongpoints, situated within the perimeter defenses, were almost independent positions composed of infantry fortifications surrounded by barbed wire and mines. Their entrances were heavily guarded. The heart of these strongpoints usually consisted of an artillery battery armed with weapons with calibers of 150-mm or more.

A *Verteidigungsbereich* included positions known as *Stützpunktgruppen* that consisted of several strongpoints occupied by a unit of battalion strength or less. Each *Stützpunkt* or strongpoint comprised all around defense, several weapons positions, crew quarters, communications and munitions bunkers, and, usually, a power source. Its garrison was up to company strength. Its weapons, mounted in the various types of concrete positions, included machine guns, anti-tank guns, old tank turrets, and flame-throwers. Some of the later positions included the small Goliath remote-controlled explosive tank.

The smaller positions of the *Verteidigungsbereich* included the *Widerstand* or resistance point designed for a well-armed platoon or smaller unit. *Widerstand*, found either on heights overlooking beaches, on the beaches, or between strong points in fortress areas, supported the stronger *Stützpunkte*.

Ports designated as fortresses were surrounded with *Stützpunkte* and included gun batteries, many of which were in casemates. Gun batteries were also placed at points outside the fortresses wherever there was a need to cover a section of coastline beyond the range of the fortresses.

Many of the heavy gun batteries mounted naval guns served by naval crews. The army manned some heavy rail-gun positions. During the war, the army took over from the navy the task of defending the coasts and organized about 800 batteries, many with captured weapons. By late 1943, the navy's hundred or so coast-defense battalions were outnumbered by about 140 army coastal-defense battalions (three or more batteries each) and a large number of coastal artillery regiments (two to three batteries and independent battalions).

Boulogne is probably one of the best examples of a fortress. It was surrounded by over forty *Stützpunkte* and *Widerstande* that included several with gun batteries. Almost half of these satellite positions were *Widerstande* and fifty percent were located on the coast or in the harbor. They included 75-mm, 88-mm, 94-mm, 105-mm, 138-mm, and 155-mm weapons and the usual assortment of anti-tank guns, mortars, and other infantry weapons.

Fortress Boulogne was home to a garrison of two battalions of a Luftwaffe regiment, three battalions of Luftwaffe Flak, and an undetermined number of fortress engineer units. The navy was represented by a flotilla of R-boats or small mine sweepers that were sheltered in concrete pens, and a naval garrison. The whole fortress was under the command of a colonel and was divided into six sectors. Naturally, the other fortresses were not exact duplicates of Fortress Boulogne for there was a certain amount of organizational variability.

Rommel changed the orientation of the defenses by turning the high water mark into the main line of defense. As a result of his decision, many new features were added, including a huge number of mines. Rommel also ordered the installation of many dummy minefields and positions and fore-shore obstacles that filled the gaps between the *Widerstand* and the *Stützpunkte*. In addition, three to six rows of underwater obstacles were placed between the high and low tide marks. Some consisted of wooden and concrete stakes placed at an angle, sometimes mounting mines, others consisted of old artillery shells anchored to metal structures. Finally, there were also pyramids, tetrahedrons, and Belgian Gates. The obstacles on the Channel beaches alone reached a total of over 500,000; more than 30,000 held mines. Tall pointed stakes, known as "Rommel Asparagus," were installed in open fields to prevent glider and parachute landings.

The OKW's *Regulations Governing the Army's Standard Design as of Autumn 1942*, set the standard for most of the construction on the Atlantic Wall. The designs and specifications set out in this document were, to a great extent, developed on the East and the West Wall. There were too many variants of fortifications on the Atlantic Wall to cover in the present work. However, there are a number of fundamental types, such as troop shelters, ammunition magazines, weapons bunkers, positions for machinery and searchlights, supply and kitchen positions, infirmaries, command posts, observation and fire direction positions, command posts for anti-aircraft units, combat bunkers with cloches or turrets, combat bunkers with frontal embrasures and others with flanking embrasures, combat positions for naval artillery turrets, open concrete artillery positions, and command posts with communications equipment. Most of these types usually had ten or more variants that included the design Series 100, 200, 300, 400, 500, 600 and 700 bunkers. The casemates for the huge artillery batteries, and the concrete positions for the artillery turrets were not usually standardized. One of the most unusual positions was a special concrete turret built for Battery Waldham at Fort Vert, in the vicinity of Calais, which was not approved for use until April 1944. Another unusual position consisted of several larger domed turrets in Norway that were not approved until 1944.

Many of these bunkers had protected entrances, air locks, and, in some cases, Tobruk positions. The Tobruck was a circular open machine gun position, sometimes placed on the roof of, or adjacent to, a bunker designed for local defense. Some of the first Tobruk positions to appear on the Atlantic Wall were the Series 100 of 1939 that included Czech 4.7-mm anti-tank guns and M-19 automatic mortars. Series 400 and 500, which required less armor, replaced Series 100 in 1942 and were used with coastal batteries.

Coastal positions used the standard protection that consisted of as much as 3.5 meters of concrete and 600-mm to 350-mm of armor thickness in Type A structures, and as little as .3 meters of concrete and 60-mm to 30-mm of armor thickness in the small Type D.

The Kriegsmarine and Luftwaffe, who developed their own designs, began setting up radar positions during 1942. They used concrete positions for the radar masts, and communications and command blocks. The navy's gun casemates faced the coast for maximum range, while the army's tended to be concealed. As a result the naval range-finding positions operated more effectively than the army's, against naval units. The radars that were deployed along the coast in concrete positions, and even atop large concrete observation posts, yielded disappointing results.

Among the most impressive, if not unusual, positions of the Atlantic Wall were the batteries defending the approaches to Narvik, which included Battery Dietl (three guns) and Battery Trondenes (four guns). These mounted their naval guns in turrets on large two-level concrete installations. The Gneisenau batteries, also quite uncommon, were created with two turrets salvaged from the badly damaged warship *Gneisenau*. One turret was placed on an island west of Bergen, the other at Austrått, Norway. The guns from the forward turret went to the Fortress of Hoek van Holland. The secondary armament of the ship went to various locations, including Denmark. The emplacement of the 280-mm triple-gun turret of the battery at Austrått, which went into operation in late 1943, was blasted into the rock. The interior rooms were concreted. The battery was complemented by anti-aircraft weapons and anti-tank guns that were set up at the fort. Along with other 280-mm batteries and medium artillery positions, the Austrått site played a key role in barring access to Trondheim and its submarine pens through the fjord.

The area between Calais and Boulogne was home to Batteries Todt and Lindemann, a battery of 305-mm guns, another of 280-mm guns, and a few domed bunkers for heavy rail guns, the heaviest concentration of big guns on the Atlantic Wall. Battery Todt, located near Cap Gris Nez, consisted of four casemates, each containing a 380-mm gun in a turret. The completed positions went into operation in the spring of 1942. Wire obstacles and minefields surrounded the battery, and other bunkers served various types of weapons, including anti-aircraft guns. There were also troop shelters, munitions storage, and other supporting positions to complete this strongpoint.

Located near Sangatte, Battery Lindemann was the heaviest gun battery on the French coast. Unlike similar 406-mm guns near Narvik, these weapons were in three single gun turrets, mounted individually in large three-level casemates. Additional bunkers in and around the battery site formed a strongpoint that included anti-aircraft batteries, machine gun positions, a concrete anti-tank ditch with wire obstacles, and an electrified fence protecting each gun casemate.

Further to the west, atop a hill overlooking the harbor of Cherbourg, old Fort Roule was equipped with defensive positions, including concrete emplacements for anti-aircraft guns. Just below the fort, a rough gallery was excavated in the rock and four concrete 105-mm gun casemates with an observation position between them were built into the side of the hill. In addition to Fort Roule, other positions surrounded the city of Cherbourg, including concrete gun batteries, and reinforced positions on old forts which occupied the jetties.

The fortress area of the Channel Islands was also unique. The Mirus Battery, located on the island of Guernsey, mounted 305-mm guns salvaged from the old Russian battleship *Imperator Alexander*, which had been scrapped in Bizerte, Tunisia. The guns had been sent by the Allies to Northern Finland during the Winter War, but were captured by the Germans after they invaded Norway. The weapons were refurbished and sent to the Channel Islands where they were mounted in turrets atop a large underground concrete support area. This massive construction fitted well with the large multi-level observation and range-finding stations on the islands.

The largest of all the Atlantic Wall concrete structures were the submarine pens. The most unusual of these pens were those of Lorient, where only one set was on the water. The other two were only reached by a slipway. The submarines were pulled out of the water on "chariots" and shifted along a set of rails into one of the pens. Another position included unusual dome bunkers for U-boats, where they were also pulled out of the water and moved on to a round table from which a chariot carried them into one of the two shelters.

Other large submarine pens in France were located at Bordeaux, La Pallice, St. Nazaire, and Brest. Along the Channel coast, concrete pens for R-boats were built at Cherbourg, Le Havre, Boulogne, and Dunkirk. Outside of France, the Germans built submarine pens at Trondheim, Norway and R-boat pens at Rotterdam and Ijmuiden in the Netherlands.

Most of the artillery was concentrated on the Channel Coast. Only about one third of the artillery allotted to the area was placed in Normandy, between the Seine and the Belgian border. Even the Channel Islands had more super-heavy batteries than the Normandy coast west of the Seine. More importantly, Norway received almost as much heavy artillery as the remainder of the Atlantic Wall.

Heavy and Super Heavy Gun Batteries of the Atlantic Wall in 1944 included:

	100-mm/130-mm	150-mm/155-mm	170-mm	210-mm or larger
Norway	183	114	5	44
Denmark	31	4		3***
NW Germany	22	11	1	5
Netherlands	41	9	2	2***
Belgium	14	14	2	5*** ++
France-Dunkirk to Le Havre	34	60	8+++	19++++
-Normandy west of Seine	21	20	5	4++
-Channel Islands	9	7	1	11
-Brittany & West France	36	28	7+++	13***
Southern France (The South Wall)				
-Sete-Marseille	33*	4	4	5
-Toulon-Nice	14*	4	5+++	2

The South Wall's heavy weapons consisted mostly of French guns.

In addition to these batteries, many others consisted of guns ranging from 75-mm to 88-mm (including Flak). Many weapons were mounted in casemates or on concrete platforms with supporting facilities in concrete positions.

SUPER HEAVY BATTERIES

Norway	Type	
Kiberg	3 x 280-mm SKL/45	Naval
Trondenes I	4 x 406-mm SKC/34	Naval Turret
Lödingen	4 x 305-mm L/30 Bofor	Naval
Engelöy I	3 x 406-mm SKC/34	Naval Turret
Orlandet	3 x 280-mm SKC/34	Naval Turret
Jusöen	3 x 280-mm SKL/45	Naval
Fjell (Bergen)	3 x 280-mm SKC/34	Naval Turret
Mövik Vara	3 x 380-mm SKC/34	Naval Turret
	1 x 305-mm	& Casemate

Oscarsborg	3 x 280-mm K L/40	Naval
Nötteröy	3 x 380-mm K M36/35f	Naval
Knatteröd	2 x 280-mm Heavy Bruno	Rail Guns
Denmark+		
Oksby	4 x 380-mm SKC/34	Naval Turret
Hanstholm	4 x 380-mm SKC/34	Naval Turret
NW Germany		
Helgoland-		
Von Schröder	3 x 305-mm	Naval
Wangerooge-		
Fredrich August	2 x 305-mm	Naval
Sylt	3 x 381-mm	Naval Turret
Borkum		
Coronel	4 x 280-mm	Naval
Belgium		
Schelde	4 x 280-mm SKC/34	Naval Turret
Bredene	4 x 280-mm Heavy Bruno	RR
France - Dunkirk to Le Havre		
Gravelines	2 x 280-mm Heavy Bruno	RR
Colequelles	2 x 280-mm K 5	RR
Nieulay	2 x 280-mm New Bruno	RR
Lindemann	3 x 406-mm SKC/34	Naval Turret in Casemate
Les Alleux	2 x 280-mm	RR
Grosser Kurfürst	4 x 280-mm SKL/50	Naval Turret
Todt	4 x 380-mm SKC/34	Naval Turret in Casemate
Hydrequent	2 x 280-mm K 5	RR
Friedrich August	3 x 305-mm SKL/50	Naval Casemate
Wimereaux	3 x 380-mm SKC/34	Naval Turret
Bléville Il-la-Corvée	3 x 380-mm SKC/34	Naval Turret
France - Normandy West of the Seine		
Beuzeville	2 x 280-mm Heavy Bruno	RR
Tourville (incomplete)	2 x 340-mm	Naval Turret
British Channel Islands -Guernsey		
Mirus	4 x 305-mm K626r	Naval Turret
France - Brittany and Western France		
Paimpol II (incomplete)	4 x 380-mm	Naval Turret
Kéringar	4 x 280-mm SKL/40	Naval Casemate
Plouharnel	3 x 340-mm K 675f	RR
Batz sur Mer	2 x 305-mm Skoda	Naval
South Wall of France		
Cépet	4 x 340-mm K M/12f	

*includes a number of 130-mm K L/55r and 138-mm K M/24f.
**include a number of 145-mm K 405f
***includes a battery of 194-mm K 486f Army
+Other batteries on the Baltic side included 7 x 305-mm Danish guns at Fort Middelgrunds, and 6 x 210-mm Danish

395

guns at Flak Fort and 4 x 305-mm turret guns on Bornholm. Over a dozen other batteries were at Fyn and Seeland.

++includes 203-mm rail gun battery.

+++includes batteries of 164-mm K 454f. (South Wall 164-mm K M93/96f)

++++includes batteries of 194-mm K 486

ff=French h=Dutch r=Russian t=Czech

WEAPONS AND EQUIPMENT

Naval bunkers with the following prefixes

    M - for medium coastal batteries

    S - for heavy coastal batteries

    Fl - for anti-aircraft units

    V - infirmary

Air Force bunkers had a prefix of L.

Construction Types:

	Concrete Thickness	Maximum armor thickness
E	5.0 meters	
A	3.5 meters	600 mm
A1	2.5 meters	420 mm
B	2.0 meters	250 mm
B1	1.0 meters	120 mm
C	0.6 meters	60 mm
D	0.3 meters	60 mm

Type E was used for V weapons sites and HQ, while A was for heavy gun batteries, and sub and E-boat pens. Type B was for most positions in strong points and resistance nests

WEAPONS	RANGE (METERS)
406-mm SK C/34	56,000
380-mm SK C/34	55,700
340-mm KM 12f	35,000
305-mm SK L/50	51,000
305-mm How. M. 16 (Bofors)	30,000
280-mm SK L/50	39,100
280-mm SK L/45	36,100
240-mm SK L/40	26,750
210-mm Skoda	23,000
170-mm SK L/40 (also includes RR)	27,200
164-mm K 454f	20,000
164-mm KM 93/96f	17,000

155-mm SFH 414f	19,500
150-mm K L/45	16,000
50-mm K C/36	19,525
150-mm SK L/45	18,000
150-mm SK L/40	20,000
105-mm SK L/60	17,500
105-mm SK C/32	9,500
105-mm K 331(f) Schneider	12,000

T-10 Spinne Torpedo - Designed for coastal defense and wire guided. One man could direct three torpedoes. Had 5,000 meter range.

WORLD WAR II

After 1941, most of the German units in the West consisted of veterans of the Russian front who needed rest, or older men. In 1943, Ost Battalions, consisting of prisoners from the East, were incorporated into many of the static divisions manning the coast defenses. The loyalty of these prisoners was dubious at best, but under the supervision of German officers and NCOs they could be kept working. Better quality troops usually manned the artillery batteries.

The command of the Atlantic Wall was also problematic because the army and the navy squabbled over jurisdiction over the coastal batteries and tactical control. This would eventually create difficulties during the invasion of Normandy because it would affect the selection of enemy targets.

The last British raid before D-Day involving regular army or large commando units, took place at Dieppe in August 1942. The operation demonstrated the futility of attacking a defended port, even with its fortifications still under construction. However, it also exposed some of the weaknesses of the Atlantic Wall, which would not be corrected until Rommel's arrival.

Although the Atlantic Wall was still incomplete on D-Day, it presented a formidable obstacle to the Allies and determined their strategy. Rommel's dummy positions successfully diverted many aerial bombs, while his improved defenses caused the Allies some serious problems. If the super-heavy artillery had been installed in the casemates or armored turrets of Normandy, it would probably have caused serious disruptions to the disembarkation process. It is true that the Longues Battery was eliminated by Allied naval bombardment, but a greater number of heavy batteries would have been more difficult to silence.

There can be no question that the Atlantic Wall played a significant role in the events of June 1944 and influenced the decisions of the Allied leaders. The German defenses and strong points at Omaha Beach amply demonstrated the difficulty of an opposed landing. If the Americans had better luck at Utah Beach, it was because they just missed the more heavily defended areas. Had the invasion targeted the heavily fortified Boulogne-Calais coastline, it may well have been as disastrous as the attack on Dieppe, despite Allied air superiority. The fortress areas of the Atlantic Wall proved to be particularly hard nuts to crack. Some of the first that the Allied came across were Cherbourg and Brest, whose ports were left in ruins after the battle. Once the Allied supply lines were established, the other coastal fortresses were largely bypassed, foiling the German strategists who had hoped to tie up their adversary on the coast.

The truth is that Hitler over-committed vital forces to the Atlantic Wall in Norway, diverting valuable resources and troops that would have been better used in the West. Thus while the British and Canadians eliminated most of the heavy batteries on the Channel coast, the German troops in Norway sat idle, braced for an invasion that never came. The Atlantic Wall almost succeeded in its mission, but, as Rommel had predicted, the outcome of the invasion was decided in the first twenty-four hours.

Atlantic Wall Bunker, B-werk, Regelbau 634 with a 6 embrasure cloche and armored plate.

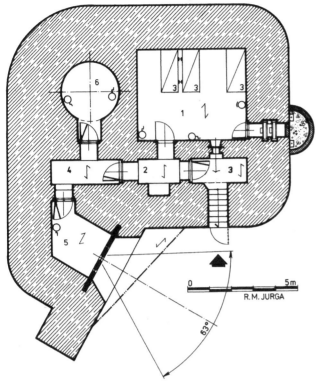

1. Crew's quarters (9 men) and emermgency exit
2. Gas lock
3. Defended entrance
4. Corridor
5. Firing room for MG-34 behind armored plate 78P9 (20-cm thick)
6. 6 embrasure cloche 20P7 for two MG-34 on fortress mounting

Atlantic Wall Bunker
Standard Doppelgruppenunterstand, Regelbau 622, B-werk.

1. Crew's quarters (9 men)
2. Defended entrance
3. Gas lock
4. Ring stand (Tobruk 58c) for MG

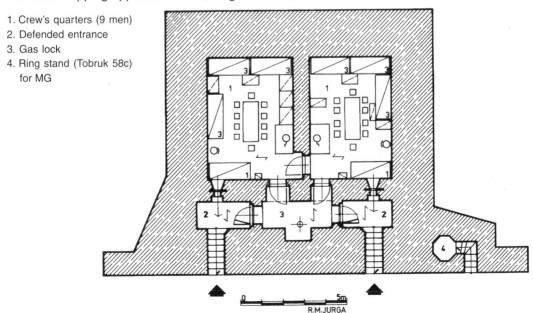

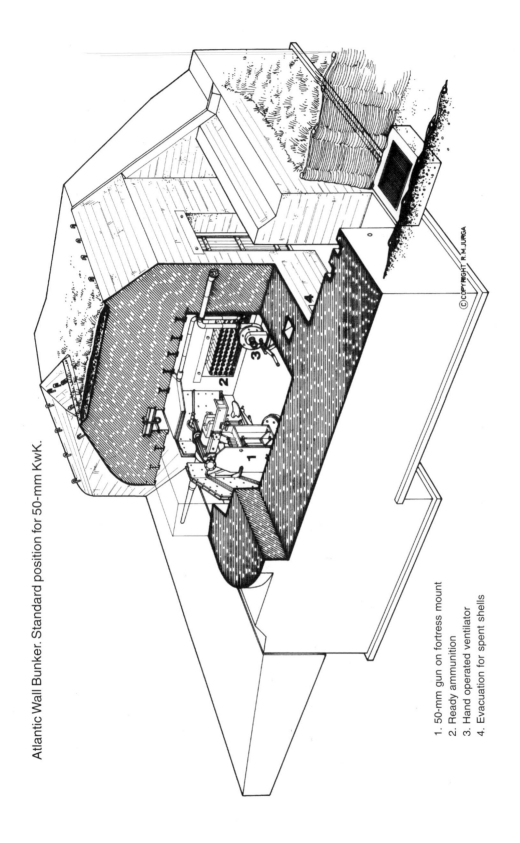

Atlantic Wall Bunker. Standard position for 50-mm KwK.

1. 50-mm gun on fortress mount
2. Ready ammunition
3. Hand operated ventilator
4. Evacuation for spent shells

© COPYRIGHT R.M.JURGA

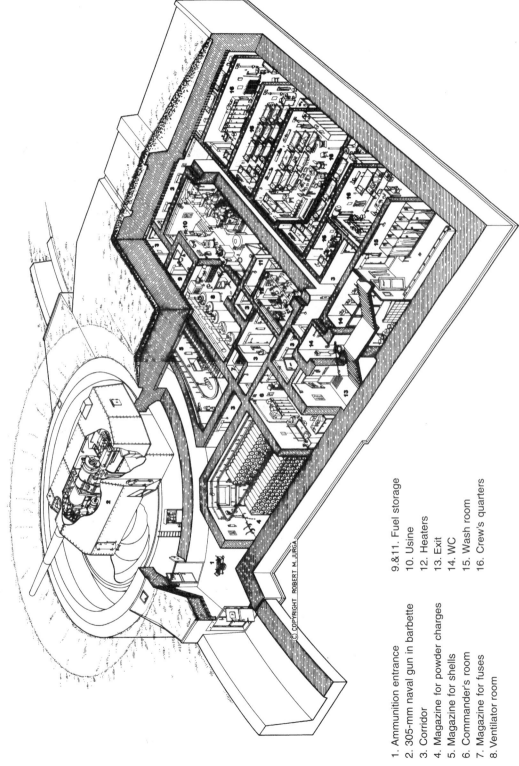

Atlantic Wall- Battery Mirus on Guernsey Island with 4 x 305-mm.

1. Ammunition entrance
2. 305-mm naval gun in barbette
3. Corridor
4. Magazine for powder charges
5. Magazine for shells
6. Commander's room
7. Magazine for fuses
8. Ventilator room

9.&11. Fuel storage
10. Usine
12. Heaters
13. Exit
14. WC
15. Wash room
16. Crew's quarters

© COPYRIGHT ROBERT M. JURGA

Atlantic Wall.
Universal emplacement of Ring Stand type for tank turrets.

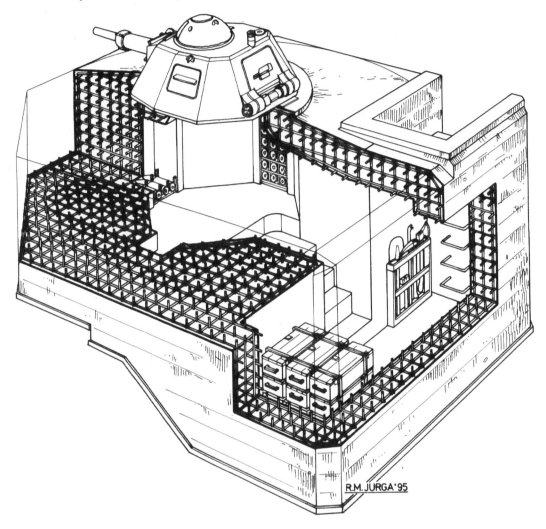

R.M. JURGA '95

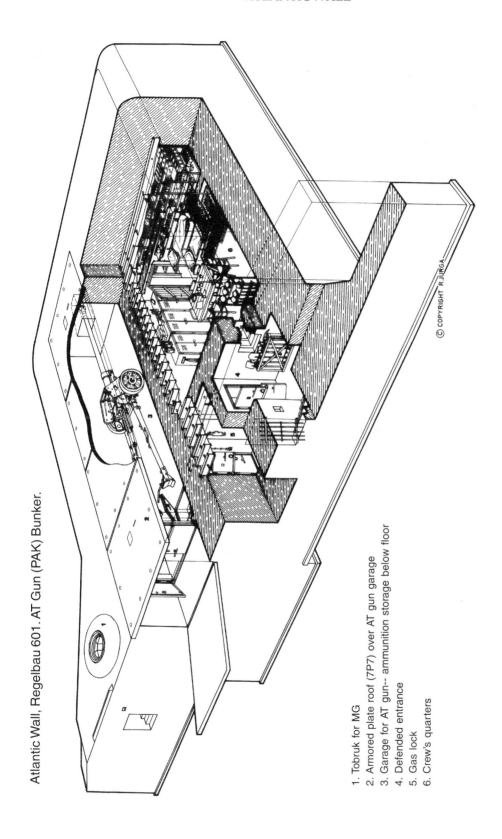

Atlantic Wall, Regelbau 601. AT Gun (PAK) Bunker.

1. Tobruk for MG
2. Armored plate roof (7P7) over AT gun garage
3. Garage for AT gun-- ammunition storage below floor
4. Defended entrance
5. Gas lock
6. Crew's quarters

© COPYRIGHT R.JURGA

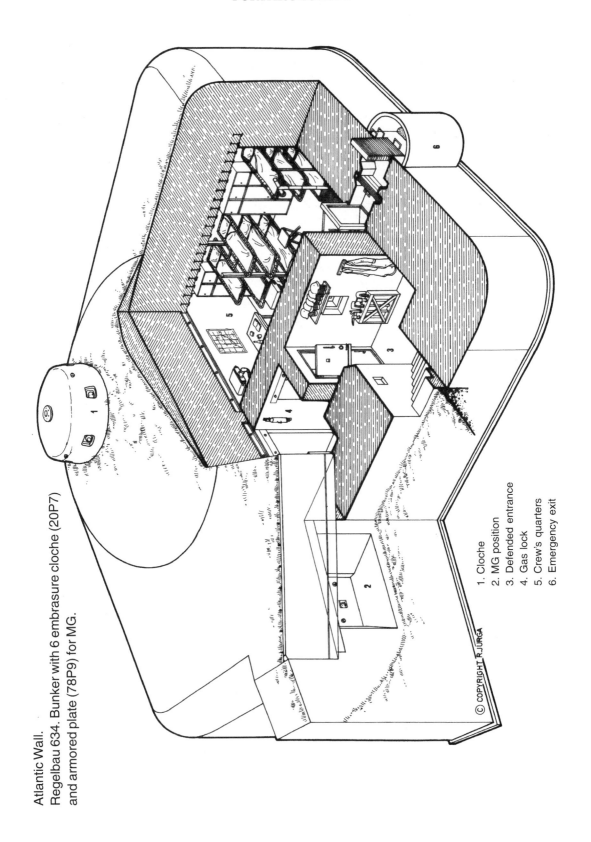

Atlantic Wall.
Regelbau 634. Bunker with 6 embrasure cloche (20P7)
and armored plate (78P9) for MG.

1. Cloche
2. MG position
3. Defended entrance
4. Gas lock
5. Crew's quarters
6. Emergency exit

© COPYRIGHT R.JURGA

APPENDIX

THE IBERIAN PENINSULA

1. Background

The neutral countries of the Iberian Peninsula, Spain and Portugal, provided a secure anchor for Germany's Atlantic Wall. Dominated by rugged terrain, the Iberian Peninsula favored the defender. An allied invasion force that managed to take over the peninsula would still have to pass the formidable and easily defended barrier of the Pyrenees stretching across the Franco-Spanish border.

The fact that Spain refrained from becoming an active member of the Axis, saved Germany the enormous expense in manpower and resources of defending the long Iberian coastline. Spain's coastal defenses were quite modest and consisted of old weapons from the early 1920s. They were augmented with eighteen 15-inch guns purchased from the British Vickers company between 1929 and 1935.

Late in the war, with Germany moving closer toward defeat, Franco had the army create a barrier along the Pyrenees, known as "Linea P."

2. Description

The Spanish coastline was defended by a number of adequate, if antiquated positions. Spain's counterpart of Gibraltar at Ceuta, in Spanish Morocco, allowed it to keep an eye on shipping through the straits. Ceuta's gun batteries included two with four 150-mm guns with armored shields, two batteries believed to be of 9-inch guns (six and four gun batteries), and five batteries with a total of ten 305-mm guns. Although they were old, these weapons were still effective.

The port of Cadiz, which served as a proving ground, had a variety of different caliber weapons, many of which were obsolete by 1940. Its three old 305-mm guns were probably its most effective weapons. There were also a variety of coast defense weapons in other Spanish ports. The 15-inch Vickers guns that defended a few key ports and the regular artillery weapons of the Spanish army served as the most effective units for coast defense on the peninsula. The Spanish also installed some of the new Vickers 15-inch guns in the Balearic Islands early in the 1930s, particularly at Majorca and Minorca.

Barcelona's coastal defenses centered on the old fort of Montjuic, overlooking the city from the south. Further to the north of Barcelona, not far from the border, were the beaches of the Gulf of Roses that were vulnerable to sea-borne invasion. Here, the military deployed about five batteries, some in concrete casements. North of Roses, on the outside of the peninsula, stood another battery with 100-mm guns near Port de la Selva.

The port on the island of Tenerife in the strategic Canary Islands in the Atlantic was defended by three forts. In addition, work began on two coast defense batteries to the northeast of the port in 1940. Three batteries observed in 1941 were believed to have 8-inch to 10-inch caliber guns mounted on barbettes or pedestal mounts. The city of Las Palmas and its port on the island of Gran Canaria had several coast defense batteries situated above 150 meters elevation over 1000 meters inland. In addition, three batteries were placed on the crests of a peninsula to the north of the port.

The land defenses consisted of Linea P (the P may have referred to Pyrenees) with several thousand blockhouses stretching from the Atlantic to the Mediterranean across the Pyrenees mountains. Presently little information is available on Linea P, although the Spanish government has recently facilitated access to information on the subject. Almost all of the research and articles written on this subject come from Colonel Arcadio del Pozo y Senillosa and the team of Jean-Louis Blanchon, Pierre Serrat, and Louis Esteve. The frontier included three military regions: Region IV ran from the Mediterranean to Vielha, Region V started west of Vielha and ended at Valle de Anso, and Region VI continued on to the Atlantic coast.

3. History

Spain did not succumb to the fortress-building craze because it was involved in a bloody civil war that lasted three years and precluded extensive public projects like fortified lines. When it emerged bloodied and exhausted from the civil war in 1939, the reins of government were in the iron grip of Generalissimo Francisco Franco, the leader of the Fascist faction.

Beginning on January 3, 1940, Fascist Spain allowed German U-boats to resupply in ports such as Cadiz, Vigo, Cartagena, and Las Palmas, in the Canaries. The Allies did not find it worth their while to stop the military and economic aid that Spain lent the Axis. As the war came to a close, the Spanish became concerned about an invasion of pro-Republican forces from France. So in 1945, at a time when many fortifications were being dismantled or destroyed in various parts of Europe, Spain began to work on its first line of fortifications, Linea P. It was the last major European defensive line of the war and the first of the post-war era.

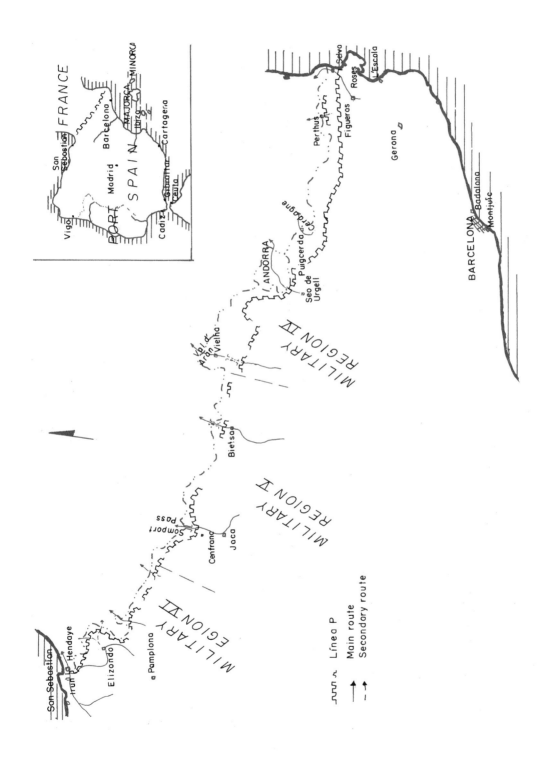

NOTES

Chapter 1:

1. See chapter on Belgium.
2. The fort had the following armament: 2 old cast iron Mougin turrets with 2 x 155-mm guns each; 2 new disappearing steel turrets with 2 x 155-mm guns each; 2 new disappearing steel turrets with 2 x 57-mm guns; 1 new disappearing steel turrets with a machine gun; two 80-mm guns in open position; six 220-mm mortars; four 150-mm mortars; 12 machine guns
3. These names were not applied to these sections before the war, but were adopted after the war for convenience's sake.
4. At least one had three entrances.
5. In 1933, the short-barrel German 105-mm guns (100-mm according to German nomenclature) of Ft. Guentrange were replaced with long-barrel weapons. It appears that the German-built complex at Mutzig also maintained a few batteries in a supporting role.
6. The term main d'oeuvre or MOM creates some confusion. It refers to military labor, and some works have been identified as MOM bunkers, abris, etc. This only means that military labor built them and the design could have come from the STG or there regions' engineer command. In many cases groups of MOM bunkers would be named for a commander such as Billotte Bunkers.
7. The German First Army had two 420-mm pieces. One was a Czech Skoda weapon and the other of German origin (possibly a Big Bertha?).

Chapter 2:

1. The Eifel is an extension of the Belgian Ardennes and provided an excellent defensive shield for the Germans between the Mosel River and a point near Aachen. It also served as an excellent area to conceal the massing of German troops for offensives in 1940 and 1944.
2. Except for the OWB Line, which was identified as a fortified front, the other positions of the East and West Wall were not broken into special sectors. These other defenses were also intended for use by field units and the only type of sectors set up would relate to Festung Pioneer (Fortress Engineer) headquarters responsible for their construction and maintenance.
3. The term werkgruppe was not actually applied to those positions on the East Wall until 1944.
4. The categories of strength were created before 1935. In June 1939 Hitler directed that all positions be called Panzerwerke to create confusion among his enemies. Any position with a cloche was to be called a Panzerwerke. The term was nothing more than propaganda when used during the war. To avoid confusion Panzerwerke will only refer to heavy independent works in this manuscripts, but the proper term should be B-Werke or A-Werke depending on the type of structure.
5. Two other positions were labeled as werkgruppen for propaganda reasons, but one had a single block and the other had no links between its three blocks.
6. German reports state it was actually 200 kilometers in length with four positions per kilometer.
7. The French term cloche is used to avoid confusion. The German terms are quite specific, but also sometimes confusing. A non-moveable cupola or cloche for weapons is identified as a Schartenturm. The standard type was a six-embrasure model known as a Sechsschartenturm. The other type with three embrasures, and actually only half a cupola or cloche, was known as a Dreischartenturm. As can be seen, it is not always possible to identify whether this was actually a regular cupola for roof mounting or a more unusual type of armor designed to be used like a casemate position. The Germans identified their special observation cupolas or cloches by the distinctive term Beobachtungsglocken and their rotating turrets by the name of Panzerdrechturms. The main problem is that in many cases they often identify all of these as Turms orturrets, making it impossible for the reader to distinguish one type from the other. Hence, we use the French term cloche for clarification.
8. According to some sources, the length of the Oder Line was 285 km with up to three structures per kilometer.

9. Manually it fired 30 to 60 rounds per minute, while electronically it fired up to 120 rounds a minute.
10. The Germans call these cloches cupolas and make no significant distinction between turrets and these fixed non-rotating armored positions. In the present text the French term will be used to avoid confusion.
11. When the Central Sector is listed as two sectors, the West Wall totals four sectors.
12. This is a term used by Bettinger and Büren in their book, but apparently not one used before or during the war.
13. This unusual type was the culmination of bunkers with tank turrets. The Panther turret from a Panzer V tank was not only used in a concrete shelter, but it was also setup with a steel box-like structure. A few of these were used on the Eastern Front and the Italian Front. Most, which is over 150, were set up on the Western Front, mainly on the West Wall and inside of Germany

Chapter 3:

1. The Belgian debacle caused the French to abandon many of their own forts, despite the fact that they were actually superior to Brialmont. This explains why Fort Douaumount, which had only a skeleton garrison, fell so quickly in the battle of Verdun.
2. The PFL II, as described in this text, actually consisted of PFL II, PFL III and PLF IV. PLF III was a third line that included large casemates with 47-mm Anti-Tank of two types which protected the city. It included over 40 concrete positions. PFL IV consisted of forts Flémalle and Pontisse and the defenses of the left bank of the Meuse between Fort Flémalle, southwest of Liege and Lanaye next to Eben Emael. The PFL IV included three sections with machine gun bunkers and some anti-tank bunkers on the Meuse, and the Albert Canal (some on bridges). Usually, these two PFLs are overlooked and included as part of the PFL II.
3. Initially, the French had only wanted to take up positions along the Schelde, but in the first months of the war they decided to advance to the Dyle.
4. Pontisse and Flémalle were actually part of PFL IV.

Chapter 4:

1. After 1940 they were used by the Germans for antiaircraft guns.
2. In some cases, such as the Bath and Zendijk Positions, the 1941 German toponymy is used, which may not reflect the actual Dutch 1939-1940 name for a particular position.
3. According to some sources, the Grebbe Line is not part of Fortress Holland.
4. Brongers call these lines the Betuwe Positions and the Maas-Waal Positions.
5. Fort Vechten still has three of its armored turrets.
6. The Neder later changes names and becomes the Lek.

Chapter 5:

1. These camouflage methods were commonly used on other Swiss forts as well.
2. Swiss army units were linguistically and ethnically homogeneous, speaking the language of their canton of origin. German cantons were the most numerous, followed by French, Italian, and Romanish.

Chapter 6:

1. Before the war began 9.2-inch, 6-inch, 4.7-inch and 6-pounder Quick Fire gun batteries had been set up although some old muzzle loaders remained in service.
2. The general Headquarters Line, after the war was known as the Ironside Line (after the C-in-C of Home Forces, Edmund Ironside.)
3. The invasion of North Africa began on November 8, 1942. The airstrip had about 1,350 meters completed then and ready for use.
4. The British, like the French, had not yet perfected an anti-personnel mine in mid-1940.
5. Pooh was not installed until February 1941.

6. The guns were turned over to the army in 1942. A late arrival in 1944, the 13.5-inch gun named "Bruce," was designed for extremely long range but not much of a success.
7. This was also the main armament of Singapore.
8. Like many of these weapons, these were old, but this model originated in 1894 with modifications and many more were brought back into service after the war began.

Chapter 7:

1. I (Bassa Roja), II (Alta Roja-Gessi), III (Stura), IV (Maria-Po), V Media Roja), VI (Germanasca-Pellice), VII (Monginevro), VIII (Bardonecchia), IX (Moncenisio) and X (Baltea).
2. Little research has been done on the full extent of the Vallo Alpino and most of Italy's other World War II fortifications, as of this date. Most of the details in this chapter on sectors, types of fortifications, and numbers have been provided by Dr. Carlo Alfredo Clerici who has done considerable research on this subject and is now publishing it.
3. According to a 1942 Italian report of the Stato Maggiore, the Northern Front included the Swiss and German borders, and the Eastern Front covered the Yugoslav border.
4. In 1928 the 1st Coast Artillery Regiment was at La Spezia with a detached groups at Savona, and another at La Maddalana. The 2nd was at Venice with a group at Pola, and the 3rd was at Messina with a group at Reggio Calabria, one at Taranto and another at Brindisi. At that time 400-mm guns were still in use.The defenses of the port of Taranto were considered weak, and Pola impregnable. Brindisi was protected heavily by sea mines and Venice was considered modern, but Trieste was stripped of its weapons. La Maddalena was strongly mined, and Tropania was being fortified.
5. It is difficult to identify individual opere because most were assigned a number designation that referred to the particular sector and defensive system to which they belonged. These numbers were repeated in other sectors. The opera described here is #17 at Gravere in the IX Covering Section of Susa and the III Defensive System.
6. Many of these opere are so small they should not be classified as forts.

Chapter 8:

1. The actual name of the fort was Ingstadkleven, but the English language news media changed it to something more pronounceable in 1940.
2. The Coast Artillery troops retained an organization and uniforms similar to the army's.
3. Fort Skjellanger, north of Bergen, was to receive a three-gun battery of Armstrong guns and Fort Korsneset, south of Bergen, a battery of Bofors guns. The Germans completed the forts and used them in the Atlantic Wall.
4. These searchlights probably could be found in most other coastal forts, but at this time the data is not available.
5. There were only two other 75-mm AA gun batteries near Bergen. Kvarven, which was the largest fort, also had six 7.92 mm machine guns for use as AA and Fort Hellen had three of these weapons.
6. John Cockerill's company was Belgian.
7. In comparison to Boden, in 1914 the Verdun fortress ring had a circumference of 42 km, Przemysl 48 km, and Antwerp 100 km.
8. Only the one to Ft. Rödberget was completed. Those for other forts were cancelled.

Chapter 9:

1. It must be emphasized that the Czechs refer to all the border defenses as their Maginot Line, but we are not doing this in order to avoid confusion regarding the location of the heavy defenses.
2. The Czech term "tvrz" is similar to the French term "ouvrage" which refers to "a work". This term is generally used with the heaviest Czech fortifications, hence the Czechs identify them as fortresses although that term is a slight exaggeration.
3. These 100-mm caliber howitzers had a designation of 105 mm which has created some confusion.

Chapter 10:

1. Polish terminology for twentieth century defenses is not very precise. The term objektcan refer to one or more structures considered as a position. The term schron refers to a structure usually classified as a bunker by the Germans, which itself is a vague description. Polish writers have used the terms objekt and schron interchangeablyand translated them into English as casemate, bunker, shelter (like a French abri),and blockhouse without distinguishing between them. Gun casemates are calledtradytor, a term traditionally applied to to the section mounting guns and givingflanking fires and later extended to the whole structure, which, technically speaking,should be called ostróg. To avoid confusion, we will use the French terminology.

Chapter 11:

1. German sources estimated that the Yugoslav population in 1941 numbered 6.4 millionSerbs, 4.4 million Croats, 1.3 milion Slovenes, and 2.4 million other ethnic groups,for a total of 15.6 million.
2. In a 1942 German report on Yugoslavia, the sectors were listed in a different order. The 1st Sector was placed on the coast and the others ran northward in logical sequence. The information quoted here comes from a 1940 American intelligence report based on Yugoslav sources.
3. German sources do not show or mention an 8th Sector.
4. This table is based on German wartime estimates and Polish post-war estimates and it is possible the Yugoslavs did not use the ratings of I through IV as indicated by the Germans.

Chapter 12:

1. The Positions of the Metaxas Line are still largely secret since the positions were modernized for nuclear war. Because of this information is lacking and only a few good photos are available. They appear to be distinctive from the works of other nations. They may have had both telephone and radio communication, and also included air tight doors for use against gas attack. Some Greek veterans claim that machine gun bunkers had a periscope for directing the weapons fire. Presently it is not possible to verify this information.
2. The information on the Greek gun positions mentioned in the text comes from an American intelligence report of November 1938. Except for most of the 305-mm weapons in the Athens Piraeus area, the Greeks probably used some of the other naval guns removed from ships.
3. Greek sources claim that one position continued to resist after the cease fire inflicting additional casualties on the Germans. When the commanding officer was convinced the war was over and surrendered his small garrison, the German officer supposedly paid him tribute for his gallant resistance and then had him shot.

Chapter 13:

1. Actually, the Swedish government had planned to send 9,000 workers and finance part of the construction. Norwegian volunteers did not arrive because of Hitler's invasion of Norway, which forced the Swedes to concentrate on Sweden's defenses.
2. Further down the coast was the Soviet fort of Yhinmaki (Krasaj Gorka), sister fort to the one guarding the southern end of the Gulf of Finland.
3. Fort Kuivasaari protected the outer coastal defenses of Helsenki, while the older fortress of Soumelinna, which occupied several islands, formed the obsolete inner defenses.

Chapter 14:

1. Information on the Soviet fortifications has not been abundant, although the Russian archives are now open. Since many works were not complete, details are lacking. Most secondary sources have heavily relied upon the German Denkshrift on Russian fortifications which, like other German Denkshrifts, has many errors and cannot be considered very reliable. Unfortunately, because of the lack of sources, especially primary ones, we have had to rely on this German

document for much of this chapter. So it is possible, as more information comes to light from the Russian archives, that some of parts of this chapter may prove innaccurate.

2. According to the March 1940 issue of Time, the Soviets had sabotaged the route by creating break downs and looting rail cars, in the hope of making the Germans use the longer Danube route. In 1940 the Soviet Union began shipping oil to Romania by sea and to Germany by rail sea and to Germany by rail, so the railroad began to function with fewer problems.

3. Dnepr is also spelled Dniepr or Dnieper. The spelling for Dniestr is also Dniester. Transcriptions from the Cyrillic alphabet can be rendered in several ways and the ones selected in this chapter may not be the best. Lvov is spelled Lwów in Polish and there may be some mixing of Polish and Russian spellings presented here in border areas.

4. The Germans called it the Petersburg Military District.

5. In the fall of 1939, the Baltic States had been forced into an alliance. They were annexed the next year, in June, as Soviet troops marched in.

6. The defenses of the east are beyond the scope of this book.

7. According to German sources, these fortifications were not built until October, but the concrete could not have cured on the bunkers, nor would they have been ready   when the Germans arrived in the same month. In addition it is likely that preparations would have had to be made before the invasion, if the proper amount of equipment and materials were to be ready for this construction.

8. The Finns and Estonians intended completing this barrier with smaller batteries and minefields laid by submarines.

9. This system was listed in the German Denkshrift and also used by Czech historian M. John, but it may not have been what the Soviets used.

10. According to Tarleton, the blockhouses were two-level structures and the bunkers were one-level. The lower level was below ground and the upper level was earth covered except for the facade with the weapons embrasure.

11. The odd calibers of 132-mm, 185-mm, etc. were identified in German documents, but may have other designations.

Chapter 15:

1. The seventh Army also covered Brittany.

Appendix:

1. Presently little information is available on the Línea P. Almost all of the research and articles written on this subject come from Colonel Arcadio del Pozo y Senillosa and the team of Jean-Louis Blanchon, Pierre Serrat, and Louis Estève. The information included here is largely based on their work.

FURTHER READING

Chapter 1:

ENGLISH LANGUAGE

Kaufmann, J.E. and H.W. Kaufmann. *Hitler's Blitzkrieg Campaigns*. Conshohocken, PA: Combined Books, 1993. An analysis of the French military, the Maginot Line, and the reasons for German success in 1940.

—*The Maginot Line: None Shall Pass*. Westport: Greenwood, 1997. First detailed description of the Maginot Line in English.

Rowe, Vivian. *The Great Wall of France*. New York: Putman's Sons, 1961. The first English description of the Maginot Line, with good background information and a detailed account of the campaign.

FRENCH LANGUAGE

Jean-Bernard Wahl, *La Ligne Maginot en Basse Alsace*. France: Éditions du Rhin, 1987. Excellent book on the Maginot Line and the RF of the Lauter.

Hohnadel, Alain and Michel Truttmann. *Guide de la Ligne Maginot: des Ardennes au Rhin, dans les Alpes*. Bayeux, France: Editions Hemidal, 1988. An excellent guide for visiting the fortifications. Well illustrated.

Plan, E. and Eric Lefègvre. *La Bataille des Alpes: 10-25 Juin 1940*. Paris: Charles-Lavauzelle, 1982. The best account of the Alpine campaign.

Truttmann, LTC Philippe. *La Muraille de France: ou la Ligne Maginot*. Thionville: Éditions Klopp, 1982. The best description of the Maginot Line by the leading authority on the subject. Excellent illustrations.

Chapter 2:

ENGLISH LANGUAGE

Gander, Terry and Peter Chamberlain. *Weapons of the Third Reich*. Garden City, New York: Doubleday and Company, Inc. 1979. Excellent descriptions of various types of German weapons, and captured ones, which were used in World War II with a section on those for fortifications.

Kaufmann, J.E. and H.W. *Maginot Imitations*. Westport: Greenwood, 1997. A description of the East and West Walls.

GERMAN LANGUAGE

Bettinger, Dieter and Martin Büren. *Der Westwall*. Vol 1-2 Osnabrück, Germany: Biblio Verlag 1990. The most detailed book on the West Wall including a large number of illustrations.

Burk, K. *Die Deutsche Landbefestigungen im Osten*. Osnabrück, Germany: Biblio Verlag, 1993. The most complete book on the East Wall.

Jäger, Herbert, Gerd Wildfang and Robert Jurga. *Die Küstenbatterie Fort Kugelbake in Cuxhaven*. Cuxhaven, Germany: 1996. Well illustrated book describing the evolution of a coast defense fort.

POLISH LANGUAGE

Kedryna, Anna and Robert Jurga. *Grupa Warowna Werkgruppe Scharnhorst*. Krakow, Poland: Donjon, 1994a.

—*Grupa Warowna Werkgruppe Schill*. Krakow, Poland:Donjon, 1994b.

—*Grupa Warowna Werkgruppe Ludendorff*. Krakow, Poland: Donjon, 1995. All three booklets include excellent drawings and descriptions of the East Wall werkgruppen.

Chapter 3:

ENGLISH LANGUAGE

Kaufmann, J.E. and H.W. Kaufmann. *Hitler's Blitzkrieg Campaigns*. Conshohocken, PA: Combined Books, 1993. A description of the events of the German campaign in the West.

—*Maginot Imitations*. Westport: Greenwood, 1997. Detailed description of Belgian forts and smaller defensive positions.

Mrazek, James E. *The Fall of Eben Emael*. Novato, CA: Presidio, 1970 (1991 reprint). Detailed account of German assault on Eben Emael.

Vliegen, René. *Fort Eben-Emael*. Maastricht, Neth.: Koninklijke Nederlandse Papierfabrieken, 1993. Presents a complete account of the German operations against Fort Eben Emael.

FRENCH LANGUAGE
Anonymous. *Ceux du Fort D'Eben-Emael*. Liege: Imprimerie MASSOZ, 1978. Complete and full description of Eben Emael's blocks and their activities on May 10-11, 1940.

GERMAN LANGUAGE
Melzer, Walter. *Albert Kanal und Eben-Emael*. Frankfurt: Kurt Wohlwinckel, 1957.

Chapter 4:

ENGLISH LANGUAGE
Kaufmann, J.E. and H.W. Kaufmann. *Hitler's Blitzkrieg Campaigns*. Conshohocken, PA: Combined Books, 1993. A description of the campaign of 1940.
—*The Maginot Imitations*. Westport: Greenwood, 1997. A detailed description Dutch positions.

DUTCH LANGUAGE
Brongers, E.H. *Afslluitdijk 1940*. Baarn, Neth.: Hollandia B.V., 1977.
—Grebbelinie 1940. Baarn, Neth.: Hollandia B.V., 1977.

Chapter 5:

ENGLISH LANGUAGE
Kaufmann, J.E. and H.W. *Maginot Imitations* Westport: Greenwood, 1997. A description of Swiss fortifications.
Schwarz, Uris. *The Eye of the Hurricane*. Boulder: Westview Press, 1980.

Chapter 6:

ENGLISH LANGUAGE
Mallory, Keith, and Arvid Ottar. *The Architecture of War*. New York: Pantheon Books, 1973.
Hogg, Ian V., *British & American Artillery of World War II*. New York, Hippocrene Book. 1978. Excellent description of artillery used in coast defense.
Saunders, Andrew. *The Book of Channel Defences*. London: English Heritage, 1997.
Willis, Henry. *Pillboxes: A Study of U.K. Defences 1940*. Trowbridge, UK: Leo Cooper, 1985. Complete listing and descritpions.

Chapter 7:

ITALIAN LANGUAGE
Castellano, Edoardo. *Distruggete lo Chaberton!*. Torino: Edizioni il capitello, 1984. Good account of the fort and the role it played.
Clerici, Carlo Alfredo. *Le Difese Costiere Italiane Nelle Due Guerre Mondiali*. Parma: Albertelli Edizioni, 1996. Excellent description of all the Italian coastal defenses of both World Wars.
Fenoglio, Alberto. Il *Vallo Alpino*. Cuno, Italy: Susalibri, 1993. A good description of some of the opere in the Alpine Wall, but lacks maps.
Lazzarini, Furio and Carlo Alfredo Clerici. *The Lion's Claws*. Parma Albertelli Edizioni, 1997. Excellent description of defenses of Venice in both wars and their use by Italians and Germans in World War II.

Chapter 8:

DANISH LANGUAGE

Frantzen, Ole L. and Bjorn A. Nielsen. *Kobenhavns befaestining 1886-1986*. Copenhagen: Tojusmuseet, 1986. Covers the only major fortified area in Denmark, Copenhagen.

NORWEGIAN LANGUAGE

Fjortoft, Jan-Egil. *Kystforsvaret I: 1905*. Arendal, Norway: Agdin, 1980. One of a series of books written by Fjortoft that covers the Norwegian fortifications. This book included the background for the coastal forts created at the beginning of the century.

SWEDISH LANGUAGE

Danckwardt, Jean-Carlos. *Kustartilleriet i Sverige under andra världskriget*. Karlskrona, Sweden: Abrahamsons Tryckeri AB, 1992. This book, written by a member of the Swedish military, is the first, and to date, the only complete description of Swedish coastal defenses. It is an excellent description and the only reference material now available.

Chapter 9:

ENGLISH LANGUAGE

Kaufmann, J.E. and H.W. *Maginot Imitations*. Westport: Greenwood, 1997. Decribes the Czech fortifications.

CZECH LANGUAGE

Aron, Lubomir, et. al. *Ceskoslovenske Opneni 1935-1938*. Nachod: 1990. Covers the history and details of the fortifications.

Rábon, Martin, Tomás Svoboda et.al. Ceskoslovenska Zed. Brno, Czech Rep.: FORTprint 1993. Detailed description of the fortifications.

GERMAN LANGUAGE

Rábon, Martin, Tomás Svoboda, Karel Vancura and Milam Blum. *Der Tsechehoslowakische Wall*. Brno, Czech Rep.: FORT Print, 1994. German version of Czech book and contains less data.

Chapter 10:

POLISH LANGUAGE:

Jurga, Tadeusz. *Obrona Polski 1939*. Warsaw: Instytut Wydawniczy PAX, 1990.

Chapter 13:

ENGLISH LANGUAGE

Trotter, William. *A Frozen Hell*. Chapel Hill, N.C.: Algonquin Books, 1991.

FINNISH LANGUAGE

Arimo, Reino. *Suomen linnoittamisen historia 1918-1944*. Helsinki: Otava Publishing Company, 1981. The most complete history of the fortifications.

Chapter 14:

ENGLISH LANGUAGE

Fugate, Bryan and Lev Dvoretsky. *Thunder on the Dnepr*. Novato, CA: Presidio, 1997. Presently the only book in English with any information on the Russian fortifications, although that is only secondary to the thesis of the book. The book reveals the true role of the Border Defenses in relation to Russian strategy.

Tsouras, Peter. *Fighting in Hell*. Mechanicsburg, PA: Stackpole Books, 1995. This includes four U.S. Dept. of the Army publications, some of which cover operations against fortifications. These publications are difficult to find individually.

Chapter 15:

ENGLISH LANGUAGE

Chicken, Steven. *Overlord Coastline*. New York: Hippocrene Books, 1993. One of the few good books in English describing the fortifications.

Partridge, Colin. *Hitler's Atlantic Wall*. Guernsey, Channel Islands: D.I. Publications, 1976. An excellent descriptive history.

CZECH LANGUAGE

Kupka, Vladimÿiar. *Atlanticky Val*. Prague: FORTprint, 1995. Good summary with complete lists.

FRENCH LANGUAGE

Gamelin, Paul. *Objectif Douvres*. Nantes: l'imprimerie Le Pape, 1976. Describes the Channel coast.

GERMAN LANGUAGE

Zimmermann, R. Heinz. *Der Atlantikwall*. Munich: Schild-Verlag GmbH, 1982. Good account of German defenses on the Channel. A second volume covers the remainder of fortifications on French coast.

TRILINGUAL: ENGLISH-FRENCH-GERMAN

Rolf, Rudi. *Atlantic Wall Typology*. Beetsterzwaag, Netherlands: AMA, 1997. Excellent.

BIBLIOGRAPHY

Arimo, Reino. *Suomen linnoittamisen historia 1918-1944*. Helsenki, Finland: Otava Publishing Co. 1981.

Aron, Lubomir, et. al. *Ceskoslovenske opneni 1935-1938*. Nachod: 1990.

Axworthy, Mark, Cornel Scafes and Cristian Craciunoiu. *Third Axis Fourth Ally*. London: Arms and Armour Press, 1995.

Bettinger, Dieter R. *Der Westwall*. Unpublished manuscript, 1993.

Bettinger, Dieter and Martin Büren. *Der Westwall*. Vol 1-2 Osnabrück, Germany: Biblio Verlag 1990.

Bilek, Jiri. *Evropská stálá opevneni 1918-1945*. Nachod:Czech Rep 1988.

Blau, George. *Invasion Balkans!* Shippensburg, PA: Burd Press 1997.

Bond, Brian. *France and Belgium 1939-1940*. Newark: University of Delaware Press, 1975.

Bogdanowski, Janusz. *Architektura obronna*. Warsaw: Wydawnictwo Naukowe PWN, 1996.

Bour, Bernard and Günther Fischer. *Le fort de Mutzig 1893-1945*. Mutzig, France: 1991.

Brongers, E.H. *Grebbelinie 1940*. Baarn, Netherlands: Hollandia N.V. 1971.

Bruge, Roger. *Faites sauter la Ligne Maginot!* Paris: Fayard, 1973.

—*On a livré la Ligne Maginot*. France: Fayard, 1975.

Burk, K. *Die Deutsche Landbefestigungen im Osten*. Osnabrück, Germany: Biblio Verlag, 1993.

Campbell, John. *Naval Weapons of World War Two*. London: Conway Maritime Press, 1985.

Castellano, Edoardo. *Distruggete lo Chaberton!* Torino: Il Capitello, 1984.

Ceux du fort D'Eben-Emael. Liege, Belgium: Imprimerie MASSOZ, 1978.

Chazette, Alain. *1940-1944 Les Batteries allemandes*. Tours, France: Editions Hemidal.

Chazette, Alain and Alain Destouches. 1944: *Le Mur de l'Altantique en Normandie*. Tours, France: Editions Heimdal, 1989.

Chicken, Stephen. *Overlord Coastline*. New York: Hippocrene Books Inc., 1993.

Cine, Bernard and Raymond Cine. *Ouvrage du Barbonnet*. Menton, France: Auto-Edition, 1988.

Clarke, George Sydenham. *Fortification: Its Past Achievements, Recent Developments and Future Progress*. (Reprint of 1907 edition.) Liphook, UK: Beaufort.

Claudel, Louis. *La Ligne Maginot: conception-réalisation*. Lausanne, Switzerland: Association Saint Maurice la Recherche de Documents Sur la Fortresse, 1974.

Clerici, Carlo Alfredo. *Le difese costiere italiane nelle due guerre mondiali*. Parma, Italy: Albertelli Edizioni, 1996."

Collin, LTC Georges and Jean-Bernard Wahl, *The Ligne Maginot in Basse Alsace*. France: Association des Amis de la Ligne Maginot d'Alsace, 1981.

Corvisier, André. *The Dictionary of Military History*. Cambridge, Mass.: Blackwell Publishers, 1994.

Danckwardt, Jean-Carlos. *Kustartilleriet i Sverige under andra Världskriget*. Karlskrona, Sweden: Abrahamsons Tryckeri AB, 1992.

Deventer V. Mart, and Marina Fermo. *De Stelling Kornwerderzand, Betonnen verdedigingswerken op de Afsluitdijk 1923-1936*. Leeuwarden, Neth.: Monument van de Maand, 1990.

Durcak, Josef. *Openovani ostravska v letach 1935 az 1938* AVE. Opava, Czech Rep.: Informacni centrum Opavska, 1995.

Eastwood, James. *The Maginot and Siegfried Line: Walls of Deaths*. London: Pallas Publishing Co. Ltd, 1939.

Eden, Anthony. *The Eden Memoirs: Facing the Dictators*. London: Cassell and Company, 1962.

Edwards, Roger. *German Airborne Troops 1936-45*. Garden City, NY: Doubleday & Company, Inc., 1974.

Egger, Martin ed. *Festung Sewastopol: Eine Dokumentation ihrer Befestigungsanlagen und der Kaempfe von 1942*. Köln, Germany: Lippmann, 1995.

Ehrhardt, Traugott. *Die Geschichte Der Festung Konigsberg/Pr. 1257-1945*. Frankfurt, Germany: E.S. Mittler & Sohn GmbH., 1960. New York: Viking 1944.

Epididis, Alexandros General. *The History of the Greek-Italian War and the German-Italian War 1940-1941*. Athens, Greece: Paypros Press, 1952.

Etat-Major de L'Armeé de Terre, *Service Historique. Les Grandes Unites Francaises: Guerre 1939-1945*. Paris: Imprimerie Nationale, 1967.

Etlin, John R. *Battles for Scandinavia*. Chicago: Time-Life Books, 1981.

Fenoglio, Alberto. *Il Vallo Alpino: le fortificazioni delle Alpi Occidentali durante la seconda guerra mondiale*. Cuneo, Italy: Susalibri, 1992.

Fjeld. Odd T. Captain. *Fort Austrått*. Orland, Norway: Municipality of Orland, 1992.

Fjortoft, Jan Egil. *Tyske kystfort i Norge*. Arendal, Norway: Agder Press, 1982.

Fodor, Denis J. *The Neutrals*. Chicago: Time-Life Books Inc., 1982.

Förster, Otto-Wilhelm. *Das Befestigungswesen*. Neckargemünd: Kurt Vowinckel Verlag, 1960.

Fjortoft, J.E. *Kanonene Ved Skagerak*. Arendal, Norway: Agdin.

Fröhle, C. and H.J. Kühn. *Die Befestigungen des Isteiner Klotzes*, Herbolzheim, Germany: Druck, 1996.

Fugate, Bryan and Lev Dvoretsky. *Thunder on the Dnepr*. Novato, CA: Presidio Press, 1997.

Fuhrer, Hans R., Walter Lüem, Jean-Jacques Rapin, Hans Rapold, and Hans Senn. *Die Geschichte Der Schweizerischen Landesbefestigung*. Zurich: Orell Fÿuussli, 1992.

Gamelin, Paul. *Objectif Douvres*. Nantes, France: Le Pape, 1976.

—*La Ligne Maginot: Images d'Hier et d'Aujourd'hui*. Paris: Argout Éditíons, 1979.

Gander, Terry and Peter Chamberlain. *Weapons of the Third Reich*. Garden City, NY: Doubleday and Company, Inc., 1979.

Gariglio, Dario and Mauro Minola. *Le Fortezze Delle Alpi Occidentali*. Vol. 1 and 2. Cueno, Italy: Edizioni L'Arciere 1996."

Gilbert, Martin. *Marching to War 1933-1939*. New York: Military Heritage Press, 1989.

Ginns, Michael and Peter Bryans. *German Fortifications in Jersey*. Jersey, Channel Islands: Meadowbank Trading Co., 1978.

Goralski, Robert. *World War II Almanac 1931-1945*. New York: G.P. Putnam and Sons, 1981.

Goerlitz, Walter. *History of the German General Staff: 1657-1945*. New York: Barnes & Noble Books, 1995.

Grasser, Kurt and Jürgen Stahlmann. *Westwall, Maginot-Linie, Atlantikwall*. Leoni am Starnberger See: Druffel-Verlag, 1983.

Grimnes, Ole Kristian, *The Battle of Hegra 1940*. Oslo, Norway: Forsvarets Pressetjeneste, 1994.

Grimes, Ole Kristian and Odd T. Fjeld. *Oscarsbourg Festing: 9. April 1940*. Oslo, Norway: Informasjonskonsulentene, 1990.

Gryner, Peter. "Czechoslovakia '38", *Hitler's Army*. Conshohocken, PA: Combined Books, 1995."

Gunsburg, Jeffery A. *Divided and Conquered: The French High Command and the Defeat of the West, 1940*. Westport, CT: Greenwood Press, 1979.

Hakala, Jaakko and Martti Santavuori. *Summa*. Helsinki, Finland: Otava Publishing Company, 1960.

Halle, Guy le. *Précis de la fortification*. Paris: PCV Éditions, 1983.

Harrison, Gordon A. *Cross-Channel Attack*. Washington,D.C.: US Government Printing office, 1951.

Hart, Liddell. *The Defence of Britain*. London: Faber and Faber Ltd., 1939.

Högberg, Leif. *Skånelinjen*. Unpublished manuscript (to be published in 1999)

Hogg, Ian. *British & American Artillery of World War 2*. New York: Hippocrene Books, Inc., 1978.

—*The History of Fortification*. New York: St. Martin's Press Inc., 1981.

—*German Artillery of World War II*. Mechanicsburg, PA: Stackpole Books, 1997.

Hohnadel, Alain and Michel Truttmann. *Guide de la Ligne Maginot: des Ardennes au Rhin, dans les Alpes*. Bayeux, France: Editions Heimdal, 1988.

Hohnadel, A. and R. Varoqui. *Le fort du Hackenberg*. Veckring, France: AMIFORT, 1986.

Holub, Ota. *Trutnovosti hranicari*. Trutnov: 1995.

Horne, Alistair. *The Price of Glory*. Boston: Little, Brown and Co., 1962.

—*To Lose a Battle: France 1940*. Boston: Little, Brown and Co, 1969.

Hughes, Judith M. *To the Maginot Line*. Cambridge, Mass.: Harvard University Press, 1971.

Jäger, Herbert, Gerd Wildfan and Robert Jurga. *Die Küstenbatterie Fort Kugelbake in Cuxhaven*. Cuxhaven, Germany: 1996.

Jaillet, André. *Pourquoi une forteresse à Pré-Giroud, Vallorbe?* Brassus, Switzerland: R. Dupuis, 1988.

Jurga, Tadeusz. *Obrona Polski 1939*. Warsaw, Poland: Instytut Wydawniczy PAX, 1990.

Kaplan, Václav. *Delostrelecka Tvrz Dobrosov*. Náchod, Czech Rep.: Okresni Muzeum v Nachode, 1989.

Kaplan, Václav and Broz Jaroslav. *Opevneni z let 1936-38 na Sumave Náchod*, Czech Rep.: Oresny Muezeum w nachode, 1988.

Kaufmann, J.E. and H.W. Kaufmann. *Hitler's Blitzkrieg Campaigns*. Conshohocken, PA: Combined Books, 1993.

—*The Maginot Line: None Shall Pass*. Westport: Greenwood, 1997.

—*Maginot Imitations*. Westport: Greenwood, 1997.

Kedryna, Anna and Robert Jurga. *Grupa warowna Werkgruppe Scharnhorst*. Krakow, Poland: Donjon, 1994a.

—*Grupa warowna Werkgruppe Schill*. Krakow, Poland: Donjon, 1994b.

—*Grupa warowna Werkgruppe Ludendorff*. Krakow, Poland: Donjon, 1995.

Keegan, John. *World Armies*. New York: Facts on File Inc., 1979.

Kemp, Anthony. *The Unknown Battle: Metz, 1944*. New York: Stein and Day, 1981a.

—*The Maginot Line*. London: Fredrick Warne, 1981b.

Kesselring, Albert. *The Memoirs of Field-Marshal Kesselring*. Novato, CA: Presidio, 1989

Kleczke, Major Carol and Major Wladystaw Wyszynski. *Fortyfickacja stala*. Warsaw, Poland: Wojskowy Institut Naukowo-Oswiatowy, 1937.

Komjathy, Anthony T. *The Crises of France's East Central European Diplomacy 1933-1938*. New York: Columbia University Press, 1976.

Kornwerderzand: Geschiedenis van de verdeigingswerken. Netherlands: De Stichting Kornwerderzand, undated (circa 1985).

Kühne, Rudolf Theodor. *Der West Wall: Unbezmingbare Abwehrzone von Stahl und Beton an Deutschlands Westgrenze*. Munich: J.F. Lehmans, 1939.

Kupka, Vladimÿiar. *Atlanticky Val*. Prague: FORTprint, 1995.

La battaglia delle Alpi Occidental: giugno 1940. Rome: Ministero Della Difesa, 1947.

Länsivaara, Iikka and Arvo Tolmunen. *Salpa-Asema—Sodan Monumentti*. Finland: Hansaprint Salo, 1996.

Lásek, Radan. *Prazská Cára Ceskoslovenské opevení let 1936-38*. Praha, Czech Rep.: FORT Print, 1995.

Leach, Barry. *The German General Staff*. New York: Ballantine Books, 1973.

Levaux, Louis. *Ceux des dorts de Liege*. Brussels, Belgium: Edition CAREYMA, 1978.

Linklater, Eric. *The Highland Division*. London: HMSO, 1942.

Lüem, Walter and Andreas Steigmeier. *Die Limmatstellung im Zweiten Weltkrieg*. Baden, Switz.: Baden-Verlag, 1997.

Madej, W. Victor, ed. *Italian Army Handbook, 1940-1943*. Allentown, PA: Game Publishing Co., 1984.

Maistret, Georges. *Le gros ouvrage A-2 Fermont de la Ligne Maginot*. France: Association des Amis de l'Ouvrage de Fermont et de la Ligne Maginot, 1978.

Mallory, Keith and Arvid Ottar. *The Architecture of War*. New York: Pantheon Books, 1973.

Manstein, Erich von. *Lost Victories*. Novato, CA: Presido Press, 1982.

Mary, J.Y. *La Ligne Maginot*. Cuneo, Italy: SERCAP, 1980.

Mayer, S.L. ed. *Signal: Years of Triumph 1940-42*. Englewood Cliffs, New Jersey: Prentice Hall, 1978.

McEntee, Girard L. *Italy's Part in Winning the World War*. Princeton: Princeton University Press, 1934.

Meehan, Patricia. *The Unnecessary War*. London: Sinclair Stevenson, 1992.

Memorial of the Maginot Line, Marckolsheim (Alsace). Colmar, France: S.A.E.P., 1983.

Miniewicz, Janusz and Boguslaw Perzyk. *Miedzyrzecki Rejon Umocniony 1934-1945*. Warsaw, Poland: "ME-GI" Sp. Cyw. 1993.

—*Wal Pomorski*. Warsaw, Poland: Militaria Boguguslawa Perzyka, 1997.

Mrazek, James E. *The Fall of Eben Emael*. Novato, CA: Presido Press, 1970 (1991 reprint).

1929 World Almanac and Book of Facts. New York: Workman Publishing Co., Inc., 1929 (1971 reprint).

Novák, Jiri. *Opevnení na Králícu: Befestigung In Der Gegend Von Králíky*. Králové nad Labem, Czech Rep.: Fort Print, 1994.

Office of Military History. *Sotatieteen laitoksen julkaisuja*. Volumes 1-4. Helsinki, Finland: Werner Söderström Co., 1977.

Partridge, Colin. *Hitler's Atlantic Wall*. Guernsey, Channel Islands: D.I. Publications, 1976.

Perrett, Bryan. *Knights of the Black Cross*. New York: St. Martin's Press, 1986.

Pimlott, John. *Rommel In His Own Words*. London: Greenhill Books, 1994.

Plan, E. and Eric Lefevre. *La Bataille des Alpes: 10-25 juin 1940*. Paris: Charles-Lavauzelle, 1982.

Prásil, Michal. *Tezká dela Skoda*. Brno-Nachod, Czech: Prvnÿia, 1995.

Puelinckx, Jean. *Fort Aubin-Neufchateau: Mind Out!* Belgium: Privately published, 1995.

Rábon, Martin. *Prehled Tezkeho Opeveni*. Brno: Military Club Brno, 1994.

Rábon, Martin, Tomás Svoboda et.al. *Ceskoslovenska Zed*. Brno, Czech Rep.: FORTprint 1993.

Rábon, Martin, Tomás Svoboda, Karel Vancura and Milam Blum. *Der Tsechehoslowakische Wall*. Brno, Czech Rep.: FORT Print, 1994.

Rábon, Martin, Tomás Svoboda and Ladislav Cermák. *Pevnosti*. Brno Nachod, Czech Rep.: Prvni, 1995.

Rocolle, Col. Pierre. *2000 ans de la fortification française*. Paris: Charles-Lavauzelle, 1974.

—*Les Guerre de 1940: les illusions*. Paris: Armand Colin, 1990a.

—*La Guerre de 1940: la defaite*. Paris: Armand Colin, 1990b.

Rodolphe, René. *Combats dans la Ligne Maginot*. Switzerland: Association Saint-Maurice pour la recherche de documents sur la fortresse, 1981.

Rogelski, Marian and Maciej Zaborowski. *Fortyfikacja wczoraj Idzis*. Warsaw, Poland: Ministerstwo Obrony, 1972.

Rolf, Rudi. *Der Atlantikwall: Perlenschnur aus Stahlbeton*. Amsterdam, Netherlands: AMA, 1983

—*Der Atlantikwall: Diet Bauten der deutschen Küstenbefestigungen 1940-1945*. Osnabrück, Germany: Biblio Verlag, 1998.

—*Atlantikwall - Typenheft*. Beetsterzwaag, Netherlands: AMA, 1988.

Rose, Yannick. *Quatre ans d'occupation pour: "la vigie Du Val De-Saire"*. Alençon, France: Alençonnaise, 1990.

Rothstein, Andrew. *The Munich Conspiracy*. London: Lawrence & Wishart, 1958.

Rowe, Vivian. *The Great Wall of France*. New York: Putman and Sons, 1961.

Sakkers, Hans. *Festung Hoek Van Holland*. Middleburg, Neth: 1992.

Salmond, J.B. *The History of the 51st Highland Division*. Edinburgh: William Blackwood and Sons Ltd., 1953.

The Salpa Line. Finnish military booklet for foreigners.

Saunders, Andrew. *Channel Defences*. London: English Heritage, 1997.

Schwarz, Urs. *The Eye of the Hurricane: Switzerland in World War Two*. Colorado: Westview Press, 1980.

Senger und Etterlin, F.M. von. *German Tanks of World War II*. New York: Galahad Books, 1969.

Showell, Jak P. Mallmann. *The German Navy in World War Two*. Annapolis: Naval Institute Press, 1979.

Silvast, Pekka. Hangöudd Som Sovjetisk Örlogsbas 22.3. 1940-2.12.1941. Sweden: Hangö Muesum Publication 2.

The Simershof Fort. France: 1988. (Guide booklet).

The Small Fortification of Immerhof. France: Township of Hettange Grande, 1979.

Stato Maggiore Dell'Esercito. *Memorie Storiche Militari 1983*. Rome: 1984.

Stehlík, Eduard. *Lexikon tvrzi cs. opeveni let 1935-38*. Králové nad Labem, Czech Rep.: FORT Print, 1992.

Stehlík, Eduard and Vladimír Kupka. *Pechotní Srub: R-S 74, Na Holém*. Praha, Czech Rep.: FORT Print, 1994.

Stehlík, Eduard and Jirï Novák. *Delostrelecká Tvrz Hanicka*. 1995.

—*Delostrelecka Tvrz Bouda*. 1995.

Tarnstrom, Ronald. *The Sword of Scandinavia*. Lindsburg, KS: Trogen Books, 1996.

Taube, Gerhard. *Festung Sevastopol*. Berlin: E.S. Mittler & Sohn GmbH, 1995.

Taylor, James and Warren Shaw. *The Third Reich Almanac*. New York: World Almanac, 1987.

Taylor, Telford. *Munich: The Price of Peace*. Garden City, New York: Doubleday and Company, Inc. 1979.

Trojan, Emil. *Betonová Hranice: Concrete Frontier*. Ustí nad Orlicí, Czech Rep.: OFTIS 1994.

Trotter, William. *A Frozen Hell*. Chapel Hill, NC: Alqounquin Books, 1991.

Truttmann, Michel. *Le Fort de Guentrange*. France: Impriemerie Henz, 1977.

Truttmann, LTC Philippe. *La fortification francaise de 1940 sa place dans l'evolution des systemes fortifies d'Europe Occidentale de 1880 a 1945*. University of Metz: Doctoral Thesis, 1979.

Trye, Rex. *Mussolini's Soldiers*. Osceola, WI: Motorbooks, 1995.

Vliegen, René. *Fort Eben-Emael*. Maastricht, Neth.: Koninklijke Nederlandse Papierfabrieken, 1993

Vondrovsky, Ivo. *Opevneni z let 1936 - 38 na Slovensku*. Králové nad Laubem, Czech Rep.: FORT Print 1993.

Wahl, Jean Bernard. *La Ligne Maginot en Alsace*. Steinbrunn-le-Haut, France: Editions Rhin, 1987.

Weisbecker, A. *Ligne Maginot: Ouvrage du Four a Chaux*. Lembach, France; Syndicat d'Initiative de Lembach et Environs, 1985.

Wetzig, Sonja. *Die Stalin-Linie 1941*. Germany:Podzun-Pallas,1997.

Whitaker, Joseph. Whitaker's Almanack 1941. London: Whitmanaack, 1940.

Wills, Henry. *Pillboxes: A Study of U.K. Defences 1940*. Trowbridge, UK: Leo Cooper, 1985.

Wilt, Alan F. *The Atlantic Wall: Hitler's Defenses in the West*. Ames, Iowa: Iowa State Univ. Press., 1975.

World Almanac and Book of Facts, volumes for years 1928-1946. New York: The New York World Telegram.

Zimmermann, R. Heinz. *Der Atlantikwall von Dunkirchen bis Cherbourg*. Munich, Germany: Schild, 1982.

Documents

Brown, LTC Robert D. "Published or Spoken Views on National Defense Preparedness. Study on Possibilities of Invasion of Netherlands in Present War". Brussels, Military Attaché Report 7563, September 18, 1939.

Center of Military History. The German Campaigns in the Balkans (Spring 1941). Reprint of DA Pam 20-260, November 1953, Facsimile Edition. Washington D.C.: U.S. Army, 1986.

Colbern, Major William H. "Land Frontiers and Interior Defense System". The Hague, Military Attache Report 4552, February 15, 1940.

—"Land Frontiers and Interior Defense System." The Hague, Military Attache Report No. 4578, April 19, 1940.

Denkschrift: über die belgische: Landesbefestigung. Berlin: Oberkommando des Heeres, 1941.

Denkschrift: über die franzosische, Landefestigung. Berlin: Oberkommando des Heeres, 1941.

Denkschrift: über die jugoslawische: Landesbefestigung. Berlin: Oberkommando des Heeres, 1942.

Denkschrift: über die niederlandische: Landesbefestigung. Berlin: Oberkommando des Heeres, 1941.

Denkschrift: über die polnische: Landesbefestigung. Berlin: Oberkommando des Heeres, 1941.

Denkschrift: über die russische: Landesbefestigung. Berlin: Oberkommando des Heeres, 1942.

Denkschrift: über die tschecho-slowakische: Landesbefestigung. Berlin: Oberkommando des Heeres, 1941.

Department of the Army. *German Anti Guerrilla Operations in the Balkans 1941-1944*. Pamphlet No. 29-243 Washington D.C. Department of the Army, 1954.

Die Französische Kriegswehrmacht 1939. Berlin: Oberkommando des Heeres, April 30, 1939.

Durchbruchschlact der l.Armee: Stabsbildmeldung Nr. 16 von 1-25 Juni 1940. AOK 1 Koluft Stabsabtielung, 1940.

Ford, Colonel Stanley H. "Systems of Organization for Defense of Coast in Certain Foreign Countries".*Memorandum for the A. C. of S.*, War Plans Division, January 25, 1928.

Fortier, Major Louis J. "Frontier Defense System: Fortified Area near Italian and Hungarian Frontiers". *Belgrade: Military Attache Report No. 4787*, July 13, 1939.

—"Frontier Defense System". Belgrade: Military Attache Report No. 4830, October 5, 1939.

—"Coast Defense System: The Coast Defense System of Yugoslavia". *Belgrade: Military Attache Report No. 4929*, April 9, 1940.

—"Fortifications: Defense System Opposite Hungarian Frontier". *Belgrade: Military Attache Report No. 4939*, May 20, 1940.

—"The Coast Defense Outpost Line". *Belgrade: Military Attache Report No. 4965*, July 15, 1940.

—"The Land Fortifications System of North and Northwest Yugoslavia". *Belgrade: Military Attache Report No. 4995*, September 30, 1940.

Fuller, LTC H.H. "Land Frontiers and Interior Defense Systems. Northern Defense of Belgium." *Belgium: Military Attache Report No. 24,106-W*, March 14, 1938.

—"Land Frontiers and Interior Defense Systems. Cointet Mobile Anti-tank Barrage". *Report No. 25,569-W*, March 19, 1940.

GMDS. *German Permanent Fortifications*. Washington D.C.: Intelligence Division, War Department, undated.

Grosses Orienterungshft Frankreich: Ausgabe 1935/1936. Berlin: Oberkommando des Heeres, August 1, 1936.

Grosses Orienterungshft Frankreich: Ausgabe 1935/1937. Berlin: Oberkommando des Heeres, August 1, 1937.

Guenther, Major G.B. "Soviet Russia: Fortifications—Construction of Fortifications and Organization of War Industries". *Riga: Military Attache Report No. 9663* January 16, 1937.

Historique et déstruction de la forteresse d'Istein. Direction de Traveaux du Genié de Bade, Paris: Imprimerie Nationale, 1949.

Hofmann, Rudolf, Fredrick Schlieper, Fredrick Wolf, Walter Botsch and Franz Halder. *German Attacks Against Permanent and Reinforced Field Type Fortifications in World War II*. Germany: Historical Division, Headquarters U.S. Army Europe, undated.

Hohenthal, Major William D. "German Permanent Land Fortified Zone". *Berlin: Military Attache Report No. 17,269*, May 14, 1940.

—"Fortified Zones. Training Doctrines." *Berlin: Military Attache Report No. 17,300*, May 29, 1940.

Holmer, Major Frederick A. "Sweden. Fortifications - Land Frontiers and Interior. Fort Boden at Sweden Northern Frontier". *Sweden: Military Attache Report No. 388*, May 11, 1927.

Huthsteiner, LTC G.E. "USSR: Land Frontiers and Interior Defense Systems: Fortifications on Soviet-Estonian Frontier". *Riga: Military Attache Report 1042*, June 2, 1939.

—"USSR: Land Frontiers and Interior Defense Systems: Fortifications on Soviet-Latvian Frontier". *Riga: Military Attache Report 1047*, July 29, 1939.

—"USSR: Land Frontiers and Interior Defense Systems: Planned Fortified Line in Latvia and Lithuania". *Riga: Military Attache Report 0172*, July 8, 1940.

—"USSR: Coat Defense in the Baltic". *Helsinki: Military Attache Report No. 6810*, January 29, 1941.

Johnson, Captain Max S. "Armament and Equipment-Organizational Standard. Captured German Land Mines. *Paris: Military Attache Report No. 25,470-W*, January 24, 1940.

Kiel, Machiel. Excursion to the Position of Amsterdam 1897-1914. Unpublished, 1982a.

—*The Fort Rijnauwen*. Unpublished, 1982b.

—*The Fortress Works of Muiden*. Unpublished, 1982c.

—*Fortification of Holland Between 1918-1940*. Unpublished, June 10, 1982.

Kluss, Major Walter L. "Turkey: Coast Defense System, Armament and Organization of the Dardanelles, Izmir and Marmaris Areas on August 28, 1939". Istanbul, Turkey: *Military Attache Report No. 7093*, September 7, 1939.

Kroner, Major Hayes A. "Belgian Defense Works". *London: Attache Report No. 36536*, October 26, 1934. Report consists of a single clipping from the *London Times* of October 24, 1934.

Lageberichte West vom 10. Mai bis 30. Juni 1940. Berlin: Oberkommando des Heeres, 1940.

Legge, LTC B.R. "Interior Defense System". *Berne: Attache Report No. 3487*, November 18, 1939.

—"Interior Defense System". *Berne: Attache Report No. 3502*, December 2, 1939.

—"Land Frontiers and Interior Defense Systems". *Berne: Attache Report No. 3556*, January 26, 1940.

—"Land Frontiers and Interior Defense System". *Berne: Attache Report No. 3619*, April 3, 1940.

—"Land Fortifications - New Defense Plan". *Berne: Attache Report No. 3685*, September 2, 1940.

—"Land Fortifications - New Defense Plan". *Berne: Attache Report No. 3729*, November 5, 1940.

—"New Defense Plan - The National Redoubt". *Berne: Attache Report No. 3766*, December 17, 1940.

Leonger, A.L. "Swiss Fortresses". *Berlin: Military Attache Report No. 7822*, January 21, 1926.

Magruder, LTC John. "Land Frontiers and Interior Defense System: Frontier Defense Works" *Berne: Military Attache Report No. 3325*, July 13, 1937.

Paine, Colonel G.H. "Land Frontiers and Interior Defense System: Fortifications Near Tarvisio". *Rome: Military Attache Report No. 15,868*, March 11, 1937.

—"Land Frontiers and Interior Defense Systems: Italian Fortifications on Frontiers". *Rome: Military Attache Report No. 17,507*, May 10, 1940.

Peyton, Colonel B.R. "Organization, Defense and Attack on Fortified Zones such as the Siegfried and Maginot Lines." (Translation of a German magazine article of February 1941). *Berlin: Military Attache Report No. 18,126*, March 31, 1941. des Heeres, 1940.

Pillow, Colonel J.G. "Land Frontiers & Interior Defense Systems: New Element in the System of Defense at Brenner Pass". *Rome Military Attache Report 15,390*, July 10, 1936.

—"Fortifications - Land Frontiers & Interior Fortifications on Northern Italian Frontier". *Rome: Military Attache Report 14,362*, April 3, 1935.

Reiss, Günther. Unpublished notes.

Reports on Experiences Gained During World War II in the Development of Fortifications and the Demolitions of Fortress Installations in the West, January 21, 1945 and December 1940 - January 19, 1943. Undated.

Report on German Concrete Fortifications. Office of the Chief of Engineers, European Theater, U.S. Army. 1944.

Riley, Major Lowell M. "Field Fortifications". *Prague: Military Attache Report No. P-947*, October 12, 1938.

—"Rumania: Land Frontiers and Interior Defense Systems. Fortifications". *Bucharest: Military Attache Report No. B-74*, April 28, 1939.

Russian Combat Methods in Word War II. Dept. of the Army Pamphlet No. 20-230. Washington DC: Dept. of the Army, November 1950.

"Seacoast Defenses of the Netherlands". *Germany: Military Observer Berlin G-2 Report*, December 2, 1922.

Shipp, Major W.E. "Soviet Russia: Coast Defense System, Coast Defenses of the Gulf of Finland". *Riga: Military Attache Report No. 8489*, October 25, 1933.

Small Unit Actions During the German Campaign in Russia. Dept of the Army Pamphlet No. 20-269. Washington DC: Department of the Army, July 1953.

Villaret, LTC E. "Greece: Coast Defense System, Harbor Defenses". *Belgrade: Military Attache Report No. 4543*, April 15, 1938.

—"Land Frontiers and Interior Defense Systems: Greece". Belgrade: Military Attache Report No. 4545, April 18, 1938.

—"Rumania: land Frontiers and Interior Defense System. Fortifications along Hungarian Frontier". *Belgrade: Military Attache Report 4588*, July 6, 1938.

—"Greece: Coast Artillery, Harbor Defenses". *Belgrade: Military Attaché Report No. 4641*, November 23, 1938.

—"Rumania: Land Frontiers & Interior Defense System. Frontier Fortifications". *Belgrade: Military Attache Report No. 471*, March 9, 1939.

Waite, Sumner, LTC. "Land Frontiers and Interior Defense System. Eastern Defense of Belgium." *Paris: Military Attache Report No. 23,413-W*, May 11, 1937.

—"Army Establishment- Land Frontiers & Interior Defense Systems". *Paris: Military Attache Report No. 24,841-W*, February 24, 1939.

Williamson, Major Royden. "Coast Defense System. Rearmament of the Straits". *Istanbul: Military Attache Report No. 6752*, February 5, 1937.

—"Turkey: Coast Defense. Refortification of the Straits". *Istanbul: Military Attache Report No. 6796*, April 30, 1937.

—"Turkey: Armament and Equipment - General. Railway Artillery for Defense of the Dardanelles". *Istanbul: Military Attache Report No. 6847*, August 27, 1937.

Wuest, LTC Jacob W.S. "French Advise Fortifications along Swiss Border". *Berlin: Military Attache Report No. 13,710*, October 15, 1934.

Yeager, Major Emer. "Rumania: Fortifications in Bessarabia". *Warsaw: Military Attache Report No. 1393*, July 30, 1931.

—"Rumania: State of Communications and Fortifications in Bessarabia". *Warsaw: Military Attache Report No. 1759*, July 6, 1932.

Journals, Magazines, Newspapers and Pamphlets

Balace, Francis. "Description détaillée des forts de la Meuse en 1914". *Liege, Belgium: 1000 Ans de Fortifications Militaires* (16 December 1980 to 16 January 1981): 75-105.

Bagnaschino, Davide. "Il Vallo Alpino a Cima Marta". *Bollettino d'informazione Gruppo di Studio Delle Fortificazioni Moderne*. (January-April 1994): 2-8

"Belgium to Modernize Fortifications on East With Chain of Sunken Batteries and Dugouts". *New York Times* (July 30, 1932): 1.

Bikar, A. LTC. "May 1940: Pourquuoi le fort d'Eben-Emael est-il tombé si vite?" *Revue belge d'histoire militaire* (Sept-Dec 1995): 123-196.

Blanchon, Jean-Louis, Pierre Serrat and Louis Estéve. "La Línea P. Topographie et conception d'un systèm de défense." *Fortifications and Patrimoine*. (July 1997): 36-42.

Boari, Benito. "Fünfzig Jahre Wacht am Rhein" Unser Rheintal. 1993.

Bochenek, Ryszard and Stefan Fuglewicz. "The Fort Fortress Modlin". *Fortyfikacja* (1996): v IV, 71-72.

"Carol the Cocky". *Time* (January 15, 1940): 24.

Chazette, Alain. "Le musée militaire de Barcelone." *1939-45 Magazine*, (Deceper 1996), Number 126: 22-27.

Clerici, Carlo A., "Il Vallo Alpino del Littorio". Unpublished manuscript.

—"La diffesa costiera in Italia durante i due conflitti mondiali". Unpublished manusript.

Clerici, Carlo A., Valerio Giardinieri and Eugenio Vajna. "La fortificazione permanente di frontiera in Italia durante la seconda guerra mondiale; il Vallo Alpino. *Bollettino d'informazione No. 5 Gruppo di Studio Delle Fortificazioni Moderne*. (January-February 1992): 1-8.

Damilow, Igor. "Radzieckie rejony umocnione—historia terazniejszosc". *Forteca* (January 1997): 61-63.

"Decision in a Week?". *Time* (July 7, 1941): 17-19.

Egger, Martin. "Der deutsche 5cm Maschinengranatwerfer M 19". IBA-Information. Nr. 10, 1987): 47-56.

Eggimann, Pierre. "Visiting the Fort of Pré-Giroud (1939-1945)". *Guide paper*, June 1990.

"Ein kleines Volk wehrt sich: Der russisch-finnische Winterkrieg 1939/40". *Schweizer Soldat* (February 1977): 21-81.

Fischer, Günther. "Die Festungsfront Oder-Warthe-Bogen und das Hohlgangssystem Hochwalde". *Schriftenreihe Festungsforschung*. vol. 7. Wessel, Germany: 1988. (English translation by Fischer prepared in Düsseldorf, Germany).

Frobenius, Lt. von. "Die moderne Festung in Schweden." 1913.

"Fresh German Divisions Move into Western Front; Swiss Call 60,000 Troops". *New York Times* (March 5, 1940): 2.

"Germans Claim a Liege Fort..." *New York Times* (May 12, 1940): 1.

"Germany: A Stern Note". *Time* (June 15, 1925): 22.

"Germany: Glorious Garrison". *Time* (March 16, 1936b): 24.

"Germany: High Minded Dumping". *Time* (July 1, 1935): 19-20.

"Greatest Battle". *Time* (May 27, 1940): 23-25.

Gryner, Peter. "Czechoslovakia '38: What if They'd Fought?" *Command*. (Sept-Oct 1993): issue 2.4

Gwyn, Major General Charles. "French Forts Held Peace Safeguard". *New York Times* (April 19, 1936): 35.

"Happy Birthday Joe". *Time* (January 1, 1940): 20-22

"Hitler's Borodino". *Time* (July 28, 1941): 15-16.

Hitler's Hour. *Time* (May 20, 1940a): 22-25.

"Holes Ripped in Allied Lines". *New York Times* (May 16, 1940): 2.

"Hot Spot". Time (February 14, 1940): 31.

Jäger, Herbert and Terry Gander. "Atlantikwall Defender" *Fortress* (May 1992): issue 13, 55-61.

John, Miloslav. "Sovetska Opevni 1933-1941." Sonda do historie.: 10-11.

—"Sovetska permanentni predvalecna opevneni." Sonda do historie: 4-5.

Kammerer, Capt. M.R. trans. "The Carol Line" *Military Review* (June 1940): Vol XX, 62-63.

Kaufmann, J.E. "Dutch and Belgian Defences 1940" *Fort* (1989): Vol 17, 57-83.

Kemp, Anthony. "British Fortifications 1940: Part 1" AIRFIX (August 1979): 628-629.

—"British Fortifications 1940: Part 2" *AIRFIX* (September 1979): 22-24.

—"British Fortifications 1940: Part 3" *AIRFIX* (November 1979): 148-152.

Knuuttila, Jukka. "Entwicklung der Küstenartillerie in Finnland". *Marine-Rundschau* (May 1977): 1-32.

Kühn, Hans-Jürgen. "Der Isteiner Klotz in der Konzeption des Westwalls". *Zeitschrift für Festungforschung* (Germany: Deutsche Gesellschaft Für Festungsforschung e.V., 1987): 33-39.

Krupa, Lucjan and Waldemar Brozoskwinia. "Tradytory Artyleryjskie Punktu Oporu "Bobrowniki" Obszar Warownego Slask". *Forteca* (January 1997): 38-41.

"La Frontiera Italiana di Terra, Agosto 1942". Bollettino d'informazione No. 12 Gruppo Di Studio Delle Fortificazioni Moderne. (September-October 1993) 1-9.

"League of Nations: Ruptures". *Time* (March 16, 1936a): 22.

"Leopold Goes to War". *Time* (May 20, 1940b): 25-27.

Lüem, Colonel Walter. "Les origines de la fortification du Saint-Gothard". *Revue Militaire Suisse* (May 1992):No 5, 32-41.

Knuuttila, Jukka. "Entwicklung der Kÿuustenartillerie in Finnland". *Marine-Rundschau* (1977) No. 5, 227-241.

"Last Wish". *Time* (August 25, 1941): 19

McCormick, Anne O'Hare, "Belgians Agitated by New War Fears", (March 26, 1936): 14.

"Million Nazi Troops Roll Back French Line..." *Washington Post* (June 9, 1940): 5.

"Military Notes Around the World: British Sea Forts". *Military Review* (March 1945) Vol. XXIV, 80.

"Nazis Report Use of Secret Weapon". *New York Times* (May 13, 1940): 2.

"Nerve Gas?". Time (May 20, 1940c): 26.

"North of Suez." *Time* (January 29, 1940): 31-32.

Olsen, Svein Wiiger. "12 cm Schneider Gun Turrets in Norway". *Casemate* (January 1995): Number 42.

Pozo Pujol Senillosa, Col. Arocadio de. "L'artillerie côtière sur le littoral catalon." *Fortifications and Patrimoine* (January 1998) No. 5: 11-17.

Pruski Zbigniew. "Komunikacje Podziemne W Fortyfikacjach Polesia" *Forteca* (January 1997): 49-60.

Ramsey, Winston G. ed. "The War in Gibraltar." *After The Battle* (1978) Number 21.

Reiss, Günther D. "The Fortification in Switzerland from 1860 to 1945", *Fort* (1993): Vol 21, 19-53.

Rolf, Rodi. "Revolving Concrete Turrets". *Fort* (1988)): Vol. 16, 119-128.

Russian 'Oiling the War'". *Time* (March 11, 1940): 24 "San Gottardo: FORTE AIROLO". Switzerland, undated brochure.

Sauerwein, Jules. "Main Entrances Blocked, Side Doors Worry France". *New York Times* (December 10, 1933): IV-1, 12.

"The Second Agony". *Time* (July 21, 1941): 18.

"Second Wind, Third Week." *Time* (July 14, 1941): 17-18.

"Signal" German Armed Forces magazine. Various issues 1939-1940.

Stassen, P. "La Defense du Fort de Tancremont". *Le Jour* (May 10, 1979): 3-4.

Sternberg, Fritz. "Siegfried Line vs. Maginot Line. *American Mercury* (1940): 286-293.

"Sweden on the Spot". Time (April 29, 1940): 20.

"Swiss and Belgians Increase Defenses". *New York Times* (October 12, 1933): 1.

"Swiss Mobilisation". *Sunday Times* (May 12, 1940): 1.

Swiss Border Force Called into Service". *New York Times*(August 26, 1939): 2.

"Swiss Prepared by 27 Bombs Mobilize Army". *New York Times* (May 11, 1940): 2.

"Switzerland: Blacked Out". *Time* (November 18, 1940): 37.

Touissant, Pierre. "Le fort d'Eben-Emael". *Liege: 1000 ans de fortifications militaires* (16 December 1980 to 16 January 1981): 107-132.

Tarleton, Robert E. "What Really Happened to the Stalin Line?" Part I, *The Journal of Slavic Military Studies*. (June 1992) Vol 5, No 2, pp 187-219.

—Part II, *The Journal of Slavic Military Studies* (March 1993) Vol 6, No 1, pp 21-61.

Traverso, Fulvia and Davide Bagnaschineo. "Il Vallo Alpino del littorio a San Dalmazzo di Tenda". *Bollettino D'informazione No 11 Gruppo di Studio delle Fortificazioni Moderne* (May-June 1993): 1-6.

Verbeek, John R. "Kazemet met gietstalen koepel voor een pag van 4,7 cm." *Armamentaria* (1992).

Wernet, Dieter and Inge. "Maksim Gor'kii I: A Recent Example of the Re-Use of Naval Turrets in Coast Defenses". *Warship International*. (No. 1, 1997): 22-34.

Wieringen, J.S. van. "The Grebbe Line: A Long Defence Line with a Long History". *Fort* (1991): Vol. 19, 73-92).

Zorach, Jonathan. "Czechoslovakia's Fortifications". *Militärgeschichtliche Mitteilungen* (2/1976): 81-94.

Interviews and Correspondence

Allcorn, William. Correspondence December 1996.

Airila, Markku. Correspondence, 1996-1997.

Boleslav, Libor. Correspondence, February 5, 1996.

Chin, Brian Burr. Correspondence, December 15, 1996.

Clerici, Carlo A. Correspondence 1997.

Dahlquist, Olle. Correpsondence, 1997.

Egger, Martin. Correspondence, 1996-1997.

Enqvist, Ove. Correspondence, 1996-1997.

Fugate, Bryan. Correspondence, 1997.

Hasque, Joseph de. Interview in Belgium, 1982.

Heymes, Raoul. Interview at Hackenberg June 1979 and correspondence 1979-1982.

Hölberg, Leif. Correspondence 1998.

Horak, Ales. Interviewed in Czech Republic and at various Czech fortifications, June 1996.

Kedryna, Anna. Interviewed at various positions on East Wall, June 1996.

Kiel, Machiel. Interviewed at home in The Netherlands, 1982.

Lang, Patrice. Correspondence 1997.

Länsivaara, Iikka. Correspondence 1997.

Maistret, Georges. Interview 1979 at Fermont and correspondence 1979-1984.

Olsen, Svein Wiiger. Correspondence, January 24, 1997.

Pipes, Jason. E-Mail Correspondence, 1997.

Reiss, Gunther. Correspondence, 1994-1997.

Sundquist, Dag. Correspondence, 1997-1998.

Tarleton, Robert. Correspondence, 1998.

Truttmann, Phillip. Correspondence, 1982-1997.

Wahl, Jean Bernard. Interview at Schoenenbourg June 1982.

GLOSSARY

Betonhöckerhindernisse (Ger.)

Concrete-pole-barrier known as "Dragon's Teeth".

Bunkkeri (Fin.)

Concrete bunker.

Barbette mount

The gun mount fixes the weapon in a position above the parapet for both loading and firing. Gun shields can be added, but this refers mainly to a weapon in an open firing position as opposed to a casemate.

Caponier

Usually a position giving flanking fires on the counterscarp and includes an underground passage, but the term is more liberally used with modern fortifications. For the Russians it is any casemate firing to the flanks.

Caserne (Fr.)

Garrison area.

Casemate

A term with mixed meanings throughout history, it usually refers to a bunker-like position for weapons that fire through embrasures. The Germans only referred to positions that had flanking fires as casemates, but in the case of French and Czech positions some of them fired forward.

Chicane (Fr.)

Refers to a defensive feature to deny direct access. It is designed so a person will have to make one or two turns to enter a position or pass an obstacle on a road.

CKM (Pol.)

Heavy machine gun.

Cloche (Fr.)

A non-movable armored cupola mounted. This term is used to refer to any all such items in the text to avoid confusion with a movable turret.

Coffre (Fr.)

Defensive position in the counterscarp covering the moat and connected to the main work by tunnel.

DOT (Rus.)

Bunker.

Episcope

Term seldom used in English, but refered to a type of vision device used on tanks. Its optics are arranged differently than a periscope and it gives a view through slit opening.

Feste (Ger.)

German fort, usually refers to new type from turn of century.

Fossé (Fr.)

Moat used with fortifications that can vary in size. Those with combat and entrance blocks of fortifications were not very wide and were angular are called them "diamond fossé." In the text these small protective positions are called fossés to avoid confusion with a traditional moat.

Fusil Mitrailleur (Fr.)

Light machine gun or automatic rifle. Abbreviated FM.

Génie (Fr.)

French army engineers

Gross Ouvrage/GO (Fr.)

Large fort or artillery fort.

Gun House

Armored shield covering a gun on a barbette type mount, a fully enclosed gun house may give the appearance of a turret.

Half Cloche

See Half Cupola.

Half Cupola (Ger.)

Non-moveable armored cupola mounted just below a bunkers roof level on one of its walls. referred to in the text as a half cloche.

Korsu (pl. -t, Fin.)

Wooden bunker or what was known as a dugout. This term was also sometimes applied to concrete bunkers, but was actually supposed to represent a wooden fortification.

Monte Charge (Fr.)

Refers to any type of elevator or lift from those large enough for equipment to those small enough to only carry up single rounds of ammunition.

Objekt (Pol.)

Bunker or block of some type of permanent fortified position.

Obszar Warownyor/OW (Pol.)

Fortified district

Opere (pl.-e, It.)

Large Italian fortification, the same term as the French "ouvrage." In the text it refers only to the new subterranean fortifications built in the twentieth century.

Ouvrage (fr.)

means a "work". Used in text to refer for the newer type of French fort.

Panzer fort (Ger.)

An armored fort refering to a fort with positions like armored casemates and turrets.

Panzerwerke (Ger.)

Bunker or combat block of a Werkgruppen with one or more armored cupolas.

Petit Ouvrage/PO (Fr.)

Small fort.

Pillbox

British term applied to the bunkers built during World War I that looked much like a pill box. The term remained in use both in British and American English and referred to most types of machine gun or anti-tank gun shelter.

Pimples

British term for concrete AT obstacles similar to Dragon's Teeth. Not to be confused with AT cubes.

PF (Belg.)

Position Fortifiée or fortified position.

Pioneer (Ger.)

Term refers to army engineers

Punkt Oporu/PO (Polish)

Defensive Point.

Reconnaisance

Also refers to making a survey of a site.

Region Fortifiée/RF (Fr.)

Fortified region.

Sapper or Sapeur

Usually refers to British or French engineers.

Schron (pl. -y, Pol.)

A bunker or shelter.

Secteur Fortifiée/SF (Fr.)

Fortified sector.

Stützpunkt (Ger.)

Strongpoint whose positions are not linked by an underground tunnel system.

Stützpunktgruppen (Ger.)

Several strong points serving a battalion size unit.

Tobruck

(also spelled Tobruk) Refers to type of position in concrete with ring shaped opening in roof for weapon which was usually designed for a machine gun or a mortar.

Tradytor (Pol.)

Traditionally, a defensive position in a fortification similar to a caponier; modern use: artillery casemate for flanking fire.

Turret

Revolving armored position with weapons on the exposed dome area and controls below or in the turret column similar to that of a ship. Guns with a full armored shield, but no actual turret column are usually not considered turrets, but guns with a gun house. A non-moveable turret in this text is referred to as a cloche to avoid confusion.

Tvrz (Czech)

Fortress. This term was used with the new forts similar to French Maginot Line ouvrages and has the same meaning. The Czechs refer to individual independent combat blocks with their own facilities as forts which creates some confusion, just as labeling their subterraean fortifications as "fortresses."

UR (Rus.)

Ukreplinnje Rajony or fortified district

Usine (Fr.)

Engine room or Power room usually containing diesel engines, transformers, and a fuel supply.

Verteidigungsbereich (Ger.)

Defense Area

WC

Water closet i.e. urinal, toilets, and/or sinks.

Werk (Ger.)

Position. B-Werk refers to a position with one or more blocks, is considered to be an independent fort by the Germans (see Werkgruppe)

Werkgruppe/WG (Ger.)

Group of two or more blocks linked by a tunnel system with supporting facilities.

Widerstand (Ger.)

Resistance point garrisoned by a platoon sized units

INDEX